D1621353

Search Foundations

Search Foundations

Toward a Science of Technology-Mediated Experience

Sachi Arafat and Elham Ashoori

The MIT Press
Cambridge, Massachusetts
London, England

For information about special quantity discounts, please email special sales@mitpress.mit.edu.

This book was set in Stone Serif by Westchester Publishing Services. Printed and bound in the United States of America.

Library of Congress Cataloging-in-Publication Data

Names: Arafat, Sachi, author. | Ashoori, Elham, author.
Title: Search foundations : toward a science of technology-mediated experience / Sachi Arafat and Elham Ashoori.
Description: Cambridge, MA : The MIT Press, [2018] | Series: History and foundations of information science | Includes bibliographical references and index.
Identifiers: LCCN 2017061372 | ISBN 9780262038591 (hardcover : alk. paper)
Subjects: LCSH: Information science. | Information retrieval.
Classification: LCC Z665 .A69 2018 | DDC 020—dc23 LC record available at https://lccn.loc.gov/2017061372

10 9 8 7 6 5 4 3 2 1

To my parents and teachers—SA

For Mohsen and Roshanak—EA

"Ars Sine Scientia Nihil Est"
—Jean Mignot (14c.)

Contents

4   From Growth to Progress II: The Network of Discourse   187

5   Basic Questions Characterizing Foundations Discourse   211

Preface

The idea for this book began in the Senior Common Room at the Imperial College in the summer of 2011 as we acknowledged our mutual dissatisfaction with the course of research in information retrieval and science (IR&S). But this was a relative dissatisfaction brought on by our attempt to measure information retrieval against the mature science of quantum mechanics.

Our then-recent engagements in projects adapting ideas from quantum theory to information retrieval had left us with questions of a conceptual, philosophical, and a rather inconvenient type. What then proceeded was a type of nonlocal collaborative research that was wholly new to us. It was intense, sustained argumentation, based on closely reading texts, that lasted more than five years, and involved conflicting perspectives: Ashoori's flavored by a strong technical and engineering inclination (as is common to information retrieval) and Arafat's by a philosophical and humanistic bent (common to information science). The topics included specific foundations questions, questions whose answers are presumed by IR&S research discourses, ranging from those about what a user, document, or query is, to more general questions about disciplinary identity and progress. In particular, the argumentation centered increasingly on the text of the "notes" that we developed through a type of deep syntopical reading of works across disciplines from which ideas were being appropriated to address the aforementioned questions. These notes eventually became this book.

An earlier version of these notes representing preliminary discussions was first intended to be presented as a paper for an interdisciplinary workshop on the foundations of IR&S. Its purpose was to argue the need for foundations and then become the first chapter of a wider-ranging, book-length text that would comprehensively detail a new kind of science—which we argued IR&S would need to become for the sake of progress. That workshop never materialized, and that single chapter became this text, whose main purpose is to motivate such a new science. To adequately develop such a science would require a sustained community effort. Much has to be done to persuade a critical mass of scholars to pursue such a task, and then to create such a community; to divert their gaze from the intensely quantitative research programs to what appear to be "mere philosophical matters" (i.e., the foundations research discussion about progress). As one reviewer suggested, this text can be understood as a sort of manifesto. It is apt to also frame it as a prolegomenon to a new kind of science: a science of technology-mediated experience.

While quantum theory initiated our journey into the foundations of IR&S, the question of progress that became pivotal to our work was a response to what appeared to us an exigency of some tension clouding our professional and intellectual concerns. Do the multitudes of works produced in IR&S conferences and journals add up to take the respective discourses from a lesser state to a greater one, as can reasonably be argued for scientific discourses? Is this question relevant? Perhaps one should not expect technological disciplines to be like the traditional sciences, since the former are more concerned with solving practical problems than progressively discovering more facts about some part of the world. But IR&S researchers do indeed seek to unify theories and frameworks and therefore "build up." While IR&S employs technology and is moreover technology–centric, its goal ultimately is to serve humans by means of this technology. This is not something it can do without understanding technology-use with respect to the human subject. Moreover, while rarely made explicit, technological disciplines possess an underlying vision about the kind of world the technologies created therein are supposed to help build; a world that is presumably better than the current one. In this sense, progress in technological discourses appears concomitant with the socio-technical and econo-political development of cities.

Not only did the question of progress thereby appear to lack an immediate or obvious answer, it also opened up a cascade of interrelated questions resembling a mess of tangled wires. Can IR&S be a science? If so, what kind of science? Do we need to first fix what we mean by "information" before we decide what kind of science it is? How does IR&S relate precisely to information systems or web science? Is this all just about finding a grand mathematical theory? While one could start with any one of these questions, their sheer mass and complexity presents a hindrance, a fear. And while the idea that "a philosophical problem has the form: I don't know my way about" (Wittgenstein, 2010, p. 123) was comforting—since the "way about" was certainly not clear, and since we could now categorize our woes as "philosophical"—we were led to numerous inconvenient questions of an intellectual and professional type. Are these problems ours to solve? Should we leave them to the philosophers?

This complex of questions—and their often apprehensive nature—characterized the difficult yet extremely rewarding journey from which the present text emerged. A journey that began in 2003 with a rather different foundational problem. Where does information retrieval stand among the sciences, with respect to physics and psychology in particular? The nascent allure of this problem was nurtured until 2010 through sustained discussions with several interlocutors, growing eventually into a mess of concerns; our concerns. We were behooved to pursue its address together. The genealogy of this allure is therefore also that of this text.

S. Arafat and E. Ashoori
October 2017

Genealogy

The idea that appears to have determined the entire intellectual trajectory leading to this text emerged in hindsight the first time Sachi Arafat met Keith van Rijsbergen just prior to his acceptance as Keith's doctoral student in 2003 at the University of Glasgow. While discussing what technology-use has to do with both the computer and social sciences, it was proposed that information retrieval (IR) was somehow in between physics and psychology, between the discipline that helps us study both computer hardware and physical nature and the discipline pertaining to the human subject. In a reflective moment, a question presented itself as a muse, an enduring source of intellectual allure: What does this in-betweenness mean?

Arafat's (2008) ensuing doctoral work, based on van Rijsbergen's (2004) seminal work on the topic, became the first thesis work on the nascent research program of quantum theory–inspired IR (QTIR); Arafat (2011b). This program purposed to formalize the (mathematical) foundations of IR. However, the question remained unaddressed therein, and grew steadily into the elephant in the room. The more one attempts to graft mathematical models representing the physical world to the socio-psychological world, the more this question imposes itself. What is the relationship between these worlds? More specifically, what is the relationship between the discourse on physical nature and the mixed discourse pertaining to human–machine interaction? These are not questions about mathematical representation. And moreover, they point not only to the interdisciplinary space between these respective fields but also to that vast gulf between the sciences and humanities in general.

Arafat was not yet equipped with the conceptual vocabulary to adequately think about this question, let alone answer it. Having neither the training nor (at that time) the taste for the humanistic style of intellectual discourse to which the question pointed served only to instill a sense of urgency into the growing yet vexing allure of the problem.

It was around this time, during a sabbatical in Malaysia, that Arafat was introduced to several humanistic discourses by Adi Setia, a philosopher of science by training and a keen critic. This occurred after a fortuitous first meeting brought to a tension with Setia's query "You study information retrieval; what do you mean by information?" Unable to muster a rigorous response to this and several other questions (later understood to be foundational for IR&S), Arafat instigated an initial yearlong intensive study of various humanistic discourses with a focus on the philosophy of science. The elusive question of the disciplinary position of IR lurked in the background as motivation.

On returning to his postdoctoral work with a better idea of foundations and progress, the idea of contributing to the growing QTIR program (typically through applying mathematical models from QT to IR) no longer appealed—not without first settling the many foundational questions. Arafat became convinced that foundations research would be the most progressive route for IR. But it was not at all clear how others could be convinced. Research trends in IR were moving in increasingly technical directions. Not only did foundational and conceptual work appear to hold less weight, but also the existing attitudes toward them, especially those of technically inclined researchers, posed a major barrier—an intellectual as well a political one.

It was in the midst of this crisis of sorts in 2011 that Arafat met Ashoori, an IR researcher who had become interested in the QTIR program after having completed doctoral work on experimental aspects of IR (Ashoori, 2009).

Ashoori's interaction with the program was of a different nature, much of it conditioned by her experience as a postdoctoral researcher (since 2009) in Terry Rudolph's quantum information theory group at Imperial College. There she engaged in an intensive study of quantum information processing/quantum mechanics, and working closely with Rudolph, she developed a critical perspective on the QTIR program. In particular, Ashoori noticed that those with a deep understanding of the physics behind quantum theory (i.e., its original context of use) were concerned about the scientific legitimacy of applying QT to other than the physical world, by those who at most gave this context a cursory glance as they hastily adapted its mathematical framework to a wholly different context. There was indeed a marked difference between how quantum physicists (e.g., quantum information processing researchers) tended to interpret the QTIR research program and how a sizable number of IR researchers perceived it.

She found problematic the culture of adapting QT models to wholly new contexts without sufficient consideration of the original context. In particular, works in QTIR employing models in a decontextualized way lead to erroneous or ambiguous understandings of what the models depicted. The main problem here was the inadequacy of the analogy between phenomena represented by the mathematical models in QT and those phenomena in IR that were to be represented by the same models. This problem challenged the program to find analogies that convincingly relate IR phenomena to physics phenomena so as not to misrepresent them relative to their original IR-specific properties (see Ashoori and Rudolph). That this was problematic was acutely felt in later work. She faced this problem in later work (2012–2014) applying the mathematics of QT to developing community detection algorithms for complex quantum systems, but found that an adequate analogy with quantum phenomena was available. Furthermore, even if such an analogy could be found for the QTIR case, why try to draw the analogy with QT in the first place? There are several (more general) mathematical theories with features similar to QT that would be simpler to employ, because they are not tied to a specific context of use.

It was during Ashoori's subsequent work on investigating these other theories that she met with Arafat. In hindsight, the critical perspective of the QTIR program they shared was instrumental in guiding their collaborative work; it became instead a critical perspective of IR&S overall. Moreover, it was the background for their study of the foundations of IR&S. This more general perspective was additionally influenced by another consequence of their experience with QT discourse: the acutely felt absence in IR&S discourse of the rigor, theory–experiment correspondence, and disciplinary organization found in QT, which was not something that could be resolved satisfactorily by mathematical models alone. They were only lead to such a project of problematizing IR&S as a whole, where this absence was felt, through a mutual acknowledgment in their first meeting in the summer of 2010 of a creeping dissatisfaction of their inability to grasp IR&S research papers through their titles. This we realized was not simply due to our lack of familiarity with the semantic network or immediate discourse network of any particular paper. As even if one could identify a recent research trend to which the paper belonged, it was unclear how to fit it into a larger research program or how to relate between such programs. The issue was with the fragmentation across the larger discourse—QT in this sense was something that they began to think of as a scientific mirror to IR&S (Arafat, 2011b).

What does it mean for IR&S discourse to not measure up to that of a successful science such as QT? Is it still a "good" discourse? Is it perhaps on its way to a better state? These queries lead us to the central question of what it means to make progress in IR&S. From this we were led to consider foundations. This direction was influenced by the rapid growth of search and other technologies that were being used in increasingly pervasive contexts and the implications of this for basic concepts used to discuss such phenomena. For example: What ought to constitute the query and the document in the context of augmented-reality search? Moreover, our choice of direction was influenced in an indirect manner by philosophy of science discourses that viewed scientific discourses as having an "inner" or foundational aspect and an outer aspect. What is this inner aspect, the network of basic concepts and questions constituting a foundation for IR&S? This lead us in 2011 to scour the literature in IR&S and farther afield (e.g., information systems, computer science in general), starting with the earliest such papers, to create a map of discussions about progress and foundational issues, so that we could understand how to characterize the discourse as a whole. And to allow us to deduce whether discourse could be said to build up toward some ultimate purpose. The initial idea was simply to understand this overall trajectory. It was only later that we realized we were trying to understand what progress means for IR&S.

While our discussions thus moved us away from the QTIR research program, it was our experience of QT and QTIR discourse that set us on a specific research path investigating the nature of IR&S. However, our fortuitous discovery of the work of Patrick Heelan (in particular, Heelan, 1965) brought QT back to a central position for our project of developing a science of technology-mediated experience.

Arafat met with Patrick Heelan in 2011 at Georgetown University. An intense discussion over two days followed by further engagement with Heelans work has had a major influence on this text. Three points became certain through these discussions. First, that quantum mechanics (beyond quantum theory) is indeed of major importance for IR&S, not primarily due to its mathematical framework but because it is a science pertaining to the participatory relationship between humans, technology, and nature. The technology-mediated activity that IR&S focuses on thus does resemble the human observer prodding nature by using tools. Thus perhaps IR&S can also be a science, and perhaps one could borrow from the conceptual framework of quantum theory that addresses the observer and the process of observation—especially as Heelan frames it—to develop an alternative foundation for IR&S. Second, that phenomenology (i.e., the work developed primarily by Husserl as well as the hermeneutic phenomenology of Heidegger) has to play a crucial part in any such foundation. Thus, to combine the first and the second points, perhaps QT could help in setting up IR&S in a hermeneutic-phenomenological sense by focusing it on observation/experience of the world prior to lending it mathematical representations for adaptation. Third, this project has importance beyond the usual confines of IR&S: Such a project implies the need for a new kind of scientific discourse that is placed peculiarly between the humanities and the sciences. Heelan's work thus guided the synthesis of the thought previously developed from Arafat's discussions with Keith van Rijsbergen and Adi Setia. It thereby guided the synthesis of the mathematical sciences plus physics and the humanistic discourses plus philosophy. Thus Heelan's work became the background to the development of this book since 2011. Moreover, his work is understood to be crucial to the development of a future science of technology-mediated experience beyond its introduction in this book.

Acknowledgments

Our work has been shaped by numerous conversations and debates with, fortuitous meetings and reflective moments with, and facilitations and encouragement by colleagues, friends, and family.

We are indebted to Keith van Rijsbergen, who was Arafat's doctoral and postdoctoral supervisor, initially based at Arafat's home institution, the School of Computer Science at the University of Glasgow, but now at the Computer Laboratory at the University of Cambridge. His peculiar ability—stemming from of a deep sense of duty, care, and responsibility toward his students and interlocutors—to instill in them an ownership of research problems and to boldly follow intellectual paths wherever they lead brought us to this point. However, it would not have been possible without the generous support of the Royal Academy of Engineering (RAENG) and the Engineering and Physical Sciences Research Council (EPSRC); their joint postdoctoral fellowship funded Arafat from 2008 to 2014. Moreover, thanks are due to Information Retrieval group at the School of Computer Science in Glasgow, and to Paul Cockshott, Yashar Moshfeghi, and Joemon Jose in particular. We are furthermore indebted to Paul Bishop at the German Department at the same university, a scholar of Carl Jung and Ernst Cassirer. He understood the nature and purpose of this book even before it was clear to us, and he directed us to works on the memory arts and philosophy of culture, which influenced chapter 6 in particular.

Ashoori is extremely grateful to Terry Rudolph at her home institution, the Imperial College in London. She is indebted to him for teaching her how to critically analyze multidisciplinary scientific activity. Moreover, Rudolph offered a significant critique of the QTIR project early on (2010), which did much to set a standard for rigor in how we borrowed from discourses outside IR&S to make the arguments conveyed in this book. Ashoori took much from the method of and attitude of critique that she saw in the physicists and applied mathematicians at Imperial. This complemented her previous experimental research experience in computer science and engineering, for which she is grateful to Mounia Lalmas, her doctoral supervisor at Queen Mary, University of London, and also to Farhad Ooumchian, the late Caro Lucas, and Kambiz Badie at the University of Tehran. Ashoori's work at Imperial College was supported by an EPSRC strategic fund followed by an EPSRC digital economy program (EP/I017267/1). She also thanks both the Quantum Optics and Laser Science and Applied Mathematics groups. Discussions with David Jennings, the late Sean Barrett, Neill Lambert, Oscar Dahlsten, Tommaso Tufarelli, and Peter Lewis of the Quantum Optics group were particularly beneficial, as were the fruitful exchanges with Mauricio Barahona, Michael Shaub, and Sophia Yaliraki in the Applied Mathematics group. These discussions worked to further strengthen the direction she took with the foundations of IR&S.

Beyond our main home institutions, Arafat expresses his sincere gratitude to Adi Setia (now at the University of Technology in Malaysia), who offered his erudition for several hours a day over a year while working full time. His patience allowed for humanistic thinking to constructively affect a technical mindset. Thanks are furthermore due to the late Patrick Heelan of Georgetown University in Washington, DC. Patrick was a major influence on this project not only by means of his individual works, but as a scholar and person who pursued problems across the sciences and humanities as a whole over a lifetime.

Samir Mahmoud at the University of Cambridge was the first and main person through whom Arafat came to see the relevance of Heidegger's thought and specifically his theory of technology to IR&S. Andrew (Frederick) Burniston, an independent Jung scholar, devoted many hours over several years to imparting his knowledge of the psychoanalytic tradition, phenomenology, the memory arts, and related disciplines. He traveled to London every few weeks to meet with Arafat over two years (2011–2013). Arafat is indebted to their patience and generosity.

Ashoori is additionally grateful to Matthew Leifer (now at Chapman University), Bob Coecke, and Jonathan Barrett (now at the University of Oxford) for discussions on generalized probability theories, which allowed her to develop a better understanding of alternative mathematical structures to formalize the foundations of IR&S.

We are indebted to Micheal Buckland at the University of California at Berkeley for his wide-ranging help, which was instrumental from the inception of this work as a book to its publication. First was his support of our ideas about the need for foundations research in IS through his body of work and comments, then the influence of his ideas on ours (especially chapters 5 and 6). This materialized in the form of practical advice and support that lead us to MIT Press and through the entire publication process. Most significant, however, was his overall confidence in our project—in a wide-scoped discourse on the foundations of IR&S—especially given the seminal nature of his own works in the area. The works of Ronald Day at Indiana University, another key figure in IR&S foundations research, were an inspiration for this book. His comments on earlier drafts of parts of this book did much to allay our fears that we had somehow gone off course, while his patience and rigor in clarifying queries about foundational concepts in IR&S—coupled with his consistent encouragement—did much to keep us going until the end.

Gita Devi Manaktala took care of us from the MIT Press side; her patience, kindness, and assurances offered relief in the midst of our juggling several career demands, and for this we are grateful. Cyd Westmoreland did a great job with the copy editing, her many subtle rhetorical touches do much to bring-home the message of different parts of the book. We are also grateful to Susan Clark and Katie Helke at MIT Press, Marguerite Avery who was previously at MIT Press, and to Maura Neville at Westchester Publishing Services.

Moreover, we also thank Julian Warner, Justin Weisz, David Bawden, Mounia Lalmas, and Andrew Trotman for reading earlier drafts of chapters, and especially the two anonymous reviewers who provided excellent feedback and gave us hope. We are grateful to Amir Hussain at the University of Stirling who made it possible for Arafat to continue this book project to its fruition at the end of his fellowship at the University of Glasgow, and for influencing us to think about how the arguments in the book would apply to areas such as Cognitive Computing. And our thanks go to Naif Aljohani at King Abdulaziz University. He facilitated the writing of this book at Arafat's most recent place of work, providing much needed motivation in the later stages of this project.

Needless to say, we bear responsibility for any remaining mistakes, confusions, or misconstruals of borrowed concepts.

In addition to those already mentioned, each of us wishes to add several personal acknowledgments.

Sachi Arafat: I would like to express my deepest gratitude to my parents and sister, for suffering my relatively hermitic lifestyle for the last decade. And to my wife for tolerating my being distracted with this book since our first meeting. They may not have quite understood the need for such a project, but they respected my investment in it nonetheless. Without their kindness, love and support I would not have been disposed towards contemplating the bigger picture.

Elham Ashoori: I am greatly indebted to my husband, Mohsen, and our daughter, Roshanak, who supported my love of writing this book. Both have been by my side from the start to the end of this project. My warmest thanks goes to my parents, sister, brother, and my in-laws for their continuous–and endless–love and support.

Introduction

Our dependence on increasingly pervasive technology has served to make it a significant determinant of the modern human condition. To comprehend this condition, one must thus understand the human–machine relationship. This relation is actuated and upheld by the work of technology creators through augmenting existing situations of technology-use and creating new such situations. It is subsequently unfolded and amplified through use.

The study of technological discourses is therefore not only important for the immediate practical end of technology creation, but also for understanding the contemporary human condition. This book brings together ideas about the technological and human aspects of technology-use into an intellectual discourse. Its purpose is to improve the present understanding of the human–machine relationship at a conceptual level as well as to frame it in a way that could also inform the work of technologists. This discourse is situated among discussions of technology-use in information retrieval and science (IR&S), a discipline of deriving mainly from the computer and library sciences.

IR&S seeks both to understand the human use of information systems and to facilitate that use by developing tools, such as search engines, for effectively completing information tasks. It is a discipline and discourse that forms a representative microcosm of the macrocosm that is the technologists' overall engagement with society through developing technologies that shape that society toward particular ends. IR&S is representative because it is expressly concerned with the human and technological side of this engagement, blending these concerns intimately through its concepts and methods, which IR&S practitioners use to create technology and understand situations of technology-use.

As this book demonstrates, IR&S can be structured in way that relates it to the bigger questions pertaining to the human–machine relationship, yet from a perspective sensitive to technology creators, whose work engenders concrete situations of technology-use. In particular, we structure IR&S discourse by understanding how it is constituted with respect to research questions and concepts that are foundational and therefore presupposed by other questions and concepts.

While the project that instigated this book began by investigating some of these foundational questions, we realized that their resolution depended on more general problems that are shared across discourses addressing the human–machine relationship. Moreover, it became apparent that the foundations of IR&S can be perceived as common to technology-centric disciplines concerned with the contemporary socio-technical context and with situations of technology-use in particular. Other than IR&S, this includes discourses that study pervasive and ubiquitous devices, and beyond this, any discourse that seeks to examine the increasingly encompassing nature of technology-mediated living. As a result, we began to work from the perspective of these more general problems while addressing them within an IR&S context.

In particular, we began with the foundational problem of progress: What could it mean to make progress in IR&S given the contemporary reality of the human–machine relationship? Our answer is that progress at this juncture is concomitant with the critical analyses of unexamined presuppositions and the addressing of basic or foundational questions; the development of a corresponding foundations discourse and a discourse culture; and ultimately, the reorientation and re-envisioning of IR&S as a new kind of science, a science of technology-mediated experience (STME).

The investigation of IR&S's foundations thus led us to a confluence of researchers and thinkers beyond our discipline into an intellectual space centered on problematizing the human–machine relationship in a general sense. Once in this space, we felt compelled to boldly delve, among radically empirical and quantitative research trends no less (yet not against them), into rigorously investigating foundations. Not the mathematical foundations, but that which is even more foundational; and not into one or two isolated issues thereof but the whole of them. This book therefore addresses the problem of the human–machine relationship that is shared among several disciplines, but as it manifests within the discourses of our home discipline of IR&S.

Next we introduce this book from the perspective of the problems IR&S shares with other disciplines and with the general discourse on the human–machine relationship. We then reintroduce it from the perspective of specific concrete IR&S problems. The point here, as it is throughout the book, is to show the mutual interaction between these perspectives. We close this introduction with a detailed synopsis of the book's contents.

From Technology Futures to Search

Technological disciplines seek to make the tools that increasingly mediate all aspects of the human living experience. As a result, progress in such disciplines is not only intellectual progress—it ultimately also has to be concerned with human or social progress. Technology is made to effect social change, to fulfill cultural and social objectives based on an ideal vision of society or a technology future: a future enabled by the creation of technology and technology-policy. Any such vision for modern times must adopt notions of the ideal city or society. Whether or not these notions are made explicit, they nevertheless influence technologists and their creations. An influential source of discussion about these issues can be found in imaginative science fiction literature and film, which together function as a means for philosophical and intellectual contemplation about possible technology futures (i.e., perspectives on what a technology-infused society may be like in the near future). The future worlds depicted therein can be learned from: "through imagining strange worlds we come to see our own conditions of life in a new and potentially revolutionary perspective" (Parrinder, 2000, p. 4). They express collective hopes and despairs, challenge our present conceptions and habits, and by presenting an understanding of the human condition, imagine alternative possibilities of life (see. Moylan, 2000; Jameson, 2005).[1] In particular, science fiction serves to suggest both the possibilities of human–machine relationships crucial for determining such future situations and the conditions for such possibilities.[2] Beyond

1. Not only has such literature influenced technology design, but it has also influenced intellectual and industrial movements, and generations of technologists. Moreover, technology-based future visions often go hand in hand with academic, industrial, and governmental schemes to bring out new ways of life—from new educational plans to the redesign of cities, to reimagining human rights (e.g., with respect to privacy) and law in general, and to reimagining what it means to be human.

2. For example, technology as a seamless extension of the body and mind, interfacing through organic gestures—yet as "servant" of the user in the film *Minority Report* (Spielberg, 2002). In the case of the more recent film *Her* (Jonze, 2014), the technological agent or system had to pretend to be a peer for an intimate relationship to be maintained. That is, it sought to replicate the corresponding real-life human–human relationship by implementing the associated communicative behaviors to "simulate" a separate consciousness, a living entity.

such movies/media and sci-fi literature, the important topic of technology futures, conceptions of which must presuppose technology design (however implicitly), are also discussed in the academic humanities literature. But this literature is arguably a less influential source for futures than is fiction.

Given that the technologists are the ones designing the concrete products and thus the technology-use that constitutes such futures, shouldn't they appropriate discourses on technology futures in a direct and systematic manner? A consequence of the arguments made in this book is that it is crucial for them to do so. In particular, scientific progress in technological disciplines depends on it. Although this book does not further argue this corollary for technological disciplines in general, we argue it for a specific case: What does progress mean for IR&S? Given the modern context and the need to incorporate humanistic discourses into technology-centered discourses, we find that progress in IR&S is concomitant with the project of explicitly problematizing and understanding the human–machine relationship, and developing ways to explain technology-mediated activity. The ability to explain observations is not only important for IR&S to be a science, but is also of particular significance for practitioners, as it provides a rationale for developing technical or policy-based solutions to IR&S problems. These implications for progress in turn suggest a reorientation of IR&S to a new kind of science. Moreover, IR&S discourse can be understood as a microcosm for the greater discourse about the human–machine relationship. As the following chapters show (chapter 1 in particular), IR&S is a discourse in which the question of the human–machine relationship is not merely presupposed (as it is in every discourse dealing with technology-use), but is presupposed in an especially intimate way. Our findings, if confirmed, may extrapolate beyond IR&S to that greater discourse and to specific discourses dealing with this relationship, whether they seek to explain and understand it or create the technology that engenders it.

This work can thereby be understood as a first step and preliminary road map to a more thorough future engagement between technologists and technology futures than is currently the case. That this engagement is needed has been recognized by several thinkers—and not only in the humanities. Yet it has not yet been effectively undertaken as a project for any sustained period of time, nor has it become a mainstream research goal in computer science or the humanities.

Goguen is an influential example of such a thinker from computer science, and his work (Goguen, 1999) highlights what can be understood as the primary intellectual obstacle to such an effective engagement. Therein he speaks of a crisis in computer science, arguing that: The science of computer science is mainly about the technology and does little to explain the human contexts of its use. As an example of this inherent focus on technology, consider the notion of information, one of the basic concepts employed in computer science. As it is used in information technology (and also in information retrieval or science) it pertains not only to the data but also to the meaning given to data by human beings through the human experience of technology-use. Yet this meaning is not directly problematized by computer science. The result is "a great divide between theory and practice"—that is, between the technical and social—and hence an "ever declining interest shown in theory" (Goguen, 1999, p. 1). This divide has much to do with that between the sciences and humanities. And although the declining interest here pertains to the theoretical aspect of computer science, it extends to the discipline as a whole. Ultimately, a disinterest in theory means a disinterest in the basic concepts constituting that discipline (i.e., its foundations), which determine the phenomena that are relevant to the discipline. These foundations underly what is known as mathematical foundations and are therefore more fundamental than the latter. Thus, the disinterest here should be interpreted to mean that the foundations appear to not say much about the application context, that is, about how the technical products are socially situated in contexts of technology-use. The foundations of a discourse are the collection of positions presupposed by other parts of the discourse and by the related scientific-intellectual processes. Thus, the making of observations, evaluation of systems and theory development, all presuppose foundational positions about, for example, the objects or processes in the world that are supposed to be of interest.[3]

3. The notions of "fundamental," "basic," and "foundations" differ. A fundamental question is an important question, whereas a foundations question need not be. It may be resolved and no longer important to address in any immediate sense for the project at hand. Similarly, there are technical research questions that are fundamental in that their address is important for building applications, yet they may not be foundational: other concepts in the corresponding discourse may not depend on them. In one sense, "basic" implies "presupposed" and "foundational." In another sense it means "simple" as opposed to complex, i.e., having few or no additional aspects or attributes or being easy to resolve. Foundational questions are usually complex: they have many aspects or branches and are of varying difficulties. The foundations of a discipline are the set of ideas/propositions that a significant number of other propositions/ideas presuppose. For a question to be foundational means that the position one takes with respect to its resolve acts to support (significant) other dependent positions; the foundations aspect of a discourse is therefore that which supports other parts of that discourse.

What would it then mean to solve this great divide? That is, what could it mean for the foundations of technological disciplines to bridge this divide, by combining aspects of social situations and not just of the devices involved? While we did not set out to address this question, our work can be read as doing so, but for the limited context of IR&S. As this book will argue, this bridging is crucial for progress in IR&S and entails a nontrivial reorientation and reimagining of the discipline as a science of technology-mediated experience (STME).[4] Because bridging occurs primarily at the foundations level, it is a task of foundations research, as opposed to being a task primarily of empirical research, for example; and such research is rather lacking in IR&S and occupies little space in IR&S discourse.

This book is best understood as a prolegomenon to a foundations discourse for IR&S that is on its way to becoming a STME. It is therefore a preliminary foundations discourse for such a future STME. This book presents the way to a new beginning for IR&S by means of a reorientation. What we ultimately hope for from this project for a STME is to encourage a particular type of research culture based on an intellectual framework. This book presents such a framework, a pattern of thought and dialectic, as a condition of possibility for such a culture. However it is not sufficient to activate that culture. That requires people to absorb and live-out the pattern, to "speak the pattern-language" (to borrow the notion from Alexander, 1979), to engage with the intellectual framework, and to continuously change and adapt it to deal with novel contexts. We hope this book will help instill the necessary part of that culture, by inspiring scholars to engage with basic principles.

From Search to Technology-Mediated Experience

The above motivation for this book stemmed from the general discourse of human–machine relations and was only developed post hoc—as a corollary—once most of our arguments in it were already clear. We were instead motivated by a more concrete problem specific to IR&S and to the modern application context. The problem is based on an observation

---

4. It is unclear what kind of science it is to be. But what is intriguing perhaps is that it is neither a purely technical discipline nor a social or humanistic one. Nor do the labels "multi-," "plu-," or "inter-disciplinary," in their popular sense of a "roughly defined concoction of methods and concepts used to solve a problem" quite capture it.

about the nature of modern technology with respect to the technology created by IR&S (i.e., search technology): Given the increasingly pervasive nature of modern technology, applications are moving from enabling the simple finding of information to its use, enjoyment, or in general, to facilitating any type of desired experience with information. However, what actually counts as search experience or as information seeking? What phenomena ought to be delimited as search phenomena? And in general, what types of such experience are possible, and what overall aims are they based on? Unexamined answers to these basic questions are implicit in the use of every application, and the contemporary context requires that they be confronted more directly. To address these questions, one would have to designate a subset of human activities as search or seeking phenomena to be investigated through a corresponding science. This science would then, in accordance with a set of aims or values (e.g., efficiency, effectiveness, and the enjoyment of information finding) influence the design of applications that facilitate these activities and make possible the corresponding types of human experience. Therefore, the nature of the applications depend on the positions taken on the basic questions. However, these positions are routinely presupposed in a significant part of the discourse in information science (IS; which seeks to study information-related phenomena) and in information retrieval (IR; which is concerned with applying IS discourse to the creation of applications that generate and manage information phenomena).

The basic questions are not limited to the nature of search but also pertain to the cultural constitution of a person; the definitions of information, query, document, and (retrieval) application or device; and to what values should guide software design. Positions taken on the basic questions form the stable initial understandings, from which theoretical frameworks for representing the relevant empirical objects and processes are derived. This is the case whether the frameworks are mathematically rich or incline more toward nonmathematical concepts. It is to the extent that positions about these questions are presupposed in existing research that they can be understood as basic/foundational questions and investigations of them as foundations research. Foundations research therefore differs from the "theoretical research" that employs these theoretical frameworks to understand particular empirical search or seeking scenarios.

Foundations research does not only discuss specific questions about each of the entities employed in discourse. It also problematizes the discipline and discourse as a whole, and one of the most important questions that result from this is that of the overall value of the discourse and discipline.

That is, whether there is progress therein, and indeed about what progress means in the first place: Does it have more to do with the growth of application-oriented mathematical models, or to the growth of explanatory frameworks that improve our understanding of phenomena? By problematizing the discourse as a whole, foundations research investigates the logical and scientific coherence between concepts and praxis in the models and frameworks, and it studies the ontological, epistemological, and ethical positions presumed therein. By investigating progress and scientific coherence, foundations research in IR&S joins with discourses, such as with the philosophy of science, and seeks to apply their findings to IR&S. Yet such research is not limited to critique. It is also formative, since it involves the development of definitions, principles, arguments, and theories.

This book develops such a foundations research discourse by addressing the question of progress in IR&S and by establishing a network of fundamental questions pertaining to relevant phenomena, methodology, and the nature of scientific propositions therein. This discourse, cognizant of the creative fusion of interdisciplinary approaches required for addressing increasingly pervasive application contexts, seeks to reorient IR&S from focusing on search (and related processes, such as information seeking) to focusing on the more general (and encapsulating) phenomenon of technology-mediated experience. This shift is significant for two reasons. First, technology-mediated experience accounts for an increasing portion of human lived-experience. The phenomenon of mediation gets to the heart of what the human–machine relationship is about. Second, framing IR&S in this way generalizes its problems and perspectives, making them more amenable to comparison with those of related disciplines, such as information systems and web science. The book argues that such a reorientation—centered on a rigorous foundation—is paramount to significant progress in IR&S.

Synopsis

Chapter 1 introduces different ways of understanding technology, focusing on the character of modern technology as mediating between the world and the human observer. It then argues that search, the central phenomenon for IR&S, in being a meaning-suggesting process, is the most typical mediation phenomenon enabling this character. By showing the importance of the phenomenon of search for mediation and in turn for the human–machine relationship, the study of search (and related phenomena, such as information seeking) is shown to occupy a central position among technological disciplines; and it is IR&S discourse that currently focuses on such study albeit without recognizing its important role. Moreover, chapter 1 introduces the study of search as it is undertaken in IR&S, differentiating between research perspectives permeating the discourse. It characterizes foundations research as one such perspective that usually lies hidden or embedded without being explicitly exposed, and argues that the contemporary context particularly engenders foundations research. Finally, chapter 1 contextualizes the question of progress as a specific type of foundations research question and frames the remainder of the book as an attempt to expose and develop this overall foundations research perspective. Foundations research is important as without it foundations questions such as the question about the place and role of IR&S among technology discourses remain unresolved. Progress is impeded as a result.

Chapter 2 further explores the importance of foundations questions for the modern context. It demonstrates the role foundational questions play in nonfoundational research such as technical and experimental research. In particular, chapter 2 shows that IR&S discourse is guided implicitly by positions taken on the foundational question of what it means to make progress. These positions correspond to implicit notions of progress, such as discourse coherence, the effective construal of phenomena, and the generalizability and explainability of results, which are also notions common to scientific disciplines and used to assess progress therein. This chapter also discusses how positions are assumed about several other foundational questions, but it relates them back to the question of progress. It argues that progress is dependent on their resolution.

Chapter 3 explicitly raises the question of what progress means for IR&S and partially addresses this question using the ideas of scientific progress from the history and philosophy of science. It differentiates between the inner and outer parts of discourse—corresponding in some sense to the foundational and nonfoundational—showing how their relative growth contributes to the different stages of progress in scientific disciplines.

Chapter 4 further refines the arguments of chapter 3 to suggest that progress in IR&S calls for more explicit linking between technical and nontechnical aspects of discourse[5] but shows that this would require rethinking the nature of the elements of discourse (theories, propositions and such) and their interrelations. It would also require close coordination between discourse elements that have different functions. In particular,

---

5. This can be read as the linking between application and theory from Goguen's (1999) account mentioned above.

following from arguments in chapters 2 and 3 about the need for a more explanatory discourse, explanatory elements of discourse would have to be well linked to other aspects. Thus progress requires thorough linking between foundational and nonfoundational aspects of discourse. In addition, good linking in the nonfoundational part of discourse—needed for progress—is predicated on a well-linked foundational discourse.

Chapter 5 develops a network of basic questions whose address is a prerequisite for progress, and it works to "grow foundations" by further structuring this network. It does this by forming an initial discursive framework relating these questions that complements the framework developed in chapter 4 and by elaborating on the resolution of several of the most important questions about this network, focusing on explaining what their characteristics must be to successfully cater to the modern context. Moreover, it explains that there are properties that should apply to the network as a whole, such as that: It should have a hierarchical structure and be centered on questions about

1. how the technological and humanistic aspects of technology-mediated phenomena should be related;
2. what the relationship is between aspects of the general phenomenon of technology-mediation and concepts used in IR&S discourse, such as search (first introduced in chapter 1); and
3. what the disciplinary identity of IR&S should be.

It suggests that any resolution to the first two questions needs to employ a theory of technology; it adapts one such theory from philosophy of technology discourses, which induces further structure on the network.

The resultant discursive framework constituted by the foundational questions is the basis for the well-linked foundations discourse that chapter 4 supposed is necessary for progress. That is, the intellectual engagement with this overall framework would lead to the necessary progressive growth in foundations and would consequently reorient IR&S discourse to become centered on a rigorous foundation. This reorientation has an inevitable consequence that is more radical. Not only does it imply a corresponding need to reorient the research culture, but the fact that the foundations network is constituted by basic questions common to various disciplines tackling technology-mediated experience suggests that perhaps the identity of the discipline needs to be rethought. Thus the third question becomes urgent to address.

Chapter 6 contextualizes this book among prior foundational discourses focusing on the question of identity posed in chapter 5 as to what kind of field IR&S is. It argues for the continual relevance of such foundations due to the relevance of IR&S-like discourse, as the need to understand and create richer types of technology-mediated experience is not expected to subside any time soon. Chapter 6 suggests that this need will be difficult to meet without reimagining the relationship between IR and IS. First, the chapter considers them to be integrated, but more significantly, since they constitute an intellectual discipline that seeks to study phenomena, it proposes that they should be recognized as aspects of a hitherto undeveloped STME. Second, since IR&S fulfills a practical function in developing technology and modifying culture, it should be understood as a nontrivial, modern instantiation of the traditional arts of memory. Where the memory arts, a precursor to modern computation, were used to acquire experiences by means of cognitive techniques often aided by machines. The focus therein was on the relationship between humans and techniques or technology/machines, that is, on the mediated experience beyond the technology. Going back to the premodern memory arts means re-focusing on this technology-mediated experience.

Finally, chapter 7 proposes ethical, social, and disciplinary implications of not actively engaging in authoritative foundations research. These are the effects of not seeking to make progress in the ways suggested in prior chapters. It also discusses the importance of IR&S's progress for related fields.

Reading This Book

This book can be read in several ways. Consider first the following brief overview. Chapter 1 contextualizes IR&S phenomena within technology discourses in general. Chapter 2 can be read as a rational reconstruction of aspects of IR&S discourse with respect to understanding progress therein. Progress is more formally treated in chapters 3 and 4. Chapter 5 develops a framework for foundations problems in IR&S, centered on reorienting the phenomena of interest and relating these problems to general intellectual problems. Chapter 6 relates our foundational discourse to prior ones and argues for reorienting the identity of IR&S to that of a new kind of science, for the sake of progress. Chapter 7 focuses on the implications of not doing progressive research on IR&S scholarship.

This book highlights research problems in IR&S that are shared across disciplines from cognitive computation, information systems, and human-computer interaction that deal explicitly with socio-technical phenomena (i.e., both the technical and social aspects). These problems are similarly relevant for discourses that deal with such phenomena in a more implicit way, such as in the emerging area of explainable artificial intelligence. This book is therefore of relevance to researchers regardless of disciplinary association who are interested in the implications of bringing together the technical and social aspects in an intellectual framework.

Most importantly, this book is for new researchers and postgraduates who are not constrained by disciplinary boundaries and want to work on multi-faceted problems with wide remit. For such readers the best course of action is to read the book from start to finish. These are the readers who can be expected to contribute to foundations research.

Curious researchers and professionals of any discipline, who are navigating their way around problems in pervasive applications of technology and around the rapidly changing boundaries between disciplines (and between industry and academia) may wonder how to make sense of this contemporary reality and understand the near future. The best place for such a reader to start is would be at chapter 1. If they are not particularly interested in IR&S but only in the concepts therein shared by technology disciplines in general, then they should continue with chapters 5 and 7 and skim chapters 3 and 6.

Practitioners and researchers interested mainly in experimentation and technical aspects, and in general readers who require immediate IR&S-centered motivations to delve into foundations may want to begin with chapters 2 and 7. These chapters show how foundations issues relate to the technical and experimental aspects of discourse, and they explain the dangers of not doing foundations research. This should be followed by a cursory reading of chapter 5 to see what constitutes foundations research, and then of chapters 3 and 4 if the particular question of progress then appeals; chapters 1, 5 and 6 should then be read in full.

Finally, interdisciplinary scholars who study the relationship between humans and technology, especially from a humanities perspective (e.g., new media studies, digital humanities, science and technology studies, history and philosophy of science and technology, and the philosophy of technology) and who incline to critical-analytical discourse of a philosophical bent should take the following route: chapters 1, 3 and 5–7. If they are particularly interested in how foundational issues appear in IR&S research, they should also add chapter 2 to that list, and if they are interested to see how philosophy of science concepts need to be adapted for a mixed scientific-humanistic discourse like IR&S, then chapter 4 should be read as well.

1 The Embedding of the Foundational in the Ad Hoc

1.1 Introduction: The Nature of Modern Technology

The question of what technology is has occupied thinkers for millenia (Mitcham and Huning, 1986; Scharff and Dusek, 2014). The works of Martin Heidegger (and his students), in framing technology—specifically, modern technology—have arguably had the most influence in the contemporary period, on post-war philosophers and sociologists of technology (Feenberg, 2002). Heidegger takes the traditional understanding of technology to be either the means to ends or a type of human activity, corresponding respectively to the instrumental and anthropological perspectives. Instrumental perspectives frame a situation according to instrumental rationality, which in the context of critical theory is a form of rationality that focuses on the efficient means for achieving an end without itself reflecting on the value of that end (cf. Kolodny and Brunero, 2013). In the rational evaluation of actions, instrumental reasoning focuses on the "how" of an action instead of the "why": on characterizing technological situations in terms of the static configurations of actual instruments and the possible (and actual) operations performed by them. Anthropological perspectives in general focus on the human activity associated with such situations, and through this incline more toward addressing the whys.

In his seminal work on the question of technology, Heidegger suggests that the instrumental and anthropological perspectives belong together, "For to posit ends and procure and utilize the means to them is a human activity. The manufacture and utilization of equipment, tools, and machines, the manufactured and used things themselves, and the needs and ends that they serve, all belong to what technology is" (Heidegger, 1977, pp. 4–5).

Against the purely instrumental perspective, "technology" refers not only to the operations of physical machines as tools but also to a complex configuration of resources, people, designs, and physical objects (chapter 5 further characterizes this configuration). Each such configuration is a (not necessarily unique) means to solve a problem, to achieve an end. Its design reflects the interests of the actors involved: it is socially conditioned, as is the initial problem definition for which it is a solution (Feenberg, 2010). As a result, an account of the efficiency of a design or a constituting device is insufficient for explaining its success or failure (Feenberg, 2010, p. 67):

> Efficiency is not the decisive factor in explaining the success or failure of alternative designs since several viable options usually compete at the inception of a line of development. Technology is "underdetermined" by the criterion of efficiency and responsive to the various particular interests and ideologies that select among these options.

Technology then refers simultaneously to phenomena that are technical and abstract, social[1] and political (Feenberg, 2009; Day, 2008): "The domain of technology and that of everyday experience cannot be separated from each other; they are mutually constitutive" (Dourish and Bell, 2011, p. 73).

Heidegger affords technology yet another dimension. For him technology also concerns the ontological, neither in the sense of being concerned with objects in the world as such (i.e. ontology as the catalog of different things and their properties) nor with human beings vis-à-vis their activities (which the anthropological perspective already addresses). Instead, he means ontological in a fundamental sense: with respect to what it means to be for human beings (i.e., an ontology of ways of being and existing; Gelven, 1989). Technology as a particular configuration of designs, devices, and people (engineered devices, material objects, and means by which people know things and live; see Wilson, 2002) thereby conditions our overall mode of being or existing. This does not refer, for example, to particular emotions or feelings of particular people during instances of device use (i.e., properties of individual psyches) but instead to intersubjective existential regularities (which of course may also relate to psychological regularities) in groups of people or, as in Heidegger's case in particular, to large sections of

---

1. In modern times, devices have become the means by which social structures are effected and affected, societies created and known about. The study of technology in modern times has to therefore be concerned with social epistemology (Goldman and Blanchard, 2016). This concern manifests in technical discourses in different ways, often in discussions of human factors or user studies. A thorough discussion of what a device is and what it does from a perspective influenced by Heidegger's theory of technology can be found in Borgmann (2009). While the present book does not further engage with Borgmann, it can be understood as doing the preliminary work for a future such engagement.

humankind in some historical context.[2] This overall effect of technology not only manifests during device use; it also conditions the user's overall life experience beyond that particular use.[3] Thus, for Heidegger, what technology is depends on the historical context one is in, and in particular, modern technology differs from the technology of any other known period. That there is a difference (even a radical difference) in the human effects of modern technology, postindustrialization and post-Internet, is self-evident. However, the difference for Heidegger is also ontological in the sense of his fundamental ontology; this ontological dimension is further discussed in chapters 5 and 6. Technology is thereby understood to significantly influence human existence, but the particulars of this influence, especially in the context of modern technology, are not all apparent.

Technology, as a diverse configuration of elements that are means to ends, corresponds to systems of control. These systems can be understood top-down, in terms of their overall social, political, or ontological dimension, whether the scope is an office or society as a whole. However, this book will mainly take a relatively bottom-up perspective that instead considers technology with respect to the imbrication of devices, applications, interactive phenomena, and algorithms that are of immediate influence on user experience.

It is clear from this bottom-up perspective that an increasing portion of everyday human experience is mediated by these devices. If the idea of technology having ontological significance, of determining human ways of being, could be dismissed some decades ago as philosophical excess or a merely abstract hypothesis, it certainly can no longer. The idea has perhaps never been more acutely realized than in the modern context, where technology mediates in a pervasive fashion. Contemporary lived experience is conditioned by devices and applications (from the bottom up), and from top down by the sociopolitical systems such applications and devices help create and/or sustain. It is as though we are increasingly only living in the world that is revealed to us by these devices. This intimate

2. Specifically, Heidegger's analysis applies not to an individual subject (a being) which deals with objects, nor to a statistical grouping of several subjects (beings), but to a way of being that uniquely characterizes human beings. He names this Dasein.

3. The experience of a person refers to more than a purely psychological or cognitive dimension: Experience is embodied. The use of technology corresponds to an embodied experience, where "embodiment is not a property of systems, technologies, or artifacts; it is a property of interaction" (Dourish, 2004, p. 189), i.e., it is a property referring to our participation in the world, in this case through technology.

mediating character of modern technology—its salient aspect—works to reveal and hide the world, to amplify and reduce (or constrain) capabilities and actions therein (Ihde, 1979).

Section 1.1.1 further explores this revealing/hiding character of mediation, while sections 1.1.2 and 1.1.3 clarify the particulars of technologies that enable mediation focusing on how mediation phenomena can be construed; these sections describe the main aspects of the bottom-up perspective of technology. The remaining sections in the chapter further characterize modern technology from this perspective through the phenomenon of search, a particularly (and peculiarly) typical mediational phenomenon. As a representative phenomenon of mediation, it can be construed to expose the anthropological, instrumental, and as developed later in chapter 5, the ontological aspect of mediation. Moreover, as also discussed in chapter 5, the search phenomenon as a representative mediational phenomenon facilitates the linking between the bottom-up and top-down perspectives of technology, and additionally, suggests the possibility of studying technology and technology-mediation in a way that combines humanistic and scientific-technical accounts through a new kind of science (see chapter 6).

Section 1.2 introduces conceptions of search found in different discourses, identifying the semantic conception of search as central. Section 1.3 introduces information retrieval (IR) and information science (IS) as disciplines studying that particular conception. While the precise relation between IR and IS is problematized in later chapters, the proceeding introduces the composite IR&S (information retrieval and science) as an otherwise unspecified combination of whatever IR and IS are considered to be.

Section 1.3 both elaborates on discipline-specific variations of the semantic conception of search in IR&S and provides a structure for IR&S research according to a typology of research perspectives. Section 1.4 employs this typology to argue that, in spite of the overall focus of modern technological disciplines, whether toward the instrumental or anthropological, they are increasingly compelled to address questions whose subject matter go beyond these aspects toward the foundational. Research pertaining to foundational questions includes but is not limited to those about ontology in the Heideggerean sense mentioned above. The remainder of this text, particularly chapter 5, develops a foundations perspective centered on an ontological perspective of technology influenced by Heidegger. Section 1.5 discusses different types of such questions but focuses on those about the purpose, growth, and progress of a discipline. Section 1.6 summarizes the main arguments of this chapter.

By showing the place and importance of search as a phenomenon among other technological phenomena, this chapter aims to demonstrate the importance of IR&S as a discipline that both studies search and creates technologies to enable it. The problems constituting IR&S, especially the foundational problems (including those of progress addressed in the remaining chapters) are to a large extent shared by numerous other such discourses responsible for enabling and understanding the contemporary human situation as conditioned by technology-mediated living. IR&S therefore has an important but unrealized role among technology discourses. And while there is a trend towards foundational questions (see section 1.4 and chapter 2), it needs to be fully developed for the sake of progress (see chapters 3 and 4) through a reorientation of the discipline. It is only then that IR&S's role can be realized, only then that IR&S can come into its own.

1.1.1 Mediation as Revealing and Hiding

Our everyday understanding of the world is constituted by our cognizance of local social groupings (family, work, friends, and activity circles), groupings based on ethnicity or nationality, and even larger groupings based on world events and historical context. All these aspects constitute our *sociological imagination* (Mills, 2000; Aronowitz, 2003; Fuller, 2006). Given that technologically mediated living accounts for an increasing portion of lived experience, our sociological imagination is similarly increasingly determined by, and hence limited to, what technology is able to reveal about these different aspects. For example, search system recommendations that determine our choice of restaurants (or gathering places), are increasingly limited to those that have a web presence. Our interactions with others is determined by their social media representations. Basic skills, such as our way of reading books, strategies for learning and ability to comprehend, and habitual ways of thinking through ideas (i.e., cognitive processes) are highly influenced by technologies that mediate the corresponding experiences. And, in addition to our understanding of the public sphere, our self-understanding (i.e., understanding of identity), especially with respect to the difference between our identities and that of others (i.e., the construction of *otherness*; Miller, 2008), are all increasingly determined by technologically mediated experience. This construction of otherness is conditioned by opinions about world events and the like from online news media—from articles to video streams. However, this conditioning is not only through the raw content; the medium through which the content is received also conditions.

The medium corresponds to the technical design mediating between the user/observer and the basic message text or content on the other end, and determines much: from enabling modes of experience in the observer, to effecting socio-cultural or political changes (McLuhan, 1994). Technological mediation as a phenomenon is facilitated by such media. The technical design of media is therefore an important means for understanding this mediation. The study of technological mediation is thereby concerned with the role of technology in human experience and human action (Verbeek, 2009, p. 228). With respect to experience, this role is conceived as "the ways in which their world is present to them" and with respect to action as "the ways in which human beings are present in the world" (Verbeek, 2009, p. 228). Their being present in the world corresponds to what they do with or through technology, and this concerns how they interact with technology. Having the world presented to them corresponds to the way they understand the world, given their technology-mediated experiences of it. By being present in the world and having the world presented to them, the user is a participant in a tripartite relationship between human, device, and "the world." A mediational phenomenon would then be something that always involves human experience and sometimes human action.

Every act or experience mediated through technology conditions the world that is mediated. In mediating, technology reveals aspects of reality, but it simultaneously hides other aspects. This is in the sense of setting up a perspective and narrative, and therefore prioritizing some aspects of the message over others. It not only sets up the narrative, it also tends to limit other possible narratives by implicitly suggesting the importance/centrality of its own narrative. In any narrative (i.e., something that is reported) some aspects of an event are left out and others included according to the perspective and agency of the narrative's author. However, algorithms also have narrative agency: Automatically recommended videos on YouTube or books on Amazon express an interpretation of public opinion about those videos and books. These recommendations are not value neutral.

Therefore, technologies cannot be sufficiently explained or differentiated solely by reference to their technical designs. Nor is it sufficient to evaluate them by means of the value of efficiency (which underdetermines them; Feenberg, 2009). Instead they must be approached through a diverse perspective made up of ways of understanding phenomena across the humanities and sciences. It is not that these different ways would merely be useful for understanding technology, but that—given what technology is—the nature of technological phenomena demand such an approach. To study technological phenomena means to consider the dimension of the immediately empirically given in perception (as does the material device), to the sociopolitical and formal-abstract (computational and mathematical), and all the way to the dimension of the existential (or fundamental-ontological). Certainly, if any group of phenomena warrants the dissolution of disciplinary boundaries and the fusion of methodologies on either side of Snow's two cultures (Furedi et al., 2009),[4] then it is the study of technological phenomena.

1.1.2 Modern Devices as Enabling Mediation Phenomena

The bottom-up view of technology is concerned with devices, the different types of which can be understood to form a range: from specialized nonprogrammable devices (e.g., nail-cutters, sunglasses, and traditional telephones and microwaves)[5] to general programmable devices (e.g., camera-phones and personal computers; Dourish, 2004, p. 195). Our relation to a specialized device is different from a general-purpose one; they mediate our experience of the world differently. By allowing for different applications, general-purpose devices are fluid in their functionality and interactive possibilities. Therefore, what they mean to us—and our relationship with them—is changeable; this opens up a range of relational possibilities. The potentially richer interaction patterns the device may offer, conditioned by a specific application, elicit different levels of attention toward the device that make possible a much more diverse set of mediated experiences.

These experiences range from single interaction command-response type usages that are at a far lower level of communication than that between humans and domestic animals, to natural language and gesture-based interaction that resemble human conversation and perhaps even work to develop human-like relationships between human and machine.[6] The latter type of technology, by seeking to imitate or replicate human experience (or go beyond it), appears to be the end goal of modern trends in the technology industry. In this chapter, modern devices are understood to

4. Snow's two cultures are the humanistic and scientific cultures.

5. The traditional (specialized) devices are either nonprogrammable or, if programmable, then they are not usually reprogrammed or developed through software changes that can add further functionality, new interactive possibilities, or make other changes that affect the user's experience.

6. The human-machine relationship exhibited in the movie *Minority Report* (Spielberg, 2002) can be understood as a vision for ideal or effective interactions between humans and machines. Jonze's more recent film *Her* (Jonze, 2014) takes this ideal much further, envisioning a different mode of human-machine relationship, where the machine was able to create and maintain an intimate relationship with a human; the machine thus simulated a separate conscious/living entity. Personal assistant and question-answering technologies, such as Watson, Siri, and Viv, are recent examples of products inline with such technological futures.

be entities constituting this type of technology: They correspond to the whole range of general-purpose programmable devices, from desktop computers to portable augmented-reality devices that can be interacted with.[7] The type of mediation such technology engenders is what is responsible for the intensely technology-mediated nature of modern life.[8]

To understand modern technology through its mediating nature, whether from the bottom-up or top-down perspective, is to do so through mediating phenomena: specifications of regular/stable/organized events or occurrences that stipulate what it is that mediates between two distinct things and how it does so. Identifying or constructing a mediation phenomenon pertaining to technology mediation means to deduce a relation between humans, technology (devices or institutions and systems of control/influence) and the world. From the bottom-up perspective, such a phenomenon would typically refer to a user intention or interaction, a technical configuration (such as an algorithm), and a world object (or a representation thereof). Many such phenomena can be construed. For example, an augmented reality phenomenon that refers to user interaction, an object in the real world, and the augmented representation of that object on a device, would constitute such a mediation phenomenon were it to be a regular occurrence.

Any such phenomenon would presumably be facilitated by a device. Devices mediate between the world and the user. That a device is mediating a user's experience is a statement about one or more events of device/technology-use. These events together constitute the user's overall experience of technological mediated living. For technology designers who seek to modify/create devices and engender that mediation, and hence seek to design what is mediated and how it is mediated, it is insufficient to simply state that mediation is taking place. It is uninformative on its own as a fact. It is instead necessary to understand the role of applications and particular properties of devices in determining mediated experience. The next section explores how the phenomenon of mediation—which is a category

---

7. This does not include such technologies as sensor networks or cloud-based devices by themselves but only as aspects of a technological solution with an interface that provides a means of human interaction, and hence a means of mediating experience.

8. There is a wealth of philosophy of technology literature that further refine the simple picture given here of the relationships between humans and technology (see Introna, 2011). All that is required from the outset, for the purposes of this book, is to find rational the proposition that devices do mediate our experience, and that there are potentially several types of mediation and several different ways of construing mediation.

of human experience—is related to device use, by further developing the particulars of mediation and of technology-use.

1.1.3   Construing Device-Based Mediational Processes

At the level of human experience, technology-mediated experience can be understood to have its own particular modes or types; Verbeek (2010) provides such a typology of mediated modes that is fit for our purposes. Briefly, the mediation experience facilitated by the Google glasses corresponds to an embodiment type of mediation. The experience of reading a thermometer corresponds to a hermeneutic type of mediation. Experiencing subtle or non-immediately perceptible changes to an environment caused by user detection or interaction corresponds to a background mediation. Finally, the traditional user-system scenario, such as the use of an ATM machine (where the system is distinctly an "other") corresponds to an alterity type of mediation (Verbeek, 2010). In each such mode, device use can be understood and expressed in terms of physical "moves" made or behaviors exhibited by the user and system. Thus we say, at the level of human experience, device use can be construed with respect to the mode of mediation and in terms of these moves and behaviors. By construal we mean an interpretation and specification of a phenomenon by means of which the phenomenon can be understood, and by reference to which it can be discussed.[9] When such a construal instead mainly references the technical operations of the device or limits the narrative to user behaviors (interactions) in a technical sense (e.g., what kind of system inputs they pertain to), then it is relatively instrumental. When the construal instead focuses more on the human meaning of the physical actions, both of the user and the system, it is relatively more anthropological.

At a relatively instrumental level, device use can be construed in terms of requests given to the device (through interaction) combined with the received (or observed) responses from the device. In this respect, the

---

9. We take the notion of construing as being between defining and describing. A construal is a rigorous and analytical goal-oriented description of a phenomenon that refers to some aspects of a phenomenon and ignores other. The goal here would pertain to how the construal is to be used in a discourse. A construal does not purport to be a, let alone 'the,' definition of that phenomenon. A construal should therefore neither be taken as a subjective nor as an objective account of something, but instead an "intersubjective" account of it. That is, it is an account that is open to being agreed-upon between several parties upon rational argumentation without necessarily being a certain account agreed-upon by all.

requests a device can accept would be delimited by its technical configuration. For example, the form of the requests could be construed with reference to the event of a tactile movement, such as a button press, while responses/feedbacks could be specified by referring to the visual or tactile effect, such as an image of a depressed button (on screen) or the changing of screens on the interface. In particular, when construing device use for a device engendering an alterity type of mediation (i.e., the device is a clear and tangible other in a two-agent process), a request-response type of construal scheme employing simple tactile or visual events is useful. Consider instead a device that offers an embodiment type of mediation; the same scheme can also be used, except that the request construal would perhaps be constituted by the gaze position (and other details of body orientation) of a user and require specification of a series of contextual elements, and thus be more complex—even if still a relatively instrumental construal. However, the rather significant qualitative detail—and so the more intimate mode of mediation (and device use)—does not figure into such an instrumental construal. An instrumental construal of device use thereby stays close to the physical level. It is limited to referring to a set of technical operations (of the device) and system inputs corresponding to user interactions. And even if it were to mention the aspects of human beings involved in the interaction (eye movement and gaze, for example), it would not go so far as to mention what such interactions mean as human behavior. These aspects of a human user would only be mentioned to the extent that they influenced further system responses, so as to paint a picture of the instrumental reasoning that the device engages in. Thus, no mention would be made of the user's cognitive or reasoning processes that lead to their behavior.

If instead the aforementioned operations are given more meaning from a human perspective, such that device use is construed in a more cognitive-behavioral sense as an aspect of an encompassing human activity, then this would cross into a relatively more anthropological construal. For example, this would be the case where instead of requests and responses, the operation is construed as the asking of questions and receiving of answers (as opposed to technically specified requests/responses). This is because such a construal now corresponds to a predefined human social activity. Such an activity, as a concept, does not require reference to technological devices, it is conceivable without such a reference.

It is precisely in such an anthropological construal that the mode of mediation can be specified, as it pertains to the qualitative dimension of experience. That is, even though each mode of mediation requires a particular type of user–device configuration, an instrumental construal of the use of that device is inherently unable to capture this qualitative aspect of mediation, which has to do with the overall user experience.

It is important here to make explicit why instrumental construals are essentially thus limited. First, it is for a human observer that the world is mediated. Second, that the device mediates the world for human observers implies that it presents something about that world (i.e., it re-presents it) in a way that has meaning for the observers. Third, it is the signs (i.e., linguistic or nonlinguistic meaning carriers) that mean something for human observers.[10] Hence, any non-trivial construal of (device-based) mediation should refer to what is mediated and how the world is being represented or revealed (see prior section) to a human observer (i.e. what the world comes to mean for them), and this must be a relatively anthropological construal.

Not only are there many technological processes that mediate in different modes, there are several ways to construe them; some relatively more instrumental or anthropological than others. The next section focuses on one such type of mediating process: the search process. As the following will argue, search is not only a significant phenomenon of mediation, it is the most typical of the device-based mediation processes and a phenomenon whose emergence is concomitant with the use of modern devices. To study search then is to study modern technology in general, through an example typifying its character. The next section identifies several ways of construing such a process. It isolates one construal that sways just enough toward the anthropological for it to be used to understand what it means for search to mediate, while not straying too far from the instrumental as to hide how technological configurations make this mediation possible.

10. From the perspective of semiotics (the study of signs and signification) human experience has to do with the interpretive processes "mediated and sustained by signs" (Deely, 2005, p. 8), where signs bring together the natural and social. In the above case, the technology is providing the signs that mediate: it is suggesting meanings by producing signs. Or, more simply, the technology mediates the world, since the signs it generates reveal or re-present the world. A thorough analysis of the place of semiotics discourse in construing technology mediation would be of great use, especially from a foundations point of view, and while this book sets up a foundation for a later such engagement, it is beyond the scope of this book. Brier (2008) can be consulted as the initial basis for any such future engagement; see also Beuchot and Deely (1995) and Bains (2014).

1.2   Search: A Significant Phenomenon of Mediation

Search is an activity, a phenomenon pertaining to human interaction with modern devices and media. It is a means by which devices that engender it can mediate experience. Moreover, search makes it possible for those devices to mediate experience and facilitates this mediation. Thus, search is a mediational phenomenon, and it works to mediate human living. This section explores the nature of search as a mediational phenomenon. Section 1.2.1 introduces different conceptions of search using the typology developed in section 1.1.3 and shows how the different types of mediation processes discussed therein can yet be understood as types of search. It then argues that search is not only a type of mediational phenomenon, but a peculiarly typical one at that. Section 1.2.2 explains this peculiarity by introducing the semantic conception of search which is said to be presupposed by these various other processes. The salient focus of this concept is that ability of search and hence of processes that presuppose it, to generate and suggest meaning, i.e. their meaning-generating and meaning-suggesting ability. This is what makes search, construed as semantic search, peculiarly typical. Section 1.2.3 explains how this concept of search is presupposed in computational processes and applications, formal processes and concepts, and in the experience of device use, and why it is therefore a representative mediation phenomenon.

1.2.1   Conceptions of Search

Search can be understood initially, in the sense discussed in section 1.1.3, as a type of request-response process, and usually as the matching between query words given as a request (as words expressed) to a device and documents provided as a response (as words observed) from that device. This concept of search is typically employed in IR&S. That is, search is thought of as a technological process that mediates in the mode of alterity.

However, this concept of search is

(1) not the only type of search;
(2) not the only way to construe search (i.e., as requests in the form of word-based queries and responses as word-based documents);
(3) not the only mode of mediation that search engenders; and most importantly,
(4) not a specification of search that captures its special role among mediational phenomena.

Instead, the variations in each of these aspects need to be explored.

With respect to (1), IR&S does consider more complex types of search, such as ostensive/implicit search that can work with gestures,[11] as well as search as a process that is more complex than simple matching through considering, for example, searches that employ prior usage information.[12]

As for (2), search as the matching of queries and documents can be construed in many ways. As an algorithm, it refers to a computational process that compares linguistic words as data elements, whether represented as an array of strings or as matrix elements of a numerical type (as required by the algorithms associated with vector space representations), or the probabilistic representation of such words in a set of documents. Search can be specified as a static, set-theoretical (i.e., mathematical and functional) relationship between two subsets, representing parts of documents. It can also be construed as a cognitive-behavioral process that considers, for example, a user's information needs and the intentions behind their interactions that in turn influence the queries they formulate. This latter specification (like the corresponding specification in the request-response case in section 1.2.1), is relatively more anthropological than the former, and the former is relatively more instrumental than the latter. That is, the latter construal considers phenomena pertaining to the user or provides a

11. In the case of ostensive retrieval/search, where the immediate objects corresponding to requests are visual objects on screen, the response is only given through taking the word(s) corresponding to that immediate object. Since it is the underlying object/word(s) that is conditioning the response, we take it to constitute the main semantic (meaningful) aspect of the request at the semantic level of phenomena construal (see chapter 5). Clearly the immediate object (e.g., a blue circle that partially represents some book in a visual manner) can also be sufficiently meaningful and should therefore be seen as having the potential to influence user behavior. Hence it is usable by designers in that way, and can also therefore be seen as significant enough to be part of the construal of mediation phenomena at the semantic level. In addition, the immediate object can be given further meaning through adding another semiotic layer or sub-layer (within the semantic); however, this is beyond the scope of this book.

12. Search may not be the primary function of an application. It may be employed as part of another, more primary function, e.g., where word-word matching is a background process for finding related data to support the function of adding a new calendar item. In this case, search as a computational function is subsumed in another function. Search can similarly be presupposed in other senses, e.g., as a behavioral process. This is the case for information-seeking processes, which are a general class of processes that subsume search. They are further explored in IR&S discourse; see section 1.3.

more human-oriented perspective of the phenomena, whereas the former focuses on the technical or machine-related phenomena or provides a more technical perspective of the phenomena concerned.

In general, conceptions of search can be similarly compared based on whether they incline toward the anthropological or instrumental directions (see section 1.2.2). In addition, conceptions of search can be understood in terms of how abstract or concrete they are. Search construed mathematically in terms of vector spaces results in a concept that is more abstract than when it is construed as a technical design. The resultant concept is similarly more abstract, when construed in the following analogous ways, as (i) logical claims (e.g., that requests imply responses) or as mathematical objects (e.g., the response as the geometric transformation of the request as a geometric object, or as what is probabilistically inferred from the request as an event in a sample space), (ii) natural-scientific phenomena (e.g., request/response as two interacting natural, physical systems [van Rijsbergen, 2004; Arafat, 2011a]), (iii) more humanistically as meaning-making or sense-making or simply a type of hermeneutic/interpretive activity, and (iv) (philosophically or) existentially in terms of how they mediate our experience of being as human beings (Heidegger, 1977). Each such construal provides particular insights and has a particular use.

With respect to (3), consider the case where instead of a large text document, a search presents tweet-like summaries of documents in an augmented-reality environment by means of Google glasses, such that the document summary acts as a means of interpreting the actual physical environment the user locates (e.g., a museum). This is clearly not mediation in the mode of alterity but in the embodiment and hermeneutic modes: the document summary represents something in the world, it partially constitutes the medium that mediates the world for the user, and it does so in a direct visual sense.[13] It is the specific context of search use and the modifications to the search process (e.g., the employment of document summaries instead of full documents) that has greater bearing on the way the overall application serves to mediate than anything specific to the search process embedded therein.

This brings us to (4), the role of search as a mediating process among other mediating processes (i.e., any such processes that encompass or

---

13. However it is not the only thing that represents the world. The use of Google glasses here corresponds to an alternate way of living, and it is this way—with all its particulars, and not just the form of documents shown in the display—that constitutes the main aspect of the medium.

contain a search). There are indeed several ways to construe processes depicting technological mediation through devices, and such construals depict phenomena central to various fields beyond IR, yet are related to search in some way. In each case, the respective field can be understood to be adding layers of meaning to the request/response (input/output) concept. In IR, this concept becomes a query-document relation, and is termed "search." In the natural language processing (NLP) context, this search is understood as a question-answer process. Similarly, it is a learning or classification problem for data science and statistical learning (e.g., the assignment of a class or category to a previously unseen item after training on other items and their classes). It is proposed that these processes do indeed involve a kind of search; a tacit concept of search that denotes the linking of entities in general, not only of queries and documents as for IR&S. Moreover, this tacit notion also appears to be analogous to concepts such as (i–iv) in (2) above. What then is this tacit concept of search, if it is not primarily concerned with query-document relations? The conception of search that is in question, defined in the next section, will be from hereon known as the semantic conception of search.[14] It is a conception and specification of search that leans sufficiently toward the anthropological to indicate the meaning-generating/meaning-suggesting nature of search, yet it stays close to the instrumental to indicate its relation to more technically specified mediation processes (such as encompassing processes).

This semantic conception occupies a central position among other conceptions of search and exemplifies what technological mediation is about. As discussed, it not only pervades the various conceptions of search and discussions of technology-mediation as a concept, but refers to concrete aspects of real-life technology-mediated processes that technologists facilitate and optimize through practical work.

1.2.2 A Semantic Conception of Search: Search as Meaning-Generating and Meaning-Suggesting

Consider a typical algorithmic (or technical) specification or conception of search that depicts a typical search engine; a specification that would be a product of research discourse in IR&S. It would refer to a set of words, interactions, images and the like, as queries, and their relationship with a set of corresponding words, interactions, images and the like, but as documents.

---

14. This should not be confused with "semantic search" (Guha et al., 2003; Dong et al., 2008; Schoefegger et al., 2013).

It would also usually refer to an order for the documents, such as by means of a ranked list, where the rank would supposedly depict the linguistic or semantic closeness of the documents to the given query. Moreover, such a concept would also usually refer to the process or algorithm that shows how the matching is done.

This specification of search thus refers to a semantic operation, that is, an act that has to do with the meaning of linguistic entities.[15] It is semantic first by virtue of the fact that the specification specifies relations among sets of words or meaningful entities proposed through a request by the user to a system in the form of queries, and sets of words or meaningful entities that correspond to system responses (e.g., in the form of documents).[16] Second, it is semantic not merely because the specification refers to meaningful entities and relations between them, but because it serves to generate or suggest new meaningful associations between them, that is, between queries and documents. Let these two senses of "semantic" together constitute the semantic function of search. There is indeed an implication here, since it is only for the human (user) that something can have meaning (Heidegger, 1962, I.1–I.4; Gelven, 1989, 21–34),[17] that the presence of a user is implied in any search that is characterized by the semantic function. However, even if an algorithmic conception depicts a search engine (and corresponding search event) that takes a previously-gathered set of queries in an automated fashion (without a live user entering the queries), it can

15. This is the case even if the specification is more abstract, such as a mathematical specification of relations between two elements in different sets (documents or queries) leading to a resultant set fulfilling particular characteristics. The existence of linguistic elements and the derivation of new relations between such objects implies a semantic operation.

16. It is not only the queries that have been related to documents here by this semantic act, but also queries and documents among themselves. For a ranked list of documents serves not only to relate such documents to a query, but also to relate documents with other documents. Similarly, the issued query is related to all other queries that produce the same or similar ranked lists.

17. The use of search, through the use of a search engine on a device, as an instance of technology mediated living, and therefore, as a meaningful activity: is a language activity (linguistic game playing, or play in general, see Huizinga, 1949). There is a strong connection between the meaning of words and their use in human activities that is the basis for this claim. This connection is beyond the scope of this book, but the connection was explored rigorously by Wittgenstein. An introduction to this work can be found in Stroud (1996). The relation between that work and IR&S is explored in Blair (2006).

still be characterized by the semantic function. This is because both the queries and documents would be meaningful to a user were they involved in this process. In addition, it would be meaningful to them because the search process would serve to suggest new meaningful associations. In contrast, it would not be meaningful to a system. The human actor is therefore assumed even if not explicitly referred to in such algorithmic conceptions, especially for the majority of modern search engines and the contexts of their use.[18]

The physical event of a search corresponding to some algorithmic specification/concept may not always suggest an association to a user (i.e., documents for their query) that is new for the user. However, it may nevertheless lead to new meanings in another sense. Even if all such an event were to do was to confirm what the user already knows, this confirmation would itself confer a new meaning: that the user's understanding is coherent with that of the system. It is also possible that a search generates no recognizable new meanings, however slight. Yet in general, search has the potential to deliver such new meanings. More importantly, the whole raison d'être of search engines is to facilitate search events where new meanings are suggested. Thus, we contend that all search events are characterized by this semantic function, to relate between meaningful entities and to generate new meanings. This is done in the same way as for all computational systems, generally speaking: through automating human processes and seeking to reduce

18. There are indeed cases where, for example, system-generated queries need to be matched to documents, and the queries are perhaps not what real users would ever issue to a typical search engine, but instead concern technical items (e.g., system-generated descriptions of application errors). The documents could perhaps contain technical information about how to resolve these errors and are only to be used by the system without ever being seen by the user. In this case, to the extent that the queries are indirectly and implicitly generated by user action, and the documents implicitly conditioning the user's usage experience (however remotely) through informing the system how to act, we say that the user is merely distant. This type of search could still be characterized as functioning semantically except in a less direct way than the above example. Additionally, even if there is no live user implicitly responsible for the queries and whose experience is being conditioned in a live sense, the user could be responsible and be conditioned in a non-live sense. For example, the queries could derive in some way from the use of the system in one spatiotemporal context and could be used to generate the documents in a completely different context, and nevertheless lead to the conditioning of the usage experience, however indirectly, in yet another context.

human labor (even though they may end up increasing it in concrete cases).

Consider instead the following toy conception of search, the semantic conception of search, that is also characterized by the semantic function but in a purer way. Let the semantic conception of search be a conception that depicts a search event and refers to two associated groups of meaningful items and relations between these two groups. Moreover, let the first such group be typically associated with human users and the second with devices and the world. Finally, suppose that, were a search event to be characterizable according to the semantic conception, that this would entail a physical or computational process that selectively relates between the aforementioned entities. Thus, any conception that were to only mention the meaningful entities and their relations would not be semantic: there must be some reference to a context of technology-use (see Simon, 1999, p. 51).

This semantic conception is purer than the algorithmic one, as it does not further abstract the idea of meaningful entities as queries or documents. Also, although it still refers to a situation of technology-use and assumes the user/device/world relation that is a feature of technology-mediated human experience, it does not further specify these aspects (e.g., by referring to a search engine to specify the device).[19]

This toy conception nevertheless relates to more practical or realistic (i.e., further specified) search conceptions. As the typical algorithmic conception can be characterized by the semantic function, we say that it also presupposes this semantic conception of search. This means that it is reasonable to presume that everything entailed by the semantic conception is also entailed by the typical algorithmic conception (section 1.2.3 further details the idea of presupposition). Hence, the typical algorithmic conception depicts a search event, even though it focuses on the system-side

---

19. The semantic conception of search is fitting for the arguments in this chapter pertaining to the relationship between search and mediational processes, and useful for bringing-out the meaning-suggesting ability of search and its presupposing processes. It does not however, adequately consider the possibility of meaning pertaining to different aspects of mediated experience such as the medium in addition to the content (e.g., document), let alone exposing the relations between these aspects. As such, it does not capture sufficient aspects of technology mediated experience. 5.3.1 and 5.3.2 address this problem through developing a richer characterization of situations of technology-use to address this issue. Indeed, the following chapters, chapter 5 specifically, argue that IR&S must consider the overall technology mediated activity and experience beyond its important but limited aspect of search.

aspects of this event by mention of queries, documents, and algorithms (or explicit computational processes). In addition, although the typical algorithmic specification may not explicitly refer to users, the first set of meaningful entities therein—the queries—do entail a human actor, even if that actor was not directly responsible for the query (see footnote 18). Furthermore, also implied in the typical algorithmic specification is a device and "the world": the source or background for the documents. Finally, it is clear that such an algorithm will selectively pick documents—that there is a rationale for selecting some documents and not others.

We thereby contend that any conception of search corresponding-to or seeking to depict some real-life process or event that presupposes the semantic conception (i.e., that is characterized by the semantic function) refers to a meaning-generating or meaning-suggesting process or event. A distinction should be made between the terms "meaning-generating" and "meaning-suggesting." The latter implies a meaning that is presented to an observer (whether it is newly generated or already existing). We presume here that in most modern contexts, where search processes (or other encompassing processes) are interactive, that the user is presented with results—with meanings. Thus, to simplify, throughout this book any reference to meaning-generating indicates that the meaning was additionally suggested, and all references to meaning-suggesting imply that the generation of meaning has taken place (with respect to an observer/user). As apparent especially in the typical algorithmic conception, search as conceived in IR&S refers to a physical process that is literally meaning-generating. That is, it generates—by physically suggesting—new associations between meaningful entities.[20] In general, any process (or concept thereof), whether termed search or otherwise, that contains or presupposes the semantic notion in this way and concerns the establishment of a relation between meaningful entities should be understood as specifying a meaning-generating process.

It is further contended that all conceptions of search employed in IR&S discourse presuppose the semantic, and that in particular, they are all meaning-generating. However, even though two conceptions of search may presuppose the semantic, they are not equivalent except with respect to

20. The meaning-generation occurs as a result of an application, such as a search engine, selecting a smaller set of documents from a larger set. This is analogous to the human act of deliberately choosing items from a set, which is a defining quality for human intelligence (Warner, 2010, pp. 17–22).

being characterized by the semantic function. They can differ in several ways, such as with respect to their referent, the search event or process, or with respect to what they choose to capture, specify, or represent about that event or process. With respect to the latter, for example, a mathematical specification of search (e.g., by means of a set-theoretic specification of queries and documents and the relation between them) is more abstract than the typical algorithmic conception of search. Whereas the former may be of use for quantitative analysis, the latter would be more suited for implementation by software. Yet the mathematical specification still presupposes the semantic; the quantities represent meaningful entities.[21] Similarly, the typical algorithmic conception is more clearly specified than the semantic; it is more technical, practical, and hence concrete. It is easier to use the former to create search software than the latter, while the latter captures an aspect of search that is not explicit in the former.

The typical algorithmic specification of search, more qualified than the semantic conception in the technical or instrumental direction, is yet less technically/instrumentally qualified than most other concepts common in IR&S discourse.[22] Moreover, there are conceptions of search that are instead further qualified in the opposite, anthropological, direction. They refer more to the meaningful entities *as* meaningful entities, such as by discussing how users interpret documents or the social context that leads users to issue particular queries. In particular, such anthropologically inclined specifications serve to specify processes in a semantically richer sense, because they relate between numerous human factors (and not just between queries and documents). For example, in question answering, the meaning generated, in addition to being a relation between two meaningful entities, is furthermore the answer to a question. Specifications such as these are semantically richer for researchers, not users participating in the search process. Similarly, any conception that is further qualified—in whatever direction—is more semantically rich for the researcher than one that is not. Thus, although the characterizations of specifications as concrete versus abstract and anthropological versus instrumental may imply the

---

21. The mathematical terms are of course also meaningful, but they are so from the perspective of a researcher modeling a search event, whereas the meaningful entities they represent are also and primarily meaningful for the users issuing queries.

22. For example, the ad hoc search concept is an elementary and foundational search concept, around which much historical and modern IR&S discourse revolves, usually by contrasting new concepts with it (see section 1.3.1). It is less qualified than most search concepts and is more technically qualified than the semantic conception.

mutually opposing character of these property pairs, this is not quite accurate. One conception can be simultaneously more anthropological and more instrumental, or more abstract and more concrete, than another. It merely requires specifying an increased variety of aspects corresponding to these categories. Thus, these categories should be taken only as an initial, convenient way to differentiate particular types of search concepts when the concepts have similar degrees of qualification.

The semantic conception of search in this regard is semantically richer (for researchers) and also more anthropologically inclined than, say, one in which search is conceived in terms of requests and responses without explicit mention of linguistic entities involved, such that the meaning of these interactions is unclear (i.e., as to what kind of search task the user was trying to do). Because this conception requires reference or association to devices or a context of technology-use, it is more operational than conceptions that refer to meaningful entities or meaning-generation (or semantic operations in general, as in linguistics or humanistic discourse) without situating these entities in a context of technology-use. The semantic concept is arguably just adequate to capture the idea of meaningful technology-use (or meaningful interaction between human and device). Technology-use here, meant in the context of devices as discussed in prior sections, is about technology-mediated human living. Thus, we propose that technology-mediated human living can be characterized by the semantic function. Specifically, the concept of living processes presupposes the semantic concept that all such processes and events involve the relating between meaningful entities. Thus the semantic conception of search depicts a significant aspect of the phenomenon of technological mediation, or more generally, it specifies a significant phenomenon of technology mediation.

The semantic conception is "just adequate" for the following reasons. First, it is minimally abstract: neither mathematical representation nor the use of numerous concepts (e.g., those pertaining to user cognition or action) are involved. Second, specific technologies are not mentioned—only that there is a user/device/world—so no technical specification or a reference to one needs to be unpacked. Third, the conception retains reference to both the human activity as that of interacting (or providing meaningful entities) to the device, and the basic function of the device as that of relating meaningful entities. As a result, the semantic conception preserves the instrumental and anthropological senses in an explicit way such that, in addition to being a significant phenomenon of technological mediation, search can be understood as a highly typical mediation phenomenon and an interaction-based application for modern (information technology) devices.[23]

In addition to being presupposed in and 'in between' other conceptions as the notion of typical supports, the semantic conception is also commonly present in both other conceptions and concrete applications. It is present in applications in the sense that it (at least) partially specifies the function of those applications. Conversely, as we argue in the next section, interactive data-based applications can be said to somehow extend (or more accurately, presuppose) this conception.

1.2.3   Search as Presupposed

At the application level, search engines are usually fully specified by search conceptions. That is, there exists a conception of search that accounts for what a search application does and how it behaves. Several such conceptions may be required to fully capture both the idea of a search engine and account for its empirical behavior as it is put to use.

Search engines make search processes possible; they bring about search phenomena. However, as other applications also presuppose search conceptions, search should be understood instead as a cross-application phenomenon not limited to only specifying applications that only relate queries and documents. Thus, by being highly typical, conceptions of search are commonly presupposed in various mediation processes beyond search processes. This presupposition has at least three senses. Search can be understood as (1) a function or subapplication of an encompassing application, (2) a subprocess of application-use whose encompassing process is studied as a formal process/concept (as introduced in section 1.2.3), or (3) an aspect of an overall usage experience. The following explicates these types of presupposition.

1.2.3.1   Presupposition within applications   Technology mediation accounts for an increasing share of everyday experience, and information finding or knowledge acquisition is central to this experience. From the finding of applications on the Windows start menu, to documents on the desktop, to words inside a web page, or friends on Facebook, the semantic conception of search perhaps specifies the most typical (sub-) application

---

23. This typicality can be further understood by using an analogy involving the mathematical notions of supremum and infimum. It is like a supremum of a hypothetical set of instrumental and concrete construals (separately) and an infimum for the set of anthropological and abstract construals (separately).

therein. As such, all these applications presuppose search; search is embedded therein. Thus they can be said, at least, to relate between objects that have meaning to a user. In particular, they relate between the meanings pertaining to an initial object on screen and another object presented to the user as a response. This is the case even in applications that do not accept words as input, where the input is physical (e.g., clicking on an icon or other object), as such objects can be reconstrued in the former sense by assigning meaningful descriptors.

Take the case of clicking a menu item leading to the opening of a dialog box (or that of clicking and dragging an avatar in a game, which leads to an updated/moved image). Both the initial action and object, and the response, can be given a descriptor indicating their meaning in context. The clicking of a menu item is like a query or request that can be represented by the menu text, whereas the application that opens as a response can be represented by a construal of its function or interface elements. Similarly, the interaction with the avatar could be represented by a construal of the request it is making of the game (e.g., "move avatar into attack formation"), while the response from the game could be represented by a construal of the in-game effect (e.g., "avatar set to attack enemy").

1.2.3.2 Presupposition within formal processes or concepts The semantic conception of search is presupposed by (the formal specification of) processes, such as information-seeking processes that explicitly feature search processes. This is regardless of how such processes are modeled, for example, as information foraging (Pirolli and Card, 1999), sense making (Dervin, 1999), or resolving anomalous states of knowledge (Oddy et al., 1982). Similarly, any formal process that is relatively more anthropological than the one specified by the semantic conception (e.g., question answering) could be understood as presupposing it.

1.2.3.3 Presupposition within experience It is not only the search application and process that is presupposed by other applications and processes. The experience of being engaged with a search process is also presupposed by the experience of being engaged in other processes. If one considers the experience of using an application as being the experience of using a tool, then this experiential presupposition can be further explicated by Heidegger's analyses of tool use.

An experience of tool use can be understood to be presupposed by another experience, when in the latter, the tool in the former withdraws from the user's explicit attention, such that while they may use it, they do not focus on its use explicitly. Instead, they focus on the use of another tool that may include the former as a component, the overall or encompassing task, or on the object to which the tool is applied. Tools used in such a way, removed from explicit attention, are said to be *phenomenologically transparent*. Heidegger calls this mode of tool use "ready-to-hand" (Wheeler, 2014).

For a user engaged in processes that presuppose search (i.e., they are using a tool with search as its component), their experience of search is transparent when they are not explicitly attentive to its search aspect. The search aspect of this larger process could of course catch the user's attention if it were to behave differently than expected or get in the way. If this did happen, the relation between this search component (as a tool) and the user would then be one of "unreadiness-to-hand" wherein the tool draws attention as a separate component in its own right. It would then lead to the user reflecting on why it acted the way it did.[24] This would be the case if the user were to feel the need to revise the steps that lead to an unexpected state by reflecting on the search aspect of their experience (e.g., when unsatisfactory results lead the user to refine query terms).

The phenomenon of search as experienced involves the expression of words/interactions and observation of words/documents or meaningful forms on screen (i.e., as per the semantic conception of search). Most technology-mediated experiences can be understood to contain or presuppose this phenomenon, but this is mainly as an instance of phenomenologically transparent tool use. Thus the search phenomenon is near omnipresent in the experience of using modern applications/devices in technology-mediated living.[25] As to why search features in this way in contemporary, technology-mediated living, it is perhaps because the

24. More accurately, the mode of tool use changes from "ready-to-hand" to either "unreadiness-to-hand" or "presence-at-hand" when the tool fails, to work as expected, stop working at all, or when it works but becomes an obstacle to the use of other tools (Wheeler, 2014).

25. Search is presupposed in general, in all three senses of section 1.2.3, in the above types of mediational phenomena (i.e., alterity, hermeneutic, etc.). One may object to there being meaning generated in the typical example of the ATM machine pertaining to the mediation of alterity. However, this objection can be resolved as follows. The query here corresponds to an already available word or item choice corresponding to a menu item, and the document—the matched element—is similarly a predetermined visual element/screen that is always linked to that menu item. The meaning generation is, for example, the

search phenomenon appears to capture our fundamental inclination to know something about something through technology.

Next, we map out the discipline of IR&S, which studies conceptions of search and search events that all presuppose the semantic. These notions are important, because the search phenomenon they focus on is increasingly predominant in expanding spheres of contemporary lived experience.

1.3   Studying the Semantic Conception of Search: Information Retrieval and Science (IR&S)

The arguments in this chapter thus far lead us to suppose that perhaps search—as per its semantic conception if not also as the process of relating queries and documents—is more than just a significant phenomenon of mediation. Because it is so commonly presupposed by other such phenomena, it is perhaps also the most typical mediational phenomenon (i.e., concept and process) and interaction-based (sub-)application.[26] Even though the semantic conception is significant, it is not studied directly by any discipline. There are however disciplines that study related, more qualified conceptions. And to the extent that it is important to study technology-use and technological mediation, these disciplines become important. They are important both in their own right and as a basis from which a discourse more directly relevant to technology mediation can be created. This book focuses on both these values of IR&S and works especially to explore

---

new information produced by the ATM, such as the current account balance. An interactive thermometer that responds according to user input induces hermeneutic mediation, since the generated meanings (temperature, humidity etc.) are a means by which a user reads or interprets their world context. One may object that unlike the search example, no lack of word-matching is going on. However, this is a type of ostensive search (Campbell and van Rijsbergen, 1996). Queries for ostensive search may be gestures and responses, and the documents are not necessarily word-based but instead some arbitrary yet informative response. Background mediation thus involves an ostensively given query or input that results in a response to the user. Embodiment type relations (e.g., in the context of Google glasses), due to their rich interactive possibilities and clear word/image/meaningful responses, constitute scenarios in which the semantic conception of search is a clearly presupposed phenomenon.

26. However, the user experience of search—of the linking between meaningful entities— is hidden in the experience of engaging with search processes; it is not something users are attentive to in particular. Instead, the search part of that experience is transparent, because it is encompassed by other processes that are more immediately experienced.

IR&S for this second purpose. This section examines the main phenomena of search employed in IR&S (in IR specifically) and briefly describes the research perspectives and styles employed therein.

Consider first the concepts of search in IR&S: they are all more qualified than the semantic. Yet we contend that IR&S is predominantly about the semantic notion. This is because IR&S, especially IR research (the more instrumental aspect of IR&S) still considers the user's perspective, even when employing mathematically abstract or experimentally concrete conceptions of search. Queries are thus understood as objects that are meaningful to users in addition to being technical objects. Thus, IR&S cares about search concepts to the extent they are semantic. In contrast, the general concern about search processes from a systems perspective (which is arguably the standard computer science perspective) is less about its semantic function and more about its computational details: how fast it is, how much data it uses, the correctness of the algorithm, etc.

In addition to IR&S, the discipline of human-computer interaction (HCI) also focuses on the user's perspective of technology-use, and to the extent HCI addresses interactive processes from this perspective, those processes can also be understood to presuppose semantic search. There are of course many differences between HCI and IR&S. The latter considers a rich range of search concepts, including abstract mathematical specifications, detailed instrumental specifications involving numerous technical details, concrete specifications that express details of experimental situations (of technology-use) involving real search events, and anthropologically detailed accounts of arbitrary complexity (see the many methods discussed in Fisher et al., 2005). However, HCI tends instead to exhibit more anthropologically inclined and (often more) concrete specifications than does the technically inclined research in IR, and does not otherwise address the wide range of concepts common to IR&S (see chapter 6 for further comments on the relationship between HCI and IR&S). Moreover, while several discourses in the fields of the philosophy of technology (PhilTech) and science and technology studies (STS) discuss technology mediation[27] and could be understood as referring to the semantic conceptions of search, the situation for IR&S is presently different. First, while some discourses of PhilTech/STS can be understood as discussing semantic conceptions, the norm is not to focus on technical details of processes; these studies are instead generally more

---

27. These discourses discuss mediation and not only conceptually/philosophically but also by using empirical data (e.g., by considering specific technical details of processes cf. Verbeek, 2016).

anthropologically oriented. Second, the focus of IR&S is limited to the meaningful entities being related, the relation, and the meaning generated by technology-use. The context of technology-use (as further discussed below) is important for IR&S as well as being an important aspect of the semantic conception. Third, IR&S seeks not only to conduct humanistic analysis of semantic conceptions (as PhilTech and STS discourses do) but also to create software and tools, technically analyze these tools, and scientifically explain the operation and effect of these tools and of tool use. To this end IR&S discourse has a stronger focus on concepts more instrumentally, abstractly, and concretely (e.g., by experimenting with users) inclined than common in more humanistic discourses.

How did IR&S come to be interested in conceptions of semantic search thus qualified? Search as a phenomenon, that is, as an intellectual and technical concept, began to be discussed in an academic or industrial discourse in the contemporary period[28] due to the prevalence of technology-use in libraries. In its initial context, search referred to the activity of querying a computer to find library books. It was only later abstracted as a phenomenon and concept for analysis. The technology-mediated human activity of searching for books in libraries was the precursor to Internet search and was one of the initial public manifestations of the information technology revolution; it exhibited the defining capabilities of computers as efficient means to store, retrieve, transmit, and manipulate data. However, online search is functionally different from library search: while the latter directs a user to the location of a preexisting physical place (which could nevertheless be visited or accessed by walking/browsing), online search is usually the only effective way to access information in the first place or to gage what exists out there. In addition to being a popular initial application of information technology and a key application of the Internet, online search is additionally the condition of possibility of the Internet-as-information store: without search engines enabling the activity of search, even though the data is potentially existent, it does not become actualized (or its existence confirmed) in the knowledge and experience of users/observers until it is made accessible through a link from an initial search (or an initial website that exposes the links).[29] Thus, not only

28. The discussion in chapter 6 understands modern search, as a typical technology-mediated process, to be similar to the premodern processes of using memory techniques for various purposes.

29. This initial website is nevertheless accessed through providing words to the system, to which words/media/websites are returned.

is search a highly typical contemporary mediational phenomenon, it was concomitant to and a condition of possibility of, the historical uptake of information technologies through the generation and normalization of technology-mediated subcultures.

IR, coming from library and information science, is a discipline that specifically studies the above notion of search that emerged through technology-use for the sake of automating library practices. IR interprets search as an information retrieval process. Hence, it characterizes the response as information, and the process of relating the request to the response—which it further conceptualizes in terms of queries and documents, respectively—as a retrieval process.

The notions of query, document, and information, relative to the semantic concept, further qualifies IR's concept of search (as retrieval), as well as making it lean further in the anthropological direction. The notion of information here implies that the retrieved items have the potential to be informative to someone in addition to being meaningful.[30] However, beyond this default conception that IR adopts (which is a step more anthropological than the semantic conception), the variety of other search conceptions employed in discourse, owing to the computer science orientation of IR, are more instrumentally inclined (see section 1.2.1) while still presupposing the semantic.

There are indeed a wide range of search concepts employed in IR. This is a natural consequence of studying search both theoretically, (i.e., as a phenomenon to be analyzed and modeled) and practically (as an application or technological process to be designed and engineered that makes it possible for the phenomenon to manifest). Thus, while the typical focus is on search as understood at the device level, corresponding to matching between word sets (queries and documents), IR's scope extends beyond the queries and documents (and document collections) to consider the human contexts of queries and documents. Where an IR study seeks to understand human factors, it approaches the territory of IS, its originating discipline. While IR can be understood to gravitate toward the instrumental view of technology, IS has generally inclined more toward the anthropological by additionally focusing on the various encompassing processes, phenomena that presuppose algorithmic conceptions of search (e.g., information seeking)

---

30. This can be understood as implying, as per the second aspect of the semantic conception, that the retrieved item serves to suggest new meanings to the user, that it is informative by virtue of these new meanings.

and the various aspects of the human end of search (e.g., user cognition and culture). IS's broad scope means that it is not limited to examining documents but extends to understanding the social and disciplinary systems that are responsible for producing a collection of documents.

The difference between the methodologies of IR and IS are influenced by intellectual trends characterizing the sciences and humanities, respectively. Through computer science, IR was influenced by what Winograd and Flores (1986) call the "rationalistic tradition." In particular it was influenced by the positivist trend in science that was particularly influential during its time of inception.[31] In particular, IR was influenced both by the idea of scientific theories being primarily a collection of sentences/axioms and the follow-up idea of the semantic conception of science, which understood theories as corresponding to a class of structures/models that instead took central place, even though the discourse surrounding them may employ an axiomatic language. IR mainly inclined to the latter trend, preferring to express search phenomenon through mathematical models—in particular, set-theoretic structures (vector spaces, probability spaces, etc.). IS was instead influenced by the humanistic tradition, including anthropology, history, philosophy, the social sciences, and sociology.

In addition to discussing their contrasting intellectual influences, affinities, and indebtednesses, the next section presents several views of IR and IS. Section 1.3.1 frames IR discourse as either being about ad hoc search (a more specific version of the semantic conception of search) or about non–ad hoc search. Section 1.3.2 further arranges IR discourse according to research perspectives, defining IS discourse as being continuous with it by extending IR's scope of concern. Together, sections 1.3.1 and 1.3.2 work to structure IR&S discourse in a way that exposes salient research focuses and trends, and their relations to the same in external discourses. The following arrangement of IR&S discourse also sets it up for the analysis of its progress in chapter 2 and for the discussion on foundational questions in section 1.4 and chapter 5.

---

31. In fact, M. E. Maron, one of the key early researchers and creator of one of the earliest probabilistic models for retrieval (Maron and Kuhns, 1960)—one that heavily influenced future such approaches (Robertson et al., 1982; see also Buettcher et al., 2010, p. 280)—was a doctoral student of Hans Reichenbach. Reichenbach was a seminal philosopher of the past century and a central figure in the logical positivist school, from which came the syntactic view of science (Salmon, 1979).

1.3.1 Structuring Phenomena around Ad Hoc Search

Conceptions of search found in practice and in IR discourse have usually been understood in relation to the standard, basic conception of ad hoc search or retrieval. This formal notion, elaborated below, is the typical search phenomenon studied by IR. It is a more specified version of the semantic conception of search, approaching the anthropological by referring to the qualitative user aspect of information need, and approaching the instrumental by qualifying the system processes and characteristics. While the semantic conception depicts the most typical mediational phenomenon in general, the notion of ad hoc search depicts specifically—and in the context of IR discourse—the most common means of Internet use and perhaps, the most typical means of mediation through information technology. This section develops a precise definition of ad hoc search, a phenomenon that is central to IR research in the way we earlier understood the semantic conception of search to be among mediational phenomena (i.e., such that other phenomena can be understood in contradistinction to it).

Ad hoc retrieval was originally defined, according to TREC, as "the task of finding a number of documents that are relevant to a particular information need."[32] Manning et al. (2008) construe the common/regular information needs of a person/community as standing queries corresponding to standing query retrieval tasks or as a routing (or ranked filtering) task (Baeza-Yates and Ribeiro-Neto, 1999, pp. 163–164) operating in the context of a changing environment (that is regularly filtered according to the standing query). All other needs that elicit queries are characterized instead as being irregular (i.e., transient, temporary, short-term, short-lived, or fleeting). These irregular queries, resulting from nonregular needs, are said to constitute ad hoc (retrieval) tasks, "the most standard" type of retrieval task. In particular, these tasks correspond to a system response constituted by (links to) documents from a collection that are relevant to "an arbitrary user information need," where the response is due to an initial "one-off, user-initiated query" (Manning et al., 2008, p. 5). This irregularity of ad hoc search is a simulation of the classic search activity in a library, where user goals/queries can change but the environment, the physical set of books, remains stable (during the execution of a sequence of such activities; Baeza-Yates and Ribeiro-Neto, 1999, pp. 163–164). Thus the ad hoc search task corresponds to a technology-mediated task that is engaged in as a result of changing

---

32. While this task was the basis of evaluation for retrieval models since the 1960s, it only came to be called "ad hoc" when described on the TREC website, and has been known as such since.

goals against the background of a fixed environment (document set, library, or web, etc.) or with no particular reference to an environment. The particular information need that leads to such a task is taken to be represented by a query (e.g., a set of words), which the retrieval system is then tasked to relate to documents that are said to be relevant to that query and hence to that information need. Like the semantic conception, ad hoc search refers to the process of relating words/meanings to documents that hold further words/meanings. The difference is in (1) the technical details, for example, documents are represented as a set of links or pointers according to interface design practice and the links are usually ranked; or in (2) the disciplinary convention of "ad hoc" referring to the case of changing goals/queries and relatively fixed environment (although this is less relevant for the Internet context).

The notion of ad hoc search can be made more precise: a set of particular qualities can be derived from the discourse in Manning et al. (2008) and Baeza-Yates and Ribeiro-Neto (1999) that differentiate it from other types of search. That the user goals/queries change (unlike filtering) can be taken to imply three properties of ad hoc search. First, ad hoc search is memory less: it does not keep details on the current user or session information; thus there is no intrasessional memory. Second, ad hoc search does not involve a comparison of one user's search to information of the search behavior of another user, as this would correspond to using information from another session. Hence, unlike recommendation tasks—a common phenomenon for study in contemporary IR—ad hoc search does not maintain intersessional memory.[33] Third, ad hoc search presumes a specific information need, such that the process does not require to include browsing or disambiguation subprocesses at the beginning to reduce an ambiguous or complex need into a simple one. Any such disambiguation process would usually correspond to an additional search process (ad hoc or otherwise) but would not be part of the same process. If it were understood to be part of the same process whereby there was some memory kept of the initial browsing which then affected the documents returned upon the issue of a query, this would correspond to intrasessional memory; so the process would not be ad hoc. If instead no memory was kept, and yet the initial browsing process helped the user disambiguate their information need and therefore

---

33. Thus, standing-query tasks are the opposite of ad hoc tasks, as in the former the memory of the query—from an initial session—is maintained and strongly determines the outcome of future sessions, whereas ad hoc tasks are only determined by the query at hand.

purposefully affected their query formulation process, then this would also be something other than an ad hoc search. Thus ad hoc search responds only once with results, whereas such phenomena as exploratory and interactive search present multiple responses: they provide intermittent results in different forms according to several goals (e.g., disambiguating the initial or subsequent needs and addressing complex or multiple needs). This final property of ad hoc search stems from the corresponding experience of the historical library user that the initial ad hoc TREC task was attempting to resemble in order to automate library processes.

The three properties refine the received definition of ad hoc search and make it more compatible with the meaning of "ad hoc," from the Latin meaning *for this*, which gives the sense of being about the case at hand. Thus ad hoc search is a phenomenon that only considers the immediate observed aspects of user requests and system responses (i.e., user and system concerns). This compatibility is in particular due to the properties specified, which work to (1) limit the scope of the search task as being strictly for this session, in that it does not refer to other than the scenario at hand (the first two properties); and (2) construe the user as only being concerned about their immediate (initial) request/query (and information need) and the corresponding system response, and not, for example, with the "real need," which may require further interaction with the system to manifest. The properties thereby imply that there is no pre-planning either on behalf of the user or the system, that the task is for this query (and no other, either from this session or others) and information need. In addition, it implies that in analyzing ad hoc search phenomena, the IR researcher is thereby not concerned about the user need beyond what is expressed in a given query, nor does the researcher construe the user as being concerned about the system response except for immediate results given by it. Furthermore, these properties of ad hoc search are also compatible, indirectly, with the semantic conception of search, since ad hoc search presupposes semantic search. Were inter- and intrasessional memory and "real user needs" to be included, this richer/wider phenomenon would not correspond only to the relation between a query and a set of documents. Such a conception would appear to go beyond the semantic conception, which pertains to the relationship between two meaningful entities. However, the semantic conception does not specify whether these meaningful entities have to be simple, nor does it qualify the device or system processes and their properties. Thus, such a conception would still presuppose the semantic but be specified further both in the instrumental and anthropological senses than the ad hoc conception, which is already more specified than the semantic in those directions.

As in the case of recommendation, the difference between exploratory/interactive search, browsing, and classification phenomena and ad hoc search is on account of the violation of one or more of the properties of the latter. Similarly, search phenomena studied in IR (i.e., non–ad hoc searches) can be identified by which of these properties they violate and to what extent. Browsing/classification systems preserve intrasessional information for individual users while possibly also allowing for initial disambiguation (contrary to its first and final property). Filtering systems preserve fixed intersessional information through standing queries (Manning et al., 2008; contrary to the first property), and recommender-systems—especially collaborative filtering systems—preserve information on multiple users (contrary to the second property).

There are some cases of systems that may not appear to fit the above restrictions of ad hoc systems but are nevertheless tacitly understood to be ad hoc in the literature. For example, with respect to inter- or intrasessional memory, the assumption is that ad hoc search systems do not use it in a search session, so that such data do not influence document selection when a query is issued. However, consider the case of systems tuned to a domain prior to the actual search session. The matching subsystem of such systems would inevitably employ information pertaining to the "average use" of searches over that domain which are hard-coded upon tuning. Its use of such information is what supposedly would improve search results over that domain. Yet, the literature may still regard this case as ad hoc, since there is no live usage of that information. This tuning (or training)—which would usually be detailed in the discourse—may still be called ad hoc to differentiate it from similar search algorithms that use inter- or intrasessional information in a live sense. Furthermore, were a retrieval task to be technically ad hoc according to the above definition, researchers may incline not to identify it as such when there are marked differences from the original ad hoc TREC task. For example, in Singhal and Kaszkiel (2001), the difference in document type between the original TREC scenario and the web is enough to cause reserve in equating the latter with ad hoc retrieval.[34]

---

34. TREC evaluation contains various tasks that are differentiated from ad hoc search through the three properties as well several other properties, such as document type (web, video/audio), query type, and context type.

Structuring search phenomena of relevance to IR&S only paints a partial picture of the discourse. An understanding of the different ways such phenomena can be studied, and their interrelationships, substantially adds to that picture. It helps contextualize research claims.[35] But then what types of research are there? The next section develops a characterization of the varying ways search conceptions are investigated in research discourse using the ad-hoc research perspective as a center.

1.3.2   Structuring Information Retrieval Research around Ad Hoc Research

While ad hoc search is a typical phenomenon for study in IR, numerous variations thereof, such as interactive and exploratory search, are also studied. In general, IR investigates the relations between one or more queries, documents, users, and contexts, where context refers to anything from user interfaces and social backgrounds to facts about the domain from which documents originate. IR researchers and practitioners additionally engineer applications implementing the technical designs derived from the findings of these investigations, designs that specify how the system is to react to user input. In both the phase of investigating relationships and that of

---

35. Consider the following account pertaining to "empirical research" which constitutes the most common form of research in IR (further detailed in sections 1.3.2.2 and 1.3.2.3). Empirical research on ad hoc tasks, understood in the tacit (TREC) sense, is claimed to be saturated in that there has been a "plateauing of improvements" (Armstrong et al., 2009, p. 602), that there is "no evidence that ad-hoc retrieval technology has improved during the past decade or more" (Armstrong et al., 2009, p. 606). Although research efforts aim to improve on ad hoc retrieval, even statistically significant improvements may not imply actual improvement, as the baselines used to judge improvement are often weak, which brings into question "the value of achieving even a statistically significant result" (Armstrong et al., 2009, p. 601). Furthermore, attempts to use novel techniques, such as latent-semantic indexing (LSI; not directly related to the semantic conception of search), do not help: "no way of using LSI achieves a worthwhile improvement in retrieval accuracy over BM25" (Atreya and Elkan, 2011, p. 5). As a result, there is little room for improvement in ad hoc search (Trotman and Keeler, 2011). These critiques are aimed at the empirical research-based conclusions about improving the operational aspects of search, which deal with techniques for matching queries to documents. This type of research differs from research addressing, for example, subtle points about the user or document domains, or research that conducts formal comparative analyses of mathematical theories used to model a specific scenario. Thus, the prior critiques are of a particular type of research pertaining to the ad hoc retrieval task, and it is that type of research that has perhaps plateaued.

creating designs, IR research is guided (usually explicitly) by theories or models (or both) depicting relationships among these objects. For example, theories of relevance suggest how queries and documents are to be related to each other based on their content.

We next seek to characterize IR—and in a more partial manner, IS discourse—through a discourse typology that stays close to the typology of the search conceptions (i.e., denoting search phenomena) previously introduced. In doing so, we discuss semantic and pragmatic conceptions of science—not to be confused with the semantic concept of search—as capturing the nature of IR discourse. Section 1.3.2.1 explores the sense in which mathematical models are central guiding entities for IR research, arguing that they are increasingly less central. Instead, as section 1.3.2.2 proposes, it is the more subsuming, mixed subdiscourse entity of the research process (i.e., not only mathematical structures) led by a research perspective, such as an empirical or a formal mathematical perspective, that should be seen as the guiding entity. Section 1.3.2.3 explains how research perspectives relate to one another: they are co-constitutive. Section 1.3.2.4 proposes to understand the space of research perspectives in terms of their relation to the "ad hoc research perspective," a typical perspective employed in IR, in a way analogous to how other search phenomena are understood in relation to the ad hoc search task. IS research is then understood in section 1.3.2.5 as being continuous with, but on the other end of the spectrum from, IR. Finally, a type of subtle research perspective, embedded in other perspectives, is identified in section 1.3.2.6 as denoting the increasingly rich and complex set of unaddressed (often humanistic) contextual factors that inevitably condition even the most technical researches. The remainder of the chapter discusses how research that seeks to investigate these factors follows a different perspective, a perspective that remains hidden and embedded without being explicitly brought out. This perspective is that of foundations research. The remainder of this book works both to make this perspective explicit and to develop it further.

1.3.2.1 IR discourse and the semantic conception of science There are several conceptions characterizing how scientific practice and discourse—the complex consisting of phenomena representations, argumentation, explanation, and prediction—work. The main conceptions—the syntactic, semantic, and pragmatic conceptions—of scientific theories, assuming that theories are the main constituents of discourse, are all relevant for understanding IR discourse. They are not only ways to depict such practice in retrospect but can also act as a means for actively developing methodology for practice and discourse. The syntactic conception characterizes scientific discourses as being centered on axiomatic systems (Chakravartty, 2001) and is characteristic of several influential works in IR that develop comprehensive retrieval theories (recent examples include Huibers, 1996 and Fang, 2007). These sorts of works are a means of, and showcase both practice/engineering and intellectual discourse. IR is, however, more influenced by the semantic conception of scientific theories which understand theories "as what their formulations refer to when the formulations are given a (formal) *semantic* interpretation (Suppe, 1989, p. 4)"[36] (Chakravartty, 2001). According to this view, theories in IR—supposedly, the main building blocks of discourse—generally correspond to one or more (or a family of) mathematical models. A model here is both the representation of some part of the world as data or phenomena (such as queries, documents, users, and context) as well as the representation of "laws" or regularities (e.g., with respect to user or system behavior) and axioms of a theory.[37]

In IR, models are used for formal analysis, for reasoning about relationships between search processes or their components, and for representing how a retrieval application should behave with respect to an overall picture of relationships among queries, documents, users, and contexts. Hence, both senses of model are applicable to IR. For example, the vector space family of models employed in IR uses vectors to represent queries and documents in a space of their features, such as words. These vectors can also be implemented as a data structure and employed in an algorithm that takes user feedback as input such that the vectors are seen as representing empirical/observed regularities pertaining to user interest in an abstract way. In this way, IR discourses are centered around one or more models representing relations between sets of search components defined by the particular conception of search that is chosen.

A model for the ad hoc conception of search would represent relations over sets of queries [q] and documents [d]. The users [u] and contextual factors [c] are usually implied by the model specification.[38] Thus, even if

36. The term "semantic" here comes from the idea of formal semantics in model theory, a branch of mathematical logic (Hodges, 2013).

37. Further discussion about what models model, i.e., different senses of modeling, can be found in Frigg and Hartmann (2012).

38. That the set of documents [d] here refers to a purposeful collection would be such a contextual fact. In general, there are two senses of context used commonly in IR discourse. First, context as referring to contextual factors beyond the minimal factors (i.e., the query

the system implementing the model does not have an explicit data structure or variable pertaining to a user, it presumes that a user will use it (see footnote 18 in section 1.2.2) or that the researcher studying the model will find it natural to consider the usage of such a system or the contextual factors involved. With respect to the relations, however, one such relation can denote a computational instance or run of a search application, an empirical search event, or a hypothetical instance of a query/request followed by a response. A subset r then depicts all the relationships the model could propose between the respective entities. Thus, each such model should thereby be characterized as presupposing a subset of relations $r \subseteq [([q], [d], [u], [c])]$ from the of set of all possible relations between all actual instances or hypothetical construals of each entity in the respective conception of search. Each element of the relation subset r (i.e., a 4-tuple $([q], [d], [u], [c])$) relates a subset of queries (or single queries) to a subset of documents (or single documents) due to their being relevant to one another (or simply, related), given a particular user group or group of user profiles (or single user/user profile) and a set of contextual factors. If instead the model is strictly ad hoc without extending to users and context, it should instead be understood to presuppose the relation $r_{ad\ hoc} \subseteq [([q], [d])]$, since no inter- or intrasessional memory is kept. That is, there is no specific user or contextual information involved in the search process, and research is based on the relation $([q], [d])$.

IR research discourse about a particular phenomenon however, does not limit itself to only commenting on relations among entities that concern a conception of search, whereby the entities and the relation admit normative mathematical construals. Instead, research can reference many different aspects with or without such construals. For example, consider research on a search scenario generated by a system supporting only ad hoc search, where the ad hoc search conception and its models otherwise represent the scope of research. It would not be unusual for such research to comment on users and contexts; this would rather be expected. A reference such as this need not present a model, but instead supplies

---

and document models) required to specify an ad hoc retrieval task. These factors can be divided into user/query–side factors and document/system–side factors. A user-side contextual factor could be a sociocultural fact about a group of users not already captured by a u component, whereas systems-side factors include, for example, a model of the user interface, document-collection domain, and environmental aspects. Second, there is a notion of context that is used in a relative sense, e.g., "this search context versus that search context," to mean the entirety of factors constituting a search process; see section 5.3.9.

a preliminary discussion for the sake of explaining or understanding technical results. The corresponding research discourse would therefore be said to presuppose the general relation r, not only $r_{\text{ad hoc}}$. Hence, the research discourse would be about a wider range of phenomena, even though the model or conception of search employed by the system therein has a smaller scope (i.e., even though it presupposes $r_{\text{ad hoc}}$).

Furthermore, if research on an ad hoc search task compares instances of a search task in different settings/scenarios that may involve different users, it would be presupposing a relation between two search scenarios, each such scenario itself defined by a relation between the relevant entities. Or it would be presupposing one relation, where the relation identifies different users and the queries/documents involved in their usage experiences, so as to differentiate two separate usage scenarios.[39] In this case where two search tasks are compared, information about the non-immediate search process— the one being compared to—is understood to contribute models of users and contextual factors for the immediate search process. Research comparing search instances is said to have a wider scope, as are search applications that consider a wider array of contextual factors. The respective research discourse or application would thereby be presupposing a relationship contextually richer than $([q],[d])$. For example, exploratory and interactive search applications have greater scope than systems implementing ad hoc search, such that even if their research is limited to analyzing one scenario, since it is usually concerned with additional contextual factors, the research process is instead about exploring relations $[([q],[d],[u],[c])]$.[40]

To sum up, the semantic conception of research—not to be confused with the semantic conception of search—a way of looking at research through centralizing the models (usually mathematical models), has been the way IR research is typically perceived. This conception, however, does

39. Thus, the research presupposes the relation $(([q],[d]),([q'],[d']))$ or $([q],[d],[u],[c])$, respectively.
40. Because it consists of propositions about relationships between elements of arbitrary conceptions of search, IR discourse as a whole can be characterized as follows. It is research that presupposes the set of relations $[R]$ with $R \subseteq [([r_1],[r_2],[r_3],[r_4],\dots)]$, where the r_i are the elements constituting the respective conception of search. That is, an instance of IR research is about R: it concerns the relationships between one or more instances/qualifications of different conceptions or types of search (r_1, r_2). Thus, one instance of research R can be about, for example, the comparison of two specifications each, of two concepts of search r_1 and r_2, such that the research can be said to presuppose the relation $R = (([r_{1a},r_{1b}]),([r_{2a},r_{2b}]))$.

not quite capture IR research. Research therein does discuss search conceptions and their constituents (queries, documents, and such), entities that are usually mathematically modeled for the sake of technical discussion and machine implementation. However, researchers now significantly and increasingly discuss things beyond what the mathematical models here represent; thus perhaps the pragmatic conception is a more suitable way to understand IR research, as it certainly is for IS research, as discussed below. Moreover, to better characterize IR research, in addition to the language of relational sets employed above, the higher level notion of the research perspective, defined next, is effective for mapping discourse.

1.3.2.2 From models to research perspectives Consider the notion of empirical research in IR. This corresponds to observing user and system behavior in the event of a search scenario made possible by the use of a search system, and requires the construction and implementation of technical designs (e.g., in the form of algorithms). While such research is guided by models, the mathematical structures constituting the models rarely suffice to capture the research process as a whole. Not only do they omit details for realizing the model as a technical design, they also tend not to capture the numerous aspects of the search process needed to explain, predict, or analyze search-related events. Thus, models are at most a partial representation of the entire phenomenon, process/activity, and software application of search.

Instead, IR discourse is formed from a complex of mathematical structures; diagrams; algorithms and pseudocode; narratives; experimental results; and in general, propositions detailing the abstraction from phenomena or data to mathematical objects and the assumptions involved,[41] and other elements that make it possible for the model to be used adequately both in different types of research (e.g., formal versus empirical research) and in the design and engineering of systems. IR research is thereby better understood according to the pragmatic conception of science, which de-emphasizes the mathematical structure as the sole, central entity guiding research. This is especially germaine if IR is understood in the context of being a sub-discourse of IS (see section 1.3.2.5), a more

---

41. Mathematical abstraction is a type of phenomena construal whereby particular aspects of the phenomena are left out and others chosen to be represented. Within this process there are assumptions and idealizations. See section 1.1.3 and specially footnote 9.

anthropological discourse.[42] These core discourse complexes should be understood as networks of propositions generated from different research perspectives that are associated with different types of research goals.

In addition, each perspective is biased due to its particular goals: some aspects of phenomena are important/relevant, while others are not. For example, in the case of empirical research, the goal is to record observed user/system behavior and find regularities therein. Research perspectives can be understood to characterize parts of research discourse better than the mathematical structures constituting models; each type of research is therefore said to presuppose the corresponding perspective.

1.3.2.3 Research perspectives and their co-constitution   Empirical researchers are thereby following an empirical perspective that focuses on the actual decisions made by an application given user input, the observed behaviors of users (and their representations as variables in algorithms), and what they may mean with respect to the goals of retrieval (e.g., as to whether the decisions imply efficient or effective behavior on the part of the application, or as to whether the user's experience of the search was adequate/optimal). Empirical research can also refer to user-studies research, which is concerned with how users experience search processes. This type of research is also common to humanities and social-science–oriented discourses found in IS. In particular, it can be understood as bridging IR and IS discourses.

The empirical perspective still employs mathematical structures and formal expressions, which become a means of conducting empirical research. For example, with respect to documents found to be relevant, a comparative evaluation of two systems relates the formal models of relevance they presuppose to numerical values through analyzing the difference between them and some other model m_j representing an ideal (e.g., the relation between queries and documents as judged by human judges, as is the case in TREC-style evaluation; Voorhees et al., 2005). The difference is calculated through a function that would take as input the structures of constituent components (i.e., of queries, documents, etc.) and return a value.

---

42. Even though the nonmathematical aspects imply that the pragmatic conception is more suitable for understanding IR discourse, from the formal and empirical (algorithmic) perspectives, the model or its algorithmic equivalent is still the focal point of IR research practice for a significant number of researchers—it is closer to how IR researchers perceive their own work.

In addition to being used to specify models of search processes through mathematical shorthand in mainly empirical researches, formal expressions are also used in formal analysis research, which presupposes a formal-analytical perspective. Formal analysis research refers to the investigation of the proper mathematical abstractions/representations for phenomena, such as hypothetical application decisions (as rational processes),[43] the search process in general, and search goals in terms of mathematical functions/structures (e.g., geometric structures), and techniques that indicate how the mathematical objects are to be used in a discourse. For example, given any two models m_1 and m_2, formal analysis research could seek to compare the representations of objects between the models, the query-document relations in either model (i.e., between matching models), or the representations of the relation between objects in one model with that in the other model. It would seek to understand whether, for example, subsets of queries and documents can be grouped by clusters (representing similar meaning) or defined by a small set of eigenvectors or a probability distribution.

The formal and empirical (whether user-focused or otherwise) perspectives are *co-constitutive*. Any search process (i.e., any decision process in a search application or retrieval algorithm) presupposes a model, and any model, being a formal specification and representation of relationships between real-life objects, presupposes an abstraction of an empirical (real-life) scenario. The two perspectives are commonly found in practice: mathematical/formal models are used to express technical designs for applications and methods of evaluating those systems, and they are further developed through empirical results.

Furthermore, any other research perspectives (such as humanistic perspectives) that include accounts of user behavior, culture, and other aspects that can be further categorized as, for example, sociological or cognitive-scientific, along with the formal and empirical, can be seen as co-constitutive. The simple model of a user—in an empirical or formal perspective—as a set of queries presupposes a conception of the user as a cognitive entity. This simply means that one can attach cognitive models or subjective accounts—as would be typical of humanistic research perspectives—to enhance a simpler empirical/formal model. Hence, to say that perspectives are co-constitutive means that they are complementary.

---

43. Empirical research on ad hoc search is generally restricted to instrumental rationality, i.e., the immediate application-level effects, and is less concerned, e.g., with the effect on users.

Not only can one perspective be employed to explain, interpret, or otherwise enhance the findings from another in part, but the mutually-referring set of such perspectives comprise a whole that imparts an overall account of a phenomenon that can be other than the partial accounts.

While such co-constitution could be understood as the default case for research in general (in IR or elsewhere), research discourse in IR and its parent field of IS is of such a diverse nature that it is common for co-constitutive perspectives to be regularly employed to mutual benefit. Mixing research perspectives is typical and not something that is seen as particularly interesting by itself. This is in contrast to other computer science discourses, where mixing anthropological and instrumental perspectives has traditionally only been common in limited sub-discourses (e.g., in human-computer interaction research).

Retrieval research discourse as a whole is thereby constituted by mathematical structures (models), descriptions, explanations, diagrams, and such, relating to the empirical, formal, and other perspectives that are co-constitutive. Yet, just as the notion of ad hoc search, as developed above, can be understood to center the numerous conceptions of search studied by IR, the diverse assemblage that is IR research can be understood to be centered by the ad hoc (empirical) research perspective as *the* basic research perspective typical of and extended by IR discourse.

1.3.2.4 The ad hoc research perspective This section develops a notion of research perspective that can be understood as being typical of IR, the ad hoc research perspective. In the way the concept of ad hoc search was used above to differentiate search conceptions, this notion is used here to differentiate research perspectives by indicating whether one research scenario is more or less ad hoc than another.

Let the **ad hoc research perspective** be a limited empirical research perspective, construed as follows. First, let it be limited to being concerned with the relatively instrumental aspects of that part of a search process that is equivalent to an ad hoc retrieval task, and let it be concerned with how that aspect of the task manifests in a live usage scenario. It then need only consider models of documents, queries, of ways to relate between them through what is known as a "matching function," and possibly retrieval goals around which a search application can be empirically evaluated as well as the data that can be used for such an evaluation. If the search conception it is exploring extends beyond an ad hoc search task (e.g., due to the conception considering user models), then this perspective would ignore those aspects: it would only consider what documents were ultimately matched to queries presented without considering how user profiles were used to do so. Furthermore, when referring to an actual usage scenario—which could be a user-less or user-inclusive evaluation process by researchers in addition to (or instead of) a usage session involving real users—the research perspective would need to take into account what actually happened in that scenario (e.g., the queries given and documents suggested in response, and the evaluations conducted on such responses). An ad hoc empirical research perspective therefore deals with one or more concrete, live events, of search-application use.

Second, let the ad hoc research perspective be additionally limited in scope by requiring that it not seek to compare different search processes. Thus, not only is it limited to considering the queries and documents—and not user and contextual factors—of a search process, thereby being characterized as research on relations $[(\lfloor q \rfloor, \lfloor d \rfloor)]$, it also does not even indirectly consider another search process (i.e., relations $[(\lfloor q' \rfloor, \lfloor d' \rfloor)]$) for comparison.

Finally, assume that ad hoc research does not engage in formal analysis (e.g., it does not seek to find optimal representations) or seek to find out what queries and documents may mean with respect to a usage domain or user (which would take it beyond $[(\lfloor q \rfloor, \lfloor d \rfloor)]$). Instead it is only concerned with the immediate empirical results.

The above conditions are proposed to capture the sense of immediacy implied by the term "ad hoc" in an ad hoc (empirical) research perspective (presupposed by a corresponding research scenario). This immediacy is reflected in the perspective being limited to one usage or evaluative scenario (or both), in research being limited to instrumentally inclined empirical investigations, and to consideration being limited to only that part of the search process that is equivalent to an ad hoc search task. Therefore, while ad hoc research can be applied to non–ad hoc search tasks (e.g., to exploratory search, which involves relevance feedback and intrasessional memory), it would only consider the query–document relations that the corresponding matching function generated in a live scenario without considering user models (and hence not consider the intra-sessional memory due to user feedback) or how such models were used to generate these relations. Ad hoc research thus would be ignorant of any facts beyond those typically associated to an ad hoc search task.

Suppose instead that it sought to investigate—given an ad hoc retrieval scenario—the user or their cultural backgrounds (the "why" over "how" with respect to user interaction, i.e., through an anthropological perspective), or to focus on possible mathematical representations for the corresponding search scenarios. Then such user research or theoretical research would be an example of **non–ad hoc research**. Similarly, if the research comments on the commonalities of several search scenarios, whether these concern overall frameworks (mathematical or otherwise), this research would also not be ad hoc research, because being concerned about multiple scenarios or contexts is not "for this" immediate scenario or search process.

Due to both the specific-problem–centered development of retrieval systems in industry and the domain-specific and often contextually limited research common in traditional IR discourses, the empirical research perspective is still dominant and typical. In addition, as discussed in the next chapter (see section 2.3.3), a significant proportion of IR research can be described as presupposing research perspectives not significantly different from the ad hoc empirical perspective (i.e., the limited empirical perspective). Furthermore, some research can be understood as more ad hoc than other research.

For example, consider research that consists mainly of a highly empirical tweaking process that slightly modifies a typical matching function that relates queries and documents (such as a function based on the BM25 measure, see Robertson and Zaragoza 2009) for an ad hoc retrieval task. This research presupposes a perspective that is relatively more ad hoc (if not merely ad hoc) and also relatively more instrumental than most other research, such as research that includes user studies or the mere mention of context or other search processes. This difference arises because most other research either considers more than the ad hoc part of the search task, or if limited to the ad hoc task, comments on more than the immediate empirical scenario. Hence, this type of empirical-tweaking research is at the other end of the spectrum from, say, philosophical speculation about the nature of information and technology (something uncommon to IR but not to IS).[44] Most IR research is relatively more ad hoc than such research. Thus, the movement from ad hoc to non–ad hoc corresponds to

(1) moving beyond the operational from research about the relationships within/between queries and documents to research relating the deeper contextual factors pertaining to queries to those pertaining to documents[45] and

---

44. Such philosophical speculation may not even specify any particular search scenario, but yet it studies a concept (information or technology) presupposed in any understanding of a search process.

45. These contextual factors for queries would include for example, details about the social group to which the corresponding users belong. And for documents it would include for example, details about the social processes that lead to the creation of that document. This would be deduced from domain analysis (Hjørland and Albrechtsen, 1995; Hjørland, 2004; cf. section 2.3.5).

(2) moving toward conducting research concerned with the commonalities and differences between search contexts (i.e., beyond the singular), whether these contexts be the understanding of the basic objects involved (documents, queries, users, information), adequate mathematical representations for formal analysis, or the research methods used.

In addition, even though formal expressions as mathematical shorthand are common to a relatively ad hoc empirical research discourse, formal analysis corresponds to a different type of research. Discussion of mathematical properties of different models as opposed to whether the models fit an empirical scenario or how to implement them algorithmically, presupposes perspectives that are instead relatively more non–ad hoc than is typical in IR discourse.

However, even relatively ad hoc research can hide aspects that would reveal the research to instead presuppose non–ad hoc research perspectives. Thus, even though research discourses could ideally be structured according to how ad hoc their research perspectives are, one has to acknowledge the pervasive nature of co-constitutive, non–ad hoc perspectives.

1.3.2.5 Information science as non–ad hoc IR developed from the discourse in IS and library and information science (LIS) as the technological/practical end of that humanistic discourse. IS discourses, owing to practitioners from the library sciences and others trained in the social sciences and humanities traditions, are thus framed by humanistic research perspectives. Although often understood as separate disciplines, IR and IS can be understood as complementary aspects of the same discipline (IR&S). If we take Wilson's depiction of IS as a "fascinating combination of engineering, an odd kind of materials science and social epistemology" (Wilson, 2002, p. 11), IR would be the engineering aspect, and can therefore be perceived as a sub-discipline of IS.

Regardless of their exact relation, IR and IS are differentiated by research perspectives. There is a separation between tasks and hence a division of labor. IR focuses on the pragmatic or empirical aspects of search processes, and IS on the humanistic aspects of search and more general phenomena pertaining to the contemporary information-technology–mediated human experience. IS research perspectives can be understood as non–ad hoc continuations of IR research perspectives by clothing existing relations presupposed by IR perspectives in humanistic terms. For example, empirical research investigating relations between queries and documents is ultimately investigating the relationship between semantically rich cultural items (albeit not as cultural items—IS instead addresses them as such). IS also tends to focus on conceptions of search that are relatively more anthropological and abstract than in IR, as its goal is often analysis rather than the solution of specific technical problems by system building. In this way, from the IS-oriented research perspective, the relation between queries and documents that searches ought to generate are cultural relations that instead answer how a particular type of technology (machine/software) ought to respond to an external entity (the user) in a given interaction so as to fulfill social values. IS naturally inclines to move discourse from the analysis of particular usage contexts to commenting on (search) technology in general (i.e., from studying one technical process to an entire category of social processes in which that technical process is embedded). By tending to add layers of social context to the typical ad hoc research of IR, IS research is by default relatively more non–ad hoc than is most IR research.

Suppose that IS is continuous with IR, or complementary in some way (or both), such that it is reasonable to refer to the juxtaposition of their discourses as one discourse, and to denote that as IR&S (as we have done above). The discourse then, of IR&S as a whole, is less dependent on mathematical structures than for IR. Empirical researchers in IR are particularly interested in techniques that enable a particular model of search to work in a practical setting, whether this means the tuning of matching techniques, designing interfaces and evaluation experiments, or the processing of documents and queries to prepare them for matching. IS-oriented research typically deals more with conceptual structures expressed through diagrams, metaphors, and analogies for construing search and often looks to conceptions that are a richly qualified version of the semantic conception of search concerning coarse-grained processes, such as information seeking, of which search was an aspect. Where section 1.3.2.1 argues that IR research should no longer be best characterized by the semantic conception of science, we meant that discourse in IR was typically concerned with aspects of entities beyond what was represented about them in mathematical models. And as in the case of IS, IR represents those entities and related discussions by means of such nonmathematical forms. In the case of IS—and increasingly, therefore of IR—the discourse is conducted less in terms of a central mathematical model or theory, and instead in terms of a rough collection of discourse elements. This is what the pragmatic conception of science takes to be typical for scientific theories. These items include "(i) a language; (ii) questions; (iii) statements (pictures, diagrams); (iv) explanatory patterns;

(v) standard examples; (vi) paradigms of experimentation and observation, plus instruments and tools; and (vii) methodology" (Kitcher, 1993, p. 74, as quoted in Winther, 2015). Thus, contemporary IR research, IS research, or IR&S discourse as a whole—where the relatively technical discourse of IR is seen as a part or aspect of IS—would be better characterized by the pragmatic conception of science (Winther, 2015) than the semantic. The later chapters, 4 and 5 in particular, further develop ways of understanding the constituents of IR&S discourse in terms of discourse elements akin to such a pragmatic conception of science.

Other than the typical ad hoc and non–ad hoc research perspectives of IR and the rather explicit non–ad hoc type of humanistic perspectives typical of IS research, there are subtler types of non–ad hoc perspectives. They are peculiar in that they appear to implicitly mediate research, even seemingly ad hoc research.

1.3.2.6 Non–ad hoc research perspectives as pervasive yet hidden

Research adopting a purely ad hoc research perspective is quite rare, especially in modern IR discourses. There is a trend toward systematic consideration of an entire session or scenario with all its contextual elements, where this scenario is extended to capture "larger slices" of the lives of users or documents. The aspirations of IR researchers to employ increasingly non–ad hoc perspectives (Belkin, 2016) mean not only that new research seeks to capture factors for the scenarios that they design and study. It additionally suggests an emerging tendency to broaden research perspectives, even when considering prior research. And as we will show, this is because (1) research that appears to be ad hoc could be laden with, or presuppose, non–ad hoc perspectives, and similarly (2) non–ad hoc research could presuppose research perspectives that are relatively/even more non–ad hoc. Thus there is a range of such perspectives that leads to what the remainder of this book labels as "foundations research (perspectives)."

Consider an ad hoc research scenario incorporating an evaluation process where the relations between documents and queries, as suggested by a system, are evaluated against corresponding "idealized" relations previously recommended by human "relevance judges." The judges' human judgment processes are akin to research processes, and since they pertain to relating queries to documents, they presuppose relations $[(\lfloor q \rfloor, \lfloor d \rfloor)]$. Hence, when comparing its results against relevance judgments, this evaluation process involves comparisons with other search processes—albeit indirectly. If an otherwise ad hoc research process were to involve such evaluations (as its construal allows for and as is common), it could not be understood strictly as being ad hoc. In a similarly indirect manner, a clearly non–ad hoc research process could be presupposed by perspectives that are relatively more non–ad hoc.

The following defines a relation that is commonly presupposed (i.e., that commonly characterizes) in either a non–ad hoc research process or the non–ad hoc search process that the research is about. It discusses the sense in which these relations can be said to presuppose perspectives that are even more non–ad hoc, meaning that the research indirectly considers aspects that are beyond those characterized by these relations.

Consider the research discourse that studies a non–ad hoc search scenario generated by an application employing a particular set of contextual factors $[c]_1$, such that the discourse can be described as being guided by a model that presupposes the relation set $m_1 : [([q], [d], [u], [c]_1)]$. Then m_1 refines and particularizes the general relations presumed in the more typical model $m : [([q], [d], [u], [c])]$ by making the contextual factors more concrete.[46] The replacement of $[c]$ with $[c]_1$ means that a non-arbitrary and defined set of actual factors are being considered in the research design presupposing m_1. These factors condition the response of the application presupposing these relations: m_1 is thereby presupposed both by the technical design of the search application and the corresponding research process.

Search applications such as this (e.g., an interactive search application that appropriates user feedback) that consider factors beyond queries, documents, and users, are common. First, interaction/feedback could be depicted in terms of elements from $[u]$ or $[c]_1$ depending on how one construes the user model.[47] Second, one contextual factor (i.e., an element of $[c]_1$), would be the assumption and experimental/social fact of the search being an interactive one. Other facts could correspond to live factors, such as about the user's changing information needs during a search session. A less obvious case is that of search applications that use smoothing techniques to condition inner product functions that weigh the relevance of a document to a query, or other query–document relating functions (if the model is not a vector space model). The contextual factors here are the

---

46. The factors are made more concrete by identifying a particular set $[c]_1$ (a symbol standing in for a well-defined set of factors) instead of $[c]$ (which merely depicts an undefined set). The set $[c]$ can be understood to denote the universe of all possible contextual factors.
47. For example, feedback as constituting a growing set of facts about users or as constituting facts observed about the context, given fixed user profiles $[u]$.

actual smoothing parameters, understood as being insights generated from analyzing the given documents [d] (Zhai and Lafferty, 2004): they are contextual facts about the documents employed by the system in the search process and are either derived by this or some other system in a previous process.

Consider also an alternative case where m_1 is presupposed by a research discourse studying an ad hoc search process.[48] In both the case of non–ad hoc research about non–ad hoc searches and non–ad hoc research about ad hoc searches, any particularization such as m_1 of a standard model presupposing m—whether that is through specifying contextual factors (as above) or users/documents etc.—represents a corresponding real-life, pre-represented scenario, of which it is a reduced understanding through mathematical abstraction, of the (real) relations particular to that scenario. To the extent that it tells us more than ad hoc research would (e.g., by giving meaning to a set [d] as a collection of a particular type or to a set [q] by indicating regularities of human behavior) a particularization is relatively more non–ad hoc than the standard ad hoc research case. For example, if the collection of documents consisted of medical documents, a particular type of documentation practice common to health care (or to a specific hospital) is implied. And if queries are focused on issues of medical diagnosis instead of general medical research, a particular regularity in human behavior (of medical staff) is suggested. Research that is more situated or contextualized is relatively more non–ad hoc than research that is less so.

Finally, consider again the typical IR research situation where a model is evaluated by means of the relevance judgments of humans. This latter judgment implicitly corresponds to an alternative research process. This would be the process that presupposes some m_j which depicts relations between human judges (as if they were users) and their judgments (e.g., that a particular set [d] is related to or relevant to some q). Judges and their judgments are also conditioned by such factors as their different socio-psychological backgrounds that effect their understanding of the task of judgment. Hence, in evaluating some m_a by an m_j—as chapter 2 details further (cf. section 2.5.1)—the relations in the former are valued according to value framework stemming from the social background of the judges and their judgments. If,

---

48. Research on ad hoc tasks that at least comment on users and contextual factors (i.e., on other than the given queries and documents) or reference another search process would presuppose m. Similarly, research on a non–ad hoc task that considers users and particular contextual factors could also be said to presuppose m generally, although more specifically, it also presupposes m_1.

for example, some subset of $q\text{-}d$ relations generated by m_a are "effective" or "adequate," more so than in a corresponding m_b, then this must be understood as only being the case with respect to the value framework underlying the corresponding m_j.

This is similarly the case for any evaluatory comparison between models (or researches) presupposing m_a and m_b, respectively, where human beings are used directly or indirectly to relate queries and documents; or when the comparison is done indirectly using previously specified heuristics or rules (instead of live human judges) to automatically relate queries and documents. These cases would entail the implicit comparison between two real-life scenarios, re-presented in terms of m_b and m_a. It is not common for the corresponding IR research to explicitly discuss these two latent scenarios. It could merely discuss ad hoc aspects (i.e., $q\text{-}d$ relations) and hence be ad hoc research. However, in spite of this, this research would nevertheless be strongly dependent on these background (real) scenarios with all their unrepresented factors. To the extent that such a real scenario can be expressed as a research perspective, it corresponds to something further out in the direction of the non–ad hoc—as a relatively more non–ad hoc perspective pervading already non–ad hoc research.

Much of IR research can be said to presuppose, specifically, relations such as m_a, and to commonly include evaluations wherein applications/models are judged through comparing them to one another and to the idealized case of human-judgment–based relevance judgments. However, the (relatively) ad hoc evaluative comparisons therein—which may appear strictly ad hoc due to their focus on experimental parameters and such and are ubiquitous to empirical research in IR—incidentally make implicit comparisons to multiple scenarios that relate to one another in nontrivial ways. Therefore it can be argued that all such research is relatively non–ad hoc in a nontrivial sense. These hidden contextual factors are embedded in most research; they mediate such research, even if the research does not make the factors explicit or seek to discuss them. As we have argued, the nature of the modern application environment is such that it increasingly harbors many such factors. That is, modern systems, ubiquitous and embedded as they are in social processes, can increasingly only be understood by considering these processes. Hence, research that does not actively make these aspects explicit—that does not actively construe and study them—risks becoming uncognizant of its subject area and of the modern context.

1.4   The Modern Trend Away from Ad Hoc Research

The emerging technological reality exhibits an increasingly wide variation of devices, social contexts, and user and data types, where users seek
richer informational experiences. Search phenomena are becoming richer
and more complex because applications involving search are moving from
enabling the simple finding of information to facilitating complex modes of
information use. As a result, existing research concerns in IR have become
broader in scope:

(1) from seeking to understand details of particular search contexts for
    which an application is being developed (whether the questions are
    of an empirical nature or are formal analytical) to deciding what
    phenomena can count as search;

(2) from developing particular document representations to determining
    possible types of media or media experiences that can also be counted
    as documents and hence presented to the user; and

(3) from being concerned with evaluations involving a small set of users or
    relevance judgments to discovering how generalizable these results are,
    given large variation in contexts.

There is indeed a strong tendency to move away from the relatively ad hoc
toward the relatively non–ad hoc. From focusing on relationships between
queries and documents $[([q], [d])]$ to relations between their (often not
explicitly construed) respective background contexts. This tendency occurs
on both the query/user sides and the system/document side (e.g., through
domain analysis, see section 2.3.5).

These more broadly scoped questions about search phenomena in general, which are on the other end of the spectrum from ad hoc research,
are the foundational or basic questions; they and their answers are presupposed by most IR research. For example, the questions (and corresponding
answers) about what a search, document, query, or a good experimental
result is, are presupposed in all research that uses these terms or concepts.
Questions about the values on which search technology should be evaluated, theory construction (and theoretical growth), the nature of IR as a
science, and so forth, are also foundational. They are presupposed in IR
research practice. And while IR discourses explicitly discussing them are
not common, their being presupposed means that they appear implicitly
in a pervasive manner. Sections 1.4.1 and 1.4.2 suggest how foundational
issues underlie common research processes in IR and IS.

1.4.1 The Foundational in Ad Hoc Information Retrieval Research

Although lead by technological and practical needs, IR has never been purely restricted to ad hoc research perspectives. Nevertheless, the tacit understanding arguably is that "IR proper" is or should be largely be an ad hoc empirical endeavor. Empirical research in IR tends to remain close to the phenomena and take an instrumental perspective, wherein the common, technically inclined discourse, prioritizes the quantitative description of observed phenomena (e.g., through statistical description of the observations of a phenomenon or its features) over qualitative understanding or explanation of what a phenomenon may mean from a humanistic/anthropological perspective.

IR discourse and practice are still driven mainly by empirical results. Although this means that IR is rather sensitive to the changing technological reality, the predominance of instrumental perspectives therein limit its scope for fully examining and understanding this reality. As chapter 2 seeks to show, this sensitivity is reflected by the many foundational issues and progressively non–ad hoc perspectives that linger implicitly in research, and that lack systematic exposition. These issues and perspectives are instead situated indirectly (and implicitly) in a specific and relatively instrumentalist fashion within application contexts.

For example, take the technically inclined question about what kind of search functionality may suit an existing set of business processes in a firm. This question presupposes a more general one about what information retrieval/seeking or information management in general may mean to users in the firm, given their working practices and corporate/institutional structure. IR researchers would attempt to understand the information practices of the firm for whom the search application is to be designed, and one would expect that the evaluation process for any solution to involve potential future users. The research process therein of modifying standard models to cater to this new context, will tend to construe information practices and other contextual information in a technical way that aids the adaptation of existing mathematical models and techniques to this new context. This technical/instrumental perspective of information practices tends to hide other, nontechnical aspects of those practices.

For example, consider the process of construing phenomena (i.e., interpreting and specifying phenomena), such as in terms of a set of relations between elements q, d, u, c. This seeks to determine a set of possible construals, or the most suitable construal (or both), of relevant phenomena. A construal research process initially involves the development of a conceptual specification of phenomena, followed perhaps by the creation of specific mathematical models. Compared to experimentation processes, these sub-processes are relatively non–ad hoc. Conceptual specification involves understanding the kinds of ways in which users may seek to interact with a search system and the kinds of responses that may be most beneficial to them. This in turn involves understanding, not in a technical/instrumental fashion but in a humanistic way, what kind of social/work (and business) processes constitute the overall context of the search system to be developed. Answers to questions about users, their practices, social context, sought informational experiences, and other user aspects are presupposed in this understanding, and they then characterize the technical research processes. It is in the resolution of these questions through relatively non–ad hoc research processes (more so than through formal analysis) that the foundational questions appear. These are questions whose answers are presupposed by the above questions; they concern, for example, what a user or practice or social context is in the first place. Foundational questions are those questions that have the greatest scope among all research questions such that the research processes seeking to address them are the most non–ad hoc. Answers to foundational questions are presumed by nonfoundational research, that is, by research that is not as non–ad hoc as the foundational. However, they nevertheless appear; they are asked by nonfoundational research, but they are usually not critically addressed. Instead, answers are assumed. This is an indirect type of address. The questions are not identified as foundational and hence are not studied as foundational questions (e.g., the question of what a user is cannot be studied purely as a question about technical or mathematical representation but must refer in some way to cognition). Thus, the usual way of addressing foundational questions that appear is rather indirect; it is usually specific to the application context and takes the form of innovative algorithms and models (i.e., through empirical or formal approaches). In this way, the corresponding foundational questions—which are largely of the noninstrumental variety—are presupposed in the specific, application-oriented (and hence empirically grounded) questions.

Foundational questions, by definition, presuppose all research concerns in IR. What is of particular relevance however, is their increasingly frequent (albeit indirect) appearance in the modern context. Researchers in IS (as well as related disciplines, e.g., information systems) are more inclined to problematize these pre-technical (and prerepresentational)[49] subprocesses

---

49. Meaning premathematical representation.

of research than are IR researchers. Thus, even though IR depends on foundational questions and their answers, they are outside its scope. They appear to be outsourced, delegated to IS. This suggests that there is a disciplinary boundary between IR and IS, a particular relationship between them. Yet the precise nature of that relationship, a foundational concern, remains unresolved. Moreover, since the modern context requires a more acute sense of the relation between technology and its users, there is a specific demand for its resolution. Resolving this question means problematizing presumed ideas about disciplinary identity and disciplinary responsibilities.

1.4.2   The Foundational in Information Science Research

IS research focuses on a humanistic understanding of those (social) objects and processes of concern to IR research. It seeks to understand them in a pre-mathematical way, without immediate recourse to a reduced perspective that mathematical representation entails, and hence IS is open to considering them in a fuller way from the outset than is common practice in IR. Foundational issues are, however, a step beyond this level of focus common to IS. They expand into understanding the fundamental nature of those objects and processes, and require one to consult discourses from the philosophy of technology to politics. Technical questions on interface and algorithm design, or about the functionality and usability of a search interface, presuppose more basic questions. They presuppose questions about the kind of relationship the user should/can/will develop with the system; questions common to philosophy of technology discourses. This is because the user's regular experience of using an application, which is conditioned by the functionality and usability of that application, engenders a particular type of human–application relationship. Consider, for example, any set of technical questions about recommendation algorithms and the proper way to express recommendations for paid-for search results on Google searches. The selection of results is influenced by profiles created from user emails. These questions presuppose a wide range of ethical, political, and sociological questions about trust, security, identity, privacy, and public policy. They therefore link to discourses in ethics, politics, and the social sciences in general.

Although IS discourses do address such questions in a more direct manner than do IR discourses, and while many works have been written on foundational issues (e.g., the epistemological and ontological foundations of IS), there are some hindrances to effective mutual engagement between the disciplines. First, works on foundational topics tend to use a wide range of metatheoretical frameworks (from the humanities). Although a pluralist set of approaches to foundational questions is important to gather a wide range of insights, the works (1) are difficult to appraise in a comparative fashion (see, e.g., the range in Fisher et al., 2005) in a way that is intelligible to a range of research backgrounds, and (2) do not engage the empirical world of IR researchers (or if they do, the language is often far from the thought patterns of most IR researchers). Second, IS works on foundational topics tend not to be found in the collective memory of empirical (or formal) researchers in IR. This absence is due to the disconnect between current IR and IS discourses, which itself partly reflects the cultural and methodological separation between the mathematical sciences and the humanities.

For example, take the evaluation culture in IR generated through the TREC evaluation scheme. This culture acts as a way of keeping the most optimal approaches for problem contexts in the collective memory of IR researchers. There is no equivalent research culture that effectively keeps foundational issues in the joint collective memory of both IR and IS researchers, except perhaps occasional works on foundations that are of interest to a relatively small group.[50] This is not primarily because humanistic approaches—which one may suppose are the means of addressing foundational questions—are difficult to appraise or compare, as discussed above. Instead, it is mainly because of the lack of a consistent and persistent authoritative discourse on foundations and the lack of a corresponding foundational research culture. Such a discourse and culture would presumably be of particular benefit for those perusing the relatively non–ad hoc (and foundational) research questions, in a way similar to how the TREC-led evaluation culture is of benefit to those focused on systems research and those who have research concerns more akin to ad hoc research. One of the aims of this book is to address this problem by creating an initial foundational research discourse.

1.5 Foundations Research

Foundations research questions pertain not to any one search context but (possibly) to all contexts. As a result, they are on the opposite end of the spectrum from ad hoc research. Moreover, in addition to being

---

50. The History and Foundations of Information Science (HFIS) research group, supported by the main IS research body, the Association for Information Science and Technology (ASIS&T), is one such group.

concerned with particular phenomena, foundations research also pertains to how the corresponding research discourse is conducted; it is concerned with the discipline as a whole. What we call foundational questions have sometimes been associated with "theoretical studies." Currás (1993, 430) laments

> How can practice advance, if it is not supported by theoretical and scientific studies that foster invention and explain discoveries? How can we reach that new level of civilization and culture where the present crisis of mankind is left behind, without studying the scientific and philosophical foundations that help us to form new paradigms?

Relatively ad hoc empirical research is necessary to make progress in the sense of building the best search system for a particular search context. However, theoretical studies, which are the hallmark of the sciences (in addition to experimental work), are also important for progress (Currás, 1993).[51] They not only advance practice (i.e., aid with empirical progress, by explaining practical results), as Currás indicates, but also work toward creating theoretical progress. This book explores what empirical and theoretical progress, and hence progress in general, could mean for IR&S. The next section further outlines the reasoning for addressing this foundational question: What is progress for IR&S?

1.5.1 Fieldwide Questions and Their Modern Relevance

Emerging disciplines with their corresponding systems and practices—such as cognitive computing, data science, and web science—employ or study search phenomena. They generally work with an instrumental perspective, as does IR. Moreover, social science and humanities fields also study technological mediation from the anthropological and other angles, as does IS. To the extent it that is important to understand the place of IR&S among these disciplines, questions about the purposes of IR&S that relate

---

51. Currás (1993, p. 430) continues:

> In any science, theoretical studies are important, as are those who volunteer to study. It is not often an exciting task, nor are fascinating and spectacular results routinely obtained. Progress is generally long-term and often the author of basic theoretical research (unlike his counterpart in the technological area) is neither recognized nor recompensed. But without such study and research, for how much longer can we refer to ourselves as information scientists if we are just highly experienced and skillful technicians?

it to and differentiate it from these other discourses require address. These are fieldwide foundations questions; their scope is the IR&S discourse as a whole. Although such questions are not new, the emerging technological and disciplinary context not only demands that the questions be investigated, but also implies that they require regular perusal, given the rapidly changing nature of the relationship between humans and technology. In addition to the question of purpose and disciplinary identity, questions regarding the nature of IR&S (e.g., whether it is a science, and what counts or should count as progress in research therein) are also (related) fieldwide foundations questions.

Furthermore, no consensus has formed about the answers to these questions. For example, as to whether IR&S is a science, it can be understood as a science of the artificial (Buckland, 2012), but is it a science of the artificial in the way a natural science is a science of natural things? What constitutes this artificial world, and what demarcates it from the natural world? Unlike a natural science, which focuses on natural world objects, IR&S not only deals with an equally well-defined world of artifacts but is additionally concerned about the relationship between highly variable artifacts (from artificial documents to actual restaurants in an Internet of Things, to artificial avatars that represent people, e.g., in SecondLife; Boellstorff, 2008), people, and the built and natural environments. Moreover, the artifacts are of a peculiar nature. Whereas some are sought as an end in themselves (such as documents), others are only important to the extent that they mediate our experience of something else, such as objects that augment our experience of real-world objects (e.g., by means of Google glasses). Some artificial objects involved in mediation are things that have highly specific technical designs (e.g., interface objects representing a response to a user request). This means that it is possible to have complete prior knowledge of what such systems will do in all possible situations. The artificial world is quite unlike the natural world in this respect. They differ in their epistemology, ontology, and in the relationship they exhibit between observers and the observed phenomena. This foundational question about what kind of science IR&S is, is only partly about the observable entities with which it is concerned, and it remains unresolved. As argued in chapters 5 and 6, IR&S is not so much a science of the artificial, as it is a precursor to a science of technology-mediated experience and activity. This is because it is concerned with the user's experience of technological artifacts or contexts (and the corresponding activity), over and above the artifacts themselves.

Chapter 6 discusses the particulars of characterizing such a science as a science of technology-mediated experience.

1.5.2 Making Foundations Research Explicit

Consider the foundations questions about which phenomena are search-like, what contextual aspects should be considered, and whether fragmented construals/studies (anthropological and instrumental, corresponding to work in IS and IR, respectively) can be stitched together. These questions are not only relevant to IR&S but are also important from a general philosophy of science and technology perspective. They have become important in IR&S, because the concern therein is shifting from the immediate instrumental understanding of aspects of search toward richer understandings concerning the full range of search phenomena (i.e., with respect to more anthropological and abstract conceptions; see section 1.2.1).

We contend that, if these questions and concerns were made explicit, related to one another, and problematized, the resulting discursive framework around foundations questions would be highly beneficial. Not least since such a framework, and the foundation discourse it would engender, would act as a bridging discourse between IR, IS, and other disciplines. In particular it would

(1) address modern contexts that we contend require foundational issues to be resolved in order to effect better technology;

(2) work to understand IR and IS in an integrated manner, so that research can be mutually beneficial as the instrumentalist/anthropological aspects are complementary; and

(3) relate IR&S research concerns in a direct and active way with similar concerns in other fields, thereby allowing IR&S to contribute to the larger discourse on technology.

This book works to develop a foundational discursive framework, foundations research perspective, and implicitly, the rudiments of a situating foundations research *culture*, to fulfill these aims. However, neither the respective discursive framework nor the surrounding foundations discourse should be understood as a new sub-discipline in IR and/or IS. Instead, they amount to a recentering and restructuring of the existing discourse and of research perspectives around some basic questions.

Although there are numerous ways to problematize foundational questions and hence create such a discursive framework, the strategy employed here is to initially pursue a foundational question presupposed even by other foundational questions: a root question. And then to proceed to draw out a space of interconnected questions, problems, and concepts.

The question of purpose is just such a root question with which to start the process. However, for several reasons, including the difficulty of defining purposes for the modern context and the importance of making progress, the question of progress is more appropriate.

1.5.2.1 The question of purpose The fieldwide question about the purposes of IR&S could perhaps be a root question. It arguably precedes the question about the nature of the field (i.e., whether a science, and if so, of what kind). However, this choice faces an immediate hurdle. The primary phenomenon of search that IR&S focuses on is pervasive due to the proliferation of technological mediation. The purposes of search are therefore not limited to finding documents but also include enabling very diverse types of user experiences, whose purposes are beyond the basic ad hoc search and are therefore not easy to generalize. Therefore the purposes of search research also vary widely. Moreover, a wide variety of methodologies are used by IR&S researchers—from the instrumental/technical to the anthropological and philosophical—each accompanied by its own set of goals. Additionally, the technological and disciplinary landscape has undergone dramatic change since IR&S research began, with numerous other disciplines working on similar phenomena. Purposes have therefore changed and will continue to grow and evolve. Perhaps only a few generic purposes can be said to have remained invariant,[52] for example, that IR&S exists to study information-related phenomena and to create the corresponding technology.

But if we seek to create an authoritative vision of IR&S in a prescriptive rather than descriptive manner, then we can develop a set of compatible ontological, epistemological, ethical, and so forth perspectives that work to construe the aspect of reality that IR&S ought to deal with and how it ought to do so. This task depends on the question about purposes and the closely related question about what kind of discipline (if at all one discipline) IR&S ought to be. It also depends on deeper questions about the type of (technology-mediated) society that is sought—that is to be enabled by technologies that IR&S is tasked to create. This latter question is further discussed in works outside IR&S (e.g., Castells, 2000), and in IS (e.g., Day, 2008, 2014). However, while visions about the place of technology are presupposed in IR&S discourse, they tend not to be directly employed

---

52. One could claim, alternatively, that the purpose of IR&S is what IR&S scholars currently do. However, this ultimately deflects the question instead of sufficiently answering it; why do they do what they do?

in any regular fashion by IR or IS works. Instead, they remain in the background (see section 3.3). The question about the purposes of IR&S therefore depends on authoritative overall visions of IR&S given a technologically mediated society, and in addition seems less important in (or "too abstract" for) the existing, generally empirical discourse.

1.5.2.2 The question of progress   Consider the complementary matter of whether a particular research project is "good" or conducive to progress. Any definition of progress here must depend on corresponding notions of purpose and value: research is progressive to the extent that it fulfills a corresponding set of purposes/aims and values. However, the question of progress, while it tends not to be asked explicitly, participates more directly in research practice than do questions of purpose and values. This is because researchers presume there to be a benefit to the conduct of their research activities. They assume that it is better to do than to not do, that it will lead to progress toward the solution of a problem, or lead to the discovery of other problems. There are tacit understandings of what progress means, and for IR, they revolve around an empirically oriented idea, that a more efficient or effective search system is more progressive (or makes a greater contribution to the overall progress of the discipline) than a less effective/efficient one. This idea, commonly presupposed, is clearly incomplete. For example, it does not account for theoretical or humanistic research with little or no focus on system creation or improvement. Moreover, as chapter 2 argues, even if only empirical progress is sought, with modern applications seeking to satisfy an increasing variety of usage goals, it is not appropriate to reduce this complex of goals under the rubric of "effectiveness." Instead, a framework of concepts is required to take the place of "effectiveness." The idea of progress, as to what progress is, therefore requires to be problematized, especially for the modern context.

The question of progress is therefore a good one, as it is not only a theoretical concern. It is instead a relatively immediate research concern pertaining to the development and analysis of applications situated in contexts exhibiting greater varieties of usage needs. Moreover, it is an unresolved question, and due to such emerging contexts, the idea of progress is increasingly a source of contention. However, it is also a good question, as it is a foundational question with fieldwide scope. In particular, progress is almost as foundational as the question of purposes and closely mirrors the latter's concerns. The purposes of IR&S and of any discipline enabling technological mediation are sensitive to emerging contexts of technology-use and their effects on society. Conceptions of progress follow these changing purposes. The question of progress is therefore linked closely to the "low-down" (the foundations) as well as to the "high-up" (the everyday research); from system building to theoretical and humanistic research, progress is a particularly central issue for all of IR&S.

As foundations discourse underpins other nonfoundational types of research (e.g., empirical research), one would expect it to bridge not only discourses in IR and IS, but also between IR&S discourse and that of other fields. It has been supposed that tackling the question of progress, as opposed to that of purpose—due to the centrality of progress—would be good way to unravel such a foundations discourse. This centrality also means that it relates to the instrumental and anthropological dimensions of technology creation and use as pertaining to IR and IS; that is, progress is about fulfilling humanistic as well as technological values. Furthermore, there is a rich philosophy of science discourse (Niiniluoto, 2011) that can be employed, as chapters 3 and 4 do, to understand progress in IR&S in a standard way. Hence, there are preexisting schemas for addressing progress, whereas the question of purpose appears to be more elusive. Progress is therefore an effective way into foundations. It is the path we take in this book to create an initial discursive framework on the way to a full-fledged foundations discourse.

For all research discourses, any research project therein that aims to work out what progress means in the first place for that discourse would presumably itself be progressive research.[53] While we were undertaking the work for this book, we assumed that our work (and any project with similar aims) would indeed be of benefit to the greater IR&S discourse. However, in the course of writing this book, it became more than a weakly tacit assumption. It was something about which we became convinced. The perusal of the question of progress, other basic questions, and in general, developing of a foundations research discourse, if it done properly, is a significantly progressive move at this time for IR&S. This claim is further elaborated in later chapters, especially in chapters 3 and 4.

1.6 Conclusion

Understanding what technology is requires multiple perspectives across disciplines to be brought together. From the bottom-up perspective, the

---

53. Unless notions of progress were already well understood etc.

phenomenon of mediation, characterizing the particular nature of modern technology, captures something of the complex relationship between humans and devices. And this mediation, although it can be understood in many (complementary) ways, should be framed in terms of search phenomena in order to understand it in a way closest to how it is experienced in practice. This is because search is a highly typical mediational phenomenon commonly presupposed in other mediational phenomena. Relating search to mediation in this way makes mediation over and above devices, the salient aspect of modern technology around which to arrange IR&S phenomena and discourse.[54]

As a significant phenomenon of technological mediation, search phenomena, enabled by search applications prevalent in modern applications of various functions, are central to our increasingly technology-mediated lived experience. The designs of applications, through the use of which this mediation happens, conditions the type of search phenomenon a device engenders, which allows for the meaningful exchange of information between user and system. The evolving set of such applications, which condition the use of the devices they inhabit, reflect the changing nature of the human-machine relationship. That relationship, once restricted to a specific physical location (as for desktop computers), is instead now active regardless of the user's physical location (through portable devices and "tangible bits"; Ishii and Ullmer, 1997). And it is now heading toward being present out there in the world—in an "always there" sense—[55] through applications that inhabit devices in the Internet of Things. In addition, instead of applications accessing previously stored data, they are heading toward live, recently generated, socially verified local information that can affect lived experience in a dynamic sense.[56] Devices thus change from being physical points for the display of information to invisible-in-themselves revealers of information. Instead of being limited to simple requests and responses, applications tend toward facilitating natural language communication that would make devices more human-like

---

54. Kember and Zylinska (2012) suggest a similar reorientation for the related discipline of new media studies.

55. This property is enabled by relevant user information being shared among a multitude of publicly accessible devices that are regularly available.

56. This includes applications working in a smart-city infrastructure that, e.g., serves drivers by providing traffic information based on the application's immediate prior communications with other users that are spatially and temporally close and whose interactions are then used to make in decisions about traffic flow, traffic jams, etc.

(Turkle, 2005, 2011). And they go even further: from offering immersive augmented-reality experiences (e.g., as do the Google glasses) to experiences in virtual worlds in which to dwell in a serious normative manner (e.g, in SecondLife type contexts). If these trends are understood to characterize modern and near-future technologies, where the corresponding applications are extensions of basic search applications, then the study of the subsequent phenomena become increasingly important. Their study is already being conducted in disciplines looking at different aspects of these developments, from IR&S to related disciplines, such as cognitive computing, data science, natural language processing, and human-computer interaction. It is important therefore, to critically examine the structure and overall direction of these disciplines, specially IR&S.

This chapter framed IR&S in two ways. It discerned its phenomena of concern by reference to the central phenomenon of ad hoc search, and it framed its research discourse through a typology of research perspectives centered around the perspective of ad hoc research. With respect to overall direction, what is vital to understand is what drives research in that direction, and this is encompassed in the question of progress in IR&S. What this progress may mean is the subject of the following chapters. However, as we have argued in this chapter, the development of a foundations research discourse has something to do with it.

2 Notions of Progress in Information Retrieval

2.1 Introduction

The modern technological context demands a type of research that is not only far from ad hoc research but also inclines toward foundations, and in particular, as chapter 1 argued, toward addressing foundations questions that apply fieldwide, such as that of progress. What then is progress? What could it mean for IR&S? The analysis in this chapter finds that, in a nutshell, progress in IR&S corresponds to the growth of techniques, theoretical frameworks, and so forth, that enable the discourse to deal with (study and design for) a widening range of phenomena in a rigorous and coherent fashion. We also find, moreover, that this growth is premised on the development of a foundations discourse that both supports it and works to address questions presupposed therein.

Specifically, this chapter addresses the question of progress through developing several key notions of progress through an analysis of IR&S discourses that explicitly or implicitly refer to current and possible future directions for research. It does this through critical-interpretive readings of particular representative works in IR through using the visions of IR research characterized as research directions in Crestani et al. (2003). A generalization of these directions, developed in the following, can be understood to apply also to IS discourse (and indeed, any serious intellectual discourse) and hence to IR&S. While they do not exhaust notions of progress for IR, let alone IS, we contend that they nevertheless are significant to both discourses.

Progress in IR is usually associated with empirically characterizable improvements to the operation of a retrieval system, as deduced through experiments and the formal and empirical research perspectives employed to interpret experimental results.[1]

These aspects are of course complementary (and co-constitutive; see section 1.3.2.3). Crestani et al. (2003, p. 281) state:

> Research on the use of mathematical, logical, and formal methods, has been central to Information Retrieval research for a long time…[it]…is important not only because it helps enhancing retrieval effectiveness, but also because it helps clarify the underlying concepts of Information Retrieval.

They suggest that the future of research in what is usually understood as "formal IR" (or "IR formal methods") lies in the following three research directions: "(1) increasing the integration between different formal approaches to IR; (2) capturing user modelling and issues of context in IR; and (3) exploring links with other mathematical, logical, and engineering disciplines" (Crestani et al., 2003, p. 284). Since the formal and the empirical in IR are co-constitutive, advancement according to one perspective is likely to correspond to (or result in) some development (if not advancement) in another, and thus, these directions can be seen to apply to the discipline of IR as a whole and not just to the formal aspect of IR. The proceeding relates these research directions to three corresponding aims that are pursued by scientific disciplines, and therefore pertain to related discussions in the philosophy of science (Toulmin, 1982; Cartwright, 1983; Pietarinen, 2006; Thagard, 2007; Dawson and Gregory, 2009).

The first direction mentioned above corresponds to the general scientific aim of coherence among theories, propositions generated from theories, and coherence in the overall discourse involving theories and propositions. The second direction corresponds to the aim of effective construal or objectification of relevant phenomena, whether for study or for (empirical) use through technical designs that determine corresponding applications. A phenomenon here is any appearance or happening of interest to researchers or developers or the like (i.e., to those tasked to study technology whether for scientific/academic or commercial purposes, whether this study is motivated by user/application requirements, technical or scientific curiosity or other factors). The notion of construal was introduced in section 1.1.3 (cf. footnote 9 in chapter 1). Objectification is a specific type of construal. It is the process of depicting particular phenomena (e.g., user interactions) in

---

1. Progress is also often associated with the development of one or more such (or other, e.g., sociological) perspectives that may offer insights or alternative interpretations of the same empirical results, or of other empirical/real-life scenarios of interest.

terms of interrelated objects for study, capture, processing, or for placing in a technical design which can be implemented as an application.[2] Thus, not all construals are objectifications (they do not all have to specify specific objects), but each objectification is the construal of a phenomenon. Both notions, construal and objectification will be employed below. While they are mostly interchangeable, the use of the latter will serve to emphasize a more specific form of output from an intellectual process.

Construal always involves the study of phenomena according to the over-all purposes of IR&S, which in turn are conditioned by values (e.g., efficiency and user satisfaction). Construal or objectification does not only concern the study of what is "out there," such as observable, objective user input, but also the subjective and inter-subjective interpretations of it. A construal is effective to the extent that the overall purposes of the discipline are met through its study, capture, and processing. For example, the discussion in section 1.2 construed search as a relation between sets of words, and this was effective to the extent that it met the purpose of connecting between search as a phenomenon of mediation and search as a technical phenomenon understood in IR. The problem of construal then raises the basic/foundational question as to what these purposes and values are, since positions on these questions are presupposed in any particular construal of a phenomenon.

The third direction is concerned with effective borrowing from outside the discipline. Not only is borrowing frequent, but it is also an inherent part of the process of theoretical development: "scientific theories do not spring from the void—but from the development and reworking of cognitive material that pre-exists them, necessitating the creative employment of ideas from adjacent fields" (Bhaskar, 2010, p. 25). However, in matching concepts and models from elsewhere there is, implicitly or explicitly, (1) a comparison between disciplines, (2) the development of an understanding of the place of the discipline among other disciplines, and (3) the development of an understanding about the similarities and differences between the natures of the relevant phenomena, their objectifications, or both. If the borrowing is done more self-consciously, this would lead to an inquiry into ontology—as to how phenomena relevant for IR&S relate to other objects in the world (as mentioned in Brookes (1980a); Buckland (2012)). The borrowing from elsewhere and its integration into IR

---

2. This is a vastly simplified version of the notion of objectification used in phenomenological discourses (see Heelan, 2003; Salice, 2016 and Husserl, 2002, pp. 251–260) but it is adequate for characterizing a type of progress in this chapter. The notion is further developed in section 5.1.1 for the purpose of characterizing researchers.

discourse is effective, just as for the problem of construal, to the extent that the overall purposes of the discipline are satisfied. Thus, this aim is not only about exploring other disciplines for tools and mathematical methods to aid modeling, it is also concomitant with addressing the fundamental questions: "What kind of science and what kind of discipline is IR?," and "What kind of science/discipline should it be?" These questions are implicit in this aim due to the inevitable comparison between the different kinds of disciplines involved in the borrowing process (see chapter 5).[3]

Whereas the first research direction pertains to coherence within the discipline, the third pertains to coherence between this discipline and others. This is with respect to how one understands the similarities and differences between IR and other relevant disciplines as to their chosen phenomena, ways of construing/modeling/capturing them, styles of discourse about them, and the strategies for affecting them (through technologies). Accordingly, from here on the first aim shall be referred to as internal coherence and the third as external coherence.

The following sections further develop the above aims as notions of progress for IR&S. The aims are contextualized through critical interpretation of IR researches wherein they are frequently problematized, albeit often implicitly. The aims are detailed therein through an exploration of their particulars and interdependencies, related research problems (whether foundational or otherwise), and an analysis of the implications of these aims with respect to the research culture in IR&S.

One such implication is that the fulfillment of these aims is dependent on the perusal of additional foundations questions through foundations research. This is because there are foundations questions (other than those about progress) presupposed by researches in which these progress-related aims appear to be important. For the discourse therein to be coherent (both externally and internally), or the phenomena construal to be effective (especially with respect to the modern context) further foundations questions must be resolved.

In particular, section 2.2 elaborates on the nature of internal coherence in the varied discourse of IR&S and its relation to effective construal (the second aim); section 2.3 then problematizes construal in a broad fashion, relating its concerns to various research problems, persisting and modern.

---

3. Meaning that they are among the most important or fundamental of the foundational questions. In addition, they are among the most foundational since addressing them will influence the position one takes with respect to the many other foundational questions that depend on them.

Section 2.4 explains that external coherence requires a metatheory that can ensure coherence in the process of borrowing between discourses. It identifies this with the idea of an overarching discourse corresponding to what we have called a foundations discourse. Section 2.5 explains how the indicators of progress that pertain to experiments (specifically, generalizability, repeatability, and the accurate interpretation of results) branch off from the three overall notions of progress. Relations between these notions, as this chapter elaborates, offer particular insights into the modern research context.

The relatively ad hoc (and often tacit) understanding of progress in IR as improvement of ranking, and of the growth of theories as indicating progress, are addressed in section 2.6. Their limitation as notions of progress are briefly discussed there by relating them to the other notions explored in this chapter. Growth in the empirical or formal levels may not automatically entail progress, and as section 2.7 concludes, a more refined understanding of growth in terms of facts and propositions as the units of research is required to further explore the idea of growth and that of progress; this is attempted in chapter 4.

2.2 Integrating Approaches (Internal Coherence)

The need for the unification or integration of approaches (or of theories, models, etc.) pertains to the scientific aim of coherence among these formal entities, as well as the discourse that surrounds and supports them. This discourse refers in part to the propositions generated by the application of, or thinking by means of, these models/theories/approaches. Integration therefore should not be taken to refer only to the unification of mathematical models: a model may not fully capture the corresponding search scenario, software applications, or the discourse about that scenario. Instead, as per the pragmatic view of science, integration should be understood to refer to the systematic configuration of various discourse elements, from diagrams to explanatory patterns to tools (Winther, 2015). The idea of internal coherence or integration thereby presupposes, a conception of science, and furthermore, an idea of how a discourse is supposed to fit together. Seeking a unification of approaches thereby depends on the resolution of the foundational question about what conception of science and scientific discourse should be adopted. Moreover, as argued below, the goal of integration is concomitant with finding a "true" depiction of the reality of whatever is being studied. The development of an internally coherent or integrated discourse thus means to take a position regarding the idea of truth that is to be attributed to the resultant discourse. This means resolving foundational questions about the conceptions of science and truth that befit IR&S, as well as several of the other questions discussed in this chapter.

With respect to the foundational position regarding a conception of science, as section 1.3.2 argued, the pragmatic conception is most suitable for IR&S.[4] Integration in IR&S should be understood in terms of this conception. This is because IR discourses centered on mathematical models appear to follow the semantic conception of science (see section 1.3.2), as is common in the natural sciences. However, the social/psychological phenomena that are central to IR&S, and greatly differ from natural phenomena (Little, 1993; Danermark, 2002; Porpora, 1998), imply the need for the broader pragmatic conception. One of the main reasons for forgoing the semantic conception is that mathematical models of social phenomena generally capture less than they do of natural phenomena. As unlike in the natural world, where empirical regularities in observed phenomena can be captured by universal laws (which are effectively captured by mathematical models) the socio-psychological world is not as law-like; social regularities are instead highly contextual. In particular, mathematical models of the physical aspects of a social activity explain less than they do for the natural world: "The social world is meaningful in a way the natural world is not" (Gorton, 2015). Take, for example, the typical model in IR, which models the set of physical interactions with a search engine as a moving vector in the vector space of words or documents/features. The formal representations can at most tell us what physical things have happened (e.g., user interactions). The application is not able to understand or explain the activity as a whole, except simply to state what the activity was about in terms of a set of features/words, or in terms of predetermined rules that it can use to derive reasons. It is only when another human being (such as the researcher) employs their experience and a corresponding social/psychological perspective to interpret the activity that the "why" and even the "what" (in terms of social/psychological events) of the activity can be understood.

---

4. While the pragmatic conception of science provides some specification of this idea, it should not be seen as complete. IR&S discourse includes a wide variety of perspectives spanning the sciences and humanities. Hence, the related basic question of what coherence could mean beyond the prior discussion and with respect to such a diverse discourse is a nontrivial question that is far from being a concern particular to IR&S. Chapters 3 and 4 elaborate on the different types of discourse elements to be integrated, and what their coherent combination could mean, beyond the pragmatic conception. Chapter 5 refines these elements in terms of foundations questions.

Regularities pertaining to IR&S phenomena therefore pertain to what people or search algorithms actually do in real-life/empirical retrieval scenarios. These regularities depend on a particular perspective of the phenomena and a particular objectification of that phenomena. That particular way of construing and objectifying phenomena is presupposed and hence is more primary/fundamental than its representation in models.[5] Beyond relatively ad hoc research contexts, much of the IR&S discourse concerns (1) user experience analysis through the study of an increasing number of complex human factors that constitute the context of search scenarios, and (2) the study of complex concepts, such as relevance, that mediate the understanding of these scenarios. Although much of the IR&S discourse is not about mathematical models, there must be an investigation into the adequacy of the received conception of scientific theorizing and representation for retrieval phenomena. If conceptions centered on mathematical models are accepted uncritically, then an incoherence will develop between the actual nature of social phenomena that pertain to search and their presumed nature of being natural-scientific. As a result, the aim of seeking integration between approaches will not properly address the social meaning that the mathematical models fail to capture; it will not be able to effectively integrate the large nonmathematical parts of the discourse.

Furthermore, whatever the appropriate conception of IR&S discourse is, the aim of internal coherence corresponds to properly arranging ideas, discussions, and structures into an order. It is this arrangement that often involves integration or unification of paradigms, technical approaches, conceptual frameworks, theories, and models. Integration corresponds to finding relationships among these entities such that one can be understood in terms of the other or in terms of a more generalized such entity (approach/theory/model) within which several of them fit, or from which several prior approaches/ theories/ models can be generated.

This seeking of proper arrangement within a discourse is a seeking of a coherent discourse. A coherent discourse is not only favorable due to being clearer—and hence presumably easier to understand—than a less coherent one. According to the coherence theory of truth (Young, 2013; Glanzberg, 2014) (see also Haack, 1978, pp. 94–97), a coherent discourse is also somehow "more true" (than a less coherent discourse). Thus, as expected of a scientific or intellectual discourse, such as IR&S, "truth" is sought (see

---

5. This is also the case for the natural sciences, where the phenomena exhibit particular types of regularities (van Fraassen, 1980).

chapter 3 for a broader discussion of how truth relates to theories of scientific progress).[6] An IR&S researcher's search for a coherent discourse is a means of seeking a "true" discourse. A notion of truth—a foundational notion as to what one's conception of truth is that mediates their truth-seeking activity—underlies IR&S research. However, in addition to seeking truth according to the coherence theory, IR&S discourse can also be understood as seeking truth according to the correspondence theory of truth (David, 2015), by which the truth of a discourse (or some part of it, like a theory) pertains to the level of its correspondence with facts about the real world. This correspondence is judged in IR by the process of evaluating retrieval/matching models, by checking the correspondence between retrieval results and human relevance judgments (the latter being the facts in this context). That truth, both as coherence and correspondence is sought, would imply that the underlying notion of truth in IR is better characterized by the pragmatist notion of truth (Haack, 1978, pp. 86–89 and pp. 97–99) that combines the correspondence and coherence accounts. However, to limit terminology and to retain the potency of the concept of coherence, consider the following generalization, which will be employed for the remainder of this text.

Let the received notion of coherence be generalized to also include correspondence, so that the seeking of this coherence is the seeking of truth in a pragmatist sense. This expanded notion of coherence refers therefore both to proper arrangement and relation to reality. These two aspects should be understood to be related in the following way: to correspond with reality is to "cohere with" it, that is, to be arranged in a way as to mirror it (i.e., to be "properly arranged" with respect to reality). This generalized coherence as the pragmatist sense of truth should be taken to be the encompassing category of truth for IR&S.

A particular benefit of this expanded version of coherence is that IR's goal of integration also comes to mean correspondence-as-integration between discourse and observed phenomena (as opposed to just among different discourses). As a consequence, the judgment about whether a discourse is

---

6. Thus, if the truth of a scientific or intellectual discourse is important for judging its value, or for judging its progress, it is therefore important to understand both whether the discourse admits a proper arrangement and to what extent it relates to reality, and therefore to understand how coherent it is. The seeking of proper arrangement or coherence is therefore not only a goal pertaining to readability/usability of the discourse, but also pertains strongly to its truth, and by extension, to its validity. And as implied below with respect to an expanded notion of coherence, to its verifiability and viability.

coherent—in this general sense—with respect to some part of the world becomes dependent on further foundational positions. First, it is dependent on understanding the ontology of that part of the world and second, the epistemology pertaining to understanding it. That is, it is dependent on understanding, respectively, how one can go about describing the constituents and particulars of that part, and how accurately (whether and in what ways) it can be known. In particular, as a result, the judgment of coherence is dependent on an understanding of the relevant phenomena. The theories, models, technical designs, and their supporting discourse (in terms of diagrams and concepts that constitute the retrieval discourse) are dependent on the construal of phenomena that they particularly seek to capture. Thus, the aim of internal coherence is dependent on the aim of proper/effective (phenomena) construal.

As the proceeding argues, in addition to aim presupposing an understanding of construal, several types of regular discussions in IR&S, including empirical-experimental discussions in IR, also presuppose it.

2.3   Capturing Users and Context (Effective Construal and Objectification)

In modern times, there is a radical shift in the use of IR systems through ubiquitous social and augmented-reality applications that not only work on the space of electronic objects but also on real-life objects through the Internet of Things (Holler et al., 2014). This has expanded the space of objects of user expression and system expression from simple queries and documents, respectively, to possibly the entirety of objects in the real world, all of which can be construed as objects in some search process.

Take, for example, the case of an augmented-reality system, such as the Google glasses. A user expression could correspond simply to gazing in a particular direction. If something from the real world is found in that gaze that also has an associated meaning as an information-based entity through being connected to the Internet of Things, then a visualization of that object may augment the user's gaze. This visualization would then be the system's expression or response to the user's query or "expression." Instead of being one particular visualization, the system expression may consist of a set of visuals that work to lead the user through the real world to a particular place.

In this case, the user expressions are multiple, but the usage journey they constitute is something additional to the individual expressions (i.e., the whole is additional to and not completely equivalent to its parts). The "document" here is not only a set of words or features, nor only structured data or graphical objects, but is also an augmented-reality experience based on augmented real-world objects. The context here includes location and prior user history, but can also include social information left behind in the corresponding real-world place by prior users. The glance or gaze is an orientation of the user's body, and this takes the place of the query. But the goal of this search (if it can still be called that) is not so much an immediate set of documents or information items, expressed in a particular mode or through a particular medium. The goal is a type of experience over and above a final destination. Goals can be understood to constitute different user types. There is the user looking for immediate information (as in ad hoc retrieval), and at the other end of the spectrum there are users looking for extensively interactive and immersive experiences (e.g., the prior example or SecondLife).

All such complex scenarios can be represented and discussed at the level of queries and documents, because ultimately, the underlying retrieval system is responsible for a semantic matching between words or features. However, to employ this reduced perspective would be to ignore much of what the matching means at the human level. That it is inadequate to deal with such complex modern scenarios in an ad hoc research fashion (see chapter 1) implies that one must be open to considering the vast possibilities of objects associated with a user or system expression—as objects given or indicated by an application.

Moreover, the rich variation in the ways of expressing such objects must be dealt with. For example, there is the augmented-reality object that is expressed through visual cues and has several features: All these details have a programmatic/algorithmic representation as well as representation as a discrete or continuous mathematical structure (e.g., a probability function). The object may also have a normative description associated with it that reflects the social and cultural meanings of the real-world entity that it is supposed to augment. It may also be associated with various subjective meanings due to the many users who have attached their own descriptions to it by having previously interacted with it. The object may be a continuously developing entity, such as an avatar representing a real or fictitious person that changes according to real-life (or, e.g., Second Life) events. In addition, the object may be given further meaning through social-psychological and cultural studies, for example, as an object of affection for a particular user or user group, or a symbol of an unconscious desire in the psychoanalytic sense (Ffytche, 2011; Mills, 2014).

As the scope of research inclines away from ad hoc research to consider the meaning of user, query, and context, through understanding the corresponding objects according to different perspectives, the question pertaining to aim two of how to construe the relevant objects for study or use (through applications) becomes a significant problem. The following deliberates on the problem of construal. Section 2.3.1 introduces the notion of phenomena construal, section 2.3.2 works to distinguish it from being restricted to a technical or mathematical task; in particular, it is understood as a problem that mainly pertains to the (mathematically) prerepresentational. Section 2.3.3 details how the problem of construal, in particular, system construal, is raised—mainly indirectly—in the context of empirical and experimental IR, reading key works therein as suggesting that addressing the problem of construal (of system and user side phenomena) is important for progress. Section 2.3.4 instead focuses on the construal of search as a whole, reading several recent and important IR works as suggesting the centrality of addressing construal for progress. Section 2.3.4 also elucidates the different guises this problem takes in the literature. Finally, section 2.3.5 argues that construal is ultimately a foundational problem, as opposed to an empirical, theoretical, or technical one.

2.3.1 What Is Construal?

For the researcher, the phenomena or objects of interest for study not only include real-world or virtual objects that users can interact with, but also user behaviors and experiences,[7] which pertain to the way users react to, interpret, and understand these objects. The effective construal or objectification of phenomena pertains first to interpreting and understanding how the object is presented to consciousness. Second, it pertains to deciding which aspects of potentially observable (or observed) user behavior (or experience) to problematize for study or to cater to when designing systems. And finally, it pertains to characterizing that object in a normative way, so that it can be used in further discourse or system design. The construal or objectification is effective to the extent that the overall purposes of the discipline are fulfilled through studying them (or designing and using them), as construed. System designers or user-experience designers, IR&S researchers in general, and the end user are all beneficiaries of construal, and construal must proceed according to their needs in order to be effective.

Construal therefore does not only refer to selecting phenomena for mathematical representation, but mainly involves investigating how they

---

7. An experience does not only refer to a user's state of knowledge or mind. It also refers to their overall dynamic, process of cogitation that is the "whole," that subsumes and integrates subprocesses of knowing, feeling, perceiving, imagining, and the like; and which acts as the background to (static) states of cognition.

are presented in the first place, and as such it is an empirical activity. However, although this is strictly speaking empirical, IR tends to understand the empirical as primarily referring to objective (or objective aspects of) phenomena, rather than to subjective or intersubjective (or such aspects of) phenomena. The "empirical" at the level of the presentation of objects refers instead to the human (subjective and intersubjective) understanding of this presentation (see footnote 9 in chapter 1, and Gupta, 2000; Oksala, 2003). This includes understanding (i) how one can come to know about the particulars of the objects, (ii) the different ways the same object or its properties may appear in particular contexts, and (iii) how they thereby may be interpreted and understood by different individuals. Aim 2 is hence concerned, through (i) with epistemology, which is the study of knowledge and justified beliefs, and through (ii) with phenomenology, which is the study of our experience of the appearances of things (e.g., objects and their properties),[8] and (iii) with ontology, the study of what there is and how to categorize it (see also, the discussion of comportment in section 5.1.1).[9] And this is with respect to the different perspectives: the researcher's and the user's. It pertains to the former perspective, since researchers are responsible for creating applications and studying their effects. The user's experience of the application and the world through mediation of the application are also important to consider for researchers, and so the way objects may be presented to them—the way in which users may construe things—is also of relevance to researchers. For example, the investigation of the method by which researchers deduce opinions about what users supposedly know about a corpus (or what they take to be relevant) is an investigation of an epistemological variety. It is epistemological in two ways, first since the researcher's way of knowing is being investigated and second since the user's way of knowing is also being investigated. If the investigation is extended to analyze research methodology that captures not only what the users know

8. In addition, a phenomenological investigation would be concerned with structures of consciousness through the study of intentionality. Given our current context, a phenomenology of search would not only study the (technological) objects "out there" that mediate the user's experience of the world, user and system expressions, and the corresponding objects in the world, but also the cognitive structure of the information needs behind user expressions.

9. Phenomenology is used to reveal objects that are stable in experience, which then become part of an ontology. In addition, given the discussion in section 1.2.3, this also concerns fundamental ontology, i.e., the modes of being, since the way things appear to experience, in the phenomenological sense, depends on the mode of being.

or believe, but also other aspects of their experience (e.g., from emotion aspects of their cognition to how they perceive objects etc.), then this is an investigation of a phenomenological variety.[10] If this requires an understanding of possible objects in the world that concern user experience, then an ontological investigation is required.

2.3.2 Construal as Pre-Theoretical, Culturally Informed, and Nontechnical

Construal comes before mathematical representation and theorization. This is especially the case for phenomena that are not natural-scientific, and therefore do not exhibit universal regularities. The highly contextualized nature of social regularities means that, in general, mathematical forms are less representative of the overall social phenomenon (as section 2.2 mentions) than they are for the natural-scientific case. Mathematical representation may be necessary for the purposes of a social-scientific discourse, but is less satisfactory in general than when referring to natural phenomena in a natural-scientific discourse.

As such, internal coherence (aim 1) among theories/models of observed phenomena (and the discourse surrounding them)—such as phenomena pertaining to user behaviors/experiences—is dependent on the coherence of the prerepresentational and pretheoretical investigation of the space of phenomena. It is this investigation to which construal (aim 2) pertains. With IR&S phenomena radically changing in the modern context, not only are there strong practical demands on IR&S theory (as can be expected for theories involving real-world entities) but also the question of construal intervenes in a particularly strong way in the creation of theories and models. It could indeed be adequate for the study of search in limited (nonubiquitous) contexts to employ traditional understandings of user, query, and document, without needing to address construal as anything other than formal representation for study and technical design, or for the statistical summarization of user surveys for evaluation. For the modern context, however, the problem of construal presents itself in every new context of search use—which is often due to search technology becoming more pervasive.

As chapter 1 argued, this is due to (1) the complexity of phenomena pertaining to IR&S, (2) search becoming the most typical technology-mediated

---

10. Being of the phenomenological variety does not immediately imply that it needs to conform to the phenomenological tradition in contemporary philosophy (Smith, 2013), but that it is concerned with subject matter to which that tradition pertains.

activity (see section 1.2), and (3) technological mediation accounting for an increasingly large share of lived-experience. The upshot of (2) and (3), is that search is a phenomenon that both informs and is informed by social practices/habits and attitudes (i.e., culture). It informs culture as IR&S discourse informs technological designs for applications, and therefore conditions what is put out into society. It is informed by culture, as understanding the space of objects in a construal discourse (especially for ubiquitous and augmented reality contexts) requires an understanding of the preexisting culture of activities and attitudes that will be catered to by new applications.

"Informing culture" here not only refers to, for example Googling as a cultural phenomenon (Brabazon, 2006; Drotner et al., 2008; Lupton, 2013; Van Dijck, 2013), but also to various types of use of applications that involve search in some way. This includes applications that provide online product recommendations and friend suggestions (collaborative filtering), (possibly expert) answers to questions that are relevant on a daily basis (e.g., health questions), health trackers (which involve collaborative filtering), personal information organizers, augmented-reality recommendations for real-life places and events, and live restaurant-booking applications. All such applications are increasingly embedded in the everyday lived experience of modern technology users.

Search has become about far more than receiving queries and providing ranked documents; it is a phenomenon of technological mediation that has become enmeshed, or more accurately, sedimented among other cultural phenomena. Here *sedimentation* is when something "becomes a hidden presupposition that enables something higher to come to light" (Sokolowski, 2000, p. 166). To construe a search scenario is then to isolate a phenomenon from within technologically influenced cultural phenomena, and therefore to distinguish between cultural practices that are to be called "search" and those that are not. Presupposed in such a construal is the basic question: What is search? The construal of search as a phenomenon and a practice is more primary than the construal of other phenomena, such as user interactions, queries, and documents. The problem of search construal is then primarily not a technical problem but, as in Buckland (2012), a cultural and anthropological one. However, it is precisely because there are several such modes of construing search that it is supposed to transcend these modes to become a foundational concern.

While search construal is problematized directly in foundational works in IR&S, it is the implicit cases that serve to demonstrate its relevance and prevalence across IR&S discourse. The next section engages literature mainly from experimental and empirical IR, which implicitly raise the issue of the construal of the components of search and hence of search itself.

2.3.3   Construal Problems in Experimental IR

Practical research, that is, research about empirically realized (observed) user and system acts, makes demands both on theoretical and foundational research. This section studies several works by empirically oriented IR&S scholars and reads them as suggesting the need to problematize construal. This is an issue that pertains neither to empirical nor theoretical research—both these types of research presuppose particular construals of phenomena—but to foundational research. The respective works are moreover read as suggesting that such a problematization is important for progress both with regard to empirical research and to IR research in general. Section 2.3.3.1 shows how the general inclination in these works to go both beyond ad hoc search scenarios and ad hoc research leads to their implicit problematization of construal. In contrast, section 2.3.3.2 discusses specific inclinations to reconstrue systems and users. Finally, section 2.3.3.3 discusses how the understanding of the idea of substantivity corresponds to foundational questions that are also related to construal and also require resolution. Substantive results are those needed for progress to be made in experimental IR and whose definition depend on addressing construal.

2.3.3.1   Empirical progress is limited without going beyond ad hoc search and research   Commenting on the current situation in IR research, Belkin (2008, 2010)[11] argues that in spite of the success of IR—as is clear from its effect on everyday life—"there still remain substantial challenges." He refers to Karen Spärck-Jones's 1988 Salton Award speech (Spärck-Jones, 1988), which he interprets as suggesting that (emphasis ours)

> substantial progress in information retrieval was likely only to come through **addressing issues associated with users (actual or potential)**, rather than continuing IR research with an almost exclusive focus on document representation and matching and ranking techniques.

---

11. Belkin (2010) revised the claims of Belkin (2008) to suggest that there is indeed evidence that IR researchers are developing user-studies research in the form of conferences or workshops recently established. However, the main critiques in Belkin (2008) about the noncentrality of the user in IR research (and related critiques presented here) appear to still stand, according to Belkin (2010). More recent work (Belkin, 2016) implies that this

Moreover, further commenting on Spärck-Jones's 1988 position, Belkin (2008, 2010) remarks about IR research, controversially perhaps, that there are still relatively few substantive results. He continues quoting Spärck-Jones's critique about prior IR research (from the 1970s) as being abstract/reductionist where there was a lack of adequate consideration of the user's need for information (Belkin, 2008, p. 49). Spärck-Jones (1988, p. 19) expresses frustration about the perspective that IR research is purely about working with such simplified models (narrow construals) of phenomena:

> It is impossible not to feel that continuing research on probabilistic weighting in the style in which it has been conducted, however good in itself in aims and conduct, is just bombinating in the void.

For the focus of research to remain on weighting documents and terms for matching purposes, without considering information need and other user aspects, means for it to remain within a particular, limited, research perspective. This is a research perspective that stays close to the ad hoc, as discussed in chapter 1. For the focus of research to remain on such a perspective is to impede progress. While the critique in the above quote refers to research predating the 1990s, it clearly applies to similar research done since. This is not to suggest that there should not be any simplifications or reductions in experimental IR with respect to how users or other phenomena are construed and studied. There is indeed a limit to what systems can know about users to make decisions about relevant documents, and a limit due to experimental control (Järvelin, 2011). However, these aspects alone should not, generally speaking, define the boundaries of IR&S. What would it then mean to expand the existing research perspective in experimental IR while acknowledging such necessary limits?

To understand what expanding this perspective would mean, consider the idea of investigating issues associated with potential users (as in the above quote) of actual or by extension, potential IR systems. Any such investigation pertains to non–ad hoc research. This is first because it deals with hypothetical and general sets of scenarios beyond the immediate and particular scenarios of application, and second because it not only deals with the query but also with user and contextual factors—as Belkin (2008) further explains—beyond queries and documents. Thus, Spärck-Jones's

---

challenge to user centricity remains, but that, as also indicated in Belkin (2010), there is a "newly found commitment to accepting and addressing these challenges" (Belkin, 2016, p. 19).

comment can be understood as suggesting the need to shift from dealing with relationships of the type (q, d) toward those of type (u, q, d), where knowledge about users behind the queries (represented by u) is needed to deal with user issues. This shift is from ad hoc research to non–ad hoc research (see section 1.3.2, section 1.3.2.6 specifically, and section 1.4). However, this can be generalized further by using the same reasoning in a way that can be taken to be implied by Spärck-Jones (1988): To understand what users do, one needs to understand their context beyond what a system understands to be their immediate interests. Similarly, to understand why they choose particular documents, it is important to know background information, for example, about the collection that is the origin of the documents. This shifts research further from (u, q, d) to (u, q, d, c), so that it considers the relevant contextual factors c, or to (c_1, u, q, d, c_2) where c is replaced by its constituents corresponding to user- and document-side contextual factors, as previously discussed in section 1.3.2.6. The variable c_1 could denote any query-side knowledge, including, for example, information about the cultural/social backgrounds of users and environmental factors affecting use. In contrast, c_2 would denote, for example, information about the collection containing the document and the corresponding domain, where domain refers to such things as business/work processes responsible for generating the document.[12] Thus, as section 2.3.5 further discusses, domains pertain to discourse practices on either the user or system sides that help explain user behavior and collections/documents, respectively. However, the notion of context has a wider remit, as it also includes (among other things) any relevant factor that can be used to explain the search activity linking query to document.

Moreover, Spärck-Jones's apparent suggestion to include user factors, generalized above to include an arbitrary assortment of contextual factors, can be further extended. If studying individual contextual factors on either side is relevant for modern times, especially given the diverse contexts of technology-use, then so is the study of contexts on each side as wholes. For example, studies about how the sociological factors that were required for a collection to take shape compare to the social factors that lead users to employ a particular set of key terms as queries (or to adopt a particular set of regular usage behaviors). A study that focuses on comparing background contexts on either side may only care in a secondary

---

12. The division of context c into two parts, c_1 and c_2, should not be taken to be the only way to divide up the context.

way about the specific queries and documents in a particular retrieval scenario, and instead may focus on the backgrounds that make many retrieval scenarios possible at once. Thus, such studies are not adequately captured as being about (c_1, u, q, d, c_2). Instead, they are better expressed as being about $(c_1, \dots, c_2)$, that is, relations between contexts, where the contexts can support an arbitrary number (represented by the ...) of retrieval scenarios.

This shift from studying queries and documents to the factors that make them possible as a whole, from (q, d) to (c_1, u, q, d, c_2) to $(c_1, \dots, c_2)$ (i.e., from ad hoc to increasingly non–ad hoc types of research) has implications for research methodology. As section 1.3.2 discussed, it entails a shift away from a immediate or quantitative perspective, as is common in empirical/technical research about (q, d) relations. Understanding (c_1, u, q, d, c_2) or $(c_1, \dots, c_2)$ relations is not primarily a problem of formal analysis and (mathematical) representation (see section 1.3.2.1), even though it could include them. It is first a problem of understanding and construing humanistic phenomena (the relevant user-and document-side phenomena) at a prerepresentational level (Apel, 1984). It adjoins them to formal specifications and technical designs; this is the subject of both section 2.3.3.2 and chapter 5.

2.3.3.2 Construal on the system and user sides In a more recent paper, Spärck-Jones (2001), addresses what can be considered the issue of construal as it pertains to context, both on the user and system sides, as delineated above. The issue of construal is implicit in the discussion therein about the need to reconsider the relation between technology and its use (i.e., systems and their contexts of use). In particular, Spärck-Jones problematizes the construal of context by suggesting that inadequate understanding of context jeopardizes the coherence of evaluation results. She argues that reducing different usage scenarios (differentiated by task-as-context) into a single evaluation scheme focused on appraising technology leads to problematic results: whatever congruences such evaluation may show between the scenarios "conceals significant differences in the task areas" (Spärck-Jones, 2001, p. 2). Considering context means going beyond ad hoc search, but by problematizing the construal of context, one moves beyond ad hoc research.

Yet, as Spärck-Jones (2001) argues, the preexisting and dominant construal of "the system"—or what Spärck-Jones calls the "task core"—as the traditional ad hoc search system is still quite prevalent in discourse. And even when the system concerned is non–ad hoc, (e.g., information filtering or collaborative recommendation systems), often only its ad hoc aspect (i.e., the query-document relation) is evaluated while the contextual factors are ignored (Spärck-Jones, 2001, p. 3). Moreover, even in the modern situation, in which search is increasingly embedded in other applications and has pervasive usage contexts, the study of such systems is often limited to their ad hoc aspect.

Consider, for example, the modern situation in which search is a phenomenon of mediation (see chapter 1). For technology to mediate between the user and the world such that the world is only revealed to them through such technology, the user is required to use it a nontrivial number of times. Hence, this technology, generally speaking, more closely resembles an interactive system that elicits continuous feedback from a user than it does a noninteractive system. In such a system, the ad hoc search part is but one small aspect of other (inevitably interactive) activities performed with/through the system, and so one would expect that the system (and its study/evaluation) to consider other such complex activities. While user interactions are considered in the study and evaluation of such systems, either through user surveys or live interaction recordings, there is as yet no rigorous standard method for the study of interactive systems and interactive search, taking full account of the dynamism of user experience. The standard way of understanding and judging such systems is still often limited to being in terms of the performance of their ad hoc task core, albeit combined with a user survey to add a postscenario account of user experience.

To establish a rigorous standardized method for studying interactive search, akin to those already present for ad hoc search, some problems must first be resolved. The main problem arguably pertains to the construal of the task core (i.e., about what is understood to be the main function of a system). If it should not only be the relating of queries to relevant documents, then what other functions should come within its ambit? Thus, the construal-specific foundational question here is: What should the task core for a retrieval system be, given the pervasive role of modern technology? In particular, as Spärck-Jones (2001, p. 4) asks, what should be the relative sizes of (task) core versus context? That is, how should a search scenario consisting of the elements that one can control (i.e., the system parts or task-core) be construed vis-à-vis the overall scenario for study that also includes what cannot be controlled (i.e., the task context). Moreover, how important is this core in its context? What is the relation between the system aspect (the controlled part) and its function in the overall human activity or task? This is a question about construing "the system," about where—between (q, d)

and $(c_1, \ldots, c_2)$—the retrieval system can be cut out. That is, which aspects, among the background of users, their actions, technological devices, and a multitude of other possible things, should be designated as "system?"[13] The cut out part is that which makes the core contribution to the task at hand (Spärck-Jones, 2001; e.g., for the traditional IR system, it is to find relevant documents).

For traditional IR systems (i.e., only enabling ad hoc search) and more complex systems where the cut or task core is taken to be the ad hoc aspect of that system, such a cut is well established: there is a well-defined core without much space for improvement (Gordon and Pathak, 1999; Spärck-Jones et al., 2000; Spärck-Jones, 2001; Armstrong et al., 2009).[14] However, the modern context is such that the cut must be reconstrued: Where should the system stop and context begin, given that is no longer sufficient to focus only on the traditional cut/task-core? The goal therefore should be to move beyond such a core, by expanding it beyond (q, d) (i.e., non–ad hoc task core) and by looking at context (i.e., non–ad hoc research); in both cases, this amounts to problematizing construal.

As chapter 1 discussed, context is indirectly considered through the employment of evaluation schemes. For example, when using human assessors/judges, relevance assessments adopt contextual information: The judgments of judges presume contextual knowledge about the relevancy of queries to documents given a collection or user domains.[15] However, typically neither context beyond information about users, nor user experience is directly addressed. This is a deliberately unrealistic evaluation setup

13. The issue of cutting out a phenomenon pertains to the problem of construal, and it is of course central to scientific disciplines in general. In quantum theory (QT), whose techniques have been applied recently to IR (van Rijsbergen, 2004), the notion of a cut features in the same way, and various notions in QT depend on how a cut is defined (Stapp, 2007a). A brief account on applying the QT notion of cut to IR can be found in Arafat (2011b).

14. Years of extensive evaluations show the core to be a relatively well-understood statistically based technology, whose performance "at realistic output cutoff levels has reached a 30–40 per cent Precision plateau for ordinary environments, with the attainable target defined by heavy duty manual query development as only, say, 50 per cent" (Gordon and Pathak, 1999; Spärck-Jones et al., 2000; Spärck-Jones, 2001). See also section 1.3.1.

15. Similarly, contextual information is inevitably employed when configuring different aspects of evaluation schemes, "e.g. degrees of relevance to be allowed, output comparability for different strategies, the precise form of the performance measure" (Spärck-Jones, 2001, p. 3).

(Spärck-Jones, 2001, p. 3) (not least since it is done offline), as it does not capture the human experience of search.[16]

The goal then is to further understand users and their search experience in a more direct, fuller, and realistic way, to study system and usage context, which means asking questions about construal pertaining to users and contexts (i.e., about what contexts are like, and "how their properties bear on the way the task core is defined and approached," Spärck-Jones, 2001, p. 4). With respect to the task context Spärck-Jones is referring to here, one needs to know the tasks of which search is a part, or which encompasses search, why users are searching, and how they are experiencing system output (Spärck-Jones, 2001, p. 4). These questions pertain to the whole that is the user's lived experience. Ultimately, beyond the many measures used to characterize aspects of this lived experience found in more recent works (O'Brien and Toms, 2008; Kelly, 2009; Law et al., 2009; Lalmas et al., 2014), what is required is a shift in research attitude. As Belkin (2008, p. 53) argues: a shift is needed from "inherently non-interactive models of IR" toward developing models that centralize user interaction (with information), taking the user as an "active participant in the IR system"; a research task of interdisciplinary nature requiring collaboration from different research communities. This may require forgoing inclinations to build strictly formal models "in favour of realistic and useful models of IR" (Belkin, 2008, p. 53). But what is the alternative? How is a model to be judged as being realistic and useful—according to what criteria? What are the differences between realistic and useful models and strictly formal models? Is it that some aspects of real/useful models are not easily amenable to formal representation? These questions all pertain to phenomena construal. They concern the pretheoretical and theoretical/modeling stages in the construal of users and the search process in general. In addition, they complement Spärck-Jones's (2001) summarizing questions pertaining to system and context construal.

Beyond Spärck-Jones (1988), more recent work that considers such factors as novelty and diversity (Clarke et al., 2008), and those that study work tasks (Järvelin, 2011) are indicative of the ongoing exploration of the role and notion of a system beyond being an ad hoc task core. These works are and simultaneously indicative of a growing inclination to understand users

16. Spärck-Jones additionally says about this that it is done "without any reference to retrieval as an interactive human activity. Thus assessment is done offline on the combined output of the systems tested, rather than online against individual system output" (Spärck-Jones, 2001, p. 3).

and their (task) context. These trends collectively demonstrate the increasing importance of settling the foundational questions of construal. Thus, whether one agrees with Spärck-Jones (1988, 2001) and Belkin (2008) about the lack of substantive results, and/or with Spärck-Jones (2001) about the limitations (and plateauing) of ad hoc systems and research, a less controversial proposition can perhaps be readily accepted. This is that Belkin's idea of substantivity in IR&S research, about which it is supposed that substantive results lead more to progress than nonsubstantive results, strongly imply that the path of progress requires research to go beyond the ad hoc task core. It implies the need to focus on system and user context: from studying (q, d) relationships toward studying $(c_1, \ldots, c_2)$ relationships. And this is dependent on addressing the foundational question of construal. Thus, the substantivity of results leading thereby to progressive empirical research depends on adequately addressing construal.

2.3.3.3 Construal and the substantivity of (experimental) results   It is not only because substantive results depend on construal that empirical progress requires addressing foundations. The inclination toward substantive results leads to foundations from another angle: It is important to have a way of rigorously understanding what "substantivity of results" and research progress means in the first place. While defining these aspects is a separate enterprise from construing the basic phenomena of users and systems, they are closely linked. First, a result can only be deemed substantive with respect to a particular construal of an experimental scenario, which in turn employs construals of basic phenomena. Second, as discussed below, definitions of substantivity depend on a construal of values, not just on notions of user and system.

While substantivity and progress are further explored in section 2.5 and chapter 3, respectively, there is some indication of what they correspond to in the context of empirical research. Consider the argument by Spärck-Jones (2007) that the challenge to IR&S is not only the development of commercial systems that give good precision/recall results, but also to explain why such systems work. Thus, a result that explains why something works, i.e., an explanatory result, can be understood to be more substantive than one that simply states that something works. If the satisfaction of user needs is the means for judging whether a system works, then explaining why it works must relate back to those needs, to explaining something about the user cognition and behavior (chapter 5 explores this in more detail).

A result can be similarly substantive, adding scientific value to a research plan or program and leading to its progress, if it (1) helps explain or interpret why a system works with respect to user or contextual aspects,

(2) applies to a large number of cases (i.e., is generalizable), or (3) indicates a persistent or regular property (i.e., the result is repeatable to some degree). The notion of substantivity as corresponding to the scientific values of interpretive/explanatory ability, generalizability, and repeatability are further explored in section 2.5. While results of scientific value may be substantive for the current stage of research (i.e., for that research to make further progress), they may not be for some other stage of research. A group of substantive results could instead correspond to results that are valuable with respect to different values. For example, they can include results that show that something works efficiently, that suggest an efficiency-improving change in the technical design, or that indicate how alternate formal models can be used to better model the search. These results have technological value. Alternatively, results that show a system to be effective, meaning that it satisfied user needs or benefitted them in some way (e.g. by predicting user needs that worked to save the user time) are instead substantive due to fulfilling values pertaining to user satisfaction (i.e., humanistic values). These two types of value correspond to the instrumental and anthropological perspectives of technology (see chapter 1). What are or ought to be the values on which the appraisal/evaluation of systems is conducted? This basic question is about value construal; its resolution is presupposed in any development of the notion of substantivity. The question of values here is closely related to that of purposes, which in turn is related to that of progress (see section 1.5.2). Thus, a result is more substantive than another when it better serves our values and purposes, and such results are more progressive or conducive to progress than are those that are not substantive. Therefore, the seeking of substantive results originating in empirical research leads to the problem of understanding users and contexts, which presupposes the problem of construal as well as the foundational questions about progress, purpose, and values. The next section further develops the construal problem: if it applies to systems, users, and context, it must then also apply to the phenomenon of search.

2.3.4   Construing Search

The problem of construing the system, users, and context is an aspect of construing the phenomenon of search in general. Section 2.3.4.1 discusses the problematization of the construal of search as it appears in the works of technically oriented IR researchers. Section 2.3.4.2 discusses it with respect to socially pervasive modes of search use as documented by IS researchers, while section 2.3.4.3 asks whether the problem of search construal, which is an IR&S problem, belongs to IR or IS.

2.3.4.1 Search construal as problematized in IR The *Meeting of the Minds* workshop (Callan et al., 2007) suggests that instead of just providing ranked lists as was the core task of traditional systems, a search engine should help in "understanding, representing and exploiting contextual information" (Callan et al., 2007, p. 29)[17] such that it mediates complex tasks pertaining to information seeking, and "information discovery, analysis and synthesis" (Callan et al., 2007, p. 29). This corresponds to Spärck-Jones's suggestion about expanding the purview of retrieval research beyond that core task, and also to suggestions in several prior works about the need to expand the phenomenon of search, such as the suggestion in Korfhage (1991, p. 140) about moving from the paradigm of "traditional query answering system to an information organization and display system." In these cases, and especially in the modern context, users are more concerned with using documents and not just finding them, and the set of documents ranked according to relevance becomes less central in the totality of an usage experience. The user model thereby must evolve from accepting simple query terms to including detailed contextual factors, such as "goals, work history, social relations, and more" (Callan et al., 2007, p. 30), while the goal of the system goes beyond finding documents to "organizing, managing, summarizing, and mining the information people find." This shift also corresponds to a shift in the type of research, from relatively ad hoc research concerned mainly with the relationships between documents and queries (q, d) in a particular search context to relatively non–ad hoc research concerned with the relationships between arbitrary contexts $(c_1, \ldots, c_2)$.

If a modern search engine does cater to this richer set of information-seeking activities pertaining to document use such that all such activities can be referred to as "modern search," then the purposes of this modern search can no longer be that of traditional search. In this case, the part of the process that concerns the use of a traditional search tool and involves the display of ranked results would only be an aspect of a broader process or set of tasks, and it is this larger process that should come under the analytical purview of a modern IR&S.

Zhai's keynote at SIGIR 2011 Zhai (2011) can be understood as developing an idea of search that considers these encompassing, broader processes. He articulates the problem of construing search as a set of theoretical

17. See also the report of a similar meeting in Allan et al. (2012) which draws many of the same conclusions but explores more of their practical implications.

or technical[18] problems pertaining to the modeling of tasks. Zhai argues that since search is generally a means of finishing a task and since search engines do not generally (yet) provide enough support for doing complex tasks, that the goal of search engines should be expanded so that they also work to transform traditional search results into "actionable knowledge." This actionable knowledge could then also feed into applications beyond traditional search such as topic trend analysis, opinion integration, impact analysis and comparative summarization. The traditional search engine then becomes a general analysis engine (Zhai, 2011) and this leads to research questions pertaining to (1) task construal and modeling, (2) formal analysis and differentiation of tasks, and (3) the structure of task spaces.

However, these issues correspond to foundational issues. In particular, they pertain to issue of the aims of IR research, to internal coherence and effective construal. First, with respect to (1), finding unified ways of modeling tasks concerns the internal coherence of the science of "general analysis engines." Second, task modeling requires understanding of context through a pretheoretical discourse before the assignment of formal mathematical structures. This involves simplification for dealing with the complexity of real-life scenarios: easily measurable goals replace real-life goals, ranked results replace a work task result, and individual queries in collections replace search tasks or work tasks (Vakkari and Järvelin, 2005; Järvelin, 2011, p. 128). Although such simplifications—already in place before Zhai's proposal—resulted in a standardization of research designs in IR, since they "drift farther away from the practical life condition" Järvelin (2011, p. 18) wonders whether their "findings still best serve the initial goal of evaluation (supporting human performance)," as "if means (outputs) replace ends (outcomes), one runs the risk of sub-optimization." Dumais (2009) issues a similar critique in her Salton Award speech on the limitations of the current simplified way of understanding search. She emphasizes the need to capture search behavior not in an idealized static sense but in its dynamism, across multiple search sessions through multiple sources and types of data. These (and other) limitations are said to be addressable by new algorithms, interaction techniques, and evaluation methods (especially for search processes, i.e., as dynamic usage experiences as opposed to static results). Dumais agrees with Zhai that "there is much to be done

---

18. By "theoretical," Zhai (2011) means mathematical theoretization or modeling. The notion of technical here, pertaining to techniques or algorithms, is closely related.

theoretically to represent knowledge about searchers and tasks" (Dumais, 2009, p. 1). However, as indicated previously, representations must be preceded by a discussion about phenomena construal or presentation.

In addition to task modeling, it is clear that user interface design becomes particularly important for a general analysis engine, since result visualization strategies would be task dependent, the strategy is not limited to a ranked list structure. In addition, because the goal is to create actionable knowledge, the experience of doing the task on a general analysis engine, an experience strongly dependent on the interface and visualization strategies, ought then lead users to effectively complete subsequent tasks by employing this newly acquired knowledge. However, we argue that, to figure out what actionable knowledge (perhaps referring to the visualization of the results of task-dependent data analyses) actually means, one needs to consider the context, in particular, the query-side context that includes user intents and information needs. The notion of actionability, used widely in the social and management sciences (Antonacopoulou, 2008), needs to be construed and entered into the discourse addressing the goals and purposes of such engines, and compared to the notion of relevance. There are several research questions that need to be addressed in this regard, such as: Do all relevant results lead to or equate to actionable knowledge? This returns back to the need to understand usage experience, in the context of information seeking as the doing of tasks, and as discussed above, this leads beyond what is currently understood as IR research into the arena of IS research (see section 2.3.4.3).

Understanding search engines to be general analysis engines, and search as tasks that search engines help complete, still leaves open the question of objectification of tasks and therefore that of search, which must precede the formal/mathematical modeling of tasks. Therefore, the question of "what is search" cannot really be addressed through mathematical modeling paradigms. Instead, such paradigms can only be used to re-present a preexisting understanding of search. Search construal is then not primarily a problem of mathematical representation or theorization, nor a problem pertaining to algorithms or techniques (i.e., not a technical problem). It is primarily a cultural or anthropological problem, and the technical/theoretical aspect of it only enters secondarily: it is here that Zhai's technical problematization of construal is appropriate.[19]

---

19. He again problematizes what search is in Zhai (2015). As to his understanding of search using the now-popular scheme of gamification, this could indeed be true or useful (or both)

Therefore, the expansion to the notion of search suggested in Callan et al. (2007), which pertains to defining a larger process and search as an aspect of this process (of which Zhai, 2011, is an example), is not only intricately bound to the problem of construal but also relates to a series of other sub-problems of a foundational nature. Thus, as with the other problems of construal discussed previously, the construal of search, in spite of what is implied in the cited IR literature, is not primarily an empirical (in the immediate quantitative sense), theoretical, or formal problem (as suggested in Zhai, 2011). However, in addition to construal requiring a different type of research, it is premised on research values that are not shared by commercially inclined empirical research.[20] Instead, the responsibility for resolving such basic questions that constitute a "basic science" falls on the corresponding scientific community (Callan et al., 2007, p. 28):

> Society has a long history of conducting basic science and making it available for others to build upon. The scientific community's responsibility is to discover new knowledge about how people seek, use, and organize information, and to develop new tools that assist people in achieving their goals. Some of what the scientific community discovers will be immediately useful to today's commercial search engines; some of it may be the seeds of tomorrow's new companies.

In particular, research into basic science that is about understanding the user, culture, and technology mediation is important and relevant in spite of lacking immediate commercial benefit. Moreover, in addition to the problematization of the construal of search from the mainly technical and experimental researchers as represented by Callan et al. (2007), the question of search construal is also strongly raised by what is known as the sociological turn in IR&S research.

2.3.4.2 Search construal problematized by the sociological turn There are now a multitude of scenarios facilitated by applications supporting cultures of anything from social networking to augmented-reality living, where search tools are used to mediate social life, and as such, the notion

---

in particular search/seeking contexts. Its scope beyond these contexts is another foundational inquiry requiring investigation, i.e., as to when search/seeking is game-like, in what sense it is so, and when it is not so. Zhai (2011, 2015) thereby worked to demonstrate the relevance and importance of search construal as a problem.

20. That is, "it would be foolish to expect commercial search engines to do all that needs to be done in the coming years; they are profit-driven companies with specific objectives" (Callan et al., 2007, p. 28).

of social/sociological becomes important for IR&S. These notions are not new. Cronin (2008) speaks of the sociological turn in the IS discourse—the long-established infusion of sociological ideas and the continuing appropriation of both theoretical and methodological insights from such domains as sociology, and science and technology studies—as something that began in the 1980s. These notions are clearly more important and more representative of the reality of IR&S in the modern context than at any previous time. Whereas the borrowing of ideas from such fields is not new for IR&S. However, what is new is the place of search phenomena: They are a pervasive aspect of modern culture due to being a central facilitating factor for technology-mediated living (as discussed in section 2.3.2). More specifically, the sociological turn means that the semantic construal of search can no longer be taken as being sufficiently representative of what search means in the modern context; the notion of search must instead be problematized. If search is more than the linking of queries to (relevant) documents, and is something that is, very generally, the means to a particular "usage experience" (including a social experience), then its form cannot be automatically assumed to be a $R([q], [d], [u], [c])$ relation in the way q, d, u, and c are traditionally understood. Instead, what constitutes the relevant phenomena for objectification (as q, d, u, and c, or otherwise) is unclear from the outset and requires investigation. This investigation is not primarily a theoretical one in which one seeks mathematical structures for representing phenomena. Instead there is a pretheoretical or prerepresentational discourse that seeks to answer the basic question: What is (or isn't) search?

2.3.4.3 Search construal: An IR or IS problem? The report from the *Meeting of the Minds* workshop in Callan et al. (2007) suggests that the issue of construal is a job for the "scientific community." Does this refer to the academic communities identifying as IR or IS groups, or to other groups? Cronin (2008) discusses the sociological turn as taking place both in IR and IS, but as something that is problematized more explicitly in IS works. As construal, in contrast to the suggestion in Callan et al. (2007) is not strictly an empirical problem pertaining to experimentation[21] (even though it may be raised in the context of empirical research), would it be appropriate to suggest that those responsible to address it—the "scientific community"—be the IS community? Construal requires understanding phenomena that presuppose search from broader, encompassing phenomena, such as information seeking, to all other such phenomena that are a result of

---

21. It may employ experiments or use their results, but it is not strongly dependent on observational data and instead relies on conceptual organization and argumentation.

technologically mediated social experience. In addition, search, however one construes it—assuming that it refers to types of technologically mediated cultural practice—is tending toward facilitating the use of documents (as opposed to just finding them). Thus its study must tend toward understanding information seeking/use and usage experience (or social experience) as the central phenomena. The study of broader phenomena (e.g. information seeking/use), rather than ad hoc search phenomena, corresponds to the shift from studying relations of type (q, d) toward relations of type (c_1, u, q, d, c_2) and $(c_1, \ldots, c_2)$.[22] However, since IR and IS discourses parted ways some decades ago, these phenomena are known to be studied particularly in IS, as having to do with IS research problems. However, even if we thereby concede that the general problem of construal is an IS problem, since IR discourses are so dependent on it, the problem of construal in turn problematizes the (present) relationship between IR and IS—that is, construal has disciplinary implications. That is, the question of who should address construal leads to the question of what the relative responsibilities are between IR and IS, and to the general question of what the relationship is between them. Therefore, the changing nature of search carries with it the strong inclination to restructure disciplinary interactions. In fact, as argued in chapter 6, addressing the foundational questions of what should be the relation between IR&S is important for progress. Saracevic (2007, pp. 1925–1926) additionally suggests that the current use of "search" behooves us to reinvestigate the complementary nature of IR and IS, and deduce how to structure the discourse to take advantage of their relation. Deducing the relation between IR and IS, in addition to being a problem related to that of construal, is in turn a problem of internal or external coherence, depending on whether one understands the fields to be part of the same field or separate. Chapter 6 argues that IR and IS have to be understood in an integrated manner and as such the problem of their relation has to do with internal coherence (see chapter 4).

2.3.5 Construal and Foundations

As we have shown, there is a great need to reconstrue basic notions in IR&S. This section shows that it is difficult to reenvision existing such concepts on

---

22. In the (c_1, u, q, d, c_2) case, the c_1 could denote the task context (Järvelin, 2011) responsible for their information-seeking behavior. Consider instead the $(c_1, \ldots, c_2)$ case, first mentioned in section 2.3.3.1. This could correspond to research relating tasks that are an aspect of the user-side context c_1, to collections that are an aspect of the system-side context c_2. For example, it may pertain to research about how tasks and collections work together, as part of a domain, to generate or support search scenarios.

their own and that any such attempt requires consideration of related basic notions that exhibit intricate interconnections. The conclusions of several works pertaining to construal are followed to their logical ends to show the different types of foundations research they would lead to.

Consider the works of Zhai (2011) and Callan et al. (2007). Both seek to radically expand the notion of search and acknowledge the subsequent need for a host of new evaluation strategies to cater to these expanded notions. As a result they raise questions about what kind of science the study of this new kind of search can be, suggesting the need to reinvestigate what counts as progress in IR. Moreover, as section 2.5 further explains, any discussion about new evaluation strategies begs the question of what values are to be evaluated: new types of search, given the pervasiveness of search technology in everyday culture, pertain to values different from traditional search. For example, the ability of a media-based site to make its users "happy" or "entertain" them corresponds to a value in addition to that of 'topical relevance.'[23] Hence, rigorous research into new evaluation strategies ought to work to decide what values, pertaining to the lived experience mediated by information systems, are to be evaluated. This is also the case for numerous works that suggest, as does Dumais (2009), that "evaluations methodologies need to be extended to handle the scale, diversity, and user interaction that characterize information systems today."

Changes to construals of research addressing the need to reconstrue search and evaluation would not be effective were it to be limited to an inquiry into values or into a few isolated basic questions. Instead, the fundamental nature of these notions implies the need for something more comprehensive. It suggests the need (1) for a more comprehensive research program and (2) to centralize sub-discourses in IR&S that may currently only have peripheral roles.

With respect to (1), any address of values pertaining to user satisfaction, on account of the stances in Spärck-Jones and Belkin in Belkin (2008) and Saracevic (2007, pp. 1925–1926) suggests the need for a comprehensive

---

23. These abilities could be reduced to relevance, such that an entertaining site is simply 'more relevant' than a less entertaining site. This strategy would however forego capturing conceptually the different shades of meaning involved in the concept of "entertaining." Even if the corresponding measure for relevance were to accommodate empirical features pertaining to entertainment, this reductive strategy would remain conceptually impoverished. It is not simply about having measures, but about having sufficiently rich concepts to adequately construe the relevant phenomena and enable a comprehensive scientific discourse.

account of usage contexts through which the associated values can be deduced. Similarly, comprehensive accounts of system context need to be developed to understand the relevant system and scientific values (as discussed in section 2.3.3.3) for the modern situation in order to get substantive results (Belkin, 2008). As for developing such a framework for understanding both the usage and system contexts, this is one of the main purposes of domain analysis, a sub-discourse in IS. With respect to (2), while domain analysis may be peripheral to mainstream IR research, it clearly needs to be more central to help resolve construal questions.

A domain refers to a community of discourse, which includes the people involved (their training, their ways of understanding), documents (what is produced by the community), and activities (e.g., how they interact with, come to know/manipulate documents). Hjørland admits the difficulty of domain analysis as a program[24] of research but does not see any alternative (Hjørland and Albrechtsen, 1995).[25] However, domain analysis is not only a research task in IR&S but also a research orientation (Hjørland, 2004, p. 17):

> Domain analysis states that the most fruitful horizon for information science is to study the knowledge domains or thought or discourse communities that are parts of society's division of labor

This orientation is complementary to that aspect of foundations research that seeks to resolve construal problems: the study of phenomena construal entails domain analysis. However, the practice of domain analysis itself relies on numerous foundational concepts; it also depends on a

---

24. Hjørland and Albrechtsen (1995, p. 419) state that domain analysis research

should produce domain-specific handbooks and journals in all major domains of such a quality, relevance and visibility that the researchers, students, and users in the domains would find these handbooks of high importance and would depend on Research and Development in IS.

25. Domain analysis is important because so many aspects of IR&S research depend on domain-specific variables, as stated in Hjørland and Albrechtsen (1995, p. 419):

the approach domain-analysis has a continuum of problems from very simple problems that are easy to explore empirically to very complex theoretical problems. Every time you use information as the variable, i.e., every time you look at the problems of IR or knowledge organization from some kind of hypothesis about the knowledge domain as an important factor, you are contributing to this approach

A fuller, updated account of domain analysis can be found in Hjørland (2010), see also the short but important discussion in Salton (1996); Hjørland (1996).

foundation. For example, the concepts of domain (and collection; see chapter 5) and "community of discourse" are not simple. Each such community is differentiated, for example, by its respective epistemologies and discursive practices. Thus, the specification of different domains depends on the construals of such concepts.

Beyond leading to an inquiry into values, domain analysis and a network of basic questions (questions about construal in IR&S) lead to a crucial matter. They lead to disciplinary-level foundational questions, meaning that the resolution of construal questions must ultimately reference or presume answers to such crucial questions. As Belkin (2008) suggests in agreement with Saracevic (2007), IR system models and algorithms have to be integrated with information-seeking behavior research, which is the purview of IS. This is since, given that IR systems over and above general software applications, are so pervasive to modern life, IR must be seen as being more than a sub-discipline of computer science. The study of construal, being a foundational problem, cannot be limited to one type of construal (e.g., a technical or cognitive specification of a phenomenon). It must be based on the general question of what something is, prior to asking how it can best be represented for different intellectual or practical purposes (e.g., mathematical analysis or system design). Were this integration between IR and IS not to be actively developed, the critiques of Spärck-Jones (2001) would go unaddressed, and research would risk "bombinating in the void" (Spärck-Jones, 1988); IR research would be restricted to system-side values and be left with (Belkin, 2008, p. 49):

> the inability of … [the TREC] paradigm to accommodate studies of people in interaction with information systems … and a dearth of research which integrates study of user's goals, tasks and behaviors with research on models and methods which respond to results of such studies and supports those goals, tasks and behaviors.

An implication is that the complementary nature of IR and IS needs to be understood to enable progress in both fields, and this pertains to internal or external coherence (aim 1 or 3 respectively, see section 2.1) depending on the logical relationship between the disciplines, which will be addressed in section 2.4.

The problem of construal (aim 2), pertaining to the phenomenon of search and its components, thereby relates to several other foundational problems, including those at the disciplinary level. As previously discussed, its resolution requires that studies of search phenomena shift from studying (q, d) relationships to $(c_1, \ldots, c_2)$ relations. This obliges such studies to seek to understand, in terms of a pretheoretical discourse, the contextual factors depicting both the lived experience of users (and their tasks) and that pertaining to the formation of documents, before developing any structures for their representation. In addition, increasingly richer aspects of search beyond its ad hoc aspect require consideration, because retrieval in the modern context is inherently interactive. Ad hoc or system-oriented research perspectives wherein system-side values dominate are no longer tenable, not least because there is little left to do in terms of improving the performance of the ad hoc part of systems: "new models and associated representation and ranking techniques lead to only incremental (if that) improvement in performance over previous models and techniques, which is generally not statistically significant (e.g., Sparck Jones, 2005)" (Belkin, 2008, p. 49). In addition, "such improvement, as determined in TREC-style evaluation, rarely, if ever, leads to improved performance by human searchers in interactive IR systems" (Turpin and Hersh, 2001; see also Turpin and Scholer, 2006; Belkin, 2008). In particular, progress in IR (in experimental IR specifically) depends on getting "substantive results," which requires supposing non–ad hoc search scenarios and non–ad hoc research as standard. It also requires the consideration of richer accounts/construals of users and usage experiences and of contextual aspects. This in turn requires an inquiry into

- values before evaluation measures,
- the place of domain analysis as a means to extract those values and for developing the idea of context,
- the distinction between search and other practices (to understand where and how search fits into the daily life of individuals), and ultimately,
- the type of science a science of search can (or ought to) be, that is, an inquiry pertaining external coherence.

The need for an inquiry of the final type above means that addressing concerns pertaining to aim 2 leads one to be concerned with aim 3.

2.4   Exploring Links with Other Fields (External Coherence)

External coherence has two senses, both pertaining to the relation between IR&S and other disciplines. The first is concerned with coherence as it applies to the place of IR&S among other disciplines, deciding where it fits between humanistic and scientific discourses, and what its relationship is to related disciplines that also deal with technology mediated experience. It is also concerned with the problem of deciding the relationship between IR and IS. As discussed in sections 2.3.4.2 and 2.3.4.3, the resolution of the problem of effective construal ultimately depends on deciding what the relationship between IR and IS is or ought to be: this is a problem of coherence. It is a problem of external coherence if the fields are seen as separate and of internal coherence otherwise.

The second is coherence in terms of deciding how to effectively adapt concepts, epistemologies and ontologies, theoretical frameworks and methodologies, techniques, and so on, from external disciplines. What counts as relevant need to radically expand basic phenomena, with respect to search (e.g., in Callan et al., 2007; Zhai, 2011), and the natural tendency for a discipline to grow and address new problems, imply the necessity of borrowing methodology and ideas from other disciplines. If the borrowing happens haphazardly, the resultant discourse can suffer from a lack of internal coherence. Thus this second sense is related particularly to the first aim.

The seeking out of interdisciplinary approaches to solve problems in IR, such as those in recent keynotes of the Special Interest Group on Information Retrieval (SIGIR) in Dumais (2009) and Zhai (2011), or more significantly in van Rijsbergen (2006) where a radically new (formal) paradigm for IR is suggested, are discussions that can be understood to be about external coherence. Inquiries about the place of the discipline among others have also been especially persistent in the IS literature (Harmon, 1971; Arafat et al., 2014).

Integration between disciplines and borrowing from one discourse/ discipline by another pertains first to discovering connections between the disciplines, and then adapting a set of ideas, techniques, and methods for a specific purpose and expressing it into a form suitable for use in the home discipline. For example, consider the case where the research goal of an IR research project is to construe some aspect of a technology-mediated usage experience, such as the corresponding user behavior, as an "information behavior." This construal would require consulting corresponding literature in sociology, psychology, and linguistics, and appropriating the necessary concepts and methods. If this appropriation process were done adequately, then the resultant IR discourse would not only be internally coherent as per the aim 1, but also externally coherent as per aim 3. Both internal coherence and external coherence can be thought of as values pertaining to scientific discourse (see section 2.3.3.3) that must be maintained or fulfilled in this borrowing process: appropriation must make sense with respect to both the external disciplines and existing discourse in IR&S.

Given the modern context, the long tradition of borrowing approaches from the humanities and sciences, and the inter/plu/multidisciplinarity of

IR&S, external coherence is clearly not a secondary aim but is crucial to ensuring the soundness of the explanations/interpretations within IR&S. It is therefore crucial to the progress of the discipline. The basic question as to what kind of discipline IR&S is, that is not only asked in current research but has been asked consistently since the inception of these disciplines, indicates that properly understanding the place of IR&S among the disciplines— corresponding to the aim of external coherence—is important for IR&S.

Ensuring external coherence, whether that corresponds to understanding disciplinary relationships or developing ways of effectively borrowing from elsewhere, presupposes a metatheory, a method for placing different discourses among one another and choosing the appropriate theories/frameworks from therein. Section 2.4.1 discusses several notions of metatheory, concluding that it is not so much a metatheory that is required but a metadiscourse that is identified with the foundational discourse mentioned previously.

2.4.1 External Coherence Requires Metatheory
Borrowing mathematical structures and concepts from other fields is not an arbitrary process. Dow (1977, p. 323) explains that borrowing from other fields requires a consistent parallel effort to create a coherence between the different theories and discourses that enter into the discipline:

> Information science would do well to develop more and better theories, for without adequate theoretical support, we may do a technically brilliant job of solving the wrong problems. However, the interdisciplinary nature of what information science is becoming means we must use a meta-theory to guide the development of these theories. Without meta-theory we cannot compare or unify the theories.

Dow's metatheory requires among other things that the theoretical propositions constituting a scientific discourse be properly distinguished as to their function and level; as to whether they seek to make

- casual statements/propositions about phenomena (e.g., "It's a warm day"),
- macroscopic-level propositions (corresponding to, e.g., "the temperature is 29° … [as] … determined with a thermometer"; Dow, 1977, p. 326), or
- propositions at a microscopic level that are detailed and concern states and processes (e.g., "calculations show a certain mean kinetic energy of the molecules. This corresponds to a temperature of 29°"; Dow, 1977, p. 326).

A scientific discourse usually intertwines different levels of propositions; propositions therein can even pertain to several levels at once. However,

Dow's metatheory, which concerns several levels, also requires rules of transformation from level to level to adequately relate the levels. In the above example, this corresponds to relating the thermometer temperature corresponding to the macroscopic level to the mean kinetic energy of gases at the microscopic level.[26]

Dow thereby problematizes borrowing by requiring that whatever theories are used from elsewhere, their level of application in their native discourse needs to be known and clearly related to the discourse in which they are to be applied. Discourses that relate different levels of propositions, in our terminology, are said to be more internally coherent than those that do not. Dow's metatheoretical principles can then be understood to guide the process of borrowing by creating particular conditions for it that work to fulfill the overall purposes of discourse. Coherence is one such condition. In general, "metatheory is required to deepen the understanding of theory by providing perspective from a systemic whole and by permitting and encouraging meaningful comparison of parts within the whole" (Dow, 1977, p. 1).

Bates defines metatheory as "the philosophy behind the theory, the fundamental set of ideas about how phenomena of interest in a particular field should be thought about and researched" (Bates, 2005, p. 2). Her notion of metatheory can be understood as the background existing theories such as the mainly social-scientific/humanistic theories of human behavior in Fisher et al. (2005). Or it could be understood to refer to one such theory were it to sufficiently refer to its own conceptual presuppositions. Dow's principles instead apply to natural-scientific discourses, and in an analogical way to non-natural-scientific discourses. As a set of prescriptive metatheoretical principles for the natural sciences (and sciences thereby inspired), Dow's metatheory can be understood as contributing to the "fundamental set of ideas" in Bates's definition about how phenomena should be studied. The importance of understanding metatheory in this general sense, and hence the continuing relevance of metatheory, is highlighted more recently in Arafat (2011b), which addresses recent trends in applying QT to IR through the research program of QT-inspired IR (QTIR). QTIR seeks to apply notions (and techniques) relevant to the natural world in describing phenomena at what Dow would call the 'microscopic' level, to the psycho-social and computational world of IR, to what Dow would call a 'macroscopic' level. As that work suggests, although QT can be used as a

---

26. Chapter 5, expanding on the discussion in chapter 1, proposes a hierarchical framework for IR&S.

"a scientific mirror for IR" (Arafat, 2011b, p. 170), several basic questions about IR, of the epistemological and ontological variety (which Dow and Bates would understand as metatheoretical concerns) require resolution to ensure that the borrowing is coherent.

In general, to fulfill aims 1 and 3, there must be a metatheory, or as we contend, an overarching discourse that combines existing heterogeneous discourses. This is because combining a set of approaches from other disciplines into the discourse of IR&S is not simply about combining the key mathematical models constituting each approach into an overall discourse, but also about organizing associated conceptual understandings and other elements (such as methodologies) into an overall framework. This metatheoretical layer in Dow, which we generalize here to an overarching discourse, is the layer we claim pertains to a type of research that we call foundations research. If this layer is crucial in facilitating effective borrowing from other disciplines, then this overarching discourse (or foundations research) must be developed natively, from within the discipline of IR&S.

Researchers who borrow approaches from other disciplines, without sufficiently investigating how the corresponding conceptual understandings or discourses are to be adapted to IR&S, inevitably make simplifying assumptions. As such approaches come to constitute the discipline over time and are built on, and as the foundations were not rigorously established, this will eventually lead to the problem of incoherence, in the same way as the dependence on legacy code can weaken a software project over time. The borrowing from QT that occurs in the QTIR project, as critiqued in Arafat (2011b), generated problems in the interpretation of the borrowed mathematical structures. This was due to engaging in borrowing without first developing a foundational layer, an overarching discourse about the conceptual correspondences between the two respective disciplines, QT and IR. Foundations discourse has as its scope the entirety of objects, processes, research methodologies, and perspectives that are relevant for understanding some aspect of reality. As such, the task of external coherence—of ensuring coherence of borrowing from other disciplines through exploring the commitments behind the adopted methodologies, frameworks and techniques—is a task that, partly due to its wide-ranging scope, is one of foundations research.

2.4.2   External Coherence and Foundations Discourse

Due to the inevitable comparisons between the different kinds of disciplines involved in the borrowing process, the external coherence in approaches to borrowing depends on the notion of external coherence that pertains to the proper placing of IR&S among disciplines. Thus, the second, disciplinary sense of the aim of external coherence discussed in section 2.4 depends on the first. This disciplinary sense is characterized by basic question, such as "What kind of science or discipline is/should/ought IR&S (to) be?" or "What kind of science/discipline would we like it to be?" Moreover, there is a myriad of basic questions presupposed in the process of borrowing (if it is to be effective, as opposed to arbitrary) that pertain to the similarities and differences between phenomena in the respective disciplines.

As Dourish and Bell (2011, p. 62) explain:

> We need to understand the commitments involved in the various techniques that we employ, and the consequences of their combination. … Brian Cantwell Smith (1996) uses the metaphor of commercial exchange to describe this caution to methodological syncretism: when you use an idea from somewhere else, he suggests, you need to be able to say what you paid for it, how you brought it home, and what kinds of damage it suffered along the way.[27]

Similarly, not differentiating assumptions underlying our methodology and conceptualizations and the (e.g., epistemic) background of what is borrowed means that concepts eventually get confused (Hjørland, 2011b; Hjørland, 2011a; Hjørland, 2014; Hjørland, 2008, 92–95). As a result, we risk their misappropriation, misuse, and ultimately the incoherence (if not invalidity) of any propositions/conclusions that employ them. Thus, coherence aims 1 and 3 require more than theory arrangement.

Ronald Day mirrors these sentiments about incoherent borrowing. Day (2011, p. 85) problematizes unquestioned borrowing in IS, which "is a user tradition that maps onto phenomena metaphysically laden and operationalized models of reality with a conceptual logic and appropriateness that is surprisingly little questioned." This is the process whereby phenomena, conditioned by the theoretical and operational structures of "outside" disciplines employed to manifest them, are often not critically understood. As a result, it is not easy to claim scientific or scholarly status for the discourse that uses such construals (Day, 2011, pp. 85–86). Day continues:

> Instead of viewing theoretical models as subject to evaluation in terms of their empirical aptness, LIS[28] theory and practice often seems to view models as being

---

27. The reference here is to the seminal work by Brain Cantwell Smith (1996).

28. This refers to library and information science, which merges IS and library science; thus IR&S fits into LIS. However, Day's argument also applies to IR&S, i.e., not just to the library science component therein. While the majority of this book does not explicitly discuss library science, chapters 3 and 6 work to relate discussion on the foundations of IR&S to a generalized notion of the memory institution.

"foundational" frameworks through which phenomena are to be understood. And yet, then, the internal logical coherence of the models and the appropriateness of their borrowings from other sciences and from folk discourses are little critically examined. Such a hermetic disciplinary theory and practice—institutionally sealed against both empirical and conceptual critiques—constitutes a very curious understanding of scientific or even scholarly activity. And the use of "number" (as is sometimes said) in itself in the research has nothing to say as to whether scientific or scholarly work is being done. What is the answer to such a situation? As has been suggested here, in part the answer is conceptual critique, and this critique must extend to not only the theoretical models, but to research practices and methods and to the very conception of theory and the conception of disciplinary foundationality in the LIS field. There is still much work to be done here.

In addition, unquestioned borrowing, leading eventually to internal and external incoherence, tends to isolate the discipline from others as the relationships (at the conceptual and discourse level) between it and other fields (Day, 2011) are not well determined at the point of borrowing. As a result, the growth and progress in it are affected, and experts from other disciplines are not able to take the discipline seriously. Coherence helps understanding, but a highly varied discourse (as in IR&S) that is incoherent becomes especially difficult to engage with from outside the discipline. This is especially unfortunate in the case of IR&S, as its subject matter—if the suggestions of the *Meeting of the Minds* workshop (Callan et al., 2007) are to be taken seriously—pertains to technology-mediated human experience, which in turn pertains to an increasingly large part of human experience. Thus, IR&S discourse must be able to deal with perspectives from several different disciplines. Furthermore, if coherence is understood to be a sign of progress, then a more coherent discourse fares better than a less coherent one, and as the subject matter of technology-mediated experience is of increasing relevance across many disciplines, a more coherent discourse to this end is likely to replace others: it becomes about the "survival of the most coherent discourse."[29]

2.5   Notions of Progress (or Values) Pertaining to Evaluation

Each of the aims of internal coherence, effective construal of phenomena, and external coherence can be understood as corresponding to values by which IR&S discourse can be evaluated. A discourse that is more internally coherent than another is also of more value than the other. This is with

---

29. Chapter 3 discusses this point further from a philosophy of science perspective, whereas chapters 5 and 6 further explicate what this coherence means and what the future of IR&S holds, respectively.

respect to internal coherence as a value—as it is held to be by researchers—pertaining to IR&S discourse. While the scope of application of these aims, as values, was taken to be the discourse as a whole in the preceding sections of this chapter, it can instead be limited to parts of discourse. Value judgment, including the judgment of progress, can occur in modalities other than large parts of or the whole of research discourse. For example, a research paper (one small part of the greater discourse of IR&S) can be judged to be effective in how it construes phenomena and in being externally coherent, while the greater discourse to which it contributes can be judged not to be so in general.

Progress can therefore be understood as a value, as chapter 3 further elucidates. Progress is something that is sought in particular by scientific discourses. As argued in section 2.4, the three aims described in section 2.1 that correspond to three values, are pervasive to IR&S discourse. It is supposed that they must thereby be constituents of any overall understanding of progress for IR&S. They do not, however, exhaust the notions of progress that apply to IR&S. To derive other such constituents, or other notions of progress, a general strategy would be to first find instances of value judgment in IR&S discourse and practice, and then to suggest the corresponding values as also determining notions of progress.

Modalities or scopes for value judgments, in addition to the level of the whole discourse or the research paper, include sub-discourses consisting of large sets of mixed (nonspecific) propositions, all the way down to the level of particular scientific and rational research claims/arguments. Beyond research discourses and arguments are values that come into play in the evaluation of retrieval technology (i.e., software, devices, system behaviors, technical designs, and algorithms) and in the evaluation of the usage experience of a particular technology, or of technology-mediated experience in general. There is also the evaluation or judgment of results of experiments, where experiments are a particular type of controlled use of systems.

In all modalities, the corresponding objects/discourses/propositions/usage experiences are found to be contributing to progress to the extent that they fulfill a set of values. In consequence, each such value, in the context of its respective modality, can be understood as a notion of progress for that modality. Thus, there is a separation between the notions. Progress in one modality may not imply progress in another. For example, while successive improvements in ranking indicate progress in the modality of the ad hoc search aspect of a system—the traditional task core (Spärck-Jones, 2001)—it may not indicate progress in the discipline as a whole. It may not even indicate progress in an application context according to the values associated with that context. That is, improved rankings may not sufficiently improve user experience, and therefore they may not fulfill the value of effective user experience.

This section describes the relation among several modalities wherein evaluative judgments take place. The judgments considered are those that traditionally pertain to the proper conduct of scientific experimentation and reasoning, that is, what in IR&S is understood as the research activity/ practice of evaluation, a crucial component of discourse (written and spoken). In this section, we argue, given the modern context, for the need to rigorously problematize the issue of values, specifically, values pertaining to technology mediation and the study of technology-mediation. This of course is a problem for foundations research.

In particular, section 2.5.1 outlines the system of values pertaining to experimental results, indicating that the precise meaning of the values depends on the phenomena with which they are associated, and arguing the need to problematize values given the changing nature of such search phenomena. Section 2.5.2 focuses on the value of the explanatory power of statements (introduced in section 2.5.1) that are associated with experimentation and scientific discourse. It shows the particular nature of explanatory evaluation and its relation to non–ad hoc research and domain analysis. Moreover, it identifies the failure analysis evaluation program as the main program addressing this value by asking why systems failed (i.e., seeking explanation for the particular outcome of failure). Section 2.5.2.2 continues from this to discuss the evaluation of differences in results as a second program of explanatory evaluation. The effectiveness of both program is argued to depend sensitively on domain analysis.

Section 2.5.3 emphasizes the need to understand different evaluation programs as cultural forms, in that they reveal differences that are useful with respect to the values supported by an associated project that intends to solve a search-related problem, and not necessarily with respect to "real differences." Both sections 2.5.3 and 2.5.2 discuss the need for foundations research as a precursor or necessary complement to domain analysis. They suppose in addition that since the increasing variation between modern search contexts warrants domain analysis, that this implies the need for foundations research, in particular to elucidate the concepts for understanding emerging contexts/domains. This variation is further discussed in the context of the generalizability of results in section 2.5.4 and stability in section 2.5.5, both of which constitute additional notions of progress in evaluation.

In addition to deriving specific values (generalizability, explanation, etc.) that are notions of progress pertaining to the practice of evaluation and scientific reasoning, the following attempts also to relate between these values and the discourse-level values; all of which then form a complex that is the overall notion of progress in IR&S. In this regard one of the main conclusions is that, for evaluation methodologies to be coherent and thereby lead to internal coherence of the overall discourse, the research culture must focus on understanding domains. Moreover, addressing the modern context means to better understand the relationship between different emerging values and to construe new values; this is, however, a task pertaining primarily to foundations research. In particular, the current research culture must focus on understanding emerging domains and contexts of technology-use that exhibit new values. As discussed previously, the understanding of domains has much to do with foundations, as it requires deciding how search is to be construed for various contexts/domains. What it means to make progress according to the notions of progress employed in existing evaluation paradigms has to be further developed by means of understanding domains of information behavior and technology-mediated activity in general, but this presupposes the resolution of several foundational questions that are further discussed in chapter 5.

2.5.1   Emerging Phenomena Imply Changing the Space of Values and Rethinking Evaluation

This section provides a simple scheme for understanding the relation between values and evaluation results in IR&S. It uses this to explain what is required for there to be a serious problematization of evaluation, and to argue—given the changing space of values—for the need of such a problematization. This section then discusses further requirements for rigorous problematization, the insufficient scope of prior IR&S works in this regard, the relation of this task to the basic problem of phenomena construal (aim 2 from section 2.1) and explains why it belongs to foundations research. Finally, it explicates why a rigorous understanding of domains is a condition for good explanatory results and research.

IR&S experiments, whether involving users or only relevance data (queries, relevance judgments, and collections), are a means of evaluating systems or search scenarios that generate results. Evaluations can also be done through intellectual argumentation that employs results of prior such experiments or even hypothetical cases. Consider a simple attribute scheme whereby results possess (1) subject matter (i.e., they are about something, such as a search engine); (2) a function whereby they serve, for example, to explain or prove something about its subject matter; (3) a scope that specifies the breadth of its claims/application; and (4) a "strength" to indicate its truth or our certainty in it. A result can thereby be of value on account of one or more of these attributes; each such attribute then denotes a category of values that can be sought. With respect to function, suppose that, in accordance with Furner (2011) that a result is of value when it can, for example, explain the reason for a relevant state of affairs, indicate what such a state may mean, or indicate how technological designs can be changed to improve efficiency or effectiveness—which can be indicated by the mere statement of a result. That is, a result is useful to a degree reflective of its explanatory and interpretive power, and to the extent it is instrumentally effective. The explanatory, interpretive, and instrumental ability of results (i.e., their functions) can also thereby be understood as denoting three values possessed by that result; these are scientific values (see section 2.3.3.3). Similarly, a result can be of value with respect to its scope on account of its generalizability and its strength to the extent it is repeatable and reproducible. A repeated result, and especially a reproducible result (i.e., a result repeated in a separate experiment or case) indicates the verifiability and regularity or stability of an observed (or observable) pattern or fact. The generalizability of a result refers to the applicability or scope of results given a predetermined idea of contexts to which results can possibly apply. These attributes characterize a wide range of results. For example, a result of technological value, which functions to suggest improvements in efficiency or effectiveness, may have limited scope due to a lack of generalizability, and yet be strong on account of being repeatable and/or reproducible. Or, a result may have explanatory value and yet be limited in scope and weak in arguing its case. Every such result is thereby associated with the values in each value category corresponding to an attribute.[30]

The study of evaluation results involves comparing the attributes of different results, and the deriving of further results or arguments. For example, such a study may seek to adduce an explanation for a result expressing the low effectiveness of a system, or to provide an interpretation about user needs based on the examination of user interactions or queries. For any such study to be possible, there has to be a coherent way to compare

---

30. This could also apply to its subject-matter attribute: it could be of value for a result to be about one aspect of a search scenario than another, at some stage of research.

results with different attributes. That is, different subject matters (e.g., user interactions to system performance), functions (e.g., an explanation or an interpretation), scopes, and strengths. This does not merely correspond to a set of rules, but a methodological discourse and framework, which must also determine whether and how such values apply to the irrespective, predetermined set of IR&S phenomena. For example, it may be difficult to see how results about particular types of user behavior (perhaps one that functions as an interpretation) could function to suggest changes to technical designs; or how a result that functions to explain limited-scope system behavior can function to explain user behavior in a general way. Thus, such a framework and its related discourse would determine

- the kinds of things (subject matter) about which results of a particular function can be obtained (e.g., phenomena that can be explained in an IR&S context),
- the relation between such things as different result functions (e.g., results attributable by technological versus explanatory values), and
- the different possible contexts among which results pertaining to these things could possibly apply (or generalize to).

It is supposed that any significant problematization of evaluation in IR&S would entail the development of such a framework and discourse, which would relate phenomena to these scientific values and to any other relevant values. Hence, such a problematization would entail the corresponding problematization of the space of values, which in turn would depend on a problematization of the space of phenomena.

We contend not only that evaluation in IR&S should be problematized, but that it has to be quite rigorous so that it addresses the space of values and phenomena beyond metrics. This is especially pertinent in the modern context since (1) the changing nature of the phenomenon of search[31] raises the question of the purposes of search, and this in turn raises afresh the question of values. It is furthermore important as (2) problematizing evaluation and resolving the corresponding problems is important for progress; progress in a discipline is tied to evaluation. The fulfillment of values (by results) indicates a more progressive state than their nonfulfillment.

In the context of point 1, by widening the definition of search (or of a search engine) in Zhai (2011) toward the notion of a general analysis engine,

---

31. That is, search as the most typical phenomenon of technology mediation, where such mediated experience increasingly characterizes lived experience; see chapter 1.

wherein the relations between system and user differ significantly from the traditional case, one is led to a different space of associated values. A general analysis engine offers a radically new set of system behaviors and usage experiences—pertaining to this new type of (analysis) activity—that serve to problematize the idea of what a good system or usage experience is. Similarly, with systems allowing for newer types of such experiences and system behaviors, the need emerges to reconsider the existing space of values and to add to it either wholly different values or refinements of previously held values. For example, although effectiveness is a value that may remain, it still has to be defined according to the particulars of this new type of activity, and as such, the precision and recall of systems might not be sufficient to capture anything beyond an inadequately limited aspect of what the system is doing. In the case of usage experience, the increasingly pervasive contexts of search use entail the need to capture different aspects of user experience. This is a problem not only for IR&S but also for the discipline of human-computer interaction with respect to pervasive contexts of technology-use beyond search technology (see chapter 6).

For IR&S, recent works focusing on characterizing user engagement, an aspect of the overall user experience, can be seen as a sign of IR&S discourse approaching the problematization of values. In particular, the different attributes of user engagement, such as focused attention, endurability, challenge and affect (O'Brien and Toms, 2008, 2010; Attfield et al., 2011; Lalmas et al., 2014) can be understood to be part of the space of values of user engagement, although they may not necessarily also be the values sought with respect to a "good" user experience (Lalmas et al., 2014, p. 3). As chapter 1 argued and chapter 5 explicates further, the pertinent phenomenon ought to be technology-mediated user (TME) experience in general—which goes beyond user engagement. The perusal of TME corresponds to a stage of research that comes after the stage that focused on user engagement (Bødker, 2006, 2015; O'Brien and Toms, 2010, p. 65). The modern context thereby entails the explication of new values or requires adaptations of prior values; these then condition how IR&S discourse is to study and evaluate according to all their modalities: usage experiences, results, system behaviors, research statements, and discourses. Moreover, a study of the corresponding value structure for emerging conceptions of search would presumably have to precede evaluation metrics, techniques, and methods, because the methodology they serve presupposes a value structure or framework. Consequently, IR&S discourse, for the sake of the value of coherence by which it is to be valued, must first characterize a system of values: if the system of values is not well understood, then the corresponding evaluative judgments are likely to suffer—at the least—a gradually increasing incoherence with the growing set of evaluation results.[32]

With respect to point (2) (the link between evaluation and overall progress), the problematization of evaluation can only be adequate (i.e., progressive) if it is broad and rigorous. Consider the *Meeting of the Minds* workshop report in Callan et al. (2007, p. 31), which states that IR is an "empirical science" and that "the field cannot move forward unless there are means of evaluating the innovations devised by researchers." However, with Callan et al. (2007) having suggested a change in the definition of IR to include very complex tasks—to the extent that it no longer resembles any IR system—search as an activity must now be associated to a different set of values. Thus, it is not clear that the statement that IR is an empirical science means the same thing for the expanded notion of search. The empirical aspect of IR can rarely be absent; however, it is perhaps more pertinent to ask what kind of discipline/science it is (or should be). This is in order to develop an answer as opposed to assuming continuity in disciplinary structure/form and epistemology from the previous definition of IR. The discussion in the *Meeting of the Minds* workshop (Callan et al., 2007, p. 32) admits the need to change the usual function of search: "We have argued about ... having tools that help a person organize and analyze retrieved information" (cf. the followup discussion in Allan et al. (2012, pp. 24–25)). That discussion further poses the foundational questions addressed in this section: "How should such search improvements be evaluated? The use of context poses a severe challenge to the notion of a test collection, which will need to include rich user and task models. Evaluation of new tools will require development of new metrics and methodologies." Yet when the phenomenon to be studied is redefined significantly as in Callan et al. (2007) and Zhai (2011), as it was the case in the context of point (1), it is difficult to immediately address evaluation metrics without first asking what values are to be evaluated. Systems that are evaluated to be better than other systems are then said to be more progressive or more substantial (see section 2.3.3). Yet this evaluation is conditional on the corresponding values being coherent with respect to the overall aims of the field.

---

32. What if one forgoes the development of a system of values, for the sake of "pragmatic simplicity," opting instead to work with yet another effectiveness metric? Metrics work to order whatever they are used to evaluate: systems, usage experiences, etc. While this is useful, remaining at this level of research will eventually limit the growth of the discourse— as prior sections have argued—if they are not to be supplemented with by explanatory research.

Several works seek to problematize evaluation at a level beyond metrics and measures, but they do so in a partial way, for example, by suggesting a different way to construe the space of phenomena or suggesting new values. Tague-Sutcliffe (1992) argues for the idea of valuing processes (i.e., search/browsing processes) and not only documents, predating Zhai's (2011) suggestion. Robertson (1979, p. 205) as quoted in Ellis (1984, p. 28), can be understood to be exploring the implications of alternative construals of phenomena (or the adding of new phenomena or both) to evaluation. He considers that since several aspects (not just the ranked list) of the system response "contribute together to the resolution of the question," that perhaps the evaluation strategy should be modified to address the evaluation scenario wherein a group of documents can only be relevant as a group. This type of change to evaluation would "already require us to rethink most of our basic ideas in the design of IR systems" (Ellis, 1984, p. 28; Robertson, 1979, p. 205).

Beyond such explicit problematizations of evaluation by addressing values and/or alternative phenomena construals, values inevitably mediate—however implicitly—the entirety of activities associated with IR&S. Users, evaluators, systems, and researchers all perform construal activities, the key aspect of which is the selection of some aspects over others (i.e., the valuing of some aspect over another), an activity conditioned on an existing value system. User interactions, the understanding of usage processes/experiences by researchers (and users), the researcher's choosing to apply one method over another, and the system choosing one process over another are all choices guided by values, some of which may be shared. Take, for example, the choice of some documents over others as the relevant set, whether by an algorithm or a human evaluator. This comparative choice is conditioned (especially for the evaluator) by a system of values. The user may construe the relevant set differently from the researchers, evaluators, and algorithms: each actor works from a system of values. Moreover, these values can be assigned in different ways to the same phenomena space. For example, from the context of document theory, a document possesses value in addition to the value associated with it due to being the answer to a query (Lund, 2009), since a document is a cultural object and a means for social communication (and for social imagination). As such, Tague-Sutcliffe (1992), Ellis and Robertson (Ellis, 1984) and Lund (2009) can all be understood to be discussing what phenomena should or could count as "valuable" for analysis in the IR&S discourse.

Any sufficiently rigorous problematization of evaluation would go beyond the prior partial attempts and thereby seek to make the above value structures explicit. Such a task would lead to bringing out related foundational questions. For example, questions about the locus of manifestation of a phenomenon of value to IR&S discourse, as to whether the phenomenon is unique or specific to a particular domain/context or usage session, to one or more documents generated as the results of a particular query, or if the phenomenon can instead be said to occur more generally within broader processes and/or collectives (domains, documents, usage-sessions, etc). And with respect to a document object, questions about which of its parts are to be of value and how are these values to be represented and discussed? Moreover, recall from chapter 1 that the pervasiveness of technology-mediated activities means that search, as the most typical such activity, can only be fully understood by exploring the other activities that increasingly encompass it. Hence, the value of a particular type of search or information behavior must be understood in light of the values pertaining to the experience of participating in the corresponding encompassing activities that are facilitated by the device enabling this search or information behavior. The evaluation of such a device/system would then be with respect to a framework of values that must be construed to account for the relative importance of each layer of activity. There are prior works outside of IR&S (e.g., Flanagan et al., 2008; Floridi, 2008a), that investigate what there is in the space of embodied technology-use (to which values can be associated) that can be adapted for adequate problematization. The perusal of all such types of questions that involve ethical and metaethical discussion (Furner, 2011) constitute foundations research.

Finally, consider the user-experience of the judges or experts (first discussed in section 1.3.2.6) as they deliberate on their relevance judgments: these are evaluative judgments made after participating in technology-mediated activities. As such they reflect both the judges' personal value system, the values they additionally adopt for the sake of representing a domain of technology-use, and their cognitive state. Ellis (1996, p. 25) states that: "relevance judgments are a function of one's mental state at the time a reference is read. They are not fixed; they are dynamic."[33] All these aspects of relevance judgments constitute the context of the corresponding technology-mediated activities wherein that judgment takes place. This

---

33. He further critiques the way relevance judgments are used in system evaluation, quoting Harter (1992, p. 612): "Recording such judgments, treating them as permanent unchanging relations between a document set and a question set, and then using them to compute such measures as recall and precision to evaluate retrieval effectiveness, is contrary to the meaning of psychological relevance."

context conditions such evaluative judgments about the relationships between documents and queries. For retrieval systems trained on such judgments, any explanation of why they behave as they do must refer back to these evaluative judgments. Similarly, these judgments can be brought in to explain evaluation results, such as precision-recall results based on comparing such prior judgments with system decisions about an unseen document collection. Moreover, as discussed in Hjørland and Albrechtsen (1995) and Hjørland (2010), the precision and coherence of any such explanatory claims would then depend on how well the judges—and their domains—are understood. Thus the precision of explanatory statements then depends on the robustness of the framework of values (or ethical framework) and cognitive concepts used to characterize the judges and their judgments.

Explanatory evaluation of IR system performance, predicated on understanding the context of the relevance judgments and judges, thereby depends on a framework of values. What then is the importance of such evaluation in IR? As search phenomena (including user behavior) become more complex, the need to explain observations of phenomena (in experiments, for example) becomes acute.

2.5.2 Explanatory Evaluation Programs and the Value of Explanation

This section discusses the place of explanatory research in IR&S, first by discussing the existent program of failure analysis (FA) and then discussing a latent research orientation for explaining differences between results. FA seeks to determine the causal factors of a failure event, and while it is no longer a common program of evaluation in IR&S, explanatory questions and their addresses nevertheless pervade research, often in highly implicit ways. While IR typically prioritizes the instrumental value/ability of a result,[34] which indicates how a system should be modified to increase efficiency or effectiveness, results of explanatory ability are clearly also important. Robertson (2008, pp. 452–453) laments the lack of FA-based explanatory evaluation in favor of instrumentally valued evaluations:

> theories or models tend to be the subject of experimental investigation only in terms of the effectiveness of the resulting system. Seen as an application of the usual scientific method, of challenging theories by trying to derive falsifiable consequences, which may then be tested experimentally, this is extremely limited.

---

34. For example, the TREC evaluation program is mainly but not exclusively based on instrumental values.

Explanatory evaluation programs seek to explain why something happened, such as why a system failed, a user behaved a particular way, or why differences arose in a set of effectiveness results. As chapters 3 and 4 discuss, explanatory evaluation/research is a significant aspect of progressive scientific disciplines, which these chapters argue IR&S can and ought to be (or be like). This depends however on first developing the many foundational positions related to the explanation discussed below, and several other aspects further developed in chapter 5.

2.5.2.1 Explaining failure In doing failure analysis one is ultimately, as Buckley (2009) indicates, seeking to formally define relationships between domains such that the answer to why a system failed in one search scenario (with its particular domain and context) can be used to determine whether it will fail in another. Commenting from a systems perspective Buckley (2009, p. 661–662) notes that

> the root cause of poor performance on any one topic is likely to be the same for all systems … if a system can realize the problem associated with a given topic, then … current technology should be able to improve results significantly.

However, to understand why a system failed or performed poorly for a topic, it is necessary to understand the notion of poor/failure for that particular context, the relationship between topics and how they are "lead to" by the system. Unsurprisingly, this encroaches on the terrain of domain analysis. The quality of FA depends on the quality of the domain analysis that preexists and supports it.

Failure analysis limited to, for example, linking failure to system aspects, can lead to system improvements without understanding the collection a system employs, such as in terms of topic interrelations. But exploring these relations does eventually become an imperative (Buckley, 2009), presumably in order to improve or make progress in FA. This is especially the case for some topics where "understanding the semantics of the topic well enough to just identify the important aspects would seem to be crucial."(Buckley, 2009, p. 664). Moreover, if it is the case that "it may be more important … to discover what current techniques should be applied to which topics, than to come up with new techniques" (Buckley, 2009, p. 662), then the interrelations between topics and their related usage experiences must be understood. It is from this systems perspective that explanatory analysis (such as FA) entails the development of rich understanding of contexts (including their interrelations) through domain analysis. Thus, the evaluation of systems beyond their ad hoc components, in the long term, becomes about semantics or semantic networks (meaning complexes): finding comprehensive relations between domains so as to be able to explain (and predict) which usage scenarios will lead to system failures.

The same conclusion is reached from a more general point of view: as components (indexing, querying, interface, etc.) of an IR system are connected, a failure or problem (e.g., at the indexing level) is often not just a problem with that component or only a technical problem pertaining to technical design. The issue could instead be with a background of assumptions that are pre-technical and influence the design of the indexing scheme. Hjørland (2011b) makes clear that insufficient investigation of such assumptions (e.g., epistemological assumptions about theories of knowledge pertaining to the domain of interest)[35] that influence the design of components or even the definition of concepts can render incoherent the interpretation of results, and by extension, evaluation strategies such as FA.[36]

The systems perspective of FA is thereby limited, as it is difficult to pinpoint the failure if it is beyond the system aspects; thus it is hard to appreciate the larger implications of addressing the question: "why did system x fail?" This limitation is for lab experiments in general, as they inevitably require the reduction of real-life phenomena to abstractions, which creates "inevitable biases in what is studied" (Robertson, 2008, p. 15). As some aspects of reality—such as those dealing with users—are hard to abstract, they are often reduced to simplistic characterizations, such as requests and relevance judgments: a limited yet "extraordinarily powerful abstraction" (Robertson, 2008, p. 15). As a result, the effectiveness of evaluations based on (the value pertaining to) scientific explanation, such as failure analysis, is limited by the mainstream lab-based (instrumentalist)

---

35. Hjørland (2011b, p. 76) explains:

Theories of indexing in IS are mostly based on universalist, objectivist, and cognitivist assumptions that have been problematic, and may explain at least a part of the failures of the indexing … the present study … reflects domain-specific, pragmatic, and request-oriented views of indexing.

36. Hjørland (2011b, p. 75) discusses the FA in Lykke and Eslau (2010) as an example where the failure is inadequately identified, saying that the work

does not allow us to say whether the failure to identify the relevant (and only the relevant) document was because of bad indexing, of bad search profiles, or, most likely, a combination of indexing and retrieval. Because the underlying issue is the same in both indexing and retrieval[,] … to establish why the indexers failed to discriminate the relevant documents properly involves the same theory as to establish why the searchers failed to discriminate the relevant documents. We may therefore concentrate on the indexing alone.

abstractions. To move beyond this systems perspective thus means to not be limited to locating the failure in systems aspects, and to instead consider the whole domain, which then takes one beyond the ad hoc concept of search (and the ad hoc task core discussed in section 2.3.3.2). The value of FA results therefore depend on what is already understood with respect to the corresponding domain. To understand a domain entails knowing what its relation is to other domains, as to how "regular" the domain's features are, what the significance is of differences, and in particular, to understand what the results of experiments on a system actually mean: What does it signify for information needs, users, and contexts? Hence, reaching such understandings for the sake of explanatory research mean addressing these interpretive questions. The quality of the interpretation/understanding of the results (and their implications) depends on the quality of this domain understanding.[37] Thus, making progress in FA means to be able to explain a failure with respect to this larger picture.

The modern context makes the limitations of systems-based FA even more acute. The increasingly pervasive nature of search systems means increasingly complex and varied domains, diverse usage scenarios, and a corresponding increase in contextual phenomena, all of which a systems perspective would generally ignore. Moreover, this contemporary situation implies that progress in FA not only entails domain analysis using prior domain knowledge, but also the analysis must first investigate how basic concepts like domain, context, user, and system, are to be construed. Ultimately, before one asks why a search engine fails one must ask what a search engine is and what role it plays as a technology that is pervasive in an increasing range of social contexts (i.e., how it to be construed). This is also the conclusion of the extensive work of Wise and Debons (1987): the successes and failures of a system only mean something with respect to an understanding of the system's place in human activities.

2.5.2.2 Explaining differences Beyond FA a separate type of explanatory research can be delineated in IR&S discourse, although has yet to develop

---

37. For example, as Hjørland (2011b, p. 76) says about the case of Lykke and Eslau (2010): we still need to know whether this kind of understanding has penetrated to all persons and all practical procedures in thesaurus construction and indexing in this setting.... We need to know more about what is specific for this domain, its terminology, relevance criteria, documents, and genres ... there seems to be a need for research illuminating what a domain is.

into an evaluation program. This pertains to research that seeks to explain differences in results. Both FA and difference explanations pertain to the outcome(s) of one or more experimental events. Harter (1996, p. 48) argues for the need to study the causes and effects of variations in relevance judgments:

> Variations in relevance assessments can usefully be seen as a special case of the more general problem of individual differences in information retrieval. Perhaps the single most compelling conclusion that can be reached from decades of research in information retrieval is the importance of individual differences among cases.

The study of differences, however, pertains to several modalities other than relevance assessments. These include search term selections and indexing consistency studied by prior works, as cited in Harter (1996, p. 48), and to differences between experimental results in general, such as those not hinging on relevance assessments. As to why these individual differences are important, Harter reasons as follows:

> human beings involved in the information retrieval process (indexers, searchers, and users) and the products they produce (indexing records, retrieved documents, queries, and relevance judgments) vary enormously from one another. Systems need to be able to adjust to individual searchers, queries, and users.

This means that new approaches to performance measurement are needed that do not

> depend on a single set of fixed, unchanging relevance assessments from the many alternative sets of assessments that might be taken.

Moreover, he suggests that approaches are required that

> do not depend on pooling the retrieval results of many individual searches and thus destroying potentially important individual differences among problem types queries, associated relevance judgments, and the systems being compared.[38]

---

38. See also, Cleverdon (1970) and Cuadra and Katter (1967, p. 302):

relevance scores are very likely to be artifacts of particular experimental instructions and conditions and should not be offered or viewed as absolute numbers. This conclusion does not invalidate experiments in which a given group of judges makes relevance appraisals for a specific system. However, it does call into question any comparative evaluations (between systems or sub-systems) in which the attitude of the judges about the intended use of the materials was not considered and controlled, either experimentally or statistically.

In addition, he makes the strong assessment based on preceding research trends:

> Three decades of research have shown that relevance assessments are affected by a great many factors. Now we need to develop measurement instruments that are sensitive to these variations, to the individual differences that we know exist. Our approaches to evaluation must reflect the real world of real users.

The increasing pervasiveness of modern technology and the multitudes of usage contexts, user types, and the variations in search applications it exhibits, shows the increasing significance of investigating these differences. And to study such differences amounts to more than simply stating that the difference exists. It requires ultimately that the difference be understood through an explanation of its causes and effects,[39] and through interpretation of what the difference could mean (see chapter 3).

While Harter (1996) sought to question the stability of the usual IR experiments by highlighting the difference in the relevance assessments on which they depend, later works such as Voorhees (2000) showed that stability could be maintained despite these differences. However, the study of differences clearly transcends a purely instrumental goal. The ability to explain results of experiments is a hallmark of science, and hence the study of differences therein is important by itself, even if such differences do not alter their derivative effects, such as the instrumental results that depend on them.

2.5.2.3 Explanation and foundations The "why" question pertaining to the difference in results, failure, or user acts is difficult to answer in the context of rich, pervasive applications. The phenomena to which such explanations will refer are not only technical but also socio-psychological. They are, in particular, mixed phenomena, which are of concern to different disciplines. While the explanations of natural phenomena could appeal to natural laws that apply in a regular fashion to a wide scope of such phenomena, social phenomena do not generally admit such laws. They are explained by means of highly contextual reasoning: the scope of which tends to be limited. What kind of explanatory framework is then adequate for IR&S? As chapter 5 further elaborates, any rigorous address of this foundational question depends on the resolution of a broad set of preliminary questions, such as what kind of discipline IR&S is, and what phenomena

---

39. Harter (1996) does not discuss explanation explicitly, except indirectly in a quote from Smeaton (1993)—but it is clearly implied.

are therefore relevant to it. That is, how should sociological, psychological, technical, and practical reasoning be put together to explain an IR&S event?

Resolving these questions not only means developing an explanatory framework for IR&S, but also exploring its place among other disciplines (this is indeed the course that chapters 5 and 6 take) and thereby seeking to make progress through improving external coherence. Addressing explanation also serves to improve internal coherence: knowing why something happened is better than not knowing, as it improves the quality of result interpretation.

2.5.3 Useful Differences and Statistical Significance

The explanation of differences discussed above is of particular value when the differences are "real." A comparison of results that indicates a difference is akin to the comparison of domains in a reduced, quantitative way (see Hjørland, 2011a). A statistically significant difference or result—even if the statistical test is sufficiently powered (see Sakai, 2016)—may not be qualitatively or actually significant, or sufficiently meaningful. An actually or qualitatively significant difference is ultimately an experiential (empirical, see section 2.2.3.1) difference between the use of one system and the use of another, that is, between two usage experiences, with all else (the contexts of use) being equal to the extent possible. Were the user to characterize the difference here as being between two observations/experiences, of system-use (or task completion through use), then this would be a qualitatively significant difference between effectiveness results. This means more to the user than a quantitatively specified, statistically significant effectiveness result that is calculated for many contexts (i.e., statistical significance) and may not be experienceable in the same way that the average value of an attribute in a data set may not be attributed to any particular data point.[40] As Ellis (2010, p. 4) explains:

> A statistically significant result is one that is unlikely to be the result of chance. But a practically significant result is meaningful in the real world. It is quite possible, and unfortunately quite common, for a result to be statistically significant and trivial. It is also possible for a result to be statistically nonsignificant and important.

---

40. Critique pertaining to the reduction of meaningful significances and other human aspects to their mathematical equivalents go back to the early days of IR&S (Taube, 1965; Cuadra and Katter, 1967) and are even more pertinent in the modern context.

Yet, even if statistical significances are not meaningful, they do serve an important function. While dealing with real differences is necessary for good explanatory research, there is indeed a benefit, in the context of other types of research, in adopting "not necessarily real" or "useful" differences, assuming that the differences are statistically significant in an adequately powered test. Differences are useful if they, for example, can be used to structure a set of technological designs in such a way as to lead to the generation of further insights, as is the case with the differences generated by instrumentally inclined TREC evaluations. That a difference acquires a value—which "usefulness" denotes—means that there is a value framework presupposed by the corresponding experimental activity, and hence the foundational task of explicating this framework becomes necessary.

Dealing with not-necessarily-real differences through experimentation, a profoundly beneficial endeavor, serves to create a fictional yet useful narrative. As Crease (1997, p. 269) explains:

> Experiments are first and foremost material events in the world. Events do not produce numbers—they do not measure themselves—but do so only when the action is properly planned, prepared, and witnessed. An experiment therefore has the character of a performance, and like all performances must be understood as a historically and culturally situated hermeneutical process.

IR&S evaluation programs and their constituent experimental activities thereby constitute cultural forms. Observation and experimentation are activities in which human researchers participate. Thus any rigorous understanding of evaluation, such as the explanation of differences, must seek to understand the experience of researchers as they participate in such cultural forms. As chapter 5 further explicates, the researcher's observational context and experience is as important to foundations research as is user experience.

While discourse about statistical and actual/meaningful significance has become popular of late (Kelly et al., 2014a,b), it is expected to become particularly apposite as search phenomena become increasingly complex and pervasive. This discourse is also expected to become increasingly significant as understanding differences—whether in results or between all those aspects where an explanation of the difference is valued—is important for the discourses about the generalizability and repeatability of results.

2.5.4 Generalizability

A typical traditional IR&S experimental result expresses the ability of a system (or more specifically, of a search scenario) to precisely recall documents given a specific set of queries or to acquire good user opinions, as would be determined by a user study. To ask whether this result generalizes means to first determine whether there are other search scenarios with different attributes (e.g., different users or documents) that are yet similar or "relevant" to the given scenario. And second, it means to examine whether the result for the existing scenario would reflect that of a similar experiment done on these other relevant scenarios; a result is more generalizable than another when it adequately characterizes more of its associated scenarios than does the other. However, how does one determine whether another scenario is sufficiently related or relevant? Take the evaluation scenario that is depicted, as is typical, by simple user attributes, such as their number and that they are, say, postgraduate students. What other scenarios could be related to this one? Would every scenario with an arbitrary group of postgraduate students of the same number be relevant—with all other attributes remaining the same? Perhaps the other relevant scenarios are all those with "similar" document collections, regardless of the type of users involved in the evaluation. Or instead, that the relevant scenarios are those where users perform particular (similar) tasks regardless of the users and document collections involved.

Moreover, given that generalizability is concerned with how evaluative judgments made about phenomena through observation can be inferred to apply to other phenomena, the study of generalizability pertains then to studying the nature and extent of application of this judgment to other (relevant) situations. Each such situation (e.g., a search scenario) can be understood as a phenomenon or a complex of phenomena. Unlike the regularity of natural phenomena, the socio-technical phenomena that search and search technology-use is, admits only of highly contextualized regularities and no "laws" as such. The validity of results across different users and contexts/domains–as analogous to different spatiotemporal locations for natural phenomena—can rarely be presumed. Moreover, as also in the natural scientific case, any change in the construal of phenomena can effect the generalizability of evaluation results. What is not clear at the outset, however, is the extent to which one can generalize a set of results, especially given the variety of modern contexts; further investigation is entailed (Harter, 1996). In particular, as the definition of search widens (cf. section 2.3.4.1) to include diverse types of relevant phenomena and their complex interrelations, underlying notions of what it means for a result to be generalizable would require revision with respect to this new construal.

While generalizable results have always been sought in IR&S research, and the concept previously studied, it is pertinent to raise the question anew given the pervasive nature of search applications entailing a complex space of search scenarios (and phenomena) to which a result may apply in addition to its own scenario. However there are several additional foundational aspects that such a study relates to. Addressing the questions pertaining to generalizability requires the understanding of relationships (e.g., the variations) between different scenarios/domains/contexts, in order to deduce how an evaluative judgment pertaining to one context/domain may apply to another. In particular, the foundational question pertaining to the interpretation of results of "how generalizable are our results" then depends on the answer to the question "to what scenarios do the results apply," which in turn depends on "what kinds of scenarios are possible, and how do they relate to one another."[41] Moreover, a resolution of questions about generalizability is a prerequisite for developing effective evaluation strategies in IR and is therefore important for progress in IR.

It is important to study generalizability for an additional reason that is perhaps even more important for progress, especially with respect to internal coherence. The increasing variation or difference between modern search contexts (especially given the expansion of the meaning of search) means that judgments about the value of systems (i.e., existing sets of results) would become progressively incoherent as the space of possible search scenarios grows and the domain of application is not sufficiently specified and restricted. The increasing variation of search scenarios should encourage a restriction in claims—or more qualified forms in claims—about the validity of evaluative judgments to particular contexts or domains (not just to different mediums, e.g., video versus text). This entails a more fine-grained type of evaluative judgment and evaluation strategy than is common in traditional evaluation. For example, discussions about effectiveness (a value corresponding to an evaluative judgment) of systems would need to be context specific.

Effectiveness is not only a property of a system, but of human experience of search-technology mediated activity, and so it refers to the experience of effectiveness for an individual or group of users (i.e., for a domain or usage context). This is because every human activity has the potential to be seen as a search scenario, and so the corresponding notion of effectiveness of a system therein has to be extended (outside the usual precision/recall measures) to be conditioned by the particulars of the scenario. Effectiveness then would moreover be a property of the context as a whole. It is therefore more appropriate to talk about effective search behavior or effective search

---

41. Ultimately, there needs to be an ontological discourse of scenarios and their components based on first answering the question of what IR&S is about (i.e., what the relevant phenomena are); see chapter 5.

experience, which refers to the behavior or experience pertaining to a user using a system in an ideal scenario of that context. What these notions mean for some context would then have to be clarified prior to deducing effectiveness measures for representing that notion and support the making of evaluative judgments. Thus, notions of effectiveness and effectiveness measures are likely to also vary widely by context. As a result, discussions about effectiveness will then have to be tied to a discussion about usage experiences in particular domains and usage contexts. The study of variations between contexts would then have to involve domain-sensitive user studies, perhaps through studying tasks/activities.

System-based studies that do not sufficiently understand the difference between contexts limit themselves to understanding the generalizability of evaluative judgments through statistical significance. Statistically significant judgments/results may not be sufficiently qualitatively significant to users or groups, and therefore are limited in what they mean to these users (and also to researchers who are trying to deduce qualitative significance). And given the increasing variation between contexts, such results become less valid or at least less coherent, as the extent of their applicability becomes increasingly unclear. Therefore the methodological strength of system-based studies decreases. That statistical significance may not be practically significant or noticeable is a given of statistical methodology. However, the space of search phenomena in which significance is being judged is rapidly shifting, and so prior understandings of the relationship between statistical and practical significance in the IR&S context must be re-evaluated. In addition, what statistical significance means may vary across studies, given that assumptions about significance testing may differ. As a result, claims of significance—even if technically equivalent—do not imply the same thing, and the meaning of significance instead has to be established (Armstrong et al., 2009, p. 608). Thus, in addition to the difference between practical and statistical significance, the difference in assumptions of works claiming significance is also a likely source of incoherence across works.

2.5.5 Result Stability

The veracity, coherence, and significance of a discourse are dependent on the stability of the phenomena discussed. The notions of reproducibility, replicability, repeatability as applied to observable phenomena pertain to their overall stability as phenomena and work to indicate how justified one is in believing in them and relying on them. However, these notions do not admit of simple definitions (see Collins, 1992, pp. 29–49), and thus we will mainly work here with the notion of stability. A stable or regular phenomenon or result is one that shows up repeatedly in the same or similar way in different situations, with the same or different conditions, and according either to the same observer or different observers. A discourse that produces stable results or finds stable phenomena presumably has developed a "better" account of a particular phenomenon than the discourse which has not, and is therefore a more progressive discourse (see chapter 3);[42] stability is then a sign of progress. Moreover, categories of phenomena can be characterized according to their stability. Consider the case of computational phenomena: the run-time behavior of a deterministic technological design,[43] as a computational phenomenon, is stable. Every time such a program is executed and provided the same input, and on the same or similar machine with respect to hardware and software, the same or similar behavior is expected.

Of particular interest to IR&S in recent times is the problem of stability in IR&S results, which corresponds to the problem of the stability of search phenomena or search programs (Bellogín et al., 2014; Arguello et al., 2016; Lin et al., 2016). A search system may behave in an unstable way if factors (e.g., updates of software libraries on which the system depends) mean that two runs of the same system are actually that of two different programs, so that there is no guarantee that system behavior can be reproduced.[44] In general, as Callan et al. (2007) mentions, the stability (as repeatability) of experimental results is a value that is integral to the worth of IR experiments, especially for modern IR applications, which are complex and interactive. Evaluation paradigms that allow for the design of such experiments to show the stability of phenomena being observed, are thus more progressive than paradigms limited to ad hoc experiments that do not exhibit sufficiently stable results upon repetition.

In addition to system behavior, it is important for IR&S to achieve stability with respect to some invariant aspect in at least two cases. First, in usage experiences, so that different users sharing similar interests also share

42. In addition to demonstrating a phenomenon's stability, the stability of results condition the veracity of subsequent scientific statements made about it. As chapter 3 discusses, progressive scientific discourses are characterized by sufficiently verified propositions.

43. As opposed to a probabilistic or nondeterministic design.

44. Moreover, a result may not reproduce in a second case, because the latter instance may employ a different interpretation of matching models or may not use preparatory processes (such as training processes) that were used in the first case but not mentioned (Arguello et al., 2016; Di Buccio et al., 2015).

something with respect to their experience of using a search system. Second, in evaluation results (e.g., precision and recall results), so that systems that evaluate well for a particular domain or topic work similarly well for another similar domain or topic. This is so that one could expect for example, a particular precision/recall result, if the system were to be used on an unfamiliar document collection that is similar to a collection on which the system was previously tested. With respect to the invariant aspect or property, not all properties about a system or a usage experience are of the same value; the value depends on the perspective of the observer. For example, one could establish that the interface for a system is aesthetically pleasing, meaning that the aesthetic aspect of usage experience pertaining to system use is stable. This could be used to explain why users gravitate toward using it rather than another system with a different interface. This stable result may be irrelevant for a system designer trying to work out why the system performs poorly for particular queries.

Stability and its constitutive concepts, such as repeatability and reproducibility, are therefore not given concepts for IR&S. This is especially so in the growing space of phenomena that the modern context brings, where stability is particularly sought. However, neither is it a given concept in general; it has to be developed according to each field of discourse. Stability in the context of social phenomena as studied, for example, in economics, is different from that for micro-phenomena in physics. The latter exhibits more regularities (or stable results) than the former. Hence, whereas experiments that repeatedly give similar results may usually indicate progress, one has to be certain that the idea of stability is suitable for the phenomena one is considering. In this sense, IR&S is closer to economics with respect to the phenomena studied than it is to the natural sciences: social phenomena pertaining to monetary behavior exhibit relatively few regularities across all contexts (Lawson, 2003). Thus, one should expect any notion of stability for IR&S to be more like the social than the natural sciences. Yet it cannot only be like the corresponding notion in the social sphere.

IR&S phenomena are mixed; they are made up of strongly stable computational phenomena as well as highly contextual socio-psychological phenomena. Any notion of stability for such mixed phenomena has to balance between the differing natures of its constituents. Moreover, the development of such a notion is urgent in the context of progress: it is unclear how to interpret the state of progress in IR&S discourse without knowing how stable the results and phenomena are. It is unclear what a notion of progress would ultimately mean for a discourse that only consists of a series of unstable (i.e., nonrepeatable/reproducible) results. This makes it particularly important to address the representative foundational question: What kinds of stability (or reproducibility and repeatability etc.) are relevant for IR&S phenomena? Answering this question requires settling numerous related foundational concerns. Any definition of stability, or repeatability and reproducibility depends on how the observer, observation, experiment, domain, scenario, and context are defined. In addition, the foundational task of resolving the notion of stability is one on which much depends. If as prior sections discussed, IR&S evaluation ought to become more domain based (e.g., task specific), then it is the stability of results in similar domains/contexts that is the relevant indicator of veracity for statements about phenomena. Thus stable results across dissimilar domains (e.g., statistical regularities across a population of all domains that average out differences between specific domains) would generally be less important than stable results over one domain (or a group of similar domains). Stable results over a domain would directly enable judgment of the veracity of hypotheses and propositions concerning the phenomena in that domain.

The address of these foundational questions—thereby resolving the aforementioned concepts—corresponds to the problem of construing several IR&S concepts and phenomena as per aim 2 in section 2.1. However, it also concerns internal and external coherence. With respect to internal coherence, the existence of a stable phenomenon indicates a coherence between the way the phenomena are construed (i.e., propositions about their nature, attributes, and existence) and their actual nature as observed by experiment (i.e., a coherence between concept/theory and reality). Conversely, a coherent discourse—and hence the fulfillment of aim 1—is dependent on the stability of experimental results and therefore on the stability and regularity of phenomena. With respect to external coherence, the question, of result stability also depends on resolving foundational questions on which external coherence also depends. This is because an adequate account of result stability depends on understanding the relative position of IR&S phenomena among that of other disciplines, which in turn depends on the kind of science IR&S is understood to be.

That the stability and generalizability of phenomena are required for progress makes sense: The former is about justifying beliefs pertaining to observations, and the latter is about understanding the limitations of and relations between observations. Both are crucial for scientific practice. In addition to indicating progress, the stability and generalizability of results and phenomena that a discourse employs indicate its coherence and ultimately its strength (pertaining to the confidence one has in it as an intellectual discipline). Consider instead the traditional notion of progress pertaining to the improvement of system results, where the system responds to a query with a ranked list of documents, and where a more optimal result is that which better matches the result of human judges for the same query. Does the delivery of an improved system returning a more optimal ranked list indicate progress for IR&S in the same way as stability and generalizability?

2.6   Rank Improvement, Theory Growth, and Progress

Improvements in ranking in a given application context does not automatically imply an improvement in the usage experience of that application, let alone discourse-level progress. Given the variation of usage contexts, and the not necessarily actual or meaningful significance of statistical significance, ranking improvement may not correspond to an improvement at the level of running systems on average. That is, while the improved ranking corresponds to a better alignment between the algorithm and the choice of the judges in a specific usage context, this may not imply anything more about a variation of that context that still corresponds to the "same" phenomenon (i.e., the results may not be sufficiently meaningful as to be readily associated with a stable minimal variation of that phenomenon). The result is therefore limited in its generalizability and in its usefulness for understanding what a differing rank actually means or explains. Thus, incremental improvement in ranking is increasingly limited in value in the modern context without being additionally valuable according to the other value categories, such as being useful for a coherent explanation of user behavior. The discovery of good ranking functions (the best set of parameters and such) can indeed be instrumental in capturing properties of a domain. However, without a supporting discourse that offers sufficient explanation (as to why things are, why they happen, or what they mean, etc), this purely technical approach, in our view, does not contribute significantly to progress. Thus, research cultures that find value almost exclusively in regular empirical improvements are not progressive.

Consider instead research cultures that find value in developing multiple varieties of modeling apparatus or theories, without the models or theories supplying insights that help explain nontrivial (and actual) search-related phenomena pertaining mainly to user behavior. As Cornelius (2002) argues, an increase in the number of theories does not necessarily imply progress; one has to make sure that the theories are created for good reason, such as that of providing a better explanation of phenomena (see chapters 3 and 4).

The growth of theory may indicate progress when the theories are solving particular problems (e.g., by explaining a phenomenon); improvements in ranking would similarly be progressive when the rankings can be explained or given additional meaning.

2.7   Conclusion

It is neither contentious nor novel, and perhaps it will never be for any discourse, to claim that the discourse must grow and change in significant ways. The challenge is instead to understand the "why" and the "how" of this change, which requires understanding first, what it means to make progress and second, how progress can be brought about. Focusing on high-level pragmatic notions of progress, this chapter discussed the overall rationality of IR&S discourse. Progress was argued to be associated with the internal and external coherency of discourse, effective construal of relevant phenomena, and proper formulation of basic concepts and with the development of explanatory discourse.

To make progress according to these concepts, focus must broaden from relating different queries to relating different contexts. This requires understanding the context/domain and relates to the understanding of tasks at a human level (before modeling them). This requirement means focusing on domain analysis: the increasingly variegated types of phenomena relevant for the study of search entail an increase in the modes of evaluation, which would tend toward the analysis of differences between contexts. Effective domain analysis depends on a discourse that is even more fundamental: the overarching discourse we call a foundational discourse.[45] Chapters 3 and 4 refine these notions of coherence in a more formal way by using concepts from the history and philosophy of science. Chapter 5 elaborates on what effective construal and objectification mean for a network of foundational concepts.

---

45. Thus, instead of being a peripheral and optional research activity, domain analysis would become a necessary method for ensuring the coherence of claims and hence for fulfillment of aim 1. This requirement agrees with is Zhai (2011) and Järvelin (2011), who favor a task-based understanding of search, since understanding task structure beyond its significance for an ad hoc research scenario that focuses on the pragmatic is akin to studying a domain context beyond its system aspect.

3 From Growth to Progress I: Methodology for Understanding Progress

3.1 Introduction: Can IR&S Be Analyzed Using Ideas from the History and Philosophy of Science?

The question of progress is paramount to the enterprise of science, because as it is usually understood, "science is often distinguished from other domains of human culture by its progressive nature; in contrast to other endeavors, there exist clear standards or normative criteria for identifying improvements and advances in science" (Niiniluoto, 2011). Although this view of science can easily be challenged, it would be difficult to deny that progress (or advancement, or improvement) is a crucial value to scientific practice. Thus the study of scientific progress forms a central aspect of the discourse on the history and philosophy of science (HPoS).

The judgment of progress depends on analyzing the value and causes of developments in scientific discourse and practice, an analysis that is primarily historical. These developments may be caused by matters that can be understood as internal to science, such as empirical discoveries and theoretical reformulations, but also by relatively external matters, such as socioeconomic factors (Gavroglu et al., 1989, pp. 205–228).[1]

This chapter asks the question of what defines progress in IR&S from the perspective of discourses in HPoS, which are the traditional source of discussions about progress of scientific and science-like disciplines. The aim is to comparatively understand the analysis of IR&S from internal discourses as highlighted in chapter 2 with a more mainstream, explicit, and (as will

---

1. As Falzon et al. (2013, pp. 207–209) argue, the criteria for choosing one theory over another (an event signifying an instance of scientific development) "are never wholly determinate by autonomously existing empirical data, and the ultimate criteria of progress are in some significant measure internal to a research program, paradigm, or web of belief."

be explained later) a more fine-grained discourse about progress. The result is that some of the conclusions in chapters 1 and 2, such as that about the need and place of foundations research in the modern context, are given further weight from a mainstream analytical discourse of a HPoS variety that is tailored to understanding, in particular, appraising scientific discourse.

But why should techniques from HPoS be relevant for IR&S? Does IR&S not have to be a science for this to apply? Whether IR&S should be understood to constitute a science and what kind of science it may be are fundamental yet unresolved questions. These questions, initially posed in chapter 2, are further studied in chapter 5, but for the purposes of this section, we contend that for a science-like discipline, the tools for analyzing science can perhaps be used to enlighten discussions therein about progress (and other matters relevant to science).

This contention rests on two premises. First, in the case of IR&S, the use of theories and mathematical models,[2] the conducting of empirical research, and the concern with progress are properties shared with the sciences, which make IR&S science-like. Second, as demonstrated in chapter 2, apart from being dependent on the coherence of discourse and accurate phenomena construal, progress in IR&S was derived as being increasingly tied to the strength of explanatory research over and above instrumental research. In seeking explanations for phenomena in this way, IR&S shares one of the main aims of science (Randolph Mayes, 2015), which also makes it like science.

The HPoS discourse exhibits methodologies and frameworks for appraising science that seek to clarify whether a discourse, especially one that is already deemed science-like, is ultimately scientific (Hansson, 2015). The proposition that IR&S is science-like is a typical one that could be both evaluated using methods therein as to its meaning and truth, and further developed to explore the different senses of what it could mean for IR&S to be scientific.

An important characteristic for a discourse to actually be scientific beyond being science-like is that it undergoes progressive (self-conscious and self-evaluative) growth (Hansson, 2015). This is since even with theoretical models, and the seeking of explanations, sciences are attributed with a culture (and continual process) of internal evaluation of the concepts, claims, and methodologies, through which the scientific discourse (and hence science) grows. This internally reflective evaluative process does not only refer to critiquing individual claims, but to overall paradigms

---

2. Specifically, set-theoretic models, which are common to the sciences according to the semantic conception of science, see section 1.1.3.2.

that are based on basic (e.g., ontological, epistemological, and other methodological) assumptions that mediate discourse.

As chapter 1 argued, understanding what progressive growth means for IR&S is a foundational concern that remains unresolved. Addressing it is the reason for this book. However, in addition to being a foundational question, understanding what progressive growth means and then determining whether it is actually happening are necessary for understanding and deciding about the scientific status of IR&S.

To motivate the relevance of the HPoS perspective and methodology of appraisal for IR&S, section 3.2 discusses the place of two methods of historical analysis, the internal and external, and the relevance of several works in IR&S that employ such methods to understand the discipline. It then explains the overall strategy for adopting HPoS ideas from the perspective of an internal history. Section 3.3 discusses the meaning and importance of the alternative external history relative to the internal in the context of IR&S. The internal and external histories are ways of understanding scientific change. By comparing different internal understandings of scientific change, section 3.4 argues for an idea of change that is particularly suited to IR&S.

3.2   Appraising Science by Historical Analyses

There are many approaches to appraising science. They consist mainly of understanding scientific change (Niiniluoto, 2011). The historicist approach of Imre Lakatos[3] was selected for use in this book due to it being (1) more complete as a technique of appraisal than prior works (such as Kuhn, Popper, and others), (2) commented on and developed through numerous routes after Lakatos, and (3) applied in areas well beyond the natural sciences, such as economics (Khalil, 1987; Caldwell, 1991; Gonzalez, 2014), psychology (Meehl, 1978, 1990; Dar, 1987) and international relations (Elman and Elman, 2003).

As IR&S is closer to being a social science than a natural one, this last aspect was of particular influence. Lakatos's approach merges ideas about the structure of science from Kuhn (and Polanyi) with ideas about

3. While the use of historical episodes in science for making philosophical arguments about it are common, historicist approaches to understanding science take historical data to intimately constitute or support the rationality pervading that science (Matheson and Dallmann, 2015).

theory appraisal from Popper, to create a way of appraising scientific discourses: his methodology of scientific research programs (MSRP). Lakatos categorizes the types of historical analysis used to understand scientific development in terms of the resultant histories they produce: the internal and the external histories (Lakatos, 1971). Internal histories chart developments in scientific practice, whereas external histories consider outside factors that influence practice. Whereas an internal history would explain how a particular theory superseded another based on key experiments or the solutions of equations, the external history would instead focus on, for example, the econo-political situation that may have influenced scientists to prefer one set of scientific practices over another.

This distinction is useful for understanding IR&S discourse. For example, several works of critical history in the IS tradition, such as Day's (2008) work, can be considered as external histories. Yet it would be difficult to locate works of internal history. And it is this internal history that is for Lakatos the backbone of history, playing the key role in understanding scientific development. The external for him is secondary, at most aiding disambiguation when an internal history is insufficiently explanatory. Although distinguishing between the relatively more internal versus the relatively more external influences of scientific practice is immensely useful for understanding how a discourse is formed, this distinction can only be a loose one for IR&S discourse. It can be difficult to distinguish whether a change in scientific practice in IR&S is mainly due to reasons internal to the science or due to external influence. In addition, unlike Lakatos, we think that the external history is at least as important as the internal one.[4] This is because IR&S discourse is intimately tied to the use of search (and other information) technologies, and so the phenomena investigated stem from a rich mix of interactions among people, technologies, and social structures. Thus an internal history of IR&S, for example, of the theoretical development of mathematical frameworks for search, is intimately tied to the changing needs of users, which are due to changing contexts of technology-use, which are in turn driven by the external factor of changing social contexts. That IR&S discourse constitutes a mix of discourses—from those about social and cultural factors affecting technology-use (usually studied in IS) to those about technical aspects (usually investigated in IR)—attests to this close relationship between the external and internal.

---

4. Further discussion and critique of this dichotomy beyond its relation to IR&S can be found in Kulka (1977, p. 326).

3.2.1   This Work as a Rational Reconstruction

Nevertheless, in addition to being able to categorize particular IS works as external histories, Lakatos's classification has led us to understand the nature of chapters 1 and 2 as an exercise in understanding the internal history (Lakatos, 1971, p. 91) of IR&S, and in particular, as an attempt to develop a rational reconstruction of IR&S. The rational reconstruction of discourse is a restructuring of it to understand it as a coherent rational discourse. In the case of science, rational discourse is constituted by theories, propositions, paradigms, and such, and processes of theory choice, observation, and experimentation, and so forth. Rational reconstructions aim to be objective reconstructions: they are narratives about scientific practice based on arguments and evidence that are based on critical interpretation of discourse (and other accounts of practice). Thus narratives are open to critique and change based on further interpretive arguments until a consensus is reached about their appropriateness. This procedure is unlike a more subjective account of scientific practice. A rational reconstruction of a science can be understood as a narrative about what scientists do and why they do it, and ideally an agreed-on story that demonstrates that there are good reasons (e.g., seeking to improve techniques or make progress in some other way) for what they do so as to give weight to their findings and to the rationality (and perhaps coherence and truth) of their discourse.

In this regard, for example, chapter 2 can be understood to have summarized the normative methodology or overall rationality of the discourse and practice surrounding the empirical aspect of IR&S, focusing on high-level pragmatic notions of progress. Progress was argued to be associated with (1) creating coherency in discourse, (2) developing discourse that is more explanatory (answering "why" and "what it means" questions over and above "how" questions), and (3) focusing research discourses on the particulars about phenomena construal. These goals, summarizing the three main aims (see section 2.1) and other research objectives in chapter 2, can also be understood as rational explanations for the growth of discourse (objective knowledge). That is, they at least partially explain why IR&S researchers do what they do, and why particular research trends exist and not others. In addition to this high-level account about overall discourse, the goals inform the relatively lower level of practice, helping explain why particular theories or experimental/empirical setups constituting discourse were selected over others in the context of scientific practice. These goals offer an initial rational reconstruction for the development of an internal history of IR&S.

This chapter and the next take on the task of rational reconstruction more explicitly. They supplement and refine these rational explanations—as goals, aims, or notions of progress—for the growth of discourse in terms of their constituent elements. These chapters focus on theories and theory change as a relatively low-level perspective on what progressive growth can mean for IR&S. It is "lower" because it focuses on the constituent elements of these relatively higher-level goals. The constituent elements correspond to 'units of practice', meaning that each new piece of research in IR&S is developed with respect to models and theories about query–document relations, users, experimental scenarios, and so on, and not in terms of high-level research trends (as in chapter 2). Each new such research is (usually) not done with the aim of coherence (i.e., it does not take as its scope the whole discipline). It is instead undertaken to create a new theory that better explains some specific element, is an explicit construal of a phenomenon, or is a more coherent expression of a relationship between relevant elements (e.g., query and document). Chapter 4 ventures to a lower level still, exploring the propositions that theories generate as a means for developing a more detailed understanding of what theories do.

Central to the rational reconstruction of a discourse is understanding why one theory is preferred over another. While the notions of progress in chapter 2 suggest such theory preferences—such as preferring a theory as it explains more than another—this chapter elucidates the preference explicitly. In particular, it discusses different reasons for theory choice and the various ideas about why scientific change happens. However, actual theories and models of IR&S are not explicitly dealt with here or in chapter 4. Although more extensive studies could be of use to develop a more refined understanding of appraisal and progress for IR&S, this is not necessary for the key arguments of this book.

Because it is supposed to reveal the rationality of theory choice, a rational reconstruction should rationally explain what is meant by the terms and basic concepts used in discourse. The understanding of basic concepts through the practice of foundational research can then be seen as part of rational reconstruction. All of this book can be seen as an exercise in such a reconstruction. With respect to the arguments of prior chapters about the need for foundational research, both the external and internal histories are important for understanding the precise place, importance, and nature of the foundations of IR&S. This is in particular due to the mixed nature of the relevant phenomena. However, the internal history has a specific role here. As discussed in this chapter, the internal history reveals the interaction between the foundational part of a discourse (which address foundational questions) and the nonfoundational parts as the discourse grows and changes. External histories, as section 3.3 elaborates, show how basic concepts enter into the discourse and what they come to mean. Although external histories do exist for aspects of IR&S, internal histories are lacking and therefore must be created for a more complete picture of discourse. Chapters 3 and 4 work together to develop an initial such history based on some of the evidence about IR&S discourse explored in chapter 2.

3.2.2   Adopting the Basic Structure of an Internal History

There are particular challenges to adopting the idea of internal histories from HPoS for IR&S. Earlier HPoS scholars dismissed the application of their methods, which were meant for the natural sciences, to the social sciences. Internal histories are constituted by theories, propositions, and facts, where the types of theories/propositions applicable to the natural sciences differ from those in the humanities and social sciences. There are differences not only in the types of phenomena they address, but also in how their discourse develops. Kuhn identifies a significant such distinction, arguing that (broadly speaking) while continuous reinterpretation is normal scientific practice in the social sciences, the natural sciences instead construct an overall interpretation (a paradigm) and then work on details, slowly accumulating facts (Bird, 2013). If a natural science incurs a (nontrivial) change in its overall narrative, a reinterpretation results, but this tends to be an infrequent event, a revolution[5] corresponding to a paradigm shift.

Where IR&S fits among the social and natural sciences is a foundational question about what kind of science IR&S is. This question remains unresolved (see chapters 5 and 6). The difficulty in answering this question is partially due to the mixed nature of the phenomena dealt with: In addition to social phenomena, IR&S deals with artificial phenomena generated by technological designs. The regular and well-defined nature of artificial phenomena generally make them more similar to phenomena in the natural world than in the social world. But because the goal of IR&S is to understand contexts of technology-use and to create systems to satisfy users, the discourse studies social and cognitive phenomena, which are therefore primary in some sense. This makes IR&S as a whole closer to being a social science or humanities discipline than a natural science. Furthermore, IR&S is a young discipline, and even if one were to focus on its IR

---

5. Many of Kuhn's ideas can be traced back to the work of Micheal Polanyi (1964, 1967).

aspect (which is more natural scientific) identifying revolutions in it (were there to be any) is not a clear-cut task. As a result, whether the pattern for IR&S should be that of periodic revolutions interspersed with normal science or continuous reinterpretation is not clear. What kind of patterns can develop for such mixed discourses remains a foundational question. Regardless of how the discourse develops, both instrumental and social development are of crucial value. And so the discourse is dependent on both modeling paradigms (as are the natural sciences) and effective phenomena construal/re-interpretation (like the humanities and social sciences).

In light of this quality of sharing properties with the natural and social sciences, this chapter generalizes three aspects from Lakatos's idea of internal history. These aspects can be understood to apply to both types of sciences (Lakatos and Musgrave, 1970; Lakatos et al., 1980; Larvor, 1998; Matheson and Dallmann, 2015). They are aspects this chapter further develops for the IR&S context in order to refine the understanding of the current state of IR&S discussed in chapter 2. In particular, these aspects are used in chapter 4 to understand types of growth in IR&S, and the idea of progressive growth, which is a refinement of the notions of progress developed in chapter 2. These aspects are:

1. Any significant discourse is constituted by a hard core (or inner core) of propositions and concepts, around which a discourse revolves and a protective belt of theories, models, hypotheses, and facts that support this center. This protective belt denotes the positive heuristics or possible directions for research.[6] For the purposes of this text, this hard core will be known as the inner network and the protective belt as the outer network.

2. This overall structure (or discourse)—both the outer core (the network of theories, facts, and hypotheses), and the inner core (albeit less readily)—changes in different ways over time.

3. Not all such changes nor all corresponding states of discourse imply overall progress.

The first aspect categorizes the static structure of discourse, and as the next section argues, this inner network corresponds to our notion of foundational discourse. The outer network consists of the less or nonfoundational discourses that depend on (and strengthen) the foundational. The

---

6. For Lakatos, positive heuristics are based on the hard core (they are on top of the hard core), and act to lead researchers to create (to posit) the theories, models, hypotheses, and so on, that form this protective belt (Lakatos et al., 1980, p. 48).

second aspect categorizes the dynamic character (i.e., changes and growth) of discourse. The third aspect is the ethical aspect. It is about the value of a state or the value of a growth as characterized by the static and dynamic structures, respectively. Therefore, the state of a discourse or a growth therein is not automatically "good" and should instead be evaluated to understand its worth.

The first two aspects characterizing scientific practice are useful by themselves, as they indicate how parts of a discourse are related (whether they are part of the outer or inner networks) and help characterize changes in discourse (e.g., one brought on by a new and popular research trend) in terms of inner or outer changes. They are important basic characterizations for understanding the nature and development of scientific activity. For example, chapter 2 characterized particular research trends as construal seeking (aim 2 in chapter 2), coherence seeking (aims 1 and 2 in chapter 2), or explanation seeking (see section 2.5). These trends were understood as being explicitly and implicitly sought by IR&S researchers in modern times. That a trend tends to improve construal or explanatory richness is an interpretation pertaining to (or a rational reconstruction of positive heuristics indicating) the benefits sought by research. It is also possible to reconstruct from the analysis of these trends something about the hard core—about presumed basic concepts, such as that current construals do not depict the relevant or the desired phenomena adequately. The investigation of these trends in terms of the growth of theories and propositions—for which this chapter and the next provide a framework—works to clarify what the trends mean and thus to clarify the goals of overall discourse. In addition to having separate uses, the first two aspects are required for understanding the third aspect, for understanding what it means for these goals to be met and hence what it means for there to be progress, and whether progress is being made.

Whereas scientific discourse (i.e., theoretical or empirical activity) can be understood to always correspond to a growth of theories, facts, and propositions, HPoS discourses claim that not all growth is "good" (i.e., sufficiently valuable); that not all growth indicates progress.

3.2.3 From "What Is Progress?" to "What Could Progress Mean?"

To judge whether a growth of the discourse is progressive or not, HPoS discourses engage in evaluative judgments (Rescher, 2000, p. 53) about the state of a discipline. These judgments involve assessing the value of perceived changes in the research content pertaining to growth. The goal here is more modest. First, in this chapter we seek to understand through interpretive judgment—through understanding what something could mean as opposed to following the more direct route of deducing what it is—what progress could mean for IR&S in terms of scientific practice. To judge whether something is the case, it is assumed that the different possibilities of what it could be are well understood (as to what they mean). This is however not the case for the notion of progress in IR&S. The different possibilities are not clear, and therefore require to first be made clear before some of them are chosen to be the best representative of "what progress is." Understanding what progress could mean therefore precedes judgment about what it is. In particular, progress is understood in terms of the changes happening to scientific discourse. Scientific discourse reflects practice, and in this chapter we understand discourse to be based on theories. Chapter 4 refines this understanding of discourse, in terms of specific ways in which IR&S discourse could grow, and in terms of what effects progressive growth leads to, for example, explaining user behavior or developing systems designs. Second, this chapter's goal is to develop support for the understanding of progress developed in chapter 2, wherein progress meant (or was indicated by) foundational and construal-based research, explanatory research, and research that leads to a more coherent discourse.

Apart from the work of Brookes (1980a), it is difficult to locate brief analyses—let alone substantial attempts—that adopt HPoS methods for understanding progress in IR&S. The remainder of this chapter (from section 3.4), as well as the following chapter, take Brookes' work as a point of departure in IR&S, supplant it with a version of Lakatos's idea of internal history extended and generalized for purpose, and proceeds to develop an idea of what progress could mean for IR&S. Following analogous arguments in chapter 2, we then discuss in particular what progress means in the current context.

What progress means is not restricted to theory change and other aspects internal to a science, but instead, (especially for disciplines involving technology such as IR&S) relates to external factors, such as emerging application contexts (e.g., ubiquitous and pervasive technology-use). External histories of science pick up on such external factors and are a crucial complement to internal histories.

3.3   External Histories: Understanding Socio-Technical Change

External histories of science seek first to identify particular human activities, sublanguages, ideas, and concepts that correspond to the "doing" of a particular type of science, and associate it to socio-political, economic, cultural, and even urban and architectural factors that function as its condition of possibility that enable the science to exist and grow. Internal histories can be understood as a natural extension of external ones, focusing on the internal rationality particular to a science beyond such enabling factors.

The pervasive modern technologies that IR&S seeks to create—and the mixed phenomena with which it is concerned—means that researchers in the field perceive the social and technical to be intricately linked. It means that the factors particular to an external history of IR&S directly condition, (1) the creation of technology resulting from IR&S research, and (2) the analyses of the socio-technical sphere common to IR&S. Furthermore, external factors condition the value of (1) and (2) and are tightly linked to what the technology created means (see chapter 2's discussion of construal) in the rational discursive processes internal to IR&S.

That IR&S corresponds to an entire range of discourses, from technical IR works to social and humanistic IS works, is indicative of this close connection. Hence any account of IR&S discourse must contain a rational reconstruction of scientific activity therein. However, it must then also connect this to a relatively more external account of the socio-technical context that conditioned the need for the corresponding technology, technology policy and aspects that IR&S discourse addresses and affects. Both Lakatos's idea that a sharp distinction can be made between internal and external histories and his insistence that the internal (the mathematically representable theoretical structures) corresponds to the rational aspect of a science's history, do not fully capture the nature of IR&S.

There are several works in IR&S, or IS specifically, that can be understood as external histories. Day (2008) articulates socioeconomic factors that conditioned the development of key notions that IR&S is founded on; Day conducts an external analysis of the development of both the social side of IR&S (i.e., IS-oriented developments) and the empirical-theoretical side of IR&S (i.e., IR). Of particular importance is that Day understands the intricate connection between the social and the technical, which Lakatos's dichotomy does not recognize for scientific discourses, a connection that the external perspective brings to the fore.

As previously contended, internal histories are important for understanding growth and progress in the sciences. The lack of corresponding works for IR&S is a raison d'être of this book. However, to place the internal perspective of this and the following chapters in the context of the important connection in IR&S between the internal and external, section 3.3.1 briefly explores the external perspective. In particular, the perspective of external histories is explored by introducing a representative external method of historical analysis, derived in part from the work of Foucault, that is foundational for what is today known as critical theory. Critical theory is a major methodological influence in the history of the arts; cultural and anthropological studies, and critical-historical IS works such as that of Day. Section 3.3.1 introduces the main aspects of Foucault's methodology as a methodology for external history, while section 3.3.2 discusses its relation to critical theory. Sections 3.3.3 and 3.3.4 discuss how the analyses based on such methodology relate to foundational research and in what way they are relevant for modern IR&S practice, respectively. Finally, section 3.3.5 comments on the complementary nature of internal and external histories in the IR&S context.

3.3.1   Foucauldian Methodology for External Histories
Foucault, influenced by Canguilhem, Bachelard, and the French HPoS tradition (Gutting, 1989), developed the archaeological method, a method of analysis seeking to uncover the "epistemological conditions of possibility—the 'historical a prioris' " on which a set of discourses may be based (Garland, 2014, p. 369). These conditions of possibility, or "a prioris," are distinctive epistemological structures or epistemes corresponding to different historical contexts. They condition the formation of discourse if not quite determining the consciousness of thinkers/scholars themselves. Foucault used this method to classify different historical periods in European thought as corresponding to "different ways of ordering thought and producing discourse"(Garland, 2014, p. 370). Also attributed to Foucault but influenced much by the classic work of Nietschze (Mahon, 1992; Visker, 1995) is the complementary genealogical method, which traces contemporary institutions and practices to their emergence from "specific struggles, conflicts, alliances, and exercises of power, many of which are nowadays forgotten" (Garland, 2014, p. 374), in order to understand a "history of the present" (Roth, 1994).

Whereas archaeology aims to show structural order and discontinuities that differentiate present from past, genealogy instead elaborates on how "the contingencies of these processes continue to shape the present" (Garland, 2014, p. 371), that is, the dependence of contemporary practices on historical conditions of existence (Garland, 2014, p. 373). These methods are not employed to read present-day socio-cultural configurations into historical scenarios, so as to claim earlier phenomena as having a nature and significance similar to present phenomena. Nor are they intended for conducting the standard historical analysis task of questioning past narratives based on present-day interests. They are instead used to allow Foucault to effectively trace the development of a modern-day question or problem (Garland, 2014, p. 367).

3.3.2 Critical Theory and External History

Foucault's methods are a foundational aspect of the critical-theoretic method of analysis (Corradetti, 2012). As exemplified particularly by the works of Day (2008, 2014), critical theory is a popular analytic method in IS discourses. In *The Modern Invention of Information* Day (2008) seeks to trace/uncover the different streams of discourse/thought—mainly but not exclusively those constituting IR&S—that lead to the modern invention of the notion of information. Day adopts the critical method much influenced by Foucault, in both the archaeological and genealogical sense of trying to understand how contemporary IR&S emerged from discourses in the twentieth century.

As is typical for works following the critical method, the historical contingency of aspects of discourse (e.g., the key concepts and their meanings) is revealed through excavating the socio-political/cultural processes that condition the formation of a discourse. Day (2008) demonstrates the contingent nature of the shaping of the idea of information in IR&S. Discovering the contingency of such aspects leads to the questioning of the present situation in the corresponding discourse conditioned by those contingent aspects. In particular, it leads to the questioning of a situation that emerged genealogically from past processes. In the context of IR&S in Day (2008) this means that past socio-political factors (that may or may not still be relevant) are sedimented (Gutting, 1989, pp. 77–78; Flynn, 2011) not only within the received basic concepts (e.g., information, document, user, query, and context) but also within the values and attitudes shared among practitioners. Thus, they will be reflected in the discourse.

The process of understanding the way in which received discourse is contingent corresponds to a process of questioning the modern discourse. This means to not take its aspects as given and instead to adopt a critical attitude. This is crucial, because it enables and encourages the widest possible foundational questions which pertain to the purposes and conditions of possibility of the discourse. A conceptualization of the purpose of a discourse affects everything from its epistemology, ontology, methodology, and methods, to the meaning of its technical vocabulary. Furthermore, as chapters 1 and 2 argued the modern socio-technical context leads the discourse toward addressing foundational questions. This demonstrates the contemporary importance and relevance of works of critical-historical analysis as a complementary means to understand foundations, and therefore as a means to envision future directions for discourse that will be intricately conditioned by how foundational questions are addressed.

3.3.3   External Historical Analyses in Service of Foundations Research

In addition to understanding the processes that conditioned the present state of discourse, historical analysis allows disparate and forgotten ideas to be brought to light, which is of particular benefit if there is a similarity between past and modern contexts. An example of such an idea is that of the basic notion of the document, several meanings of which are discussed in Buckland (1997). In particular, Briet's work on documentation (see Briet et al., 2006) understands documents as objects taking different meanings depending on cultures (i.e., not only with respect to their linguistic content but also as a whole). Specifically, she takes the document to be "any concrete or symbolic indexical sign, preserved or recorded toward the ends of representing, of reconstituting, or of proving a physical or intellectual phenomenon." (Briet et al., 2006, p. 10) That it can correspond to "'examples'—or 'evidence'—of things or larger groupings of things" such that "a star is not a document, but a photograph of a star is; a pebble isn't a document, but a pebble in a mineralogical collection is; a wild animal isn't a document, but an animal in a zoo is" (Briet et al., 2006, p. 48). By excavating origins and genesis of basic notions, external histories form a crucial aspect of foundational research.

While Otlet (1990), Briet's predecessor and a visionary information scientist, took the book as *the* unit of scholarship—as "the document"—and the main constituent of a highly networked information-based society, Briet instead understood the book's form as being "dispersed in other documentary forms more suited to a networked and 'revolutionary' mode of intellectual production" (Briet et al., 2006, p. 52, Rayward, 2008).[7]

The book, as the document, the unit of scholarship, and the key constituent of information-based society, also represents the thing or part that is to be analyzed to understand the whole; it depicts the granularity of analysis. With their (different) respective understandings of this unit, Otlet and Briet can be understood as questioning and reconstructing/reconstruing the form and granularity of the unit of analysis by which to understand the world of information. Their ventures are useful for contemporary discourse due to the (varied) conclusions they reached, and also due to the particular foundational research attitude that lead them to question basic notions in the first place.

---

7. The revolutionary style was attributed to the natural sciences rather than to the social sciences. Prefigured in this attribution is an understanding of the nature of progress in science as incremental but punctuated by revolutions, an idea popularized by Kuhn and discussed below.

What is of particular relevance to the modern context with respect to documents is their cultural content, the meaning of a document in a system, over and above its keyword representation (as is the default meaning in the more positivistically inclined culture of IR). As chapter 1 discussed, the ubiquity of information-based devices makes relevant the question of what information is when it is seen as the content of documents, and how a document—as a response from the system to a query—can be understood given the myriad forms of interaction. That is, how should a document be construed? What would an effective construal (i.e., as per the aim of discourse, cf. chapter 2) be like?

Otlet's vision, even if overshadowed by Briet's far-reaching vision of documentation, remains relevant due to (1) its attitude of bold questioning, and (2) its conclusions about the nature of the document or the "unit of scholarship." In addition, the effect of combining (1) and (2), is to question the grander structure of the institutional setup of a networked information based society[8]—This can be seen as a necessary task—an extended domain analysis[9]—for understanding the meaning of documents. Behind Otlet's grander question is an architectural and urban vision (Rayward, 2008; Buckland, 2012; Van Acker, 2012), which in turn is based on utopian *world pictures* supported by enlightenment values (Andersen and Andersen, 1918), which are in turn supported by a worldview that assigns significant value to the sharing of information/knowledge. If a similar investigation were attempted today, it would also include diverse issues, such as the relationship between information systems and types of urban spaces, modern architectural philosophies expressed in particular architectural designs (libraries and learning spaces or other spaces), and the kinds of information behavior they encourage. It would also address what "the document" becomes in such a context.

Take, for example, the modern trend in understanding insights generated by big data as ground-truth, as an epistemological necessity for judging the state of real-world processes, from business processes to social media trends. This is arguably coherent with Otlet's positivistic worldview, because

1. Otlet understood scholarly works as being the main raw material through which the world is to be "automatically understood" through computational procedures creating insights out of them, and

---

8. This concept is treated at length by Castells (2000).

9. Recall from chapter 2 that the literature on domain analysis holds that understanding the collection and domain are of prime importance for understanding documents and

2. underlying big data and data-driven approaches is the tendency to imagine that computational statistical processes will reveal patterns in the data sufficient for understanding it (Frické, 2015).

While Otlet focused on scholarly works and the automatic answering of big questions, the big-data approach is generic: it seeks to answer arbitrary questions with any and all relevant data captured about the world. In both cases, there is a need to build narratives from data, which then allow questions to be answered and through which the world is understood. However, the automatic discovery of statistical patterns in either case is generally insufficient: layers of analysis, scientific reasoning, and interpretation—beyond computational pattern-finding—are necessary for nontrivial applications (Frické, 2015). These layers are often not mentioned explicitly; they exist tacitly. In both cases, the idea is that objective (computational) analysis of "things out there" are sufficient to address problems, a positivistic idea that ignores the dimension of human interpretation. In this way, relating between the historically held assumptions and modern trends, as revealed by uncovering relatively external factors (worldview, etc.), allows for a better understanding of the foundational aspects of modern trends.

3.3.4   Modern Application Contexts Demand Serious External Historical Analysis

Conducting a history of the present reveals the epistemes: the architectural, urban design, and enlightenment metaphors; ideas and values that are presupposed in modern industry and research trends. Such excavations allow identification of restrictive patterns of thought, the reengagement with presuppositions that may engender useful narratives for modern programs, and the discovery of useful relations/differentiations among several modern trends. This examination is particularly important: as chapter 2 explained, construal of basic phenomena and explanatory research are crucial for progress.

"Construal" here means to dig up the presentations of phenomena beyond their current reduced representational forms. It is to not take the presentations as given—to the extent that they can be understood from mere representations—and instead to seek to reinterpret the relevant

---

correctly interpreting their relevance informaton (such as what relevance judges have decided about them). In turn, this understanding is important for the evaluation of IR systems that depend on these notions.

phenomena by first identifying them from the world (or from a particular perspective of the world) and then discovering their various attributes. This arguably requires a broader outlook than Otlet and Briet present. It may not be sufficient to go back to the concepts and conclusions of Otlet and Briet and their underlying architectural/urban-theory notions that are contingent on their corresponding presupposed worldviews. Instead it may be necessary to go back further and thereby deepen our understanding of the genealogy of present concepts.

For example, in addition to the path leading back to Otlet and architecture, there is the hitherto unexplored path, briefly alluded to in Arafat et al. (2014), that leads back to the ars memoriae (memory arts) tradition in premodern Europe (Carruthers, 1990, 2000; Yates, 1992). The suggestion in Hjørland (2000) of taking the concept of memory institutions (e.g., libraries, archives, and museums) as a central object of study for IR&S can be understood to support the need to look at the memory arts that prefigured or were copresent with these institutions (Rossi, 2000). Chapter 6 provides some initial discussion of the important relationship between IR&S and the memory arts, especially given the envisioning of IR&S as a science of technology-mediated experience in this text. There are other unexplored paths, such as through the cultural anthropology work of Ernest Cassirer (Krois, 2002; Johnson, 2012), which also works as a precursor to modern discussions of information architecture, information visualization, augmented reality, and other technologies in IR&S. The upshot is to understand modern technologically motivated ideas and phenomena (e.g., Second Life or augmented-reality worlds) as examples of classic memory theaters (see Ong, 1971, pp. 104–112 and Bailey, 1989). As a result, useful critiques and recharacterizations of modern phenomena can be made. If the augmented-reality world that is lived in through Google glasses can be understood in dialectic with the idea of the classical memory theater, then the technological phenomenon of augmentation can be problematized through investigating, for example, the extent to which augmented reality fits the psychological phenomenon of fantasy projection (Bailey, 1989, p. 74) associated with memory theaters.

3.3.5   From External to Internal History and Scientific Progress
Internal histories focus on understanding scientific activity and in particular, scientific change and progress. These histories can be understood to complement methods influenced by or influencing the modern critical theory method. Whereas external histories focus on factors external to practice that influence practice, internal histories identify structures in the corresponding discourse (e.g., theories or propositional networks), map changes

in that discourse, and interpret the rationality of those changes with respect to an understanding of progress. Internal histories of science focus more explicitly on judgments pertaining to scientific progress—the subject of this book—than do their corresponding external histories. However, scientific progress is not an agreed-on concept.[10] But what different such concepts often have in common are a set of shared values that depict the kinds of developments that are significant versus developments that are not. Values are shared among practitioners of science and can be used to appraise, evaluate, and influence practices, technologies, and discourses. Prefigured in any internal history and notion of progress are values assumed to guide the participants of the discourse.

The proceeding details the structures, progress-related values, and other aspects used by HPoS methods of internal history to characterize scientific discourses, with the aim of explaining how they can be applied in the context of IR&S discourse.

3.4 Internal Histories: Understanding Scientific Change

There exist many theories of scientific change[11] for understanding scientific growth and progress; any internal history presupposes such a theory. Any such theory and the process of its application presuppose three requirements:

1. Identity: There has to be some idea about how to identity a discourse, about how it is to be differentiated from other discourses, so that theory of change has a context and scope;

2. Mereology or parts vs wholes: There has to be an understanding of the different types of constituents of discourse and the differing granularities therein; and

3. Change typology: There has to be an understanding of different possible changes or growth to the discourse, whether the changes are of particular value and are progressive or not, and what this means about the overall discourse or about some part of discourse.

---

10. Just as for other notions, there are several concepts of progress, each with their own archaeology and genealogy in the Foucauldian sense.

11. Works on internal histories of science, including those on understanding scientific progress (and related matter), are numerous. These works correspond to a tradition of discourse among HPoS scholars, such as Whewell, Meyerson, Duhem, Kuhn, Popper, Canguilhem, Lakatos, Laudan, and Kitcher.

The issue of identity (requirement 1), as to what does and what does not constitute IR&S discourse, is discussed in chapter 5. With respect to mereology (requirement 2), discourse constituents can be understood at different levels of granularity. A popular breakdown in order of decreasing generality is:

- discourse/discipline (as a whole),
- paradigms and superstructures (explored in section 3.4.2),
- research traditions (due to Laudan, 1989),
- research programs (due to Lakatos; Lakatos et al., 1980),
- theories, and
- propositions;

the last two being a common aspect in most mereologies. Thus one can talk about the growth of propositions constituting theories, theories constituting programs, or programs constituting disciplines.

With respect to change typology (requirement 3), there are numerous theories of scientific change, each differing according to its overall historiographical approach. Descriptive theories chart developments in some part of the discourse, whereas normative theories (which are dependent on such descriptions) argue about what progress ought to mean, and hence, articulate what the aims of discourse ought to be or what it should grow toward. Theories of change also differ according to what they hold to be the purpose of science, as to whether it is for figuring out how the world is actually configured or for making life easier through leading to the development of technologies (i.e., as per the utilitarian perspective of science). These theories also differ in what they consider to be significant with respect to change. For HPoS scholars like Kuhn, there are two overall types of significant change: the incremental change occurring in periods of normal science (Kuhn, 2012), and the revolutionary or paradigmatic changes between periods of normal science.

Other HPoS theories admit more types of change or assign change to a different part of discourse, for example, by suggesting that revolutionary change mainly pertains to one part (e.g., the inner part) of discourse (see section 3.4.3). Theories of change also differ in their understanding of why change happens, or what values or overall goals changes generally reflect. That a particular type of change occurs means for some that a new problem is being solved by the discourse, or that the solution to an existing problem is being improved in some way (Laudan, 1986). For Kitcher (1993), this improvement could pertain to explanations, conceptual understandings, and pragmatic/instrumental benefits. For others, like Whewell (see Whewell, 1847; Butts and Whewell, 1968; Losee, 2004), it mainly pertains to increased coherence or consilience of existing parts of discourse.

However, identity, mereology, and change typology are not independent presuppositions; they are mutually dependent. For example, the mereology followed by a theory of change depends on the kinds of changes that are to be demonstrated or suggested. Thus, if progressive theoretical change is to be discussed, then the discourse would be divided into theories as parts of discourse. Furthermore, the mereology depends on which parts of a discourse are identified as being central versus peripheral to a discipline. For example, the informal narratives used to introduce technical mathematical theories are not usually seen as being constituents of those theories.

This section discusses different theories of scientific change, arguing for the relevance of particular aspects over others for their application to IR&S. Section 3.4.1 summarizes the few prior research works on scientific change native to IR&S, and due to their inadequacy, motivates the need to look beyond these works. We therefore investigate a range of different HPoS approaches, beginning in section 3.4.2 by introducing Kuhn's theory of scientific change through the work of Brookes, who has previously applied it to the IR&S context. Section 3.4.3 introduces salient aspects of other HPoS works but focuses on the work of Laudan and Lakatos, which it adapts, in light of the other works, for the IR&S context in section 3.4.3.4. Section 3.4.4 further details the main adaptation, that of needing to work at a level below theories (i.e., in terms of propositions); section 3.5 concludes the chapter.

3.4.1 Prior Work on Understanding Scientific Change in IR&S

There are two broad categories of prior works in IR&S that can be seen as relevant to understanding scientific change. The first category is of works that explicitly talk about scientific change. The second consists of works that, while not explicitly characterizing change, nevertheless offer a mereology or discourse identification that can be used to understand change. Only the first category is of concern here,[12] and works therein can be further divided

---

12. With respect to this second category, works like Jansen and Rieh (2010) detail theoretical constructs used to understand the process of information retrieval. Numerous texts, such as Croft et al. (2010, pp. 233–297), expound the types of mathematical models that mediate between these constructs and technical designs and the evaluation of the system. A more focused account in this regard, pertaining to the linguistics aspects

into two types. There are works that provide generic accounts of change in IR&S,[13] or discuss the overall values-as-purposes in the growth of discourse, and then there are works explicitly adapting HPoS methods to understand this change in a detailed manner.

Works of Saracevic (1992) and Buckland (Buckland and Liu, 1998) that discuss progress in a general historical manner are examples of this first type, as is the work of Brookes (1980a,b,c). Brookes's work is influenced by Kuhn's notion of scientific change; he discusses the growth of discourse without significantly adapting it to the IR&S context. Furner's (2011) work—perhaps influenced by the work of Laudan (1986) and Kitcher (1993)—is also of this first type. It suggests several overall values or goals such that new theories fulfilling such a particular goal could be understood as instances of progressive growth in IR&S discourse.

In contrast, the works of Vakkari et al. (Vakkari and Kuokkanen, 1997; Vakkari, 1998; Vakkari and Järvelin, 2005), which explicitly attempt to understand growth of IR&S by adapting HPoS methods, constitute examples of the second type of work that explicitly adapt concepts from HPoS. In particular, Vakkari is influenced by Wagner et al.'s theory of growth in sociological discourses (Wagner and Berger, 1985), which itself is an adaptation of the HPoS work of Lakatos and Kuhn for the sociological context.

---

of those models and their background theoretical constructs, can be found in Manning et al. (2008). Additionally, detailed accounts of attempts to unify several of these models can be found in Dominich (2000) and van Rijsbergen (2004). All these works provide accounts of different types of theories constituting discourse, thereby providing an implicit mereology without explicitly discussing or problematizing mereology. In particular, Dominich (2000) and van Rijsbergen (2004) provide a mathematically structured mereology that places submodels in a larger model. However, both models and submodels here are at a similar level of granularity. This is as opposed to explicitly organizing discourse at different levels of granularity, such as understanding how these models would fit into larger theoretical schemes and how those schemes would fit into research programs.

Other than theoretical constructs for retrieval and corresponding IR models, several works discuss the types of social-scientific or humanistic theories—as opposed to mathematical theories that are more traditional in the HPoS context—employed in IR&S. Examples include Fisher et al. (2005) and Sonnenwald (2016). These works mainly provide an understanding of identity, and some minimal and indirect idea of mereology; they only provide a static picture of discourse and are not concerned about change.

13. Some works discuss change and progress in related areas, such as Hjørland (2016), but they are not sufficiently relevant to the discussion here.

Vakkari's works stand out, as they explicitly discuss mereology and change typology with respect to the growth of discourse in IR&S.

Vakkari understands IR&S discourse, information-seeking discourse in particular, to be constituted by studies pertaining to particular tasks. In addition to discussing static mereologies, Vakkari et al. (Vakkari and Kuokkanen, 1997; Vakkari, 1998; Vakkari and Järvelin, 2005) develop an understanding of the ways in which newer theories are constructed from the older ones; they take this from the change typology at the theory level found in Wagner and Berger (1985).[14] A recent development along this vein can be found in Savolainen (2016). Following Vakkari and Wagner, Savolainen provides an empirical study of the growth and development of one particular theory of information behavior throughout several decades of research.

The works of Vakkari and Savolainen are motivated by the idea that a lack of theoretical structure inhibits the reusability and coherency of research. They admit that where theory growth is not obvious—and this cannot be determined without first identifying the theoretical structures (mereology) and growth types (change types)—it is difficult to claim progress. The development of an understanding of what theory structures exist, and of what growth could mean, is therefore a prerequisite for determining whether there is progress. This motivation is not only in congruence with our book but strongly supports the direction of our overall argument.

However, a key point of difference exists between the work of Vakkari et al. and this book. It concerns the identity aspect in general—an aspect that conditions mereology and change typology. Vakkari et al. opt for Wagner's sociological model for theory growth. Although this model is useful and adequate for aspects of IR&S, and the available methodology (post-Wagner) is quite rich, it is not clear whether IR&S as a whole can be explained as sociological. Without understanding the identity aspect (i.e., what is included under IS and IR&S and what does not), it is difficult to understand what kinds of theories are adequate for characterizing phenomena relevant for IR&S. This point of difference means that particular key opinions of Vakkari et al. about theory growth, based on understanding IS

---

14. Wagner et al's theory of sociological theory growth is adapted in Vakkari and Kuokkanen (1997) to (1) analyze theories of information seeking in terms of such factors as tasks involved and information needs (Vakkari and Kuokkanen, 1997, p. 501), and to (2) understand ways in which such theories are successively modified or grow, in the discourse.

discourse as sociological, appear to us as ambiguous with respect to IR&S as a whole.[15]

As a result, it does not appear appropriate to treat the sub-discourses of IS (those that pertain to such phenomena as information seeking and behavior, etc.) as Vakkari et al. do, as sociological discourses, since phenomena therein concern not only the human but also technological aspects. Thus we selected as our point of departure not the works of Vakkari et al. and Wagner, but instead the HPoS works from which they derive (such as the work of Laudan and Lakatos). At this point—as IR&S is ostensibly a mixed-type discourse—the deeper foundational question of what kind of discourse and what kind of discipline IR&S is, is left unaddressed. Chapter 5 deals more directly with questions about identity and relevant phenomena. The remainder of this chapter and chapter 4 instead focus on developing a methodology for appraising discourse. This methodology is partially constituted by typologies characterizing aspects of discourse that are applicable to IR&S regardless of whatever final set of phenomena are chosen to be relevant.

Other than those mentioned above, to our knowledge, no significant works seek to understand progressive growth at any level of granularity in an explicit way. And out of all these works, it is Brookes's brief discussion (Brookes, 1980a) that is our main point of departure from IR&S. This is due in part to Brookes's generality of scope—covering IR&S in general—and his explicit reference to Kuhn's work, which makes it an apt point of departure for both developing (1) an understanding of Kuhn's ideas of scientific change (and its difference from other ideas of change), and (2) an idea for an

---

15. For example, Vakkari opines that progressive theory growth corresponds (although not exclusively) to the growth of empirically testable theories (known as unit-theories in Vakkari and Kuokkanen, 1997), and such theories presuppose (not necessarily intentionally specified) theoretical research programs that are seen to generate them (Vakkari and Kuokkanen, 1997, p. 512; Vakkari, 1998, p. 379; Vakkari and Järvelin, 2005, p. 115). In addition, Vakkari holds that such programs are said to be lacking in IS. That theories presuppose (not necessarily intentionally specified) research programs, and that neither empirically testable theories nor theoretical research programs are particularly common to IS discourse appear intuitively true. However, what are the kinds of theories that one should be looking for in IR&S discourse? This is an issue of theory identification. Without further study and some certainty about the kinds and structures of theories relevant to the IR&S context as a whole, understanding them from a sociological perspective is limiting and nonrepresentative—not just for IR&S as a whole but also for the more limited context of information seeking.

IR&S-specific understanding of scientific change. It is also due in part to the enduring nature of Brookes's conclusion about the state of theory-oriented IR&S discourse being in preliminary stages. Brookes (1980a) laments in the 1980s about the lack of theoretical structure in IS (although he appears to mean IR&S as a whole), something that puts it, in the language of Kuhn (as will be discussed further below), at a pretheoretical stage. This perception is repeated in the late 1990s in works by Vakkari et al., who point out the lack of theory structure and the lack of growth of empirically testable theories—which can be understood in the language of this book to constitute the outer network of discourse.

This perception, still shared in the early 2000s, motivates Ingwersen et al. (in Ingwersen and Järvelin, 2005) to develop a conceptual restructuralization of IR&S, which holds that the absence of empirically testable theories in IS implies the timeliness of conceptual work. That the absence of sufficient theoretical work may indicate a problem with the conceptual framework presupposed by theories is broadly in agreement with this book. The following two sections develop this argument more precisely. Foundational work is particularly needed, due to the current state of scientific discourse in IR&S, which lacks sufficient theoretical structure. The current state of IR&S is due in large to the particulars of the modern socio-technical context that IR&S as a whole seeks to address.

Next we discuss several popular theories of scientific change aiming to understand change in IR&S discourse. Section 3.4.2 introduces Kuhn's theory of scientific change through Brookes, while section 3.4.3 details other significant theories—most of which critically develop out of Kuhn's model—for understanding change. What follows section 3.4.3 is the development of our own perspective of change for IR&S, developed from adopting from the aforementioned theories of change (in particular from the work of Lakatos).

3.4.2 Brookes's Kuhnian Picture of Scientific Development in IR&S

Brookes's theory of scientific change identifies IR&S discourse as pertaining to the world of objective knowledge, "which is the totality of all human thought embodied in human artifacts, as in documents of course but also in music, the arts, the technologies" (Brookes, 1980a, p. 128). This is as opposed to the subjective world of mental events studied by psychology, for example or the physical world that is the subject of physics (Brookes, 1980a, p. 128). This tripartite division of reality is borrowed from Popper, who along with Kuhn, was a major influence on Brookes's HPoS.

With respect to mereology, for Brookes, IR&S discourse is a superstructure[16] that is mainly constituted by theories and a nucleus or foundation of basic assumptions that supports these theories. In turn, theories work to generate and support other elements of this superstructure, such as propositions and facts, presumably. Brookes's theory of scientific change admits change for both the superstructure (the theories and whatever they generate) and the foundations.

All three aspects of internal history (section 3.2.2)—the outer/inner static structure of discourse, change/growth of static structure and beneficial/progressive versus nonprogressive growth—can be extracted from the following paragraph expressing Brookes's Kuhnian theory of scientific development (Brookes, 1980a, p. 125):

> Once the nucleus of a new theory is discernibly coherent there are two ways in which it can develop: first, by growth of the superstructure resting on the initial foundations, so extending the range of the theory; and, secondly, by deepening or strengthening its foundations. These foundations are the set of basic assumptions initially taken to be self-evident. As long as the superstructure continues to grow freely—as long as the initial paradigm remains fruitful, no one worries unduly about the foundations. It is only when the growth of the superstructure begins to lose its first confident pace that we begin to question the basic assumptions. By this time, however, the basic assumptions have become implicit. We have to dig them up to see exactly what they are.

In particular, Brookes's distinction between two parts of discourse corresponds to aspect 1 (in section 3.2.2): the static structure of discourse. The recognition that there are different types of growth, that of the superstructure and (implicitly) that corresponding to questioning the foundations, corresponds to aspect 2: types of change. Finally, it is implicit in Brookes that not all growth corresponds to progress—a reference to aspect 3: Even though the superstructure may continue to grow, it may not do so at its old and therefore "better" pace, where this old pace is implied to be more progressive. With respect to growth, in the normal course of science it is the superstructure that grows, and when this happens, the foundation or paradigm is said to be fruitful. It is when this type of growth starts to lose its first confident pace that scientists then incline toward a different type of research, toward questioning the basic assumptions.

---

16. The idea of superstructure, that part of the whole structure that undergoes frequent change and is based on an underlying aspect that changes less frequently, appears to be borrowed from Marxist theory (Marx, 1971).

In addition to aligning with these three aspects, Brookes's Kuhnian borrowing (if understood more explicitly in its original sense according to Kuhn) admits a richer and in this case more useful characterization of scientific change. The proceeding introduces Kuhn's theory of scientific development.

3.4.2.1 Tracing Brookes back to Kuhn The notion of the paradigm, central to Kuhn's theory of change (Kuhn, 2012), is a notion that Brookes borrows from Kuhn and that appears to correspond to the combination of superstructure and foundations in the above quote. In its original sense, a paradigm can be understood in two senses:

> On the one hand, it stands for the entire constellation of beliefs, values, techniques and so on shared by the members of a given community. On the other, it denotes one sort of element in that constellation, the concrete puzzle-solutions which, employed as models or as examples, can replace explicit rules as a basis for the solution of the remaining puzzles of normal science. (Kuhn, 2012, p. 175)

In the first sense a paradigm is constituted not only by theories, laws, and their foundational suppositions (e.g. as worldviews and other basic assumptions or beliefs) but additionally includes the peripheral aspects needed to realize these elements in problem-solving applications (e.g., experimental or mathematical techniques; Bird, 2013). Kuhn explains this first sense as "what the members of a certain scientific community have in common ... the whole of techniques, patents and values shared."

The second sense of paradigm corresponds to a restricted version of the first sense, to those exemplary problem-solving examples, or "exemplary instances of scientific research" (Bird, 2013) or "the concrete puzzle-solutions" that classic texts typify.[17] These texts present a tightly knit problem-solving complex characterizing scientific practice for a particular discipline, a complex that not only solves current problems in exemplary fashion but suggests where to go next. It suggests new problems and their solutions, and furthermore, it contains the means for evaluating solutions.

The paradigm therefore is not only of mereological significance, it is also the identifier of a discourse. The paradigm in the first sense identifies a scientific discourse by a wide network of associated laws, theories,

---

17. In this way a paradigm can be understood as "a single element of a whole, say for instance Newton's Principia, which, acting as a common model or an example ... stands for the explicit rules and thus defines a coherent tradition of investigation" (Agamben 2002). A paradigm in this second sense can be understood as the typical language game (to use a Wittgensteinian concept) that characterizes a discipline (Kindi, 1995).

experimental and mathematical techniques, and in the second sense by exemplary concrete realizations of relevant scientific activity. As identifiers, paradigms also act as the differentiating factor between scientific communities. It is not that a paradigm defines by argument what a scientific discourse is or is not; instead it ostensibly indicates what a discourse/scientific activity is about.

The importance of the notion of paradigm is as the means by which the three different stages of scientific development are specified in Kuhn's theory. The first stage is denoted by a lack of consensus about what the representative paradigm is; it is when the foundations or fundamentals are still being worked out. Kuhn calls this the pre-paradigm phase, and Brookes describes it as the period "before the nucleus of a theory is discernibly coherent" (Brookes, 1980a, p. 125). It was also referred to as the pretheoretical stage in the prior section.

The second stage of development is the stage of normal science (Kuhn, 2012). This proceeds from a consensus about a paradigm (i.e., consensus about fundamentals, key theories, and the exemplary puzzle solutions). Normal science consists of the development of hypotheses or mini-theories, mathematical/experimental techniques, and all other aspects needed to apply the key theories representing the paradigm to numerous problem contexts. These contexts are specific empirical cases that resemble the exemplary instances of where the paradigm works well. These applications are human creative pursuits, and are generally not instances of rule following or algorithmically describable behavior. For Kuhn, normal science is not science guided by a coherent system of rules. The rules can instead stem from the paradigms. However, paradigms can guide the investigation without any rules. The stage of normal science results in the discovery of facts, ideas, and propositions and in changes to mini-theories and other aspects.

What proceeds from normal science is a third and final stage of development, during a crisis when anomalies begin to accrue, there is a revolution. While the period of crisis and revolution are two distinct periods, the crisis period will be understood here as part of the revolution period—as its beginning. The revolutionary period is when an entire paradigm is dropped for a rival paradigm, which can happen for many reasons. It is usually since the new paradigm solves more problems or solves old problems more effectively, or addresses the anomalies in the existing paradigm. The notion of paradigm then captures the identity, mereology, and change-typology aspects of Kuhn's theory of scientific change.

To what extent is Brookes's Kuhnian picture, whether as described by Brookes or some form of the richer original picture alluded to above, useful for developing an IR&S-specific understanding of change? It is argued below that Brookes's Kuhnian picture is inadequate for extrinsic and intrinsic reasons. The extrinsic reasons are those for which Kuhn's picture is problematic for describing change. These reasons are explored in comparison with other theories of change in section 3.4.3, where other HPoS scholars will disagree with Kuhn by suggesting a different structuralization of his paradigm characterizing the mereology change narrative. The intrinsic reasons for inadequacy are particular to Brookes and his analysis of IR&S. They are explored in the section 3.4.2.2.

3.4.2.2 Limitations of Brookes's picture Brookes's picture does not adequately represent the state of IR&S discourse with respect to its current stage of growth. This is because (1) the configuration of socio-technical phenomena in modern times (relevant for IR&S) and (2) the development of IR&S since Brookes have resulted in a context sufficiently different from the one in which Brookes worked. The first factor is due to the radical change in the human–machine relationship and the new types of phenomena that are therefore now addressed by IR&S (e.g., ubiquitous computing applications). The second factor means that Brookes's suggestion that IR&S is at the initial (meaning pretheoretical or preparadigmatic) stage of growth does not automatically apply to a discourse several decades into the future.

The first factor questioning the inadequacy of Brookes's theory perhaps does not require much justification, but it is alluded to when discussing some of the particulars of the modern context in chapter 5. With respect to the second factor, Brookes says about the foundations of IR&S in 1980 that there are no foundations, and so there is nothing to "dig up" (Brookes, 1980a, p. 128):[18] which leads him to propose a foundation (i.e., several foundational questions and corresponding positions), for example, on the kinds of phenomena with which IR&S should be concerned. However, it is difficult to maintain that modern IR&S still lacks any foundation. Whether foundation is defined as mathematical, theoretical, or premathematical/prerepresentational (as in this text), positions on foundational questions exist in the discourse for many basic questions. This is evidenced by several studies (Fisher et al., 2005; Ibekwe-SanJuan and Dousa, 2014), and for example, the discussion in chapter 2. Therefore if a

---

18. Brookes holds that "information science floats in a philosophical limbo. It has no theoretical foundations. That fact at least simplifies my present problems—there is nothing first to dig up! The ground is already clear" (Brookes, 1980a, p. 128).

foundation for IR&S were sought today, it is not that one would have to start afresh but instead will have to begin by "digging it up." That is what this book is doing, not only for the question of progress in IR&S on which it focuses but also more briefly for other questions (see chapter 5).

Furthermore, while Brookes's suggestion that IR&S is at the initial stages of growth may appear to be supported by recent works of Vakkari and Ingwersen (Vakkari and Kuokkanen, 1997; Ingwersen and Järvelin, 2005; see also section 3.4.1), there are in fact some important differences. For Vakkari et al., IS (information seeking in particular) is said to be lacking empirically testable theories and hence theory growth, while Ingwersen et al.'s conclusion given Vakkari's point is that more conceptual work is in order. In Vakkari's case, unlike for Brookes, it is not that the foundations (e.g., metatheoretical accounts) do not exist, but that not much has happened on top of this. In contrast, for Ingwersen (whose remit is not just IS but IR&S as a whole), it is as if some foundation does exist but is inadequate and therefore an entire foundation has to be redeveloped. However, these differences are based on differing background conceptions about the structure of scientific discourse and about how that can change. While Brookes's Kuhnian theory requires a stable foundation for theory growth, Vakkari's theory, following Wagner's sociological discourse theory, would admit growth at the metatheory level with or without complementary growth at the "higher" level of empirical/testable theories. The relation between the foundational and nonfoundational aspects differs between Brookes/Kuhn and Vakkari/Wagner, and Ingwersen appears to follow Wagner (through Vakkari).

That IR&S is at a preparadigmatic stage is therefore difficult to maintain, but that foundational work is required (albeit not because no foundation exists, but because whatever exists is inadequate or that the nonfoundational discourse is not sufficiently guided by it) is something we agree on. However, Brookes's understanding of IR&S being at a preparadigmatic stage (such that periods of normal science have yet to occur) means that he does not provide any change typology or mereology beyond the brief Kuhnian understanding of growth discussed above. This is also why there is no specific analysis of the growth of IR&S discourse—as opposed to the growth of discourse in general, which is a topic of interest for IR&S. So with respect to modern IR&S, which we contend (contrary to Brookes) to be at a later stage of growth, what that growth means (in terms of a mereology) and what it means for it to lose "its confident pace," (i.e., change typologies) still must be worked out. Brookes's identification of IR&S discourse as being about objects and relationships in Popper's third world of human-created artifacts (Brookes, 1980b,c, 1981)[19] excludes the cognitive world (user minds) and is at most at a preliminary stage. Identification therefore still remains a problem to be solved by any effective theory of scientific change for IR&S.

Following the analyses of theories of change in Losee (2004), section 3.4.3 explores theories beyond Kuhn's to understand the best ways for describing the growth of IR&S discourse. We then take the work of Laudan and Lakatos (a follower of Kuhn and Popper) as the point of departure from within HPoS, which section 3.4.3 extends to fit the IR&S case—a venture that continues into chapter 4—to understand IR&S discourse in the stages of normal science and revolution.

3.4.3 Theories of Scientific Change

A progressive scientific discourse is one in which a state of discourse is judged to be more valuable than a prior state. The transition between such states can be "gradual and incremental" or "sharply discontinuous" (Losee, 2004, pp. 1–3). Theories of scientific change, necessary for appraising science, differ through which such pattern of change they give priority to; the incorporationists focus on gradual changes, on the incorporation of prior successes into current theories; the overthrowists instead focus on discontinuous revolutionary episodes, in which prior theories are overthrown and succeeded by better ones. Theories such as Kuhn's are discerned from others in Losee (2004) as being overthrowist due to the importance given therein to revolutionary episodes that punctuate periods of normal science. There are theories of change such as that of Laudan (1986), which accept the overthrowist account but allow for partial overthrows, so that the discontinuity between states of discourse is not as sharp as Kuhn's. Theories of change also differ according to what they hold to be the quality that is improved through such change, whether gradual or revolutionary; examples include empirical adequacy (Monton and Mohler, 2014) or predictive success, coherent successive approximation toward or convergence on truth, and problem-solving effectiveness (Losee, 2004, pp. 1–3).

Furthermore, such theories differ according to whether they are merely descriptive or are also normative. Descriptive theories seek to find patterns of discourse (corresponding to historical episodes of scientific practice) understood by practitioners as being progressive, and seek to explain

---

19. He discusses measures for characterizing changes in the objective world of artifacts by measuring citation information.

these patterns through a concept of progressive change/growth. Normative theories instead prescribe recommendations about how science ought be practiced in order to be progressive according to the concept of change they espouse. The normative approach depends on the descriptive, as without the discovery of accepted development patterns, prescriptions cannot be made. In contrast, the descriptive approach can proceed without prescribing suggestions about the conduct of science. Deciding whether a theory is normative or descriptive is not necessarily a simple task. Kuhn's theory, for example, is mainly descriptive, but it can also be understood to be prescriptive (Kuhn, 2012, pp. 343–347; Tsou, 2015, p. 59).

There are no agreed-on necessary or sufficient conditions that would automatically indicate either type of change, incorporationist or overthrowist, to be progressive (Losee, 2004, p. 156). Instead, whether the change is progressive would have to be judged with respect to the quality of the discourse that the change seeks to improve. The following briefly compares different types of incorporationist and overthrowist theories (section 3.4.3.1) and theories based on different to-be-improved qualities (for a discourse), justifying properties sought for a theory of change to be developed for the IR&S context (in section 3.4.3.4). The focus is in particular on the theories of change espoused by Laudan (section 3.4.3.2) and Lakatos (section 3.4.3.3), whose ideas are crucial to IR&S-specific ideas of change summarized in section 3.4.3.4 and elaborated on in chapter 4.

3.4.3.1 From patterns or modes of change to qualities sought in change

Incorporationist theories account for successes of prior theories. Out of the many such theories, only Whewell's and Lakatos's accounts will be treated here because of their popularity in HPoS, and because we have adapted them in this book. Whewell's normative theory of scientific development understood progress as an incorporation of past achievements in present theories through a convergence or unification of evidence and concepts, which he termed consilience (Snyder, 2012). An example of consilience is when two sets of observations can be lumped together through an explanatory principle, such as planetary movements and the movement of earthly bodies through the laws of gravity (Losee, 2004, pp. 13–16). For Whewell, incorporation (e.g., previously found celestial observations with earthly ones) is progressive when consilience can be demonstrated. For Lakatos, incorporation corresponds instead to the ability of present theories to predict whatever prior theories did and more, and to have these additional predictions corroborated by experiment. Progressive incorporation then corresponds to additional corroborated predictions.[20]

Overthrowist theories hold that a revolutionary confrontation between theories tends to or ought to (if they are normative) resolve problems in prior theories. Overthrowist theories differ according to the criteria they suggest for a revolutionary episode, such as the types of things (whether they are the key theories, interpretations, methods, concepts, or otherwise) whose replacement is to signal an overthrow. They also differ in the reasons they advocate for overthrow (e.g., overthrow upon the accrual of anomalies, as in Kuhn). Kuhn's overthrowist theory suggests periods of application and growth of existing paradigms (corresponding to the key theories) punctuated by periods of conflict in which entire paradigms are replaced. Laudan's overthrowist model instead allows for partial replacement of the paradigm, such that there is still significant continuity between the pre- and post-revolution discourses. Laudan, however, emphasizes the quality being improved in scientific change over and above its character as being gradual or discontinuous.

For Laudan, incorporation and overthrow are patterns: They are modes of change, they describe how change happens. They work to describe the way that the quality, which acts as the "why" or purpose of the change (its *telos*), is established in the discourse. The quality is that which progressive change improves on; it is a response to the question: "What is the value of making scientific progress?" Lakatos's incorporationist theory values predictive success, while Whewell's values consilience. Other prominent opinions respond to this question, suggesting either that science tends to converge on truth or is a series of successive approximations to truth (Losee, 2004, pp. 98–119); or that successive developments tend toward increasing empirical adequacy, (i.e., that the theory structures, e.g., mathematical structures, increasingly cohere with what is observed of the phenomena).[21] In the latter case, empirical coherency/adequacy substitutes for truth.

Each such quality can be understood to have captured a reason that particular discourse states are valued, but they do not individually capture the

---

20. Other theories of gradual change or incorporation understand change instead as the resolution of a preexisting anomaly or when a prior theory is logically reduced to a more inclusive theory.

21. Or that the theory structure is "empirically adequate if the observable phenomena can "find a home" within the structures described by the theory—that is to say, the observable phenomena can be "embedded" in the theory" (Monton and Mohler, 2014).

full picture. For example, with respect to Lakatos's theory, the explanatory or interpretive ability of a discourse might be valuable beyond or in lieu of change in predictive ability. And with respect to Whewell's theory, even if a discourse lacks consilience or coherence,[22] it is possible that it is successively useful in some way so as to be understood as progressive.

Laudan critiques truth-based qualities (Losee, 2004, p. 120) supported by the observation that, if a sequence of theories were to demonstrate increasingly accurate predictions, this may not imply a convergence towards truth due to the difficulty in deciding what "being closer to the truth" actually means. Predictive success for him does not therefore imply truth or the convergence to truth. It is possible that while there are increasingly accurate predictions, the key notions are nevertheless poorly understood or abstract, such that what the theory actually says is ambiguous, as is therefore the "truth" that it is supposed to be approximating or converging on. For example, theories that refer to abstract objects, such as "point-masses" or other nonphysically realizable quantities, would only be true or convergent on truth if these entities were to exist, but they do not (Losee, 2004, p. 158). Laudan argued instead for understanding the value, quality, or ability that is sought to be fulfilled or improved on by change as the problem-solving ability of a discourse. It is clear that the growth of science has led to an increasing number of practical applications and tangible social improvements, and that science has solved the corresponding problems. Predictive success and consilience/coherence can also be critiqued with respect to problem solving, as discourses not attributed by the former can nevertheless be so by the latter.

With respect to the claim of progressive empirical adequacy (due to van Fraassen, 1980), while this appears less ambiguous than theories claiming to approximate truth, it leaves out the nonempirical dimension. Thus if changes did not lead to improvements in empirical adequacy but improved conceptual clarity or effectiveness of interpretation (or some other aspect), then this progress would go unrecognized. Laudan's theory insists that, other than empirical problems pertaining to relevant phenomena, there are conceptual problems pertaining to shared beliefs, problems of consistency and clarity of theories, and the relationship between theories and between theories and methodologies or cognitive aims. For Laudan, neither incorporation, (i.e., periods of normal science) nor revolution were necessary; nor

---

22. We consider Whewell's notion of consilience (Snyder, 2012) and the idea of coherence developed in this book to be analogous.

are they primary for characterizing development. They are instead modes of change serving the higher goal of problem solving. Development happens and progress is achieved when existing problems are solved, and whether this is through revolution or incorporation is secondary if not irrelevant. However, as Losee (2004) makes clear, it may not be obvious whether problems are being solved at any given time. Instead, this could be something only revealed well after the fact, through judging problem-solving effectiveness. Several key aspects of Laudan's theory are nevertheless of relevance. They are discussed next.

3.4.3.2 Laudan's theory: Discourse as network, progress as problem solving Laudan's theory of change can be understood in comparison with Kuhn's, which Laudan interprets in a particular sense. According to Laudan, the Kuhnian paradigm contains three aspects: a framework for classifying, analyzing, and explaining natural objects (this includes theories, facts, propositions, and such); a methodology (i.e., tools and techniques for the study of relevant phenomena) that supports the framework; and finally, an axiology, that is, a set of values, shared beliefs, and overall cognitive goals/aims of the discourse that are presupposed by the methodology.

These three aspects mutually determine one another. A paradigm thus represents the discipline as a whole, that is, the totality of typical scientific behavior/thinking of the corresponding discipline. A paradigm also represents or contains the typical successful applications of the discipline as captured by corresponding exemplars (i.e., the way a typical phenomenon is characterized and analyzed by the paradigm).

For Kuhn, the revolution is when the paradigm as a whole is rejected. When this happens, all three aspects are supposedly replaced at once; Kuhn thereby allows holistic change. For Laudan, such a radical change is rare, only happening when a rival theory is available; what is more typical is a partial or piecemeal replacement (Losee, 2004, p. 82).

Both Kuhn's and Laudan's theories depend on an underlying mereology, the mereology of the former characterized as hierarchical and that of the latter as reticulational or network like. The mereology works to organize discourse in a way that supports the theories' respective accounts of change. For Kuhn, there are inner and outer elements, the outer elements presupposing the inner ones. The axiological (shared values and beliefs) and methodological elements are inner elements, whereas the outer elements correspond to the theories, propositions, facts, and so forth. Thus it is the values that effect the methodology, which in turn conditions the generation of theories.

Laudan's theory similarly admits outer (theories, facts, etc.) and inner (axiological and methodological) levels. However, Kuhn's theory is relatively more hierarchical than Laudan's. This is because the inner/outer relationship for Kuhn conditions the way the discourse changes in a relatively more rigid way than it does for Laudan. For Kuhn, it is only when the paradigm stops generating useful theories and facts—and in the period of crisis just before revolution—that its inner network is questioned. This period presents itself as an opportune one, where there is some urgency to modify the network so that it can yet again be generative of outer elements.

For Laudan, any part of the discourse can affect another part (e.g., the outer elements can lead to changes in methodology or values), and one does not have to wait for a discontinuous/revolutionary phase for this to happen. Change could be triggered by everyday scientific activity such that pieces of the inner are changed and the rest is preserved. Laudan's theory thereby admits piecemeal or nonholistic changes and is relatively nonhierarchical, because there is no necessary order (between the inner and outer levels) that a change is dependent on. Inner change does not have to be preceded by slowing outer growth, nor does there need to be a replacement of the whole inner part (through revolution or such) for subsequent outer growth. It is Laudan's network-like or reticulational mereology that makes this theory possible. The network-like model means that the inner part (the methodological rules, shared beliefs, and cognitive aims) and the outer part (consisting of theories) can be "kept in dynamic equilibrium through a process of gradual, piecemeal adjustment" (Losee, 2004, p. 82), because the tension in some part of the network may be resolved by tinkering with another part. That there are existing interactions between different parts of the network across inner/outer boundaries means that if there were problems between values and methodological principles, they can be allayed by relatively minor (nonrevolutionary) adjustments to one or the other.

Laudan's theory of change, explained above, is expressed through his concept of the research tradition, which like Kuhn's paradigm, is the theoretical element representing an empirical scientific discourse. It is the research tradition that is characterized by Laudan as having a network-like as opposed to a hierarchical structure (as in Kuhn). It is the key entity in Laudan's mereology. The tradition is then constituted by a set or chain of theories (the outer element), with a common methodological and axiological base (the inner elements), without the base rigidly determining the development of theories. A research tradition thereby contains general assumptions about phenomena and processes for some region of world phenomena, and also has methods for adequate theory construction and problem analysis. Any research tradition whose successive theories solve problems in the appropriate domain qualifies as progressive.

Laudan's theory goes beyond being descriptive to being normative and prescriptive, suggesting how discussions about the inner network, the nature of cognitive values, should be conducted, if particular problems were to be discovered. It is rather inclusive: whatever scientific developments a community agrees to as having solved a problem is considered to be a progressive change. However, with this inclusiveness comes ambiguity. Laudan's model does not offer a way of discerning problems, or prioritizing the importance of one problem over another. Hence, it is not obvious how problem-solving effectiveness can be measured: Simply counting the number of solved problems does not appear to be the correct thing to do. In addition, whether a problem has been solved can only be deduced from inspecting long-term accounts of research traditions. Therefore, although it does present a comprehensive descriptive theory of scientific progress, Laudan's theory cannot be used to immediately tell us whether one tradition is more capable of problem solving than another.

3.4.3.3 Lakatos's reconciliation of Kuhn and Popper

The work of Lakatos is central to HPoS, partly because it critically combines the work of other key thinkers, such as Popper and Kuhn, and partly because significant works since Lakatos have in some way been in response to Lakatos's ideas. Lakatos's theory of scientific change, his methodology of scientific research programs (MSRP) has arguably found more popular application to intellectual discourses than have other theories. This section introduces the MSRP by discussing its genesis from other theories of change, such as those of Popper and Kuhn.

For Popper, science progresses by the rational process of falsification, a process through which one theory is preferred over another (Hansson, 2015). Theories with predictions not matching observations are promptly discarded, so that progressive science corresponds to a process of elimination. Falsification for Popper acts to demarcate scientific from unscientific discourse. If a discourse is not falsifiable, then there is no way of demonstrating the invalidity of propositions or theories therein (e.g., by observation, experiment, or argument), and the discourse cannot be judged to be a scientific discourse, that is, a discourse seeking to discover actual patterns in nature. However, from the descriptive sense, falsification is not a typical goal or process for practitioners to follow, nor is it (in the normative sense) a realistic prescription. Instead, as Kuhn holds, what is typical in the period of normal science is for scientists to preserve and not falsify their theories—even on the discovery of anomalies—in order to develop and improve on their problem-solving effectiveness. Scientists are not automatons that are persistently judging their creative outputs in order to falsify them; instead they allow work on imperfect theories, allowing their ideas to grow and mature. It is only on substantial later evidence to the contrary or the development of alternative newer theories that older efforts are abandoned.

Furthermore, in a revolutionary period, although the accrual of anomalies—each contributing to the falsification of the theories in question—is often the rationale for the replacement of the dominant paradigm, it is neither a necessary nor sufficient cause for overthrow. Kuhn's theory recognizes that revolutions need not be rational processes, or more specifically, that their rationality may lie beyond the rationality of the corresponding scientific discourse in the sociological or cognitive spheres. For example, revolutions may be politically motivated or be explained by non-rational (irrational or arational) personal choices of key practitioners. However, Lakatos's theory of change does not allow for this type of non-rationality. He does not deny that such factors can affect scientific discourse, but he categorizes them as external factors that are to be addressed by an external history of science. He understands the job of a theory of scientific change as being focused instead on determining an internal history, which for him is always a rational history. For Lakatos, a discourse representing scientific activity must be amenable to a rational reconstruction.

Lakatos's MSRP reconciles Popper's and Kuhn's views. It can be understood as being between the strongly rational and strongly social/cognitive theories of Popper and Kuhn, respectively. Popper suggests that scientists proceed through a process of elimination/falsification, and Kuhn allow for nonrational overthrows based on (possibly) subjective understandings of problem-solving effectiveness. In contrast, Lakatos suggests that theories are preferred if they have excess corroborated content (i.e., when they predict whatever the older theory did and something more), and the extra predictions are verified. Therefore, theories are not automatically abandoned when anomalies arise; they are preserved and worked on—as in Kuhn's case—but there is a specific rationality to this process: that the theories appear to cohere better with observations (by virtue of corroborated predictions).

Lakatos's incorporationist theory of development replaces Kuhn's notion of the all-encompassing paradigm (which appears to subsume the entirety of a scientific discourse) with the former's notion of the research program (which represent parts of the discourse). However, this is not the main difference. The research programs in the MSRP are "objective reconstructions," in terms of theories and heuristics, of Kuhn's paradigms; Lakatos says that the "research programme may be construed as an objective 'third world' reconstruction of Kuhn's socio-psychological concept of a paradigm" (Lakatos and Musgrave, 1970, p. 177). They correspond to a set of successive theories or experimental techniques (or both), differing slightly, that share a common hard core. Like paradigms, they contain a hard core of basic assumptions, but they also have an outer core of theories, heuristics, and so forth, whose growth and change correspond to the everyday work (and findings) of scientists.

For Lakatos, scientists work to protect the core of their research program from falsification (as opposed to trying to overthrow it). They do this by means of a protective belt of (auxiliary) hypotheses. The question of whether the worldview underlying a paradigm is true—which might be asked of Kuhn's paradigm during a revolutionary period—is now replaced. The question is now about whether a research program has become progressive or degenerative. The progressive research program is one in which successive theories predict (and are corroborated) in excess of prior theories; progress then corresponds to the prediction of novel facts. A degenerative program is instead characterized by a lack of growth. Its outer or auxiliary network no longer leads to novel predictions that are subsequently verified. Thus, Lakatos's research program engenders a richer and more nuanced narrative than does Popper's notion of falsifiability. Instead of theories being rejected at the first discovery of anomalies, science grows by the continuous adjustment and development of the outer core of research programs: this methodical process partially constitutes normal science. The effect of replacing the paradigm with a research program with outer and inner cores allows Lakatos to explain as rational the process by which practitioners expand the auxiliary belt (outer core) to preserve the hard core to the extent possible. Lakatos allows for revolutionary episodes, but the paradigm shift therein remains for him a discourse-specific rational move; he does not allow it to be nonrational, as implied by Kuhn. For Lakatos, this shift is from a research program that is degenerative to one that is more progressive. As a result, Lakatos's MSRP suggests a more rational account of scientific change than does Kuhn's picture of paradigm and paradigm shifts.

3.4.3.4 What makes a good theory of change for IR&S?   What would be a good theory of scientific change? This section argues for properties that a good theory of change should have, especially given the context of IR&S.

A theory of scientific progress can be appraised according to whether it fits with and explains the historical record of scientific activity. There are historical episodes judged to be progressive (by practitioners) that are incorporationist in character, and there are progressive episodes that instead follow the overthrowist models of change (Losee, 2004, p. 156). In addition, there are episodes that fit particular differences within each such type of change. For example, although some episodes fit Kuhn's holisitic type of overthrowist model, other episodes fit the overthrowist model but not by total replacement of one paradigm by another. Instead they proceed by a partial replacement (as Laudan's theory suggests). Similarly, there are episodes that fit overthrowist models but differ in other ways, such as when paradigms may have been rejected without a viable competing paradigm and not only due to a build up of anomalies. A good theory of change should allow for both incorporationist and overthrowist possibilities, and for such variations.

Laudan's theory is inclusive enough to allow for both general types of possibilities and most of their variations. This is first, because the meaning of problem solving (which is left up to the consensus of the scientific community), can be understood to be any combination of qualities from other theories of change. Second, the loose connection between the inner and outer elements afforded by its reticulational structure for discourse allows a richer change typology than does a hierarchical structure, where change at one level depends strongly on the state of the other level. Laudan's theory does not of course include all aspects of other theories. For example, his research traditions contain both inner (cognitive aims, values and methodology) and outer (theories and their products) elements like Kuhn's paradigms, but they do not, unlike Kuhn, emphasize the sociological (shared beliefs/practices) and pedagogical element (paradigms as exemplars). These elements are crucial in Kuhn's work for identifying a discourse and hence for differentiating discourses.

Our strategy here will nevertheless be to take Laudan's theory as a base with respect to its quality of problem solving, and yet to suggest an integration of qualities and modes of change from other theories of change as a specification of problem solving in the context of IR&S. This is not to restrict problem solving exclusively to these categories, but to contend that such a mix of aspects is required to understand the senses in which IR&S discourse is progressive with respect to the quality of problem solving.

Acknowledging various types of problem solution   Consider the following generic understanding of problem solving, which demonstrates the qualities sought by different theories of change. A set of observations without a generating principle or cause connecting them (i.e., unrelated observations of phenomena) presents a problem. The solution is a hitherto unknown theory that generates, suggests, or predicts them. The progressive growth of the respective discourse corresponds first to the development of such a theory and then to the development of a sequence of theories that are successive improvements of the initial theory; the sequence represents improvements to problem-solving effectiveness. What precisely an initial theory must do to be understood as a solution and what its successive improvements must be for that solution to be increasingly effective depend on the consensus of a particular scientific community. There are, however, conceptions of properties of initial solutions and their improvements that are commonly found in scientific discourses.

As discussed previously, theories that relate to observations by being able to predict them are one type of solution. Improvements to that type of theory are in terms of its predictive ability, such that, as in Lakatos's MSRP, successive theories predict observations of prior theories and then more, where the excess predictions are also corroborated. For Lakatos, excess corroborated predictions correspond to more effective ways to solve the problem.[23] Other ideas of solution and improvement can also be adduced. First, a theory that explains instead of predicting can also be a solution, so that successive theories present excess explanatory ability. This idea fits with Whewell's concept of development (through his theory of consilience). According to Laudan's problem-solving model of change, if successive theories present conceptual advantages (i.e., excess conceptual advantage), such as when a successive theory removes a conceptual difficulty in the former, then this could indicate progress due to a resultant improvement in predictive ability (or in empirical support, as he calls it; Laudan, 1981, pp. 145–148). In fact, Laudan holds that if successive theories were to reduce predictive ability, they could still be seen as progressive if there were some conceptual advantage.

---

23. Excess predictability is, however, not always an absolute indicator of progress in problem solving. As Popper cautions, a scientific theory that explains too much might lack falsifiability, and as such, there is reason to suspect its scientific value. Falsifiability must therefore be present as a factor in judging scientific value and hence progress. The value of predictability and explanatory ability must then be decided in comparison with the aspect of falsifiability.

Second, explanation, conceptual advantage, and prediction can be extended by using the work of Kitcher (1993). Kitcher categorizes solutions into practical, conceptual, and explanatory types. Scientific progress corresponds to practical (e.g., technological), conceptual, and explanatory gains made in scientific activity.[24] That scientific progress can be indicated by a growth in or betterment of technology rings particularly true of system building and technology-centered discourses, such as IR (and hence IR&S).

Finally, the work of Furner (2011), who can be understood to be extending the work of Laudan and Kitcher to account in particular for IR&S, can be construed as adding further solution types. In addition to the predictive, practical-technological, and explanatory, there is the "interpretive," which complements Laudan's and Kitcher's "conceptual" category. There is also the category of moral and ethical gains, and that of the practical (as meant in the sense of policy as opposed to technology). Therefore, new theories/models or in general, states of discourse (Furner, 2011) that better explain or lead to more practical (technical), policy, ethical, and interpretive benefits are also said to better solve the problem.

While these extended accounts of problem solving provide a broad understanding of qualities sought by scientific activity, the qualities only provide a very general understanding of progress in discourse. The more fine-grained characterization of discourse comes from the mereology and change typology particular to a theory of change.

Loosely coupled mereology   Although Kuhn's mereology is tightly coupled through the paradigm representing an entire discourse, Lakatos's theory breaks it into competing research programs, each with relatively explicit inner and outer cores. Laudan's notion of the research tradition is a loosened-up version of Lakatos's research program. For Laudan, scientific discourse does not need to (nor does it always) easily allow for separating into Lakatosian research programs. The research tradition also does not require sharply separated inner and outer cores, allowing for a more loosely linked inner/outer network, where the inner can change more freely (unlike in both Kuhn's paradigms and Lakatos' programs). For Lakatos, inner change usually implies the abandoning of a research

24. For Kitcher, problem-solving scientific discourse or activity can be attributed to a more general quality or goal. Problem solving is then for the sake of attainment of significant truths about the world that can be integrated into a system of knowledge (Losee, 2004, pp. 126–129).

program or the creation of a new program. Given the absence of several clear/established research programs spanning significant parts of the discourse, IR&S discourse is arguably better described as a research tradition.

Varied change typology   In all the above theories of change, the aspect that readily changes within scientific discourse are the theories in the outer network; these are empirically testable theories about the natural world. IR&S discourse does not pertain to the natural world, nor is it fully determined by empirically testable theories. This is why predictive success (as in Lakatos) can only provide a partial account of progressive change. A more complete account of change would need to consider problem-solution types in addition to prediction, such as those suggested by Kitcher and Furner. In particular, owing to the social scientific; sociological; and in general, humanistic discourse in IR&S, the change narrative for sociological discourses such as those detailed in Wagner and Berger (1985) needs to be seriously considered.

Wagner and Berger (1985) argue that sociological discourse grows more readily in its inner aspects than do natural-scientific ones; the inner aspect being constituted by metatheories. This means that progressive inner changes can occur without significant outer changes. The case of inner change without preexisting (and specifically related) outer changes can be argued to be encompassed by Laudan's theory: (progressive) inner-aspect changes can be understood as progressive because they provide successive conceptual advantages. Lauden's and Wagner's change typology could lead to conclusions significantly different from other change theories: a discourse mainly characterized by inner growth can be understood to be nonprogressive from a perspective conditioned by natural science discourses, while in fact it could be progressive from a perspective based on sociological discourses.

For a mixed discipline such as IR&S, an effective change typology not only needs to consider changes in the outer and inner (metatheory or otherwise) networks, but also needs to acknowledge less restrictive forms of change (e.g., the inner changing without the outer) as a valid mode of progressive change.

Yet, whatever change types are allowed, they tend to be difficult to detect in practice, as while empirically testable theories are the main units for the outer network (especially for natural science), Vakkari and Kuokkanen argue (Vakkari and Kuokkanen, 1997, p. 512; Vakkari, 1998, p. 379) that they are lacking in IS and are not always made explicit even when present. Outer network theories for IS would correspond to empirically testable, general theories pertaining to patterns in user behavior (e.g., information-seeking behavior), culture, and cognitive activity (e.g., a change in information needs). These are not as easily forthcoming as similarly general theories about patterns and regularities pertaining, for example, to natural or artificial (e.g., computational) phenomena.

Even if IR can be understood to have more obvious outer theories due to it being more concerned with system behavior, with respect to IR&S in general, the understanding of progress would be difficult if it were to require identifying specific, encompassing, outer theories. Instead of such general, empirically testable theories, there are narrowly scoped theories or models that apply in limited contexts (in both IR and IS). There are also heuristics that generalize between contexts and other types of structures that form the outer network. As the proceeding discusses briefly (and chapter 4 describes in detail), such structures can be understood as groups of related propositions, or a network of discourse.

3.4.4   From Theories to Propositions

The HPoS theories of change tend to understand scientific discourse in terms of general, empirically testable theories as the central structural elements of the outer network. It is not that IR&S is devoid of outer-network theories, but that it is lacking the types of theories common to natural science. Due to the mixed nature of IR&S, what a theory is first needs to be problematized beyond what it is for subaspects of IR&S, such as retrieval models for IR and metatheories for the inner network of IS. Alternative types of theories more suited to the IR&S context then have to be identified with parts of discourse. This is a foundational research task further discussed in chapter 5.

Instead of directly working at the level of theories by considering theory formations, this book opts to characterize theoretical development indirectly in terms of the facts and propositions that appear to be generated by theories. Thus to apprehend theory structure is to apprehend the network of relationships among the different propositions and facts; Laudan's reticulational model provides an apt structural fit. It also means that it may not be necessary to identify explicit theory formations, but instead to identify propositions and facts related in a way as to indicate a common generative principle or theory. This idea is developed in reference to Lakatos's MSRP, wherein successive theories are compared by their excess predictions, which correspond to a set of novel facts. These novel (meaning new and interesting) facts are the fine-grained aspect by which a sequence of theories is compared to determine whether the sequence implies progress for their related research program.

Lakatos's "novel fact" is expanded so that progressive discourse change corresponds to new facts and propositions that adequately link to the existing network; where an adequate linkage results in the overall network being sufficiently coherent. This notion of coherence expands from Whewell's notion of consilience to include the above sought-after changes to discourse. A change in the network that makes the new state of the network better in some way (e.g., in an explanatory, interpretive, practical, or conceptual sense) is said to also improve the coherence of either the overall or a specific part of the network. Improved coherence indicates a better fit among the elements of the network.

Chapter 4 develops a more detailed framework of what progressive change means for IR&S based on the above general guidelines of what makes a good theory of change. It adopts several points of departure. Lakatos's fine-grained analyses of theories through their predictions is our particular point of departure for understanding change in terms of groups of related theories and the propositions they generate. However, it will be extended to include explanatory, interpretive, conceptual, and practical benefit (etc.) in addition to the benefit from prediction. The ideas of other HPoS scholars (as discussed above), especially those of Laudan, form our general point of departure from HPoS. The work of Brookes forms our point of departure from IR&S.

3.5   Conclusion

This chapter explored the foundational question of progress for IR&S, from the perspective of the history and philosophy of science (HPoS). It argued that for the IR&S context, progress should be understood from the perspective of an internal history. This means to look at the growth of discourse as possessing an internal rationality with respect to the growth of theories and other structures constituting the discourse, in addition to being influenced by external factors (e.g., social, political). Inadequacy of the scant prior research on scientific change native to IR&S motivates the need to look beyond these works. As a result, HPoS concepts were used to develop an idea of what progress could mean for IR&S. By critically comparing the ideas of Brookes, Kuhn, Laudan, Lakatos, and others, and by arguing for the relevance of particular aspects over others for their application to IR&S, in this chapter we developed our idea of the attributes that a good theory of change and progress for IR&S should possess.

A theory of change that befits IR&S must recognizse problem solving as the key overall quality sought by the IR&S discourse, but a quality constituted by several subgoals of the discourse, such as to explain, pre-dict, interpret, or build. Owing to the lack of formal theories in IR&S, such a theory of change would mainly focus on the set of propositions. Chapter 4 further details this theory by adopting a more detailed account of growth and progress from the work of Lakatos, which is adjusted extensively to cater to the IR&S discourse. This chapter can be understood to have particularized the general notions of progress in chapter 2 in terms of theories, whereas chapter 4 further refines this in terms of propositions and propositional networks.

4 From Growth to Progress II: The Network of Discourse

4.1 Introduction

This chapter continues to develop the idea of what progress could mean for IR&S, by creating a more refined picture than in the previous chapter. Relative to preceding chapters, this chapter develops a picture of progress that is at a lower level than both the theory level in chapter 3, and the discourse level in chapter 2. Whereas chapter 2 studied the overall aims of IR&S discourse, this chapter focuses on the nature of growth with respect to propositions generated by the theories or theoretical constructs constituting IR&S discourse.

The prior chapter analyzed different theories of scientific change characterized by the way they divide up discourse (i.e., their mereology) and also by the types of changes they recognize as progressive. It found Laudan's notion of the solving of a problem as the most appropriate general explanation of what counts as a progressive change in IR&S, that is, as the main quality sought for progress. This notion can be seen to generalize several other types of progressive change—such as the prediction and explanation of facts—that can be understood as refining Laudan's notion. They can be understood as denoting types of problem solving (e.g., problem solving as prediction). It was also argued that Laudan's structuring of discourse into traditions was a better fit for IR&S discourse than Lakatos's research programs. Finally, chapter 3 argued that due to the paucity of theories in IR&S, perhaps growth would be best understood instead, in an indirect fashion, at the level of propositions. Thus, it was held that what progress could mean in IR&S has mainly to do with problem solving (in its various senses) in the structure of a research tradition, characterized as a network of discourse with inner and outer aspects. And that this should be further understood in terms of propositions constituting IR&S discourse.

This chapter further develops and refines these conclusions to offer a more detailed picture of what progress could mean for IR&S. It does this by adapting Lakatos's fine-grained theory of scientific change, his methodology of scientific research programs (MSRP) using several concepts from Laudan's work. While the MSRP works at the level of theories, it provides a way of creating detailed specifications of theory growth in terms of propositions and facts. This allows for MSRP to be extended to create a picture of progressive growth that focuses more on the propositional level, as is adequate for capturing current IR&S discourse. When creating this picture, Lakatos's prediction-centered idea of growth is extended at the level of propositions and in the context of a research tradition and not a research program. The idea is to allow for ways of solving problems in addition to solving them through prediction, such as through explanation and interpretation.

Section 4.2 addresses an objection to using the MSRP outside the natural sciences, while section 4.3 introduces the MSRP in some detail. Section 4.4 explains the specific modifications to the MSRP to cater to developing an IR&S notion of progress. Section 4.5 explicates the relationship between coherence, a high-level notion of progress from chapter 2, and notions of progress developed in this chapter. Finally, section 4.6 summarizes the narrative of progress developed from Lakatos and motivates the topic of foundational research, which is developed in chapter 5.

4.2 Applying Lakatos outside the Natural Sciences

Lakatos's concept of theory appraisal offers a way to understand progress in terms of the facts and propositions generated by theories. This is an understanding in terms of the constituents of discourse. This section adapts and develops such concepts from Lakatos to explain change/progress in IR&S and does not adopt his MSRP in a wholesale manner. Whether applying Kuhn to IR&S like Brookes, or Lakatos and Laudan, as done below, one has to address the objection of these authors to this very application of their work outside their intended context of the natural sciences. Both Lakatos and Kuhn were disinclined to the application of their methods to the social domain (Bird, 2013), due to the difficulty therein (unlike the natural sciences they worked in) of identifying an agreed-on, stable set of basic assumptions (the hard core). There are several responses to this objection.

First, IR&S does not only refer to the social domain but also to the computational; the structure of IR&S therefore does not automatically correspond to that of a social science. Yet, according to some opinions, IR may indeed not have a proper hard core (Buckland, 2012), and as is the premise of this text, the foundations (i.e., the hard core) of IR&S are unclear. However, this does not mean that a stable hard core cannot be brought out—indeed, the aim of this book is to show that it can. Second, the ideas of these HPoS scholars have nevertheless been applied successfully to the social domain (Khalil, 1987; Caldwell, 1991; Elman and Elman, 2003; Gonzalez, 2014) and psychology (Meehl, 1978, 1990; Dar, 1987). Thus the application of HPoS methods to IR&S does not immediately incur these scholars' relevant critiques. Instead, whether their application is appropriate or not requires further investigation. This chapter presents an attempt to apply these methods to IR&S. In addition, as chapter 3 discussed, it is sufficient for a discourse to be science-like for such an application to be initially reasonable. Therefore, the main import of such objections could be interpreted as calling for care in the process of borrowing such methods. Indeed a critical approach is required: IR&S is not a natural science, it does not develop like one, its theories (as argued below) are not restricted to natural-scientific or mathematical theories. If such an approach is not employed, and HPoS ideas, such as Lakatos's MSRP framework are adopted wholesale, then this would likely result in an external incoherence (to use the notion from the chapter 2). This chapter instead engages in a critical appropriation of the MSRP.

4.3   Lakatos's Methodology for Appraising Research Programs

For Lakatos, a scientific discourse is structured into research programs, each of which is constituted by a set of theories, heuristics, and other types of elements. In each such program, there is a hard core and an auxiliary/ protective belt of theories, hypothesis, and so forth. These two parts of discourse correspond to the inner network and outer network of a discourse as introduced in chapter 3. According to Lakatos's MSRP, programs can develop in different ways, and not all types of growth or development are considered to be effective or progressive.

In the (progressive) state of scientific development, a Lakatosian research program generates theories that populate the outer network/protective belt. These theories must additionally be producing novel facts, facts that are both new **and** interesting. A program would lack effective growth when, even if there were outer growth in terms of theories producing new facts, the facts failed to be interesting or empirically verified. If outer growth fails to occur in this effective manner, then degeneration could be claimed.[1] Any such claim would be an evaluative judgment based on analyzing the effectiveness of the growth in the inner and outer networks, whether in the normal (progressive) state of science or in the remedial stage. A degenerating program is, however, not immediately discarded,[2] and Lakatos does not suggest it should be discarded—only that degeneration should be admitted. Instead, it is only when a more competitive/progressive research program appears that scientists gradually discard the older one. A more complete and detailed account is provided below.

4.3.1 Lakatos's Change Narrative in Detail

This section first elucidates Lakatos's picture of a progressive research program and then explains the contrasting case of the degenerative program. For Lakatos, a research program is constituted by a sequence of theories $T_1, \ldots, T_n$, each one advancing on its predecessor. The succession from a theory to its successor, what Lakatos calls a problemshift, can be judged to be progressive in two ways: theoretically or empirically. If each new theory T_{n+1} both accounts for facts predicted in predecessor theories and in addition predicts novel facts (i.e., suggests some excess empirical content over its forerunner T_n), then it is theoretically progressive. A novel fact here is not only a new fact but also one that is unexpected from the perspective of prior theories. A problemshift is additionally empirically progressive when this excess empirical content is also supported by actual observation (i.e., when theories and their predictions lead to the "real discovery" of new facts).

For Lakatos, a research program is said to be progressive, or have an overall progressive problemshift, when each of its problemshifts are theoretically progressive and at least sometimes empirically progressive; successor theories should thus predict more than their predecessors, and at least some of these predictions should be valid (Cohen et al., 1976, p. 426). Progress is determined by the degree to which a series of theories leads to

---

1. A lack of effective outer growth could be remedied by developing new theories that instead produced interesting and verified facts, or even by making minor interpretive changes to the hard core. Unlike Laudan's narrative, Lakatos's MSRP does not accept more than minor changes to the inner core except at the stage where new research programs— with new hard cores—are formed, e.g., based on developing the hard cores of prior programs.

2. As may be the case in the Kuhnian narrative, when a sudden paradigm shift takes place; or in the Popperian narrative, when as a result of a key experiment, some basic assumptions are falsified, and a theory is discarded.

the discovery of novel facts. If a program is not theoretically and empirically progressive in a complementary manner, then it is said to be "degenerating" or "stagnating" (or said to be attributed to a "degenerating problemshift"; Lakatos, 1971, p. 100). There are therefore at least three cases indicating a degenerative program: (1) when there are a lack of novel facts from successive theories (i.e., a lack of a theoretically progressive problemshift), (2) when novel facts are predicted by theories, but this excess empirical content is not corroborated (i.e., lack of an empirically progressive problemshift), and finally (3) when such facts are discovered (empirically corroborated) but not through the guidance of preexisting theories or the preexisting research strategy,[3] meaning that there is no obvious rationale for their finding[4]—they are instead chance findings. In this final case, theoretical growth fails to anticipate or "lags behind" its empirical growth (Lakatos, 1971, p. 100).

In these three cases, it is not that scientific discourse does not happen, but that the research program lacks particular attributes. From the perspective of everyday scientific practice (which is at a lower level of granularity than the program), a degenerative state of science can be understood to correspond to the proliferation of propositions, (yet to be verified) hypotheses, or nonestablished theories. Lakatos explains[5] that a degenerative scientific discourse is usually populated with ad hoc (observational) hypotheses or (nonestablished) theories (Lakatos et al., 1980, p. 125), which are

3. This pertains to Lakatos's notion of the positive heuristic of a program, which is the intellectual and pragmatic strategy for doing science in that particular context. In particular, "the positive heuristic consists of a partially articulated set of suggestions or hints on how to change, develop the 'refutable variants' of the research-programme, how to modify, sophisticate, the 'refutable' protective belt" (Lakatos et al., 1980, p. 50), i.e., the positive heuristic acts as a strategy for producing, processing, and appraising such refutable variants, which are for Lakatos the footprints of such a heuristic. The "refutable variants" correspond to a set of (throw-away) models that attempt to capture the relevant phenomena in successively accurate ways. Although Lakatos does not rigorously differentiate between theories, hypotheses, and models, a model for him appears to be a "refutable variant of a theory," by which is meant "a set of initial conditions (possibly together with some of the observational theories) which one knows is bound to be replaced during the further development of the programme, and one even knows, more or less, how" (Lakatos and Musgrave, 1970, p. 136).

4. This means that the activities of scientists in discovering these facts are not amenable to rational reconstruction in a clear manner. That is, it is difficult to say how their findings can be rationally lead-to or acquired.

5. Although much of his idea of the ad hoc hypothesis is taken from Popper.

"fabricated only in order to accommodate known facts" instead of leading to the "discovery of hitherto unknown novel facts" (Lakatos et al., 1980, p. 5). There are three types of such hypotheses, corresponding to each of the above cases: hypothesis that (1′) account just for some recent observation and do not suggest something new; (2′) suggest something new (have excess empirical content) but are not corroborated; and finally, (3′) have excess content, at least some of which is corroborated, but "do not form an integral part of the positive heuristic."[6]

Lakatos's specification of progress in terms of theories, facts, and their novelty (and of non progress as indicated by types of ad hoc hypothesis that lack particular attributes) provides a structure for appraising scientific discourses in general, and this structure has been critically appropriated to several such disciplines, from economics (Gonzalez, 2015) and psychology (Meehl, 1967; Janoff-Bulman, 1990) to international relations (Elman and Elman, 2003). This chapter attempts to similarly appropriate it for understanding how IR&S can be appraised as to its progress, but as for other applications, some generalizations are required to allow Lakatos's notions to fit the diverse discourse of IR&S.

Lakatos provides a lot of detail on the specifics of progressive growth versus degeneration (Lakatos et al., 1980, p. 31), and although much of his analysis can possibly be adapted for IR&S, it is not immediately obvious how to do so, since it is mainly in the context of the natural sciences. For example, such notions as "empirical fact" and "theory" that are used in the MSRP discourse have a particular meaning in the natural-scientific context, and unless their corresponding meaning in IR&S can be deduced, it is unclear how further parts of his theory can be applied. In general, there are many foundational aspects to be worked out with respect to, for example, understanding the relationships between the types of phenomena of interest to IR&S versus the phenomena of the natural sciences. To some extent Brookes is accurate when he states that "it does not matter what the scientist's metaphysical position is as long as he admits the reality of

6. This third type of hypothesis is something Lakatos sees as endemic to the psychological sciences of the time (and is one of the reasons for his objection to using his MSRP in such fields). A discussion in response to this, applying Lakatos to psychology, can be found in Meehl (1967). Further critique and countercritique of Meehl's ideas can be found in Serlin and Lapsley (1985) and Dar (1987), while a full journal issue dedicated to the topic is in Janoff-Bulman (1990). As the methodology of user experimentation in IR shares much with psychological testing methodology, these discussions sourced from Meehl and Lakatos are of critical relevance.

the physical world,"(Brookes, 1980c, p. 275) but in IR&S, due to its phenomena "unavoidably straddling the boundary between the physical and mental worlds," (Brookes, 1980c, p. 275) there will be confusion in discourse until these background metaphysical and foundational positions are clarified. As a result, there is no easy wholesale mapping of Lakatosian analyses to IR&S. The only recourse is to critical appropriation, and this chapter is an initial such attempt.

4.4   Modifying Lakatos's MSRP for IR&S

Scientific development occurs through knowledge generated by the corresponding discourse. This knowledge can correspond to theories, strategies, ideas, algorithms, and so on, and it depends on the science/discourse in question. In agreement with the semantic and pragmatic conceptions of science, it is understood that the actual discursive experience of scientists is more commonly at the level of theories, overall diagrams/representations, algorithms, and the like. In other words, theories are the "unit of practice." In the context of IR&S, this theory could also be a social-science theory or metatheory and not only a natural scientific theory. While the following adopts Lakatos's framework—which is designed to appraise natural scientific theories—the arguments therein could be seen to apply in a general way. This is regardless of the theory type and the theoretical construct (Jansen and Rieh, 2010) or generative (discursive) construct (e.g., strategy or algorithm) that functions as a conventional theory (see section 4.4.2.2). The generative construct is a collection of discourse elements, such as a set of propositions, that appear, generate, or influence the creation of further propositions.

For Lakatos, it is not enough to simply identify theories; one must see whether they are "producing something," (i.e., producing new and interesting facts). Thus, ultimately, the facts that theories produce have to be identified and judged as a way of appraising the theories that generated them. This is fortunate for the IR&S case, since a wide range of theoretical constructs constitute the discourse so that they would be difficult to comparatively appraise in any direct manner. As the following argues, it is more appropriate in the IR&S case to consider these products as propositions rather than facts and so to take propositions as the unit for the analysis of change. Section 4.4.1 differentiates between propositions, facts, and statements.

The following modifies salient aspects of Lakatos's change narrative to fit the IR&S account. Section 4.4.2 suggests mereological changes by employing concepts from Laudan; section 4.4.3 extends Lakatos's account of progressive change to include research goals pertaining to other than the prediction of facts and the generation of empirical content. Section 4.4.4 explains how successive parts of discourse, with different such goals, can be compared. Sections 4.4.5 and 4.4.6 discuss how Lakatos's three types of progressive change and states of degeneration can be understood in light of these modifications.

4.4.1 From Facts to Propositions

Statements are understood to be linguistic objects; they are declarative sentences that state (assert or deny) something. Unlike statements, propositions are not only linguistic objects but also logical ones; they must be meaningful and bear truth (i.e., understood to be something that can be judged, by whatever methods of verification or argument, to be "true" or "false").[7] A hypothesis is a proposition that explains or describes a phenomenally observable or abstract (mathematical) pattern, or suggests a conceptual argument, which is to be tested accordingly. There are propositions that are not clear hypotheses, including those taken as assumptions, definitions, or heuristics. Although they can be argued for or have empirical tests designed to support them, they are not intended to be subjected to tests or argumentation, like other hypotheses.

In addition, whether or not a proposition can be understood as a hypothesis, a proposition can be judged to be true in different ways. It can be true in the sense that it (1) coheres with a set of propositions already held to be true (i.e., truth by coherence), (2) corresponds provably/demonstrably to something in the world (i.e., truth by correspondence), or (3) is useful to believe[8] (Dowden and Schwartz, 2016; e.g., it helps predict experimental outcomes or explain data). In the case of (2), where a proposition is judged to be true by correspondence with the real world, it is usually known as a "fact."

Although there are other types of truth and a wide-ranging discourse on how propositions and facts are to be related (Mulligan and Correia, 2013), these simple definitions are deemed suitable for the purpose of understanding progressive growth. This is because of a lack of discussion (and hence agreement) about how propositions (facts, hypotheses, and otherwise) and truth are to be understood in the IR&S context, and because

---

7. Several statements can express the same proposition, for example, "$1 + 1 = 2$" and "one added to one is two" are two expressions of the same proposition.

8. This is related to the notion of pragmatic truth (Hookway, 2015). See also, the discussion of truth in section 2.2.

these notions also remain ambiguous in the seminal HPoS works of Lakatos (Gonzalez, 2015, p. 110), such that their common meaning (the ones suggested here) is presumed.[9] These common meanings are also judged to be adequate for the purposes of the following discussions on progressive growth in IR&S.

4.4.2 Adjusting Mereology

The main modifications to Lakatos's MSRP are to its mereological assumptions. The other changes (e.g., to research goals) depend on the particular way the discourse is divided into parts. Section 4.4.2.1 refines the argument (from chapter 3) based on Laudan's work, for the suitability of research traditions over programs for depicting IR&S discourse, discussing why Lakatos's framework is nevertheless adopted overall. Section 4.4.2.2 introduces the generative construct as the particular unit of practice constituting discourse, while section 4.4.2.3 discusses what it would mean to work with a sequence of such units to understand progress in the same way that the MSRP works with a sequence of theories.

4.4.2.1 From research program to tradition One of the main changes in adopting Lakatos is to forgo the notion of the research program. This is since, as contended, IR&S discourse in general resembles more the notion of Laudan's research tradition than a research program. Unlike a Lakatosian research program, while the tradition is generative of theories, they need not be the exclusive or main constituents of a tradition. As a whole the tradition is a less rigid concept than a program, with a hard core that is understood to be more fluid than that of a research program. The diverse IR&S discourse is such that it is not solely constituted by natural-scientific theories that are easily grouped into Lakatosian research programs,[10] nor do theories play a central place as they do in the natural sciences. There are instead different types of theory, conceptual problems as well as empirical ones, that are given the same level of importance, and beyond these theories is a "set of ontological and methodological do's and don'ts" (Lauden,

---

9. If at a later stage more rigorous understandings of facts and propositions are to be introduced into the IR&S context, then it would be difficult to do so without correspondingly rigorous understandings of the difference between logical and linguistic objects, what the precise definitions of "meaningful," "testable," or "arguable" are for IR&S, and so on.

10. There are parts of IR&S discourse than can be considered to be research programs, such as the QT–inspired work in IR (Song et al., 2010), but these cases are rare.

1977, p. 80). All these factors make the research tradition more suitable than the program. However, even though the latter is replaced by the former, Lakatos's notion of progressive development is kept.

The objection could be raised that if the research tradition adopted, then why not the rest of Laudan's framework, given that this notion is rather central to his theory? The response is that the inherent variety of sub-discourses in IR&S does not exactly fit either Lakatos's or Laudan's accounts, hence the need for modifications. As chapter 3 discussed, Laudan's theory is attractive due to being less stringent with respect to how the inner and outer networks affect each other. Laudan readily allows for changes in both networks as part of normal science. This better represents IR&S practice, where foundational concepts (i.e., the hard core) are often modified in an ad hoc manner to enable the discourse to address immediate application contexts. Lakatos does not allow the inner network to change as freely in the course of normal science; instead Lakatos explains that scientists will try hard to preserve an existing hard core, even if it requires fudging outer-network theories to fit accepted inner-network notions. Lakatos therefore better captures the case where a discourse has a stable and strongly accepted foundation. Furthermore, Lakatos's theory also preserves Kuhn's distinction between normal science and revolution in an explicit way, and it tries especially to create a narrative that shows the rationality of change over and above non-so-rational social factors. While Laudan's looser change structure is relevant to parts of the current discourse of IR&S, Lakatos's structure instead better captures other aspects or later stages of discourse. It could further be useful for denoting an aspired state of discourse that is more rational in Lakatos's sense. Furthermore, as mentioned previously, Lakatos's MSRP offers a level of detail in dealing with the propositions that theories produce that is particularly advantageous for developing a corresponding IR&S account of change.

In adopting the MSRP as a tradition and not a research program, Lakatos's picture of development is then understood to apply to the larger structure of the IR&S discourse as a single entity. In addition, this picture must also consider looser types of theories (i.e., generative constructs) and hence an idea of progress that is in terms of the growth of constructs. The following develops the mereological aspect of scientific change with respect to how one such part of the discourse causes change in the other.

4.4.2.2 From theories to generative constructs and "bits" of discourse
Lakatos assumes that a scientific discourse can be divided (e.g., rationally reconstructed) into research programs, each working on a clear theme.

Furthermore, he assumes that the outer network of each such research program can be seen to be constituted by a set of theories that share some properties. In particular, (1) the theories share a set of common assumptions (basic concepts, etc.) as would be mentioned in the hard core or inner network, (2) they have the same subject matter, (3) they are comparable in some way either directly or indirectly with respect to what they produce, and finally (4) they exhibit an order, where one theory can be said to have improved on the other.

As the prior sections discussed, it is difficult to reconstruct IR&S discourse in terms of research programs, meaning that it is not clear how one or more of properties (1–4) could apply to IR&S. In particular, it is not easy to spot sequences of comparable theories that are about the same subject matter and work to build on one another. Let's assume that such a strict organization is not a general rule for IR&S. Is there any way to read IR&S discourse such that it exhibits the above properties? If the four properties are looked at in terms of their functions, then a more generalized version can be developed that fulfills this purpose specifically for IR&S, the following presents such a version:

- Suppose that there are parts or "bits" of IR&S discourse that can be understood as being linked or related (i.e., that IR&S does not consist of completely unrelated islands of sub-discourses). If this supposition were not true, then it would be difficult to identify different areas of research as IR&S discourse, as sharing an identity. Suppose also that these bits of discourse that are related can be reconstructed as corresponding to the units of practice in IR&S. These are the units that form everyday research, such as an empirical experimental scenario that researchers participate in and then discuss in the discourse. This unit need not depict a real experiment (one that has already happened), but it could depict a hypothetical one. It could also present a hypothetical discussion (e.g., about search scenarios), since discussion is a form of research practice. As the prior section argued, the units of practice for IR&S, to the extent they are depicted in discourse, are better understood as being depicted (written about) in terms of generative constructs than, as in the case of Lakatos, in terms of formal theories. These constructs are a weak and simple type of theory; they are a group of propositions depicting an idea that has the potential to generate further propositions.

- Let these bits of discourse that constitute IR&S then correspond to the unit of practice as a generative construct, along with its generated propositions. The outer network of IR&S discourse is then characterized as being constituted by numerous such bits. The inner network of IR&S is then those bits of discourse that have their own generative constructs that are to be presupposed by the outer network. The presupposition here does not need to be made explicit, but it must be able to be inferred from analysis. An example of these (foundational) generative constructs are the many foundational theories in Fisher et al. (2005), as well as the foundations network (the system of questions, addresses, and their relationships) discussed in chapter 5.

Let the inner and outer networks then constitute the IR&S research tradition. This depicts the static picture of a tradition.

4.4.2.3 From sequence of theories to sequence of generative constructs and/or research bits For Lakatos, research programs grow and change with respect to the addition of new theories, which offer newer perspectives to an existing problem or perhaps highlight different attributes of the problem that the other does not. Each such new theory corresponds to a problemshift. The succession of such theories are thereby connected; there is a continuity between them—they are all trying to better solve a problem. This continuity is what makes possible any comparison between the theories in the program. What could this idea of a succession of theories mean in the context of the IR&S tradition? It would correspond to new bits of discourse: instead of new theories, there would be a new generative construct or generated propositions (or both). However, what could it mean for two such bits to be related and to be seen as a sequence? One understanding of this is that a latter bit of discourse would have to share the subject matter of a former bit: They would have to be about the same problem context.

For Lakatos not only must there be a sequence of new theories, there must also be progress: The newer theories have to be seen to improve on the older ones. Thus for IR&S, at least one existing generative construct should have a particular relation to a later construct, such that the later construct can be seen to improve or build on or to have some benefit over the previous construct. If this is not true at some point, then the sequence does not show signs of progress. However, it is supposed that researchers would argue that there is some benefit to their daily work—beyond some personal and nonobjective benefit. If no such benefit was observed or expected, IR&S would not be science-like or progress seeking (see chapter 3), but this would contradict observed attitudes in research and development. Therefore, one should be able to pick out related bits of discourse that in some way depict improvements.

It is important to note here that the attempt to abstract a sequence from the discourse is only for the sake of rational reconstruction that leads to progress analysis: It interprets parts of discourse in a specific way. The underlying discourse structure is not however sequential. It is better visualized as being network-like, that is, there are arbitrary relations (edges) between discourse bits (nodes/vertices) and their groupings.[11] Hence, the discourse bits are afforded a more complex interrelationship than they are in a mere sequence. In developing sequences, one is adding an extra set of edges to this graph (directed edges in this case) to represent a progress narrative, where an order is imposed between connected nodes or discourse bits. Furthermore, it is reasonable to assume that the benefits that one bit may have over the previous one have some relation to the overall goals of research.

4.4.3 Adjusting Research Goals

The MSRP was designed with the natural sciences in mind, with respect to the goal of science being to elucidate how nature works and to do this in particular by predicting facts about nature that can be either corroborated or falsified. These facts correspond to empirical content; they refer to things or patterns in the world that can be verified by scientific observation and experimentation or by experience. For Lakatos, successive scientific theories constituting a program, were their succession to depict progress, would then have to correspond to successive improvements with respect to this prediction;[12] this works to build an increasingly better or more accurate picture of some part of the natural world. That producing empirical content is needed for progress is another way of saying that theories should be producing content that pertains to the goal of the overall science.

In the IR&S case, the goals of research are to figure out the workings of the social world (not the natural world), users (cognitive world), and the world of technology and artifacts (e.g., physical documents). While the means of doing this may include prediction, it is neither always the main goal nor readily possible due to the nature of phenomena in the social domain.[13] As

---

11. This is technically a hypergraph.

12. Lakatos takes prediction, rather than explanation and understanding, as being primary to the purpose of science. Although he requires for new theories to explain (Gonzalez, 2015, p. 106) known facts for the purpose of progress, what is important is that theories predict new facts. There are a wide range of views on the relative importance of prediction versus explanation in science, with scholars preferring one or the other as providing the main evidential support for theories.

13. This is a key way that research programs in the social sciences differ from their natural-scientific counterparts: the programs change "not only through discovery of unexplained

a result, theories pertaining to the humanistic discourses function instead to explain (Elman and Elman, 2003, pp. 381–405), understand, and to predict (where possible). As IR&S is constituted by a wide range of generative constructs from various such domains, they have a similar set of functions and include other functions that pertain to the building of systems or the designing of social policy.

Furthermore, for the IR&S case, the result of such constructs may not be best described as "empirical content," which something to do with their function and the overall goals of IR&S. For example, were a construct to explain why a user acts in a particular way, then in addition to judging the construct through empirical accounts of user behavior, one may judge it through the cogency of its argument vis-à-vis theoretical models of cognition. This explanation may not only (or primarily) pertain to empirical content. Moreover, some of the propositions that constructs generate may not relate to phenomena in a way that can be verified through the usual types of scientific observation. In addition to explanation, understanding—where the attempt is made to understand what something means and not just the immediate causal reasons as to why it happened—is not only particularly central to the humanities (e.g., history) and important for the social sciences. It is also central to science (Friedman, 1974; Apel, 1984; Faye, 2014). In IR&S, not only is it useful to try to predict what a user (or user group) will do or be characterized by at some time (e.g., how they will interact or what their information need will be); it is also useful to explain why they did something and to understand what it means for them to do so or to possess some attribute. This amounts to two particular modifications:

- Let the goals of change instead be unrestricted and include in particular: explanation, interpretation, technical designing and/or building, policy development, and ethical/social betterment as in Furner (2011).

- Let the propositions that the constructs generate also be unrestricted, in that they may be other than empirical content. And let this content be such as to reflect the purposes and values of IR&S, such that it is to be verified or evaluated based on how it fulfills those values. As a result, "discovered facts," such as facts about users (which correspond

---

empirical facts, but through changes in the very nature of the objects under study, such as the emergence of capitalism or of state sovereignty." Whatever the social theories may say about phenomena, as social generalizations they are "necessarily contingent and time-bound" (Elman and Elman, 2003, p. 489).

to empirical content) are indeed important to predict and therefore of value. However, in general, any proposition that helps explain or understand relevant phenomena is of value, as are propositions that help build systems, and so forth.

4.4.4 Adjusting How Successive Constructs Are Compared

The judgment pertaining to the improvement in a discourse, and hence among a sequence of bits of discourse, thus has to involve assessing the benefit of a later bit. And this would be with respect to the function of the construct therein and the type of content it generated (e.g., whether empirical or some other type of content that is of value). The assessment can be done directly or indirectly. The benefit can be deduced from comparing generative constructs either directly or indirectly. They can be compared directly, for example, by comparatively analyzing the generative constructs themselves (e.g., with respect to their potential to generate beneficial content). Clearly, the constructs must be comparable in the first place, and it must be meaningful to compare them. This is seldom the case for IR&S, as the two bits of discourse to be compared may have different types of generative construct. For example, one may be a system design and the other an explanatory user model, where the latter improves on the former by explaining through user factors why a system failed, meaning that the latter discourse bit provides some benefit in resolving the problem in the former. In such a case, the two bits of discourse may be compared indirectly through the propositions they generate.

In general, the numerous variations of subject matter, functions, and styles of discourse bits mean that direct comparisons are difficult. One significant method of indirect comparison is with respect to how successive constructs combine to fulfill a higher goal, a goal that transcends their individual goals. For example, were the constructs to solve a problem in a coordinated manner, this that problem would become the means for continuity between successive discourse bits.

Regardless whether constructs are compared directly or indirectly by their propositions, what we need to know to judge a sequence is how different types of constructs and propositions fit together to solve a problem; only then can they be appraised. Thus, for generated propositions to be comparable, they must be understood to work together to solve a problem; they would then be compared with respect to the relative roles they play in solving that problem. This is especially the case when they differ in subject matter, form (technical design versus social explanation), or in their other attributes.

4.4.5   Expanding the Notion of Progressive Change

For Lakatos, there are three types of progressive change, including the two types of progressive problemshift discussed above, that must be modified for the IR&S case. First, there is the case of theoretically progressive problemshift. This is when successive theories suggest excess empirical content. In Lakatos's case (that of predictive theories), this is when later theories predict whatever prior theories predicted and some more. This excess corresponds to one or more novel facts.[14] Second, there is the case of empirical problemshift, wherein the novel facts predicted by theoretical progress are also empirically corroborated (i.e., verified or supported). Finally, there is the idea of a progressive research program, which is when each successive theory in a program corresponds to a theoretically progressive problemshift, and when at least some of these shifts are also corroborated or correspond to empirically progressive problemshifts. These three types of progressive change could be adapted as follows:

• In the IR&S case, the equivalent to theoretical problemshift would be to say that a progressive problemshift (or progressive problem resolution) occurs when successive discourse bits suggest new or extra content. Whether this content is empirical or otherwise, when combined with existing content (the existing sequence of discourse bits), it can be understood to form an overall better solution to a problem shared between these bits. This is the problem that acts as a principle of continuity in that sequence. Hence, this extra suggested content works to improve the problem-solving ability of the sequence. For example, the latter bits in the sequence could explain or interpret something that the prior bits left unexplained or could suggest a system design that exemplifies the value of prior interpretations of user behavior.

14. Even though Lakatos's concept of scientific progress is dependent on the idea of novelty, there is an openness in the definition of the latter, as not only does it admit a broader meaning throughout Lakatos's later understandings (Watkins, 1989; Gonzalez, 2015, p. 110), but also later HPoS work extends the notion even further into several kinds of novelty (at least six such kinds are mentioned in Gonzalez, 2015, p. 111). In addition to having several types (which are not exhaustive), as Lakatos admits, there could be reasonable disagreement as to whether a predicted fact is novel in one such way, or as to what corroboration means and whether a fact has indeed been corroborated. The notion of "being interesting" acts as a placeholder for the wide range of ways (owing to the subjective and intersubjective nature of the value of propositions) for valuing new propositions with respect to their effect on progress. The schema developed in this and the next section to identify some of these ways for the IR&S context is an initial such categorization.

The extra content that successive bits provide (i.e., the generated propositions as opposed to the generative construct that produces them) correspond to Lakatos's novel facts. In this case, they are novel propositions. That the latter bits work with the prior bits is a way of generalizing Lakatos's idea that successive theories build on prior ones. The key difference is that for Lakatos, there is a steady accumulation of predicted novel facts, but in the IR&S case, there is a steady accumulation of propositions that have variegated functions and work to improve their predecessor bits in a way possibly different than how the prior new bit improved its own predecessor bit.

- The equivalent of the empirically progressive problemshift for IR&S would be when the new content created by successive discourse bits can be shown to actually lead to an improved problem resolution. This means that the new content has to be verified or found to be of actual (as opposed to hypothetical) value. It is contended that a prerequisite of being valuable here is to possess truthlikeness or versimilitude (Oddie, 2014),[15] as presumably propositions that are known to be false would generally not be of use.[16] Thus, when new propositions that work to suggest overall better problem solutions are both true and actually lead

---

15. To have a truthlikeness means to be true to some degree, whether by corresponding to the real world; cohering with established truths; or being true by merely being useful, where usefulness is understood in the common way. For IR&S, due to (1) the social nature of its subject matter (its involvement with users) and (2) the technical (design/development) aspects of IR&S, pragmatic truth—whereby something is true to the extent it is useful—is arguably a category of truth that is relevant for IR&S. One such understanding of "useful" is where for a proposition P, while P's truth is not yet decided, it nevertheless is successfully employed as a means to generate other propositions [Q], which are more certainly true (or useful). In this case P can be understood to be useful and true (to the extent it is useful). The notion of usefulness depends ultimately on whatever is agreed on in a particular discourse. To the extent this allows for subjective/intersubjective variation in understandings of "useful," pragmatic truth can be understood as a weaker category of truth than others that would instead require more objective verification.

16. Clearly this is not true of all cases, as a proposition that initially appears true then is found to be false, as is common in scientific development, can be more interesting than propositions that have always been true. Or as Oddie (2014) states, "Some falsehoods seem to realize the aim of getting at the truth better than others." What the point refers to, however, is that arbitrary propositions that are blatantly false or even irrelevant (i.e., they do not pertain to a context at hand) correspond to the opposite of interesting.

to a better solution, their corresponding discourse bit is said to engender the IR&S equivalent of an "empirically progressive problemshift."

- The IR&S research tradition can thereby said to be a progressive tradition to the extent that (1) the successive discourse bits therein are theoretically progressive (i.e., they indicate how to improve on existing problem solutions by suggesting how to build on past efforts to meet a common end); and (2) these successive bits can also be shown to actually improve on existing solutions (i.e., they are empirically progressive).

4.4.6 Adjusting Types of Degenerative States

When a research program is not progressive (because it lacks theoretical, empirical, or overall progress), then it is degenerative. Lakatos recognizes at least three types of degenerative state. The first case is where there could be a sequence of theories but without excessive empirical content (i.e., without newer theories saying something new and interesting). The second is the case where, even if successive theories were producing excessive empirical content, the content remained unverified. And the third case is where there is a steady accumulation of empirically verified findings but they seem not to be guided by theory (i.e., chance findings). In this case the theory seems to lag behind. Each of these degenerative states can be identified by its attributes, for example, the first case exhibits weak hypotheses or theories that tend to over fit the facts or apply to a limited number of scenarios without generalizing. The following list suggests what the equivalent of Lakatos's picture of degeneration and its signs could be for the IR&S case.

- A degenerative discourse of the first kind could correspond to the case where a set of discourse bits can be said to build on each other. For example, mathematical or social theories (or constructs) that extend each other, but are not in any clear way working to solve a common (IR&S related) problem. A sign of this state is the proliferation of discourse bits that address narrowly scoped problems (e.g., making a system that works well in one search scenario) without relating to other related problems or scenarios, such that the discourse bit is hard to generalize (as in ad hoc research; see section 1.3).

- A degenerative discourse of the second kind would be where successive discourse bits build on each other and purport to solve a shared problem, but they have not been shown to actually solve the problem or have been shown to solve it in an undesirable manner and yet, the successive bits appear to be oblivious about this fact. A sign of this state is where successive discourse bits work to make extensive problem-solution frameworks that are acutely suggestive of solutions to a common problem but the verifications are not forthcoming even after extensive framework development.

• A degenerative discourse of the third kind would correspond to chance findings (e.g., the discovery of arbitrary facts about a system) or abstract philosophical research that deliberates on particular concepts, and in either case, it is unclear how these findings work to solve an IR&S-specific problem.

Clearly, if any of these degenerate states could be attributed to either all of or a critical mass of IR&S research, then it would be a sign of degeneration of the outer network. This would require reinvestigation of the inner network of foundational assumptions. In particular, if a significant part of IR&S discourse were judged to be degenerative, it would mean that successive discourse bits therein do not sufficiently build on one another, that they were not sufficiently linked. As prior chapters discussed, such insufficient linking in discourse is indicative of a lack of coherence (see chapter 2), which itself is indicative of a difficulty relating bits of research.[17] For the IR&S case, as discussed in prior chapters, it would probably be due to the presence of different forms/styles, functions, and subject matters (e.g., of relating humanistic to technical discourse) that are nontrivial to link. This difficulty has much to do with the relation between the concepts presupposed therein (chapter 2) and is therefore a problem residing at the foundations level as depicted by the inner network of discourse. Sections 4.5–4.6 further relate progress and degeneration to notions of coherence used previously, while chapter 5 suggests how to build the inner network in a coherent manner.

4.5 Progressive Growth as Coordinated and Coherent

The notion of internal coherence from chapter 2 can be understood to pertain to the interconnectivity between bits of IR&S discourse. Every theoretically and empirically progressive (i.e., fully progressive) sequence of discourse bits that work together to solve a problem would also work to improve the internal coherence of the IR&S tradition. A maximally coherent tradition would be a maximally progressive tradition. In this case all sequences of discourse bits are fully progressive, and any one bit of discourse has a place in one or more such progressive sequences. In such an ideal state,

---

17. Presumably, researchers would readily do this linking if it were simple to do.

all sequences of discourse bits would correspond to solutions or solving strategies for IR&S-specific problems. To the extent IR&S problems interrelate, such progressive sequences are those that work together to address the overall problem of predicting, explaining, and interpreting information events and to create practical solutions, services, or social benefits (Furner, 2011). Internal coherence is thus a property of the discourse or discourse network as a whole (i.e., each node in such a network is a discourse bit; see section 4.4).[18]

To better relate between the discourse-level coherence previously discussed and the modified version of Lakatos's MSRP above, coherence must also be understood at the sub-discourse level. In this regard, as briefly mentioned in section 3.4.4, coherence should be understood to be a relation attributable to a set of two or more discourse bits (or nodes) and not just to an overall discourse. Moreover, the prior notion of coherence from chapter 2 requires refinement to a general and a specific kind, to differentiate between coherence between discourse bits as a relation depicting relevance (e.g., subject matter similarity) versus coherence in the sense of cohering in a progress narrative.

Given one discourse bit, an additional such bit is generally coherent with it if it is "sufficiently related" to it and also with the existing network of discourse, or tradition. In this case, the set itself is also generally coherent. Similarly, as research proceeds and such a set is developed, it is possible to attribute each new discourse bit and the set itself with general coherence. For a set of discourse bits to be "sufficiently" related means that they correspond to research about the same or similar subject matter, so that they can be understood as mutually relevant (e.g., one bit discusses a system design and the other a user survey pertaining to that system). For a new discourse to be sufficiently related to the existing network of discourse or tradition means that its subject matter is within the limits of whatever is considered relevant if not typical for IR&S research. In the context of the (modified) MSRP, for a theory or construct (i.e., a discourse bit) to be successive and thus become part of a sequence (see section 4.4.2.3), the bit and the

18. Thus, a discourse bit could be a generative construct or theory (see section 4.4), or possibly a group of them. For example, a discourse bit could be one particular theory of user interaction that helps predict what users may click next. Or it could be several such theories, which could all come under an organizing theme: they could all be interaction prediction theories that pertain only to particular type of social media interactions. In this sense, successive such nodes or discourse bits could correspond to different classes of theories as opposed to just individual theories.

sequence need to be generally coherent with one another. For it to be considered for rational reconstruction and as a part of a progressive research program/tradition, each new such bit or construct in the modified MSRP must first pass the test of being sufficiently related to an existing sequence which it is to extend. A generally coherent such sequence (where each successive discourse bit is generally coherent with the existing sequence; see section 4.4.2.2) need not be a progressive sequence. Yet every progressive sequence must be generally coherent.

A discourse bit is specifically coherent with the existing sequence and also with the existing network of discourse or tradition when its addition to a generally coherent sequence not only maintains its general coherence but also leads to a theoretically progressive or fully progressive problemshift. Then the respective bit has a specific place in solving the shared problem or improving an existing problem solution.

With respect to the outer network of the tradition or network of discourse, the introduction of any new discourse bit—a generative construct and some generated propositions—is a progressive move, to the extent it is generally and specifically coherent with the existing network. The notions of internal and external coherence from chapter 2, which were discussed as notions of progress, can thus be related to the notions in the modified MSRP through the further refinement into specific and general coherence. A progressive IR&S tradition is then one in which successive bits of discourse are coherent (generally and specifically) with existing bits, such that as a whole, network coherence is maintained or improved.

When successive bits are specifically coherent with existing bits of discourse, then let this be termed coordinated or complementary, that is, they fit together so as to resolve a problem. Progressive growth can then be understood as coordinated or complementary growth.

4.6   Conclusion

As chapter 3 discussed, one of the hallmarks of science is that it is a progressive discourse. Thus, the problem of understanding progress in IR&S has to do not only with its value as a discourse, but also with its identity—whether it can be called a science. This chapter argued that IR&S is a research tradition constituted by an outer and an inner layer. The outer consists of a collection of generative constructs and propositions derived from them and is supported by an inner network. In the normal course of science, progressive growth is typical, and for IR&S, it consists of successive discourse bits that work to solve IR&S problems. If this is not the case, then the discourse is said to have entered a degenerative state. These are instead periods where the network lacks general coherence, or if there is general coherence, there is insufficient coordination between bits of discourse (i.e., new bits added to discourse are not specifically coherent). The solution to such a state would be to actively develop generative constructs and propositions of different types and functions that coordinate to solve problems. If this can be achieved, then progressive growth of the outer network would again occur. If instead this is difficult or not forthcoming, the cause probably has to do with the relationship between the outer and inner networks. Then the next course of action would be to attempt to draw out these relationships between the generative constructs, their derived propositions, and their inner network of presupposed concepts (see section 4.4.6). After that, revising the inner network of foundations should be considered. If there are effective attempts at exploring inner–outer network relationships and/or the inner network itself, then progressive growth takes place, as research is being conducted to solve immediately relevant problems. However, if the foundations are not addressed, then the scientific status of the discourse would be in question.

Progressive growth for normal science is then a coordinated growth of discourse bits (see section 4.5) that keeps the network coherent, since successive bits of discourse specifically cohere with existing bits to solve problems. Progressive growth can also be understood to be creating a vertically developing (or strongly cumulative) discourse in two senses. The first is by maintaining significant continuity between different research projects or discourse bits, requiring them to build on one another; this is facilitated, among other things, by knowing how they work together to solve a problem. The second is by requiring that bits of discourse derive from "lower down" or "presupposed" aspects, building on top of foundations.

Furthermore, an internally coherent discourse, as introduced in chapter 2, can only be maximally so as a result of coordinated growth in its outer layer, between its inner and outer layers, and ultimately (if the foundations have to be addressed) in its inner layer. Coordinating growth means actively relating between generative constructs and between propositions that have different functions, subject matter, and styles, in the service of a problem solution. As prior chapters discussed, most modern problems are concerned with factors beyond system aspects, such explaining user behavior or contextual factors. Progress thereby requires that the discourse readily facilitate the answering of "why" questions, to explain why information events happen (Furner, 2011) or what they mean, especially with respect to the user aspect. Thus progressive growth as coordinated growth means actively coordinating between the technical and nontechnical aspects, and between explanatory, predictive, and interpretive works.

At the disciplinary level, seeking progressive growth means intimately coordinating between IR and IS discourses, and as chapter 6 discusses, this would mean an integrated IR&S. To seek to integrate IR and IS corresponds to seeking a common foundations that would be the basis of that relationship. It corresponds to creating a coherent and coordinated network of generative constructs for the inner layer of discourse, each such construct is a collection of foundational propositions on a particular subject matter (e.g., on the concept of a user or document). The next chapter attempts to create such a network by elaborating on the properties particular IR&S foundational concepts should be construed by in order to address the modern context. It also relates the idea of coordinated growth at the outer layer with that of the inner layer where the latter has been structured in a particular way (see sections 5.4.3 and 5.4.4). Whether the network presented in the following chapter (and by extension the book as a whole) is successful, by being generative and progressive, is for the reader to decide.

5 Basic Questions Characterizing Foundations Discourse

5.1 Introduction

Our examination of foundations questions about progress and phenomena construal has exposed the rich set of relationships among the concerns, assumptions, and basic concepts constituting IR&S. This chapter further develops this picture in a direct way. It does this through constructing a critical set of basic questions along with a discussion based on the properties necessary of any effective resolution to these questions in the modern context. This serves to build a discursive network, showing how arguments pertaining to the resolution of one question run into that of another. While the questions addressed are not exhaustive, they are the among the most pertinent for the modern context.

The perusal of basic questions, and hence of foundations research (in general), can overall be understood to be justified by the following three reasons. First, as chapter 2 argued, addressing such questions is important for resolving immediate pragmatic concerns pertaining to the building and evaluation of systems dealing with modern problem contexts, and for coherent reasoning about phenomena important for IR&S. This pragmatic perspective requires basic positions to be revised due to it being concerned with modern applications. Second, as chapters 3 and 4 suggested, foundations research is required from a disciplinary or discourse perspective, that given the modern context and the state of IR&S as a discipline or discourse, asking and addressing foundations questions correspond to drawing out an inner network of discourse, a task that is currently necessary for the discourse to be deemed progressive.

Third, foundations research is important from a logical perspective. That is, even a pragmatic discourse, such as experimental IR, must be built on clear foundational concepts and methods.[1] This is a point argued often through disdain for the lack of clarifying conceptual discourse from the inception of IR, such as in Fairthorne[2] until the present time, such as Fuhr's (2012) call for theoretical foundations. Fuhr's discussion can be interpreted as a call to establish conceptual clarification (Bodoff, 2012); conceptual clarification must arguably include clarification of foundations.[3]

As the prior chapters have explained, foundations research can be represented by the inner network of a research discourse and a supporting research culture or tradition. The nodes of this inner network can be understood as the positions (expressed as propositions) taken to resolve foundations questions. These positions are presupposed by the outer

1. It is reasonable to assume for every significant rational/intellectual discourse that it be based on a set of core concepts and principles that specify ways of making valid inferences or demonstrations based on what is known/established or assumed about what is not yet established.

2. As documented in Walker (1974, p. 130), Fairthorne laments about practitioners of IR and related disciplines: "Few intelligent groups can have achieved so slovenly and misleading a vocabulary in so short a time. Few intelligent groups can have cared less." He goes on to say that the situation of IR "is not that the emperor wears no clothes, but that some very elaborate clothing covers no emperor."

3. For Bodoff, conceptual research "leads to convergence in how a variable is to be defined and measured by all researchers in a field" (Bodoff, 2012, p. 12). Conceptualization corresponds to defining variables: their attributes, relations to other variables, etc. As the variables represent empirical reality, they have to be shown to mirror that reality, which will require testing or argumentation to show that it represents a regular phenomenon (it can be observed again and again with the same identity). Thus it has "predictive validity," a notion Bodoff gets from the psychometric literature (Cronbach and Meehl, 1955). Bodoff's notion of conceptualization thus appears to require phenomena construal, which is related to the development of basic concepts and hence to foundations research. In particular, the building of a concept requires first the process of picking out regions of the world (after deciding what the field is about), followed by the organization of that region according to the characteristics of phenomena corresponding to stable appearances/manifestations of objects that are part of an ontology of that region. In deciding the stability or regularity of a phenomenon, observational tests or arguments have to be provided. Once these basic phenomena are clear, further research about them (or research that uses them to make further arguments) can proceed. The work in Bodoff (2012) can also be adduced to make the case for foundations from a pragmatic view, since for Bodoff, the need for conceptual reorganization is also due to the lack of pragmatic progress. Without a proper inner network—what Bodoff refers to as conceptual research—research work tends to just move on from one application context to another. They "'move-on' to new phenomena" (Bodoff, 2012, p. 14) but this does not automatically mean the creation of the engineering science that is sought from IR.

network of discourse. While several such foundations questions were previously discussed, this chapter problematizes the inner network and the foundations research discourse as a whole. It argues about what this inner network, and hence foundations for IR&S, must be like to address the modern context, as reflected in the outer network of discourse (as discussed in chapter 2).

The inner network is not monolithic; it has structure. For example, for Laudan, values and basic concepts were presupposed by methodology, all three of which constituted the inner network (Laudan, 1989). While foundations issues are presupposed by other types of issues, they are not all at the same level. Some foundations issues are presupposed by others, and hence are more foundational. Perhaps the first fundamental research question that foundations discourse revolves around (and which a text on foundations such as this is supposed to address) is "What are or ought to be the foundational questions?" This question problematizes the idea of a foundation in the first place (see footnote 3 in the Introduction to this book).

Section 5.1.1 explicates two categories of foundations questions to directly address this question: (1) disciplinary questions, whose subject matter is what IR&S scholars and practitioners say and do (i.e., discourse and other activity), and what this means about the shared social phenomenon that makeup the field, discipline, or discourse; and (2) questions of comportment,[4] whose subject matter is the way that IR&S scholars and practitioners approach the world. One's comportment toward the world is a value-oriented attitude toward some region of the world that reveals that region in a particular way (*as* something). For example, to a furniture maker, a tree may appear as the material for a chair, or simply as profit; whereas for the artist, it may instead appear as a symbol of life. The IR&S scholar's view of a text, as a resource for information-seeking processes, would supposedly be different from, say, that of a literary expert, for whom the same text could instead be a socially, psychologically, and politically liberating cultural artifact. The comportment of a researcher determines their research perspective—first discussed in chapter 1 (see section 1.3.2.6). Similarly, with respect to the study of the pre representational or pre theoretical aspects of phenomena construal (as first discussed in section 2.3) this is a research task that requires a researcher comportment that is different (or that it pertains to a different aspect of a researcher's overall comportment) from

---

4. This concept is taken from the work of Heidegger. A short summary of its meaning is in Inwood (1999, p. 133). A more detailed discussion can be found in Pettigrew and Raffoul (2012, pp. 3–13).

the comportment required for mathematical representation and technical design.

Section 5.1.2 discusses the function of foundations network beyond being a static representation of foundations questions and their relations, particularly with respect to the kind of research culture it is to support.

5.1.1 Categories of Foundations Questions: Disciplinary versus Comportment Questions

Disciplinary and discourse questions are those whose primary subject matter is the scholarly and other activities of IR&S researchers relating to the field, discipline, or discourse as a shared, social phenomenon. Included are questions about what constitutes the discourse; how it grows, changes, and progresses; and how it compares with other social-scholarly phenomena such as that associated with a different field. Questions of purpose, identity, and progress are disciplinary questions, and they are also fieldwide questions (as they were denoted in chapter 1) in that they are about the field or discourse as a whole. Chapters 3 and 4 developed positions on the question of progress, a question about the character of discourse; section 5.2 instead develops ideas of identity and purpose. Disciplinary questions are, however, connected with questions in the comportment category; the foundations network is tightly linked.

Comportment questions pertain to a human agent's overall way of approaching the world; this is not only a simple perspective or "mental stance," but their overall way of being. We contend that the comportment of a typical IR&S researcher is important to understand for foundations research and hence for the foundations researcher; and as the following sections will elaborate, the comportment of the user is of importance for the typical IR&S researcher. The importance of understanding the comportment of researchers is motivated through the need to reinvestigate the nature of the components of a search process given the modern context.

Prior chapters argued that the modern context, with its richer set of phenomena associated with search applications, behooves us to reinvestigate foundations. In the set-theoretic language used to denote retrieval processes in chapter 1, this implies that the usual components in the relationship $R([q], [d], [u], [c])$ must also be reconstrued. What kind of phenomena are then to constitute q, d, u, and c? What are queries, documents, users, collections, and contexts, given the modern situation? These questions cannot be addressed in isolation. These objects are deeply intertwined with one another, and the particulars of their relationships have then to be discovered along with epistemological and other methodological assumptions that determine how one comes to know such particulars. This is not an exercise in mathematical representation, as "foundations" here does not equate to the mathematical foundations (i.e., to techniques and frameworks for representing retrieval objects and processes). Instead, it moves beyond mathematical representations to understanding the phenomena being represented. This does not only refer to the basic assumptions behind a representation (e.g., the independence of documents—as system responses—to a query), nor is it primarily concerned with the general discourse about suitable ways to mathematically represent empirical phenomena (e.g., in Krantz et al., 2006; Luce et al., 2006; Suppes et al., 2006). It is concerned instead with rigorously understanding the objects and processes themselves. As such, it is more foundational than the discourse about the details of ready-made representations (i.e., discourses on mathematical foundations).

In particular, this corresponds to studying the researcher's process of objectification: forming mathematical or other representations of objects that are observed empirically (i.e., revealed to the senses).[5] Objectification is the process through which features of the world become understood as particular objects for theoretical and scientific study (see Glazebrook, 2000, chapter 2; Heelan, 2003).[6] In addition to scientifically/theoretically

---

5. As discussed in chapter 2 (cf. section 2.3), objectification of phenomena is important to study as (1) the processes that lead to effective objectification or construal of phenomena are indicators of progress and (2) since several research problems in IR&S are primarily construal problems. The notion of objectification below develops on the corresponding discussion in chapter 2. There is yet a backward compatibility. With respect to 1, any assessment of an objectification as effective requires to also consider its different aspects as discussed below. And with respect to 2, the research problems in IR&S that boil down to construal problems can be depicted by means of the different aspects of objectification discussed below.

6. To engage in such a process is for one to partake in a theoretical (theoria) mode of being. A mode of being reveals or uncovers things in a particular way, and is guided by a corresponding mode of knowing or type of knowledge to its outcome (Volpi, 2007, p. 36). In this case, it is wisdom (sophia) that guides the theoretical mode to its outcome. Wisdom refers to a combination of scientific-knowledge where the notion of science is not restricted to the physical sciences but includes general intellectual understanding of arbitrary phenomena and intuitive understanding of things in the world (or beings). This mode of knowing will now be known as the scientific-theoretical mode; we will not have more to say about this intuitive aspect. The theoretical mode aims to engage in observation, description, and verification as means to contemplate beings/things (Volpi, 2007). In this mode, one is comported toward "theoretical and scientific study." This is a mode of pure contemplation (McNeill, 1999, pp. 19–23). Thus, a mode of being is primary, and acts as the condition of possibility for the theoretical, productive, and practical modes of comportment (the latter two are discussed below).

understanding the world and how it comes to be objectified, the researcher seeks to make things or to enact change through action. To the extent this change pertains to production (making) or manipulation it is about the póiesis mode of being, that is, the productive or making mode of comportment.[7] It is the craft or technê type of knowledge, including technical know-how, and general strategies or principles for enacting change through making/creating, that guides this mode (see footnote 6) toward its end.[8] With respect to change made through human acts without any external products, it is about the práxis mode of comportment that pertains not to activities aiming toward external beings or works/products, but to oneself; and it is practical wisdom that guides this mode to its end.[9] This is a practical sensibility that sits among an ethical-political background that determines the concrete ethos (Volpi, 2007, p. 46) for a researcher and facilitates their choosing to act in some way and not another.

The following outlines the types of questions that pertain to the modes of knowing (or knowledge types) corresponding to each mode of

---

7. As a mode of being it is "an uncovering attitude of the productive and manipulating kind, an attitude which is assumed with respect to being when one pursues the aim of the production of works" (Volpi, 2007, p. 36).

8. However, the póiesis mode is not only about making, manipulating, or in our case, technology-use. As section 5.3.2 discusses with respect to the comportment of the user (a being of interest for a researcher in their scientific-theoretical mode of comportment), this póiesis aspect of comportment toward the world, for technology users corresponds to a way of bringing-forth meanings. However, with respect to the typical researcher, only craft as making and technological manipulation is considered.

9. Practical wisdom is also known as phrònesis. (Volpi, 2007). See Simon (1986, 1999) and Mezel (1986, pp. 92-94) for a discussion of the notion of phrónesis in the Aristotelian tradition, and in the post-Aristotelian tradition as "prudence." Heidegger's adaptation of this concept is further discussed in (Coltman, 1998, chapter 1; Brogan, 2005, pp. 138–148) and Weidenfeld (2011). Note that to therefore study the pretheoretical or prerepresentational has several related meanings. Firstly, it is to study phenomena in a "scientific-theoretical" mode using the apparatus of phenomenology, so that the study pertains to that which appears to the consciousness of the researcher through basic observation. This is as opposed to their construing and thinking about phenomena using received abstract/mathematical or other theories. Secondly, it is to study phenomena, as a researcher in their póiesis and práxis modes of being; this is a more fundamental, and indeed a more foundational type of study. Finally, as users are the subject for IR&S research, a third sense pertains to studying praxis and póiesis modes of user comportment through the scientific-theoretical or other modes of researcher comportment. The first sense depicts the sense in which pretheoretical and prerepresentational was intended in prior sections and chapters. The third sense is explicitly addressed in section 5.3.2, and the second sense is not directly addressed in this book.

comportment: scientific knowledge (see footnote 6), craft and practical wisdom, and which together correspond to the categories of comportment questions.

5.1.1.1 Questions pertaining to comportment For Heidegger, the práxis mode of comportment, or práxis "way/mode of being" is fundamental or primary (Volpi, 2007, pp. 36–38), whereas the scientific-theoretical and póiesis modes are derived: they are dependent on the práxis. From the perspective of foundations research, to study the comportment of the typical IR&S researcher is then to ask questions about their different modes of comportment. To study their scientific-theoretical mode of comportment, means to consider phenomenological, epistemological, and ontological aspects of objectification. These aspects can be thought of submodes of the scientific-theoretical mode, in that they constitute the latter. In what follows, a mode (sometimes termed an "aspect") of comportment may be denoted by either the corresponding mode of being or knowing, or constituting submode. Thus, a reference to the "craft mode of comportment" or the "phenomenological aspect of comportment" is a reference to the mode of knowing pertaining to the práxis mode of being and the scientific-theoretical mode of being, respectively. Hence, a foundational question pertaining to one of these aspects belongs to the category of objectification or the scientific-theoretical mode of comportment. The phenomenological aspect of a typical researcher's scientific-theoretical comportment pertains to how they experience the world, and specifically, their phenomenon of interest, such as users and search scenarios. The epistemological aspect deliberates on the way researchers come to know their objects of interest as such (as user, document, or system, for example) on experiencing the world in a particular way. This leads to an initial construction of relevant objects. These two investigations therefore serve to generate an initial ontology, a description of the objects with their properties and inter relations that supplies the content for their further ontological investigations according to the ontological aspect of their comportment. Ontological investigations inquire about the actual and possible existence of objects (and their properties and relations), including investigations of a hypothetical nature (e.g., as to whether a particular interaction could exist or not, given a system setup). In addition, ontology as fundamental ontology considers the meaning of existing or being, as to what it means to be in the first place, and this goes back to their fundamental mode of being that pertains to práxis (see the discussion in Gelven, 1989, pp. 3–20). This would, however, be an inquiry about the práxis mode of comportment of the user from a researcher studying them from a scientific-theoretical mode of comportment. Similarly, from the perspective of a typical researcher, and certainly for the foundations researcher, all the corresponding modes of a user's comportment are of interest. For example, what it means to be a human being or technology user, or equivalently, what the user's práxis mode of comportment is like.

Closely related to a researcher's comportment, especially with respect to the scientific-theoretical mode, are the principles of reason, subsumed under a corresponding logic, that govern the proper way (for a researcher) of going about the objectification of observations with respect to thinking and discourse about them. Foundational questions can also be about these principles; about the proper way of thinking and speaking about objects, processes, and their relations.

In addition to being concerned with understanding some part of the world (through objectification), IR&S researchers are also interested in making changes thereto (i.e., acting to intervene in existing processes by creating objects, e.g., through creating technical designs or policy). This interest is a fundamental part of who they are.[10] It is in their práxis or fundamental mode of comportment: making technology or engaging culture are purposes of IR&S (see also chapter 6), and in shaping the craft aspect of IR&S researchers, the purposes determine their práxis mode as well.

The práxis mode, from whence the craft and the scientific-theoretical modes derive, conditions the latter modes, meaning that the ethical principles or ethos (i.e., principles of "practical-wisdom"—the phronetic knowledge) that guide action in the mode of práxis condition how the researchers theorize and create technological designs. Hence, the derivative modes are conditioned by those foundational positions governing the why and how of researchers' actions. These ethical principles contextualize the derivative modes according to socio-ethical concerns possessed by the researcher. For example, decisions about how created technologies ought to be engaged with or how the world is to be engaged through them, would be conditioned by their understanding of what the human-machine relationship is or ought to be.

---

10. That is, it characterizes the practically oriented IR&S researcher, in particular, the experimental IR researcher, and is thereby a researcher-type or archetype. There are of course many such types that can be adduced to IR&S research, but this book only considers the typical such IR&S researcher interested in observation and "making," and the foundations researcher. Most of the other types of researchers are somewhere in between these two types.

Foundational positions on craft are not about specific technical designs but about tacit understandings that help to further concretize the general ethical principles. For example, an ethical goal conditioning software creation could pertain to saving users time by speeding up a particular human process, whereas the craft aspect—that is, knowledge or knowing pertaining to bringing about a technological configuration or scenario (see section 1.1) that informs how the ethical goal guides its práxis mode to its end—would be concerned with the general strategy for doing this. Such a strategy could include at once, addressing bureaucratic hurdles (policy), automating parts of the process through software development, and developing a user-interaction strategy to replace prior human interaction. The technical design for the system involved would take its meaning and purpose from this general strategy.

This chapter mainly discusses the scientific-theoretic mode of comportment, focusing on the ontological aspect of the researcher's objectification as they are reflected in the basic concepts found in IR&S discourse. The focus is ontological, as it is about the nature and properties of relevant theoretical entities and their relationships (e.g., information, relevance, document, query, user, context, and collection). To the extent that the discussion therein is about researchers' knowledge, it is epistemological. In general, the following discussions often address the phenomenological, epistemological, and ontological aspects at once, as they seek to understand the ways of experiencing, understanding, knowing, and reasoning about an entity (and about what kinds of regularities or patterns the entity can have). Questions pertaining to the praxis and craft aspects are addressed in section 5.2.4.

It is our contention in this chapter that the categories of comportment and disciplinary questions account for the majority of foundational concerns in IR&S. That therefore, the inner network of discourse for IR&S is that part of discourse that addresses them. However, this network is not just a static store of foundational propositions. Instead, as the following discusses, it admits a structure that facilitates a type of dialectic and is to be used in a particular way.

5.1.2 Properties of the Foundations Network: Its Purpose, Use, and Complementary Research Culture

This section describes our proposal for the nature and properties of the foundations network, which also characterizes the discourse in the remainder of the chapter. The proposal also acts as a manifesto for the focus and style of the foundations research we deem appropriate for addressing the modern context. The foundations network is constituted by a set of positions (as propositions) taken in relation to questions or concerns that are foundational. These propositions can be understood to be related through relations of presupposition, mutual dependence, or some other unspecified relation. The network can also be understood as a discourse map. There are no set number of foundational questions and concerns from the outset, and each was chosen due to its relevance to the modern context (some having been previously raised in prior chapters). These foundational concerns are to do with the changing nature of the human-machine relationship, in particular, with the pervasive and inevitably mediating nature of technology discussed in chapter 1.

This chapter elucidates some necessary requirements for the development of existing positions to address the modern context. It also highlights dependencies between the development of different notions, forming the links in the network. In addition, where appropriate, it suggests possible specific research directions for development. It problematizes the user; system; and related notions; and in particular, notions pertaining to their relation, such as information need, document, and relevance; or notions with a key role in enabling the mediating-nature of technology, such as that of collection. Moreover, it problematizes the study of these aspects that seek to either make technology or make claims about the technology-mediated action or experience, such as to do with explaining the functioning of a system, assessing the goodness of a system, or exploring the nature of a user experience.

The network as a discourse map focuses on particular things and not on others, and it represents a specific style of discourse. This focus and style, based on an underlying interpretation of the modern context, can be understood to constitute the starting point of a critical discursive culture. The deliberations about foundations that follow from analyzing the modern context result in this overall focus being on the subject of technology-mediated experience (TME). The theme of TME thereby colors the strategies for concept development and supports the proposal in chapter 6 for a new kind of science of TME.

With respect to the culture, the type of analysis offered can be understood to be quite mixed or blended, meaning that foundational notions are investigated as cognitive, social, or machine-generated phenomena, whether in a descriptive or a more formal way. However, the analysis is closer to being phenomenological than "formal": it tends not to explain using logical analysis or using mathematical structures as metaphors. This is owing to such a style being more apt (in general) for addressing foundational positions, especially when they pertain to objectification.

The blended nature of analyses therein means that given any one aspect, such as the topic of experimentation, there is no preliminary inclination for understanding it in a particular way. The place of formalization of experimental processes can be discussed along with the social function of experimentation.

Keeping the discourse style open in this way serves also to accommodate the various ways of accounting for phenomena. IR&S phenomena can be accounted for subjectively in the first-person perspective, such as an unshared user experience (Varela and Shear, 1999). It can instead be intersubjective, being accounted for from a second-person perspective, such as when shared aspects of user experiences, such as cognitive reaction on interacting with a document, are addressed (Pauen, 2012). And finally, the account can be objective, such as the mentioning of the words in a given document or the particulars of system behavior, both of which are observable from a third-person perspective (Chalmers, 2002).

Although the main overriding phenomenon is that of search—search as meaning-generating and as the most typical mediational phenomenon—the network does not restrict focus to any one particular level of search construal (see chapter 1). For example, it may discuss the phenomenon of learning by supposing search to be a sub-phenomenon of learning. The justification for this is that the meaning of a thing (e.g., a search process), depending on the perspective, can come from an encapsulating process or a system of such processes. Moreover, the culture of foundations elicited is a self-reflective one: it problematizes its own perspective; this is partly since such a problematization is a foundational one.[11]

The above properties of the foundations network, which the remainder of this chapter develops, present a characterization that we deem important for a foundations research culture that is to equip IR&S to address the modern problem context. Chapter 6 further justifies aspects of this characterization by arguing for their importance in reimagining the discipline of IR&S.

5.1.3 Structure of This Chapter

Section 5.2 addresses disciplinary questions pertaining to identity, which are among the most presupposed of foundations questions. It relates to the purposes and ends of discourse, as well as to question of progress (as

---

11. It is also partly because, as section 5.4 explains, the study of user experience leads to the study of observation, and the latter study comes to bear on the researcher's observation process.

progress is supposedly made by fulfilling a purpose). Positions taken in regard to identity and purpose are presupposed by comportment questions. Section 5.3 discusses scientific-theoretical comportment questions, mainly with respect to the ontological aspect as it applies to specific entities and relations, while section 5.4 addresses general comportment questions to do with the epistemological aspect, in particular, those about observation and scientific theorization. It further discusses the implications for the outer layer of discourse, given the way foundations is characterized by this chapter. Finally, section 5.5 concludes with the main arguments.

Comportment questions pertaining to the ethical/practical-sense and craft modes (of researcher and user comportment) are discussed in section 5.2.4 with respect to how they relate to the identity of IR&S, and in the context of system making (as opposed to policy creation, for example) in the problematization of the notion of system in section 5.3. That foundations questions are categorizable in the way suggested and that their style of address is intended as described above (in section 5.1.2), is our own answer to the problematization of foundations. Our answer is inspired by Heelan's work on a hermeneutical understanding of how science works, that is, his hermeneutical philosophy of science (Heelan, 1991, 1997). While a fuller explanation of this borrowing is beyond the scope of this book, a basic rationale can be given. Heelan understands scientific practice as a complex interpretive dialogue between formal/mathematical theory and empirical findings through experiment. His focus on objectification was particularly suited for reinvestigating how IR&S construes its basic object and deals with complex or mixed objects that have technical and social aspects. To be clear, this book does not adapt this seminal work in any significant way; it can instead be understood as preparing the ground for any such future project.

5.2 Questions Pertaining to the Discipline and Discourse

The work in prior chapters addressed the key disciplinary question of the progress of IR&S discourse. This section instead focuses on questions about the nature of that discourse, as to its purposes, values, subject matter, and the mode of approaching the subject matter (e.g., whether it is a scientific approach), all of which serve to identify it.[12] As to the mode of approach, at the disciplinary level (i.e., about the kind of science IR&S is) it is only

---

12. A field cannot be identified by the objects it studies (Ibekwe-SanJuan, 2012)—which it may share with other disciplines—but by its purposes. In addition to purpose, positions

treated generally (and in more detail in chapter 6), and is only further specified within comportment in discussions of scientific methodology. Because IR&S also seeks to create technology, the purposes of making such technology, in addition to the purposes of studying the related phenomena, also serve to identify the discipline.

Each of the above foundational aspects of identity is discussed below and contributes to the overall position about identity. The identity serves to relate and differentiate the discipline from others, and is among the most presupposed of foundational positions. Each such aspect is also a foundational disciplinary position in its own right.

Section 5.2.1 elucidates particular concepts of IR and IS with respect to their purposes, while section 5.2.2 discusses whether their approaches can be seen as scientific. Section 5.2.3 explains the place of a concept of information in discussions about disciplinary identity. Section 5.2.4 discusses how effects of created technology inform the identity of IR&S; this pertains to the craft and its ethics and practical sense. Section 5.2.5 instead recasts the question of purpose, and hence identity, as a question of values. Purposes are generated from values. Section 5.2.5 argues that the space of values, as the source of purposes, needs to be rethought. Such a rethinking would of course have a significant impact on identity.

This problematizing of identity (i.e., as to what kind of science/discipline IR&S is) is not only useful for the sake of intellectual reasons but also for political ones. The clearer a discipline is about its identity, the stronger its case for existence, especially among related intellectual discourses.

5.2.1 Received Identities for IR and IS

This section discusses some received stances about the identities of IR and IS by examining their purpose, subject matter, and the way of studying the subject matter. As Ibekwe-SanJuan (2012) details, notions of IR&S differ across cultures, and reveal residues of preceding intellectual discourses.[13] As chapter 1 discussed, both IR and IS can be understood to be focused on the subject matter or problem of technology mediation, the purpose being

---

about the part of reality IR&S focuses on and its key phenomenon—that of the search process—are discussed below in the context of identity.

13. Such as positivist philosophy for the anglophone world, pragmatism for North America, and continental philosophies for European (especially French) conceptions of IR&S. Whereas anglophone notions of information have been associated with the mathematical and scientific, information has a more social interpretation in France, although this might be an overgeneralization (Ibekwe-SanJuan, 2012).

to solve problems pertaining to this subject matter. The style of the former is practical/technical, and the latter is more social/cultural/cognitive.

While chapter 6 critically problematizes the relation between IR and IS, and between them and other fields, the following section discusses the complementarity of their purposes in light of received stances.

5.2.1.1 The purpose and ethical imperative of IR systems: From word matching to context understanding One of the purposes of IR systems, according to Bar-Hillel (1962), was to bridge between different domains (through language-processing techniques, such as keyword matching) at a time where increasing human specializations meant that it was becoming progressively difficult to relate across the wealth of available information and to discover connections. Farradane intensifies this point. For him, retrieval technology had become a fundamental means for discovery, and hence for the growth of science (Farradane, 1961). Similarly, for Kochen (1967), IR's raison d'être was to make tools that serve to facilitate the growth of knowledge. Search-based information systems were then a necessary means for the growth and progress of science. Its purpose now has of course expanded beyond science, but how can its modern role be framed? In addition to its function as an indispensable tool for the growth of knowledge and science, it can be understood as something enabling and growing the types of possible technological/informational experiences. These experiences can then result in the growth of scientific (or other kinds of) knowledge, or more generally, the satisfaction of a variety of human needs.

Moreover, in bridging between concepts and knowledge domains, IR has evolved from bridging as superficial term matching to bridging as developing richer relationships between concepts and domains, and the creation of actionable knowledge (e.g., Wolfram).

The IR system is thereby increasingly expected to "understand" what it relates by deducing patterns[14] among material objects of knowledge. The purpose of IR can then be understood to have evolved beyond being about the study and facilitation of the growth of knowledge. It is instead heading toward being additionally about the study of relations between knowledge domains and usage contexts, and the facilitation of automatic generation of relations between particular usage contexts and domains. However, the

---

14. This can be seen as a reason for using complex machine learning approaches in IR.

relations here are not only with respect to the low-level links between queries and documents (i.e., between groups of words), but also with respect to a higher level. They are also those between the semantic networks or overall contexts on either side: between aspects that condition the user and their behavior, and those that condition the document (e.g., the collection and the document's social role).

IR systems are then moving toward relating together two overall contexts that constitute the entire set of known factors: the user-side context and the document-/collection-/system-side context. As with the original purpose of IR, this can be understood to also be a social imperative for IR practitioners. Every application creating actionable insights from data—from a music-recommendation application to service-based applications (e.g., Uber) for suggesting how one should travel (and enabling that human activity in a particular way)—is in some sense fulfilling this imperative to the extent they are relating between contexts. This relating of contexts corresponds to meaning suggestion (see chapter 1).

5.2.1.2 Information science as primarily about communication and culture This section is about the purposes of IS as they pertain to IR&S. Thus it will not focus on IR specifically, as in section 5.2.1.1, but on the combination of IR and IS. When speaking in general about its own purposes, IS discourses seldom ignore their application aspect as represented by IR. To this end, when the purpose of IR&S is mentioned, it should be taken to refer to the purpose of IS, which employs IR to partially fulfill this purpose. The following highlights three representative conceptions of purpose and argues for their complementarity, though they differ in focus.

Both Meadows (2016) and Meadow (2006) conclude, after a lifetime of thinking about IR&S, that it should be thought of primarily as a type of communications science. Human-human communication perhaps does generally serve as an ideal for human-computer communication and hence for interactive information retrieval. In this vein, Pickering (1996, p. 447) provides a manifesto for framing IR&S as "the study of the knowledge system" as a whole. This can be understood an "epistemological science" of sorts, that is, not equivalent to the philosophical discipline of epistemology but to the science complementing it. The purview of this knowledge system is that of human communication, but beginning in the mind (before behavior) of the producer of knowledge, all the way to the mind of its consumer. Everything in between that is influenced by culture—such as the expression, collection, and re-presentation of knowledge—needs to be considered. The focus here is not only on the artifacts mediating communication but also on the experience of reading or observing that artifact, including the purpose to those experiences, such as that of the satisfaction of various needs. The centrality of the notion of communication to IS, whether drawn from the cybernetics work of Wiener and the mathematical theories of communication attributed to Shannon, or from the humanities and social sciences, is accepted in both Anglophone and Francophone contexts (Ibekwe-SanJuan, 2012). Ibekwe quotes an early (1993) definition of the discipline that gained some consensus in France as "the study of information or communication processes, that arise from organized or finalized actions, that may rely or not on technical tools and that partake of social and cultural mediations" (Ibekwe-SanJuan, 2012, p. 1698).

Buckland's conception of IS is similar to these ideas, except that it focuses more on understanding this cultural (extra-cognitive) aspect. In particular, he emphasizes the craft aspect of IR&S, taking it to be "a form of cultural engagement" (Buckland, 2012, p. 1). In other words, the created technologies and policies constitute the means for such an engagement. However, these technologies have multiple roles, and they have also become artifacts of a culture and have acquired the power to generate and mediate culture.

Like Buckland, Furner suggests that IS is not particularly about information, that it is better understood as a branch of cultural studies. That it is not primarily a scientific or social-scientific but a humanities discipline that studies the cultural processes of collection, preservation, and access (whether with or without the aid of technology; Furner, 2015). What IR&S practitioners do, then, cannot quite be described as science, nor as being about information, let alone as an "information science" (Furner, 2015). In addition to being objects of study for IS, these three cultural processes can be understood to depict the general modes of the cultural engagement mentioned in Buckland (2012).

This account of the purposes of IR and IS can be understood as complementary. With respect to what IR and IS seek to do, the bridging between concepts and domains—as a purpose of traditional IR—is a form of cultural engagement of a scientific-cultural or intellectual-cultural variety. Cultural engagement in IS is partially through the technology IR creates. Moreover, with modern IR moving toward being about relating arbitrary contexts, its purpose can be understood as enabling cultural engagement in a more general sense. However, to effect such engagement, both disciplines must have an investigative component, which deliberates on shared underlying problems; problems pertaining to some region of reality. In particular, these shared problems pertain to the issue of technology mediation. IR focuses on the technical and behavioral aspects therein, while IS focuses on the cultural and cognitive.

5.2.2 What Kind of Science Can IR&S Be, If It Can Be a Science at All?

The nature of the problems and phenomena should indeed determine the character of the methodology or discipline that studies it (Buckland, 2012). With respect to the subject matter of IR&S, if it is taken to pertain to technology mediation, as chapter 1 holds, then for us it warrants a proper science. In contrast with Buckland (2012), this would not only be a science of the artificial.[15] While chapter 6 further examines this question, some necessary aspects of such a science are argued for below.

First, note that if the processes of collection, preservation, and access are taken as key to IR&S (Furner, 2015), then IR&S is less about artificial objects than it is about the relationships people have with those objects, and hence it is in a significant way a science that pertains to bodies, minds, cultures, and artifacts.

Second, the problems of IR&S warrant a proper science because the aspects involved therein already have sciences that study them, from the cognitive and neurosciences, linguistics, psychology, and anthropology for depicting the user and their context, to the mathematical and computer sciences for addressing the technological aspect. If these aspects have their own sciences, then it is not clear at the outset that their combination should not or cannot be a science; the opposite is suggested. Furthermore, the problems addressed in those sciences pertain to explaining/interpreting/predicting human or machine behavior, which is what is required for IR&S with respect to the problem of technology mediation. Therefore, what is needed for the study of technology mediation exists in piecemeal form in various scientific discourses.

Finally, as to IR&S not only being a science of the artificial, it is clear that artificial artifacts (e.g., documents, technologies) are crucial, but they are neither the only nor the central aspects of IR&S. A variety of phenomena in addition to the artificial come into play when studying technology mediation, but to what aspects of reality do they belong such that IR&S can be said to be a science of those aspects? To address this question, let us first deconstruct the idea that IR&S is a science of information and what it implies about the aspect of reality IR&S points to. Whether or not the

---

15. As developed in the seminal work by H. A. Simon (1996), this science does not only refer to artifacts but also to the interface between artifacts and their environment.

key focus of IR&S ought to be information depends first on how the concept of information is defined, and second, on the place and function of this conception among all other concepts through which the discipline is understood.[16]

5.2.3   Identity and the Concept of Information

Cornelius asks what it is that cannot be done without a theory of information (and hence a proper definition of information; Cornelius, 2002, p. 420); a theory that has to "establish a convincing relationship between information, knowledge, and models of learning" beyond technical tasks. However, if such a theory (or definition) does not appear, yet IR&S practitioners and scholars are able to continue with their work, then perhaps they do not require such a theory, nor do they even have to agree on a definition.[17]

The suggestion that information may not be a central concept for IR&S coheres with the conclusions of Buckland (2012) and Furner (2015). It can be shown to be justified for those notions of information that are absent or scarce in the discourse. However, there could be other construals of information that instead point to something—perhaps previously known in terms of other phenomena—that does have a strong presence in discourse. The absence of particular construals does not automatically imply the implausibility or impossibility of other construals.

As Ma (2013) argues, physical or mathematical notions of information do not exhaust the different possible senses of information for IR&S, implying that a more complete definition is required, and that this has to do more with the social and intentional aspects. Information may be understood to have a subjective aspect. And like the notion of "document" (which can be the source of information), information may not refer only to an objective thing (Ma, 2012). In agreement with Ma's inclination, Marchionini explains that due to the blurring of the physical and mental spaces, information becomes more "experiential, fluid and massively social" (Marchionini, 2010, p. 77).

---

16. For example, if information is that which is transferred from system to user, then the notions of user, system, transfer, and information mutually condition one another.

17. Cornelius concedes that the lack of such a theory of information may just have to be accepted and that (Cornelius, 2002, p. 420) "it may be simply a feature of the practice of information science that we need to express our regret at the absence of [a] grand theory of information, but are content to operate at the level of our own isolated technical problems."

The conclusions of Ma and Marchionini cohere with the conclusions of the more extensive analysis in Capurro and Hjørland (2003)[18] of the range of information concepts employed in IR&S and beyond. Cappuro and Hjørland's emphasis of the need to balance an objective account of information with the subjective, interpretive dimension of information is shared by works outside IR&S, such as Goguen (1997),[19] who argues for the need for a concept of information in computing discourses, where (an item of) information corresponds to "an interpretation of a configuration of signs for which members of some social group are accountable" (Goguen, 1997, p. 30).[20] Outside computation, Garfinkel and Rawls (2015) argue for the importance of including the social and subjective dimensions of information in a general concept of information. And although discourse on the notion of information is growing (Floridi, 2011, 2017; Adriaans, 2013), works exploring the subjective and social dimensions of information have been limited. Developing a rigorous concept of information that considers the subjective, intersubjective/social, and objective aspects and accounts for the modern technological context remains an important pursuit.

However, some conditions exist for an effective information concept, if it were to be expressly for IR&S. The task of developing such a notion, sensitive to the social and subjective/intentional aspects, must involve

18. The notion of information features prominently in the Aristotelian-Thomistic philosophical traditions (Capurro and Hjørland, 2003), where it is tied to a particular concept of causality (i.e., of events or actions). While this concept of causality is employed in section 5.3.2 as a way to recast basic concepts in IR&S, its use there does not include considering its relation to the notion of information. Exploring this relation would be natural next step to extending the ideas in section 5.3.2.

19. Goguen argues thus that a suitable theory of information must be a situated one; it must address "the meanings that users give to events" (Goguen, 1997, p. 28) and must therefore be a "social theory of information" (Goguen, 1997, p. 29) as opposed to a statistical one like Shannon's or (what he calls) a "representational" one (Goguen, 1997, p. 29) like that of Barwise and Perry (1983). Dretske's (1981) theory of information as an indicator of regularities from whence emerges meanings would arguably also fall into the representational category (Adams and de Moraes, 2016). While it has been influential as an objective theory of information (Capurro and Hjørland, 2003) in IR discourses (van Rijsbergen and Lalmas, 1996), as Goguen observes, it does not cater to the subjective aspect.

20. The reference to interpretation captures a subjective dimension of information that situates it in the *tacit knowledge* of a human agent, a concept borrowed from the work of Polanyi (1967). As Heelan mentions in Heelan and Babich (2002, p. 5) Polanyi affirms in Polanyi (1964, Preface) that this tacit knowledge amounts to Heidegger's being-in-the-world. In particular, this tacit knowledge includes a non-representational knowledge, which Heidegger's works deliberate on at length, see section 5.3.3.2.

looking at the entire semantic network of concepts defining an overall idea of IR&S. That is, the place of the social/intentional in different contexts of the use of the notion of information has to be discovered.

Moreover, the significance of this task should not be underestimated for an additional reason. Given the various uses of the notion of information (Adriaans, 2013), a coherent conception of IR&S with a rigorously argued concept of information at its center, could be the key intellectual identifier exposing the place of IR&S among other intellectual pursuits. This is important for the sake of external coherence (see chapter 2), but also because it could add value to IR&S through it being able to direct research in henceforth related areas (see Bawden and Robinson, 2013).

Any conception of information found to be central would strongly condition the nature of the discipline. A science of physical and mathematical information is other than a science of information when information refers to a cognitive phenomenon pertaining to human knowing. For example, even if mathematical modeling were crucial to the latter type of science, it would not primarily be a technical science but one of cognition, culture, and the subjective (and intersubjective) aspects of reality. If, as a central concept of information may reveal, the focus is mixed (i.e., on all aspects: culture, cognition, material, technology, etc.), this would make a strong statement about IR&S deserving its own logical space among existing disciplines. Perhaps then, if one were to seek the possible construal of information that is central, one would have to work out what aspect of reality IR&S points to, from whence its phenomena appear. This depends on first elucidating the metaphysical presuppositions about what regions there are, a point further discussed in chapter 6.

5.2.4   Identity through Ethics and Craft

The above claimed that the purpose of IR technology, a purpose pursued in the póiesis mode of comportment by users, should be understood to be the enabling of the ability to link up contexts through making its key phenomenon of search manifest; and the purpose of IS is the study of processes related to this technology in their social, cultural, and cognitive aspects; and that the purposes of creating technology (in IR) and for engaging culture (in IS) are similarly pursued in póiesis mode by researchers with guidance from craft knowledge. However, the purpose of this craft (i.e., its practical purposes as determined by a research ethos or practical knowledge) extends beyond the immediate technical purpose of finding relevant documents or showing relations between domains. Search systems enable search processes, and these processes in turn enable particular types of human activities with their particular benefits. The pervasive nature of modern technology means that the purpose of that technology (i.e., the ethics of the craft) has to be understood in this way with respect to their ultimate effects. What the relations are can be understood by looking at the phenomena and processes search enables. As chapter 1 argued, search is the most typical mediational phenomenon, where mediation is about linking meanings; any applications enabling this mediation thereby involve search.

In the case of IR&S in general, search is the central phenomenon either by itself (as in the classical sense of linking queries and documents) or as embedded or encapsulated in a larger phenomenon or process, such as information seeking, learning (see Hansen and Rieh, 2016), or communicating (in general). The larger phenomenon can be seen to be constituted by multiple instances of search as well as other interactive information behaviors, all organized around the single theme (learning or information seeking) that determines the phenomenon. The overall purpose of an encapsulated phenomenon derives from the purpose of its encapsulating phenomenon. IR&S is thus a science of communication[21] to the extent that the linking up of meanings, the key phenomenon pertaining to and ultimate effect of search, is a communicative action. However, the purpose that search inherits does not stop with that of its initial encapsulating phenomenon. For example, the overall purpose of a search encapsulated inside a communication phenomenon is not only communication but also includes that for which the communication was done. Thus, the various purposes for human communication are inherited by the corresponding search, and form its space of purposes. In general, whatever the encapsulating phenomenon, the purpose of search can be understood to ultimately inherit from the nontechnological human process that the technology was supposed to replace in the first place. Given that IR values its systems by means of human categories, there is a strong tacit acceptance of the ideal type of human-computer interactions in search as being those that resemble human-human interactions (Ruthven and Kelly, 2011, chapter 1). However, is the human context always the ideal? Perhaps online socializing is valued for its difference from its real-life counterpart (Turkle, 2011). Are the goals of systems perhaps even more general? If the point of technology-mediated living is ultimately to enable better modes and

---

21. The modern context with social networking, online entertainment, and the like (all of which involve search in an embedded way) however implies that search does not only serve to enable communication, unless perhaps, the notion of communication were sufficiently generalized.

forms of human life, then by definition, current nontechnological human solutions are not to be taken as absolute ideals. For example, in the movie *Her* (Jonze, 2014) the goal is to provide effective companionship, and in other visions of technology-mediated futures, it is anything from H. G. Wells's vision of a "world brain" (Wells and Mayne, 1938) with technology facilitating an oracle-like question-answering service, to technology as the means of transforming cities for the sake of world peace (Otlet, 1990; Andersen and Andersen, 1918). All of these examples correspond to creating a better or alternative version of an existing nontechnological human scenario.

Alternatively, all such technology-mediated activities can be understood-as-search: that is, their application contexts can be generalized by their encapsulated function (see discussion in section 1.2). Yet that would perhaps be too reductive and would offer insufficient explanation as to what they are about. If the meaning and purpose of search in each such embedded scenario is taken to be inherited, does IR&S then need to consider the encapsulating phenomenon or application? And if so, does the identity of IR&S then have to be additionally conditioned by the purpose of that application? Chapter 6 directly addresses this question, arguing that the differing encapsulating applications and phenomena can and should be understood in combination, in a generalized way, in terms of technology-mediated experience (TME), such that IR&S can be reimagined as a science of that generalized phenomenon (of TME). If so, then the "doing" of this science ought to determine the main mode of comportment (and hence, the specific identity) of the current IR&S researcher. In addition to conditioning the identity of the discipline and the main mode of comportment for the researcher, the "why of the craft," that is, the values intended to be fulfilled by technology, are thereby also a foundational issue in its own right.

5.2.5 Identity and the Growing Space of Values

Values and purposes mutually define each other. Values condition acts, such as the building of devices or engaging in scientific discourse, often serving as their purpose. Discussion about the ethics of a discipline pertains to moral reasoning, based on such values and purposes, for judging the merit of actions. The pervasive context of modern technology means that values conditioning human action in general readily condition technology-mediated living. Thus all the usual values pertaining to each such lived-context, and not only those read construable as pertaining to the satisfaction of needs, could be inherited by the technology created to mediate that lived-context.

Thus, as chapter 2 explains, a growing space of values encroaches on the technology space by which technology is to be evaluated. As chapter 1 mentioned, efficiency as a value underdetermines technology. In light of this pervasive context, the notion of the effectiveness of a system clearly needs to be generalized (i.e., expanded) from referring to the effectiveness of fulfilling an information need (as decided by relevance judges) to fulfilling any arbitrary purpose or value inherited from a context of technology-use.

For example, in the case of online ads based on search terms, in addition to having a topical-relevance value with respect to a query, a "document" (i.e., the result of a query) has a value with respect to the expected profit associated with the act (and event) of clicking it. This application can be understood as only having a partial IR component, such that the profit element should not be understood to be part of retrieval theory. Yet there are "users"—the clients of advertising companies—for whom an increase in relevance means an increase in profit.[22] A document then has a value according to the extent it satisfies information needs as well as other needs, such as economic needs. One can imagine many other application contexts that engender a particular value structure based on needs for the objects belonging to IR&S's ontology.

Values are associated in this way, from the viewpoint of the user and researcher, with responses from technology. There are however, values associated with user behaviors, from the perspective of the system and researcher, which leads the system to act, and also values that are associated with research or policy that are mainly relevant for the researcher. Each such observer or agent, therefore has a different space of values. Yet these values interact and depend on one another: there is a system or

---

22. Similarly, if the above application is understood according to an economic model, such a model would also have to adopt some notion of the topical relevance of information. As Braman (2006, p. 34) says, "many believe that the economics of information has fundamentally changed the field of economics itself"—including its basic concepts. The change is still ongoing, and "incorporation of the concept of information into economic theory has affected basic economic concepts, the range of applications of the economics of information is constantly expanding." Braman argues further that:

> Thinking in terms of the economics of information draws our attention to numerous linkages among social processes typically analyzed separately. When we view the economy as essentially a communication system, acknowledge the role of information flows in shaping economic power and capacity, and admit that significant asymmetries in access to information have socio economic consequences, the importance of continuing to think through the theoretical, conceptual, empirical, and methodological issues raised by information at the macro- and micro economic levels is clear.

framework of values at play. For example, while statistically significant system behavior (with respect to the values of precision and recall) might be of value to the researcher, the user might instead be seeking a qualitatively significant experience pertaining to need satisfaction that may not be considered by the researchers' investigations. User satisfaction is a goal for the researcher, albeit often in an average and not individual sense depending on the researcher. Moreover, this entire system of values is contextual: what applies in one context of technology-use or technology/policy creation may not apply in another.

The problem of values is present at a less foundational level, on the outer network (see chapter 3), for example, in research developing evaluation metrics to deal with nontopical relevance. Its prevalence is further indicated by the increasing employment of user studies, which is an attempt to study subjective (and intersubjective) user valuation of technology-use, usually through survey questionnaires and such. However, these are indirect ways to study values. A more direct and systematic study of the system of values pertaining to IR&S is needed to inform both the evaluation and creation of technology, and the study of the relevant phenomena. In particular, the foundation of IR&S needs a metaethics subdiscourse (Marturano, 2002; Sayre-McCord, 2014) subdiscourse to continually assess what values are of relevance; what they attach to; which observer they apply to; and how they interact; and in general, what the place of the ethical is for IR&S. Prior works, such as Furner (2011) suggest this need. Others develop ethical discourses for aspects of IR&S or related discourses (Froehlich, 2004; Furner, 2014), and there are general discourses on ethics and technology that can be adopted for this purpose (Bynum, 2015).

5.3　Questions about Comportment toward Specific Entities or Relations

This section addresses questions pertaining to the comportment of the researcher and only secondarily the objects studied by practitioners that follow that discipline or contribute to the corresponding discourse. In particular, it discusses why and how the traditional positions for each question (e.g., "what is a document?") need to be shifted to reflect the modern context. The main shifts suggested follow a similar theme. They indicate how the entity, relationship, or issue pertaining to the question ought to be conceptualized, given the generalization of the notion of search in chapter 1 from being a technical and system-oriented phenomenon to instead being the most typical phenomenon of mediation.

As discussed in chapter 1, the pervasive nature of modern technology means that to understand the function and effect of that technology, its human context (i.e., its relationship with humans) needs to be understood. The predominating relationship here is that of mediation. Modern technology is then about entities, systems, and the phenomena that mediate human experiences, as well as human actions. The changes in the conceptualizations of basic entities (e.g., query or document) suggested below pertain to their role in this mediation process, which itself sits in a level among different levels of phenomena relevant to the study of search. These are the human-living, mediation, semantic, and interaction levels. Section 5.3.1 discusses these levels and suggests that to properly interrelate phenomena between and within levels, a concept of technology is needed to recast the basic questions and their interrelationships. We adopt such a concept from Heidegger, and use it to reframe and restructure the basic questions relative to one another. Moreover we discuss what any modern resolution to these questions necessitates vis-à-vis this theory.

5.3.1 Different Levels of Phenomena

5.3.1.1 Introduction Foundations questions pertain to different levels of phenomena, and foundations research needs to address them, which means that such a discourse needs to clarify the similarities and differences between these levels. In this regard, this section suggests some necessary characteristics of each of these levels and argues for a specific way to relate phenomena within and between levels. The next section then shows how basic questions for search, which pertain to one level, map to other levels. It suggests the scope that any address of them must have. This in turn indicates what is necessary for addressing basic questions in the modern context, and hence, what must be understood about the inner network and how one should form it. Section 5.3.1.2 introduces the four levels of phenomena that concern IR&S discourse as it now is and as it is becoming, given the modern context. Section 5.3.1.3 presents two fundamental questions that need to be resolved to effectively characterize (and structure) the phenomena in each level.

5.3.1.2 The four levels Four general levels of phenomena can be identified.[23] Let the first and highest level, the human-activity/experience level

---

23. Each level can be understood as a level of abstraction, although this may not be entirely equivalent to the notion of the same name in Floridi (2008b).

be said to contain the most general category of phenomenon: human experience and/or activity.[24] This experience/activity as a whole will be referred to as "human living" (or as human being, i.e., human be-ing, with respect to Heidegger's fundamental ontology). Thus, the discussion of human living—and hence of level-one phenomena—is more concerned with human living or human being[25] as a whole with respect to the commonalities and invariants therein, and less with individual acts and experiences.

Human living is increasingly technology-mediated. A discourse on human living becomes about mediation phenomena when it specifically discusses the mediation aspect. That is, such a discourse refers to a human user, (a system of) devices, and a "world" that is revealed (or hidden) through the use of those devices (as introduced in chapter 1).[26]

Let the second and penultimate level containing such mediation phenomena thereby be labeled as the mediation level. Thus, any discussion specifically about mediation phenomena that does not comment on corresponding human activities/experiences that they engender as a whole and instead remains of smaller scope (as well as being mainly about the mediation aspect of the activity/experience) belongs to this second level. If the discussion were to veer into a more general discussion of human living, then its concern shifts to level-one phenomena. This second level contains both mediation phenomena pertaining to individual events (acts or experiences) where mediation takes place, and descriptions of commonalities and invariants among individual such phenomena.[27]

---

24. Recall that human activity was cited by Heidegger as one of the common ways of understanding the nature of technology (see chapter 1).

25. That is, the mode of being (verb) common to human beings, see footnote 2 in chapter 1.

26. Recall from chapter 1 that mediation as hiding and revealing has to do with the particular ways in which the world is present to humans and how they are present in the world.

27. The first- and second-level phenomena differ in their definition. Thus, even if, empirically speaking, all human living is technology-mediated, this would not mean that level-one phenomena equal level-two phenomena. Although the aspects of human living it describes may be wholly due to mediation, level-one phenomena need not be construed in a way that focuses on the mediation aspect. For example, it need not mention the device and user entities, nor how the mediation occurs. Heidegger's discussion of the effect of technology to human being in different historical contexts (see section 1.1) pertains to level-one phenomena where it does not focus on the specifics of mediation. It moves to level-two phenomena when particular technologies and modes of mediation are detailed.

Let the third level, the semantic level, contain search and related phenomena that correspond to the activity of relating meanings. All these phenomena are variations of the semantic conception of search introduced in section 1.2.2. While search is the most typical mediation phenomenon (cf. section 1.2.2), any discussion of search with respect to an encapsulating mediation phenomenon would belong to the second level. A discourse stays at this third level by limiting itself to discussing the relating of meanings (e.g., IR discourse that relates queries and documents). Any significant mention of how this amounts to mediated experiences or how such experiences correspond to general human activity, experience, or the human condition would take the corresponding discussion's subject matter to higher levels. IS discourse remains on this level when it speaks of human processes (e.g., information seeking processes) constituted by search, until, for example, it comments on the effect of these processes on society, at which stage it encroaches on level-one phenomena.

Finally, let the fourth level, the interaction level, refer to the interactions between a user and a system, the ones that constitute searches and other phenomena on the semantic level. When the discourse focuses on particular activities and behavior constituting searches, which in turn constitute mediations, and construes them in terms of interactions (actions and responses), it belongs to this level. Typical fourth level discourse in IR would be practical/empirical research discourse (such as ad hoc research discourse about ad hoc search, see section 1.3.2 and section 1.3.1 respectively).

While a phenomenon at one level is of a different type than that of another, they are nevertheless, at least partially constituted by (and therefore partially specifiable by) phenomena of a lower level. Thus, while human living is increasingly technology-mediated, not all such living is necessarily technology-mediated so as to be specifiable through a user-device-world structure. Mediation-level phenomena involve search as per the semantic conception of search (see section 1.2.2) and thus are constituted by semantic-level phenomena. Similarly, semantic-level phenomena (i.e., meaning-suggesting technology-use), involve interactions and hence, interaction-level phenomena.

The different conceptions of search processes discussed in chapter 1, most of which are of interest to IR&S discourse, are phenomena that belong to the semantic and interaction levels[28] (a few belong to the mediation

---

28. Discourse about interaction-level phenomena appears in IR&S research on user-interfaces and interaction.

level). As discussed earlier, a direct implication of the increasingly pervasive nature of modern technology, is the need for IR&S to consider phenomena that encapsulate search. This is also the implication of arguments made in chapters 1 and 2 about (1) the current research trend in IR&S, where the scope of investigation is increasingly non–ad hoc and research is moving away from query-document relations toward considering richer aspects of context, and (2) the need to actively consider such aspects, given the modern context. Part of venturing into the context of searches is to consider the human and technical processes encapsulating search. These processes are more general than search; they are at a level higher than the semantic and interactional. As chapter 1 discussed, search is the most typical phenomenon of mediation. That is, (device-based) technology-use, understood as technology-mediated activity, most typically involves search. It need not involve specification of queries and selection of documents as it does in the mainstream conception of search, but it involves something expressed by the user followed by meaning-suggestion through a system. The phenomena at the mediation level thereby become important for study, and our understanding of other layers, especially of the semantic and human-activity layer, should inform this study. All these levels are therefore important and within the scope of foundations research. Thus, while the IR&S researcher's outlook (i.e., their comportment or perspective) may usually be limited to the semantic and interaction levels, the modern context requires that it be expanded to all four levels.

Consider again the issue of context, the study and utilization of which was argued to be paramount for progress in IR&S, in a discipline that takes search (a pervasive modern technology) to be a central phenomenon. The modern situation implies the need to shift focus from query-document relations (the semantic level) toward context-context relations. Any serious discourse of such relations inevitably leads to the discussion of level-two and level-one phenomena. Thus, any significant study of context must be predicated on the consideration of the interrelationships between these four levels of phenomena, first by relating the basic concepts. This is the job of foundations research, and we are attempting to do it here. The case is similar for issues other than context such as for the human processes encapsulating search that need also to be seriously considered. Hence, if these levels were left unrelated, then foundations research (and hence IR&S research overall) would not fulfill its function at the current stage of disciplinary evolution (see chapters 3 and 4). If this stage is indeed that which requires the redefining of foundations, as prior chapters argued, then this nonfulfillment amounts to stalling overall progress.

But what does it mean to relate and consider these levels? It means that each entity (e.g., human activities, queries and documents, and interactions) or relationship, specified according to one level, must be understood as to its function with respect to other levels. Instead of only being approached by examining the related entities of users, queries, and relevance as construed by traditional retrieval theory (which works at the semantic and interaction levels), a question such as "What is a document?" needs to be reframed with respect to the entity or relationship that matches its function in other levels. Thus, answering "What is a document?" needs to be preceded by the addressing a set of corresponding prerequisite questions:

- What are the respective functions of entities resembling a document at the level of human activities (level one), technology-mediated experience (level two), meaning-relation/search or interaction (levels three and four)?, and

- What is the relation between this function and the function that other entities/relationships have at those levels?

However, as the next section argues, to effectively address such questions means to realize that they depend on yet more foundational questions, which must first be resolved.

5.3.1.3 Two key foundational questions concerning levels of phenomena
The analysis of the above questions depends on addressing questions that are even more foundational that concern the levels of phenomena. First, what are the available functions that entities can function as at each level: human acts/experience in general, mediated acts/experiences, semantic (meaning suggesting/generating) and interaction events? Second, as we are particularly interested in the mediation level, what are the characteristics shared by the phenomena therein by which this level could be characterized?

Both these questions are addressed here by employing Heidegger's concept of technology, taken from his philosophy of technology, which seeks to understand the difference between modern and premodern technology[29] and is intricately connected to his overall philosophy. Heidegger's concept of technology centers on what he designates to be the essence of technology, which has to do with what technology does. Beyond being a means to

---

29. Although "modern" for him meant before the 1950s, Heidegger's findings apply even more (and increasingly so) to our present context.

an end, what technology does is reveal truths, it brings forth true meanings into appearance and presence.[30] He further understands a technological phenomenon, which works to reveal in such a way, as being constituted by the four causes as per Aristotle's theory of causes (or causal framework), which has traditionally been employed as an explanatory theory for acts or events. The technological phenomenon here can be understood as referring to technology-use by individuals or by society at large (i.e., what technology does then refers to what is revealed to a community as a whole through such use). However, this phenomenon is not a mediation-level phenomenon; there is no particular reference to relations between user, device (medium) world entities, and hence his concept (and its related discourse) is at the human-living level.

Heidegger's concept of technology is a response to what he takes to be the common insufficient understandings of technology as either human activity or as a means to an end that were used to structure IR&S research in chapter 1, that is, in the anthropological or instrumental categories, respectively. His concept can be understood as a means for explaining what the four causes—the four types of functions of constituents of technology-mediated acts/experiences (mediation-level phenomena)—come together to effect.[31]

Heidegger's concept of technology is used here in two places. First, we take his use of Aristotle's causal framework at the human-living level to also be valid for all four levels mentioned above. The causal framework delineates the four functions that entities can function as in each such level. We take this to be the fundamental way to structure/relate phenomena in each level. Second, we take his idea of what technology does to also apply in various capacities beyond the human-living level. At the mediation level, where phenomena involve an explicit human observer as human

---

30. This refers specifically to what classical technology does; however, modern technology is different: it (typically) changes the meaning of what it reveals. The significance to IR&S of his differentiation between classical and modern technology is addressed in chapter 6.

31. Chapter 1 discussed IR&S with respect to the common understandings of the function of technology as human activities or means to ends—denoting the instrumental and anthropological aspects corresponding to IR and IS, respectively (whereas IR&S is concerned with both). In response to these preexisting notions, Heidegger develops an ontological concept of technology concerned with the notions of truth and purpose that understands technology as being primarily characterized by its ability to reveal, to bring forth or make appear (as captured by the notion of póiesis; see footnote 8). It is ontological to the extent that it reveals to us what is (i.e., the world and ourselves) in a particular way. This notion has been intimated throughout this text, particularly in chapter 1. The following sections further explicate it.

observer, the effect or result of the mediation is equivalent to the result of technology-use, and it is directed at the observer. Thus, the result of a mediation event (a technology-mediated act or experience) is also that something is brought forth to the experience of subjects, or that the experience of subjects is modified in some way such that their experience of the world (and themselves) is modified. At the semantic level, this result of technology-use corresponds to the experience of system responses on issuing a query, that is, the experience of meaning-suggestion. The mediation and semantic levels need to be differentiated in this regard. The semantic level contains phenomena that are concerned with relating meanings, where the human agent who comprehends these meanings—and due to whom the meanings have meaning in the first place—need only be implicit or presumed. The mediation level instead contains phenomena that, while they must also (most typically) relate meanings (due to which search must typically be present in all mediational phenomena), explicitly specify the human agent (or aspects thereof), the act of mediation, and aspects of the world, in addition to whatever reference they have to meaning suggestion. To further differentiate these levels, we speak of the result of a mediation event in terms of "bringing-forth" and of the result of a semantic-level event in terms of meaning-suggestion. However, in several instances they will be used synonymously to indicate that they refer to the result of technology-use, albeit at different levels of discourse. Finally, with respect to the interaction level, phenomena here are such that they mainly consist of construals that are more instrumental or abstract (see chapter 1), pertaining to low-level human behaviors and system responses without reference to human cognition. The result of a search, a semantic-level phenomenon, is a meaning-suggestion, which is partly by means of system responses: a set or sum of visual, aural, and/or tactile feedbacks that are phenomena at the interaction level. However, this sum is in a different category than the whole that is the act of meaning-suggestion (and the meaning suggested). Thus, the result of technology-use—meaning-suggestion at the semantic level and "that which is brought forth to experience" at the mediation and human-activity levels—corresponds to mere physical cues and behaviors at the interaction level. It thus can only be understood in a significantly reduced sense at this level. This reduction is in fact present from the human level down. In understanding the result of technology-use as "that which is brought forth" in terms of mediation-level phenomenon, something of its sense, as it is meant at the human-living level, is lost. Similarly, when the human agent and the act of mediation are not made explicit as in semantic-level phenomena, the full sense of meaning-suggestion as that which is brought forth to human experience is also forgone.

It would be difficult to claim that either Heidegger's concept of technology or the Aristotelian causal framework that he uses are necessary for progress in the foundations of IR&S. Yet some framework is necessary as a resolution to the two aforementioned questions about the functional constituents for phenomena at each level, and for understanding mediation phenomena (i.e., technology-mediated acts or experiences) in general. And any such resolution of what the foundational question is on which most other foundational issues addressed in this section depend in some way, and of what are nontrivial and far-reaching questions about what technology-mediated human living is and what it does in general (if anything), must be rigorously contested prior to being accepted. Below we suggest what the very basic properties of all four levels consist of, and in particular, what the mediation-level phenomena are mainly about.

The next sections show how the implications of Heidegger's concept of technology suggest changes to concepts pertaining to semantic-level phenomena in particular, such as the notions of query and document. That is, they suggest what their redefinition or reorganization should be like to adequately consider the modern context, and hence develop a proper foundation (inner network) to allow progress in the overall discourse. The following sections relate different IR&S questions, usually pertaining to semantic and interaction levels, to one of these causes, so their significance at other levels (especially human-living and mediation levels), can be better understood. By relating these questions to Heidegger's concept of technology (referring to the first level), we can begin to see what is necessary for answering them with respect to such a concept of technology.

5.3.2   Adopting a Causal Theory of Technology

Heidegger's concept of technology understands technology not primarily in terms of devices and techniques. Instead, he is concerned with how it mediates the being of human beings, part of which is concerned with our relationship with nature or the world in general. Technology as a means to control and subdue nature for particular purposes, reveals nature to us as a resource. Heidegger's concept is extensive. Chapter 6 further considers the implications of grounding IR&S in such a theory of technology, but this section brings one aspect of this theory to bear on interpreting IR&S concepts and relations in terms of their functionality in technology-mediated acts. Heidegger adopts Aristotle's framework to explain events and actions. This framework assigns four causes to each such event that serve to explain its occurrence. The following describes this framework before using it to show the positions—vis-à-vis the causes—of IR&S-specific objects and relations, relative to each other. The causal framework is a general explanatory framework for events. The idea is that by knowing the causes of an event, one knows what is to happen or is to be the case in every possible related case, whether or not they have specific experience of them (Owens, 1978, chapter 5). Thus, the framework shows how activities, whether human activities, information events or, interactions (depending on the levels) can be explained.

Heidegger takes the four Aristotelian causes (Falcon, 2015) to be responsible for bringing-forth, for bringing something from "concealment" into "unconcealment" (Heidegger, 1977, p. 10).[32] To illustrate this, consider the example, adapted from Falcon (2015), of a drinking vessel. It is brought out through the craftsman sculpting a shape in a block of stone, for example. The vessel is said to be explained by the four Aristotelian causes:

1. the material cause is the material or subject of the change (e.g., stone),
2. the efficient cause is the main source for change, such as a craftsman or the (knowledge of the) art of sculpting as known by the craftsman,
3. the formal cause is the account of the change undergone, such as the shape of the vessel, and finally
4. the final cause is the purpose or end of the change/action, which corresponds to the purpose of the vessel (i.e., to hold drink or be a means for drinking).

These four causes are responsible (Falcon, 2015) for bringing-forth or revealing the vessel, for making the vessel appear or happen. This is not so much a private act for which only the craftsman (as the efficient cause) is responsible, but a public act that happens when these four aspects come together; the craftsman merely participates. The four causes bring the vessel from potentia to actualia from nothing. Technology in the original Greek sense (from technê) corresponds to the technique or know-how (or expertise) of craftspersons, poets, artists, and designers—a technique that is involved in the above process of bringing forth (or poeisis) by the craftsman.[33] Hence knowing how is not only a knowing how-to-make or how-to-change, but a knowing how-to-bring-forth or how-to-reveal.

32. This is Heidegger's own adaptation of Aristotle's theory.
33. In particular, this is how Heidegger characterizes premodern technology; his depiction of modern technology is discussed in relation to IR&S in chapter 6.

For the case of IR&S, what is brought forth by the technology-mediated activities are meanings. Prior chapters have understood these meanings as generated or suggested. Heidegger's notion of being brought forth is truth bearing. How this would be used to speak of generated meanings, of information retrieved or knowledge learned, in search processes, is a basic question that depends ultimately on a theory of information and knowledge; and is further discussed in chapter 6. Here we instead seek to apply the causal framework to the semantic and interaction levels, to explain the information event (Furner, 2011), whether it is a retrieval or a seeking event or something else, by associating its components (queries, documents, users, and systems) to their causal role. For each such component, an argument is made about its causal role. These arguments also address how research about that component ought to be related to research about the other components, vis-à-vis their role in level one. The relating of a component, usually construed as a level three or four phenomenon, to a cause, also serves to expand the construal of that component by augmenting it with a construal of a higher-level phenomenon. The following sections can be understood as both introductions to and re-imaginings of IR&S notions. They are templates for transforming IR&S notions to concepts more amenable to a foundational investigation appropriate for the modern context. While these original notions are at the semantic or interaction levels, their construals in terms of causes works to depict them (or their equivalent) at all other levels.

At the interaction level, the causes can be understood to refer to the interaction events making up the information event at the semantic level; all IR&S events (e.g., a search event) are information events. Interactions constitute higher-level phenomena. They therefore lead to the bringing forth—of a particular change (and reaction)—from the world/environment, and this happens through a technological device or system. The interaction then reveals something, bringing it into presence. In this case, in terms of semantic-level phenomena, the event serves to suggest the meaning of a query through documents, or it brings forth meanings to the user's experience that have something to do with their interactions vis-à-vis the query they supplied. More accurately, the efficient cause is that cognitive aspect in the user that lead to their actions (see section 5.3.3). The material cause would be the system (see section 5.3.6) that is interacted with (and hence modified). The formal cause could be the changes to the interface effected through physical user action and could refer to buttons pressed or in general to state changes in interface objects, such as by issuing queries (see section 5.3.5). The final cause could denote the purpose of achieving some technical end, such as the booking of a flight, finding something, or fulfill-ing a cognitive goal. The efficient and final causes are related in that they refer to a specific user and goal, whereas the formal traditionally refers to a more universal aspect (Owens, 1978, chapter 5), an invariant form, such that it could keep causing this event beyond the context of the current user/goal. The "invariant" here could refer, for example, to social factors that incline users to participate in the technology-mediated activities or information events.[34] For our context, however, while the relative scopes are kept such that the formal cause has the largest scope, our efficient and final causes also have large scopes, since they can be concerned with the intersubjective beyond the subjective.

The final cause here brings with it some added baggage. With respect to the natural sciences, the final cause went out of fashion at least since the time of Descartes.[35] Physical events, such as the motion of an object, used to be understood in the pre-Cartesian—Aristotelian—philosophy of nature as having a goal or purpose. The geometric/abstract method of describing nature adopted by Descartes resulted in this philosophy of nature being replaced by a profoundly successful mechanistic framework for the natural sciences. However, the physical object became abstracted to a space, as a point on a line in that space, devoid of purpose. Successful frameworks tend often to be adopted outside of their original contexts. Inspired by the example of this geometrized physics, any construal of phenomena that made them amenable to "geometrization" (by which is meant an ideal form of modeling that effectively interrelates existing phenomena in a way that supports the prediction and explanation of related but unseen phenomena) would be considered as "better" than another construal. The inclination to geometrize is present across the disciplines, even when the subject mat-ter is human actions, for which ignoring final causes would significantly misrepresent the phenomenon.

To the extent that IR&S is concerned with users and user actions, final causes must be an important part of explaining information events. The growing research efforts that seek to understand information events based on tasks indicate that final causes are being taken seriously. Whereas abstract representations of user interactions are useful, their final causes

---

34. These factors need to be stable across different such activities and events, and so can be understood partially as hidden generative mechanisms, as considered in Danermark et al. (2001).

35. For some, the wholesale ignorance of final causes in the natural sciences has to do partly with a misunderstanding of Aristotle (Simon, 2001).

should always be in the picture, without which they lack sufficient meaning. Final causes are important for developing an intellectual rationale or explanation for events. The benefit of this from a systems perspective is merely secondary: a better understanding of information events can lead to algorithms that improve system responses to such events. The systems perspective has been central to IR, since its main purpose has been to support system building. As a result, the mechanistic modeling of users dominates. For example, users as "holders of opinions about relevance" are represented, from a system-oriented viewpoint, as a vector that moves continuously along a real-number line according to their interactions,[36] as per the traditional method of modeling relevance feedback in IR.

If final causes reside with the user, then the conception of the user has to be sufficiently rich to accommodate them. Section 5.3.3 discusses what such a conception needs to be sufficient.

5.3.3   What Is a User? User as Embodied-Embedded Being

Adequately understanding technological activity with respect to the four causes (discussed in section 5.3.2) requires the development of a sufficient conception of user. Final and efficient causes are immediately attributable to a user; they have a significant subjective component but are not necessarily restricted to the subjective. The formal and material causes have a significant nonsubjective component; they are not about particular users but about other aspects of the world, including other users or artifacts. However, in the context of technological activity, to the extent that technology is made for use by humans, a conception of user is presupposed even in discourses about systems—which pertain to the material cause (that which is modified or interacted with in such activities). Section 5.3.3.1 shows how this is so in IR&S discourse, while section 5.3.3.2 discusses the requirements for any modern conception of user.

36. The influential work of van Rijsbergen (2004) inspired by this idea of geometrization, can be understood to pertain to a systems view. It adopts quantum theory as an abstract formalism for describing and predicting search behavior. However, it can be understood as going beyond a strictly systems viewpoint. In mentioning the noncommutativity of observation operators depicting a fact of human interaction with a computational device (as section 6.2 further details), van Rijsbergen (2004) is making a statement about a foundational property pertaining to perception and observation. In this sense, van Rijsbergen (2004) significantly relates to the work of Heelan (specifically, Heelan, 1965, 1970, 1989, 2015), which is about understanding quantum theory (QT) in its function as a theory of (scientific) observation.

5.3.3.1 The user question as ubiquitous There are many works problematizing the notion of user, as prior chapters have mentioned. Some are explicit (Kelly, 2009) in holding that future work in IR&S will need to develop richer understandings of users (Kelly et al., 2013).[37] Other works call for this in a less explicit way when they seek better understandings of user cognition during search (Mizzaro, 1996).[38] This is since IR&S research is requiring to depend heavily on adequately modeling a diverse range of search scenarios and hence on richer methodologies for understanding users and on reasoning about user studies.

Furthermore, some works do not explicitly call for better understandings of users but they imply it. Researchers seeking to improve the effectiveness of retrieval systems are working to make a system's decision process more like that of a relevance judge. They are therefore working to make human-computer retrieval closer in some respect to human–human information retrieval. For example, consider the work of Fang et al. (2011), which focuses on general retrieval heuristics. This can be interpreted as best practices for imitating the human–human information retrieval context and can thus be taken to additionally problematize not only the ideal respondent in this specific context, but the user in general. To see this, consider that Fang et al.'s (2011) work can be taken to be about addressing the general question: What are the conditions (or enabling factors) for valuable types of search experiences? The addressing of such questions would of course include heuristics, but it could also include numerous other factors. For example, there are factors pertaining to interfaces, algorithmic principles, and the several layers of interactive behavior exhibited by the system that would partially constitute a valuable search experience (not only subjectively for an individual but intersubjectively for all).[39] This question and research based on it or more specific versions of it, such as Fang et al. (2011), presuppose an idea of user (i.e., they presuppose an answer to the question

---

37. As chapter 2 argued, although statistical characterization is a necessary aspect of representing and arguing about observed behavior, subjective understandings reveal variations lost in such a process and have to be integrated in a complementary manner. The variations have to be explained.

38. Mizzaro models this through considering a user's states and substates of knowledge, an idea that is further explored in Arafat (2008).

39. Fang et al. seek to explain why something works, i.e., why certain systems behaviors are more effective for the user (as effectiveness ultimately boils down to views expressed by humans as relevance judges). This explanation is in terms of socio-cognitive regularities that are exhibited by systems that interact with the socio-cognitive context.

of what a user is). Moreover, several of the heuristics in Fang et al. (2011) are themselves assumed in a wide range of IR systems and research, all of which thereby presuppose a concept of what a user is. Thus, while the direct basic question in Fang et al. is "What is a good system?" or more importantly, its contrastive version (see section 5.4.3): "What makes a system better than another?" to address this question means to first understand that "betterness" here must originate from a socio-cognitive context. And so the appropriate presupposed question is "What makes for good search experiences?" for one or more users, (i.e., in the subjective and intersubjective contexts). And then: "What do good experiences have to do with system behaviors?" These questions are not primarily systems questions, they are user-based ones.

The increasingly pervasive nature of systems means that answers to direct basic questions about systems (as in Fang et al., 2011) will more extensively presuppose, if not directly address, the user question. Thus, it is necessary to understand the user. And so different positions about users as human beings, as available from various intellectual discourses, have to be investigated in IR&S.

5.3.3.2 Problematizing the user   Problematizing the user means actively investigating and importing concepts and models of cognition, and choosing basic positions with respect to epistemology, psychology, and the cognitive sciences in general. For example, should a dualist or nondualist conception of cognition be adopted? As while a Cartesian dualist position— with the mind and environment being separate entities—is no longer a tenable model of the mind, it is certainly useful for talking about interaction. The pervasive nature of technology whereby technology can mediate anything from bodily movement to perception, means that investigating this mediated experience in its fullness requires considering the entire user—their physiological and psychological aspects. A user conception that works purely with mental models, or concept models, as in traditional retrieval research, where the user corresponds to a concept set derived from user interactions or as states of knowledge (e.g., Belkin's anomalous states of knowledge), would be increasingly insufficient. Moreover, it is not only the pervasive nature of technology that requires a fuller conception. Human beings are embodied (they have bodies) and are embedded in environments.

Any sufficient concept of user or more generally, a cognitive agent, cannot only consider what is "in heads" or even "in heads and bodies," but as the extended-mind idea supposes, the cognition of a cognitive agent ought to subsume (and not just interact with) things that would otherwise be considered as environment (Clark and Chalmers, 1998). A notebook on which an individual depends extensively to "save their thoughts," something outside the mind, could be considered as part of their cognition. How far should this cognition be extended? Problematizing the user means deciding where the user's cognition or mind stops and the world begins (i.e., what is the boundary and difference between the observer and observed, a question about where to cut out cognition that is of importance to cognitive theorists).[40] Taking a position about this cut is crucial for any conception of user when pervasive mediation needs to be considered, since as user dependence on tools increases, more of the world is involved—and in an increasingly intimate way—in how the user is present to the world and the world is present to the user. However, this involvement of the world cannot be fully understood in terms of mental representations, instead (nonrepresentational), "skillful, unreflective bodily activity" (Kelly, 2002, p. 377) and felt experience (McCarthy and Wright, 2007) occupies a central place.[41] Thus, an adequate discourse on what a user is needs to discuss such activity in addition to representational aspects of cognition.

Moreover, empirically speaking, cognition does not only refer to neuronal activity that is objectively construed from brain-activity read-outs. It also corresponds to first-person or subjective accounts of experience, denoting conscious (intentional) human experience, that can be discussed in a scientifically rigorous way (Bitbol, 2002), and to second-person or intersubjective accounts.[42] The work of Varela et al. discussed in Bitbol (2002), and the work on embodied cognition following it, seeks to marry the first- and third-person accounts (Varela and Shear, 1999; Varela et al., 2017). The work of neuroscientist Walter Freeman (1999, 2012), as Dreyfus (2007) asserts, also offers a way to combine (otherwise empirically informed) theoretical discourse on embodied cognition, which includes first-person accounts, to models of brain activity, which are third-person accounts.

---

40. It is also important for quantum theorists (Stapp, 2007b). Heelan's comment (Heelan, 1987) on the seminal work of cognitive science by De Mey (2012)—which is an influence for cognitivist models in IR&S—discusses the notion of this cut as presupposed in De Mey's work.

41. A detailed account of this type of activity can be found in Dreyfus (2014).

42. The responses to questionnaires in user studies common to IR&S would not normally be sufficiently rigorous to be a suitable account of first-person experience (of search, as technology-mediated activity). A further discussion of phenomenological first-person accounts referred to in (Bitbol, 2002) can be found in (Smith, 2013; Varela and Shear, 1999).

With respect not to the embodied user but the embedded user, in addition to their immediate environment, the latter is situated in a culture (i.e., in a social and political context) that conditions their actions and experience. Considering such factors requires adapting from discourses beyond the above-mentioned cognitive science works, in the humanities and social sciences and similarly considering positions on basic issues therein. As the user conception will also be employed to specify the nonsubjective aspects of the formal cause, discourse about it must have a way to characterize how social factors can generate and hence explain what users do and experience.[43] Not only social factors determine human experience and action; other nonsubjective or intersubjective factors do so as well. If one adopts a psychological theory that posits cognition as being constituted by an unconscious as well as the conscious (e.g., in the psychotherapy traditions, such as that of Jung), then unconscious mechanisms, and psychological archetypes, add to the overall set of explanatory factors (Jung, 2014).[44]

The central point here is the need to comprehensively understand human experience of the world as mediated by technology. The more pervasive technology gets, the more of human experience needs to be considered in any serious discourse about technology-mediated experience/activity. Critical appropriation from such a range of discourses is thereby necessary, as they consider different aspects that need to be brought together to solve a specific problem. Thus, to create a user concept that is based on a rigorous understanding of experience, there must first be a configuration of existing discourses that fulfills this purpose. Beyond its aesthetic and literary dimensions, a study of experience refers primarily to the discipline of phenomenology, which can be understood as being a part of theoretical psychology.[45] This should not be understood as only referring to the phenomenological tradition in contemporary philosophy since Husserl (Smith,

43. In terms of traditional IR&S discourse, understanding these generative factors corresponds to "domain understanding," discussed in chapter 2. However, they expand on the typical factors considered there, such as work tasks (Ingwersen and Järvelin, 2005; Järvelin, 2011).

44. This does not mean that one ought to accept and adapt wholesale the work of Jung, which is arguably still coherent with contemporary psychology (Knox, 2003). Instead, there needs to be some consistent account of generative factors determining regularities in human experience for the purpose of explaining that experience and thereby relating it to other experiences.

45. The notion of theoretical psychology is in contrast to practical or applied psychology. These notions are meant in the way clarified by Simon (1996, chapter 6). Simon provides a clarifying framework by which to think about the different disciplines studying human

2013), but to any discourses studying human experience in a principled fashion. Nevertheless, such (existing) phenomenological discourses can be adapted to fill this role and hence form a base (that presupposes particular fundamental positions with respect to epistemology and ontology) on which should be added methods for positing first- and third-person accounts of embodied and embedded technology-mediated experience. The base here corresponds to what is usually understood as denoting a philosophical subject area; thus one may tend to interpret this setup up as philosophical principles with (to use an IR&S-specific notion) user studies on top. This interpretation is inaccurate: a phenomenology as a base is not philosophical in the sense of literary philosophy, for example. It is more akin to a scientific endeavor that seeks systematic explanation.[46] Phenomenology here is not to be employed for descriptive, subjective studies of user experience but to help systematically and rigorously characterize intersubjective regularities and underlying principles of technology-mediated experience. Of course, there will always be a limit to understanding users, constrained to what is known by scientific investigations of consciousness, the brain, and human psychology with respect to such issues as "what their experiences are really like." Additionally, there will be limits on knowing what a user means by their behavior or what they take to be the meaning of a document. Hence there are local (or "within-discipline") limits to understanding users, on top of the more global or general limits. These are limits concerned with both what the system and researcher can know (absolutely or in some context) about a user (or users in general).[47]

In summary, to sufficiently address the problem of understanding technology-mediated experience and activity, any conception of user must

---

experience and behavior (philosophy of mind, literature, psychotherapy, moral psychology, etc.). Understanding phenomenology as having to do with 'theoretical psychology' in the sense meant by Simon, is not to equate it with psychology. Instead, phenomenology is theoretical psychology in that it deals with some of the apriori aspects of psychology (Hopkins, 2015).

46. This alludes partly to Husserl's idea of philosophy as rigorous science (Husserl, 1969) and partly to Simon's (1996) understanding of the kinship between science and philosophy.

47. Meaning that, other than the general/global limits to research on human experience, as would be defined through philosophical, psychological, and general scientific argumentation, there are local limitations due to the IR&S researcher's particular comportment. Furthermore, the limitations on the system's knowing also pertain to limitations on their practical capabilities (Swanson, 1988).

consider an embodied, embedded approach to cognition. The concept must draw from phenomenology at its base and must be usable in a way that is compatible with the coupling of first- and third-person accounts of experience, and with (social and psychological) generative structures. A user conception fulfilling these conditions can then be extended with aspects corresponding to efficient and final causes. Section 5.3.4 discusses what these aspects of the user require to be were efficient causes to be interpreted as 'desires' where desires are the immediate aspect of a user 'responsible' for drawing out their actions.

5.3.4   What Are Information Needs? Information Needs and Final and Efficient Causes

With respect to the four causes, the efficient cause (the craftsman in the section 5.3.2 example) is what is specifically responsible for bringing together the other causes. It corresponds to the need/desire aspect of the craftsman's cognition that spurs him to act. In the IR&S context, the concept of information need refers to this desire, and can be understood thereby to take the place of (or functions as) the efficient cause. Information need is a mechanism or drive that compels humans to "seek out, recognize and adapt to changes in their social and physical environments" (Cole, 2012, p. 189),[48] and its study has a central place in IR&S (Chang, 2013). Information needs are a part of cognitive needs that are further constituted by several other categories of human needs (e.g., physiological needs Wilson, 1994, 2002). Technology-mediated activity is not limited to satisfying information needs. That a particular need motivated a user to act may not be useful to know in itself, let alone to know that it was an information need. As such, understanding human motivations in terms of needs and need satisfaction[49] (as is traditional in IR&S) is perhaps too simplistic. As technology is mediating increasing portions of human experience, it must therefore consider the complex mix of human motivations beyond what can be specified by needs. This would mean considering a richer set of factors, corresponding to cognitive phenomena, as constituting this motivation.[50] That information need or whatever richer cognitive phenomenon

48. As quoted in in the review of Cole's book by Ford (Nigel, 2013, p. 2596).

49. The need to satisfy needs corresponds to the need to resolve a problem (which is co-present with the need) or to resolve a lack of homeostasis (Wiener, 1954).

50. Other than as cognitive and physiological needs, and needs such as aesthetic or visual needs—for example, the need to see something on the screen in a particular way (Albertson, 2015)—motivations can be expressed in alternative ways. One could simply be motivated to do an act or to experience something in a particular way, for example.

or motivation that replaces it—at the level of interaction—functions as the efficient cause means that it is this phenomenon or motivation, and not simply the user, that is taken to be the operative principle for user action. It is the primary aspect responsible for moving the user from a state of rest to one of movement and action. Any possible need or motivation can lead to tool use for their resolution/satisfaction or fulfillment, and this fulfillment can be understood as being part of the final cause, telos, or as the purpose of interaction. Hence, while the efficient cause is that which is responsible for the action, the final cause delineates what the action is for. The information need or desire could itself be given as both what is responsible for the act and what the act was for (i.e., to satisfy the desire). However, this is not the only possibility. A user may not immediately know the particular final cause, nor does it have to be particular to the user as an individual—they might instead be influenced by social factors that they will not readily understand or admit. Furthermore, understanding the efficient and final causes is not a matter of simply identifying a desire and purpose pair from a given set.

One strategy for developing the rich structure of motivations pertaining to the efficient cause would be to move IR&S discourse from information need to cognitive needs and to cognition in general, through the generalization of cognitive need fulfillment to the phenomenological concept of meaning-fulfillment (Mohanty, 2012). That is, our desires (from information needs to physiological needs) work to set up cognitive structures that require fulfilling. Cognition thereby pertains to a range of cognitive/mental acts, such as perceiving and imagining. Each such act is preceded by expectations (or anticipations) about what is to be perceived/imagined/known. When that thing (or some other thing) is actually perceived/imagined/known (i.e., the cognitive act is performed), it is said that the expectation has been fulfilled or satisfied. In particular, this is a meaning-fulfillment: the cognitive act resulted in meaning being conferred to the person to whom the act belongs. To fulfill the expectations of such a cognitive act, actions may be required, and this meaning-fulfillment could lead to observable physical actions. Moving from need satisfaction to meaning-fulfillment means to consider arbitrary cognitive acts (and their related physical or embodied aspects and environmental/world aspects)[51] as possible factors of an efficient cause for interaction. It also means that

---

51. These aspects could be considered to be part of the cognitive act, and hence part of the efficient cause. But if these aspects were something the system could also detect and consider, they could also be construed as being part of the formal cause.

for the context of IR&S dealing with semantic-level phenomena which in turn specify the mediated acts referred to here : IR software in its act of meaning-suggestion can be understood to respond directly to acts resulting from the need for meaning-fulfillment.

The subtly pervasive nature of modern technology (e.g., augmented-reality systems) is such that it mediates our cognitive acts in a particular way: it is as if it has become part of our cognition or has extended it (Clark and Chalmers, 1998). And as such this technology plays an intimate part in our daily living (i.e., in our experiencing and acting in the world): it becomes a means for our total being-in-the-world. Therefore we must study efficient causes using the full range of ideas available from cognitive research, but rooted ideally on existing phenomenological research discourses. Problematizing information need therefore means problematizing efficient causes of interaction, which means to study the range of cognitive acts that constitute our being-in-the-world with respect to meaning-fulfillment (and not only typical need satisfaction). This in turn means to study types of technology-mediated human living scenarios, as each will be constituted by a different set of cognitive acts. The investigation here, importantly, need not be limited to a subjective one, to each user through empirical observation—whether through first-, second- (e.g., questionnaires) or third-person accounts. It would also pertain to what the efficient cause would typically be, such that its scope of applications would be more than one actual user (i.e., it could be user groups). In this sense, the efficient cause for any particular case can be related to other cases and thus will have intersubjective significance, relating the individual to a social or cultural context. To the extent it ventures beyond the individual, it encroaches on the space of the formal cause.

5.3.5 What Is a Query? Query as Formal Cause

The notion of query in IR&S takes its meaning initially from the context of human conversation and is analogously applied to the context of human-computer use or conversation. A query usually refers to the expression of a meaning, either directly by forming words (typing or speaking them), or indirectly, by selecting words, images, or video, moving body parts, or simply looking toward a real or virtual object. It also thereby corresponds to a type of user action or interaction. Taken in this broad way, queries are units of information behavior, a concept that has been construed in numerous ways (Wilson, 1999; Fisher et al., 2005; Case, 2006). Queries as expressions or units of information behavior function as formal causes at all levels. At the interaction level, they denote the form of interaction accepted by the system, to which the system then responds. At the semantic level, they correspond to the form of the cue or question that leads to meaning suggestion. They denote the form of a technology-mediated act at the mediation level that leads to meaning being brought forth in a particular way. And at the human living level, they correspond in general to the forms of human acts (especially acts pertaining to communication).

The formal cause is closely related to the efficient cause. A query as a behavioral expression can be preceded by mental acts and content (images or words-in-mind, for example). As previously implied, this does not mean that every user interaction with the world (through a system) requires a mental representation (Dreyfus, 2014). The relation between cognition and action is something theories of information behavior readily capture (Wilson, 1999). Even in a simplistic such theory, where IR&S discourse takes user cognition to be a set of information needs, a simple cognitive-behavioral model of a user is generally assumed. To see the potentially intimate relation between these two causes, consider the following richer account of the user. Let user cognition be understood according to the phenomenological concept previously introduced, such that instead of information needs, there are a set of cognitive expectations (a desire to know particulars) related to the idea of meaning-fulfillment. These expectations correspond to an efficient cause, and are constituted, for example, by images or concepts (including words-as-conceived), which will later be expressed in specific words or acts. The more intimate the mediation of a system in technology-mediated experience, the closer will be the relationship between efficient and formal causes. For example, if brain signals were the only constituent of a query given a system, such as through a brain-computer interface, then there is no "external" form as such.

Moving from the IR&S context to that of encapsulating processes means to go from queries as information behavior to other types of behavior— to broaden the initial context beyond human conversation and beyond focusing on simple interactions, and to think about the formal cause in general. To motivate this, consider the example of an augmented-reality user experience, consisting of a walking journey wearing a pair of Google glasses (cf. sections 1.1.3, 2.3 and 3.3.4). This journey can be understood as one query or formal cause, since the whole journey pertains to "one meaning" or one narrative. It could equally correspond to an information-seeking journey or a task. The particular mereology (Varzi, 2016) of the formal cause or query here—the discussion about how to divide up the journey in terms of an ontology—would depend on what type of analysis it is to serve. This journey is a rather complex technology-mediated living process, which, like any human journey, can be analyzed as to its (personal) cognitive, socio-cultural, and other elements. The increasing frequency of such a usage scenario due to the pervasiveness of technology, and the shifting of IR&S discourse from query-document matching toward relating context to context (as discussed in prior sections, and as corresponding to a shift of discourse from level three to higher levels), work to suggest that an effective discourse on technology-mediation must be concomitant with a rigorous account of formal causes.

The forms are increasingly complex and of large scope. Any taxonomy of formal causes needs to cover (1) the range of ways a user can express themselves filtered by what of it can be 'picked-up' by a system or theorized by a researcher, and (2) the range of possible changes (interaction patterns) exposed by the system with which they interact.[52] The range of changes the system accepts would then be part of the definition of the material cause. The scope of the formal cause includes the individual as well as the social contexts. Thus, while theories of information behavior working at the IR&S level are numerous—each covering a different aspect of the user journey—they must be brought together. This is difficult since many existing theories (e.g., several from Fisher et al., 2005) are often context-specific derivations from larger intellectual trends, such as phenomenology or behaviorism, that are built on differing basic premises of an ontological and epistemological nature. The pervasive nature of modern technology means that approaches wider in scope than current information behavior models are required to describe the formal cause, and this may require going back to the source discourses. This is as opposed to the current state of juxtaposing unrelated theories to create a piecemeal picture used to interpret user behavior in empirical studies in a fragmented way. Rigorous explanatory reasoning must work with well-defined phenomena that admit to rich links with one another, especially since the move from level three to levels one and two means relating between different levels of phenomena. This admits several requirements for a sufficient discourse on formal causes. First, several existing information behavior models influenced by diverse theoretical paradigms discussed in Wilson (1999) would need to be brought into a discursive framework in a rigorous way so that one could explain behavior by cognition or social factors and such. This is a task shared with several other discourses in the human sciences. Second, the close link between the

---

52. While the system is only interested in those allowed patterns of interaction the user follows, the researcher is also interested in the degrees of freedom of user expression beyond—e.g., before and after—system use.

formal and efficient cause means that the required cognitive theory cannot be purely behaviorist. It must instead consider mental representations while accounting for embodied and embedded experience and consider linguistic and social elements all at once.

This second requirement admits to further details. The formal cause, in referring to the overall (encapsulating) human act and its particulars, barring the requirement for the close link to the efficient cause, corresponds to a public (intersubjective or objective) meaning that is open to being represented. This public aspect means that the study of the formal cause has much to do with linguistics, where the elements of the language include words as well as gestures. To the extent that this formal cause needs to be interpreted by systems and researchers, the intent behind it needs to be understood. The public aspect of the formal cause requires acts, behaviors, and expressions to be related to cultural or functional aspects of expression. This means that the linguistics used to study and frame it must accommodate these aspects. Beyond words or interactions, or even journey descriptions/narratives, a formal cause can refer to generative (social) mechanisms (Hedström and Swedberg, 1998; Blom and Morén, 2011) that lead to the act or explain its form. Thus, whereas efficient causes address the cognitive precursor to an act, the formal cause would be—in addition to a particular set of words or behaviors—the overall social setting or context that lead the user to express that need in that way. It is this context as termed in IR&S discourse, minus that part of the context represented by the efficient cause, that the aforementioned social and linguistic structures serve to describe. Formal causes are thus to relate particular expressions to general formative principles.

For the system in a technology-mediated act, a formal cause refers both to the specifics of an interaction with the system (defined as the particular choice of a set of interactive acts from a set of possible acts offered by that system) and to the principle behind that choice.[53] The scope of this principle goes beyond the relatively private scope of the efficient cause. It does

53. The work in Arafat (2008) personifies the formal cause as an "oracle," i.e., as the otherwise ambiguous or unknowable (from within the confines of a reductive model) cause or rationale from beyond the narrow picture of user-system interactions, that may be responsible for a user's cognitive/mental and behavioral activity. One of the reasons, implied in that same work, for the use of QT for IR&S—following the work of van Rijsbergen (2004)—was the existence in the latter of the analogous situation of wave-function collapse: the collapse of many possibilities for a system-state into that of one state upon a choice made manifest by the connection between nature and the observer/experimenter.

so by locating the form of the act to a larger (stratified) system of meanings (Danermark, 2002), that is, to what can be called social[54] and linguistic structures. Relating the immediate form of an act to a bigger picture, from which the formal cause is then developed, serves to classify it among other formal causes.[55]

The linguistic structures that constitute a formal cause refer not only to words of a query, for example, but also to fuller linguistic theories that identify the structures that relate these words to communicative behavior, and more generally to discourse—the written, spoken, and general behavioral patterns among entities (humans or groupings thereof).[56]

Although there are theories of information behavior offering such structures, an effective account of formal causes requires IR&S to reconsider its relation to linguistics. The use of linguistics in IR&S, closely influenced by the natural-language processing tradition, has focused on the mathematically formalizable aspects of linguistics, particularly the generative linguistics tradition represented by Chomsky and others (Warner, 2010, p. 96). The generative tradition, initially developed to understand language acquisition, focuses on rules or definitions that can be used to generate sentences. It is the main background tradition for computational linguistics (e.g., the efficient representations and automatic manipulation of documents and data). The system-functional linguistics school of Halliday (built partially on the work of Saussare and the structuralist school) instead focuses on language in terms of its function as a system for communication, that is, language as social semiotic (Eggins, 2004, p. 3). It instead focuses on different social contexts of language use. It is especially useful for explaining how language works (e.g., how a communicative scenario between people or between people and technology works). Finally, the cognitive-linguistics school of Langacker, Lakoff, and Talmy focuses on relating linguistic expressions to their cognitive origins (Evans and Green, 2006).[57]

---

54. This can include psychological archetypes in the Jungian sense, for example, as they are not specific to an individual but are shared symbols. The individual here would then be participating in that archetype, manifesting it by acting in that way.

55. At the level of traditional IR&S, this amounts to classifying queries based on domains.

56. The concept of discourse analysis perhaps covers a large part of the scope of the formal cause here, even though the current literature in the area may not; see the related literature cited in section 5.3.10.

57. In contrast to the main focus of these schools, pervasive technology-use is increasingly about gestures, and to consider gestures as formal causes means to develop a way to

In summary, queries must be treated as arbitrary expressions, as formal causes of technology-mediated activity. The trend in IR&S toward considering arbitrarily rich interactive behaviors—closely linked to cognitive states—along with the trend of moving the focus of analysis from query-document relations to context-context relations—needs to be seen as an opportunity for developing rich cognitive-behavioral theories on the way to developing an extensive account of formal causes. The formal cause of user action therefore constitutes a large part of what IR&S considers to be user-side context, where this context refers to a mix of social and linguistic phenomena (including the gestural and symbolic). Hence, any rigorous account of formal causes needs to employ appropriate social-scientific and linguistic theories to capture and study these phenomena. Unlike typical IR&S discourse (especially IR discourse), the purpose of studying such phenomena is not limited to building efficient systems (i.e., for efficient text processing and matching). It is no longer limited to deciding how to represent the formal cause by mathematical forms for technical purposes—for which the work of the generative school of linguistics is of particular use. Instead, it is about explaining and understanding the way in which the users act with respect to forms, intents (e.g., through cognitive linguistics), communicative function (e.g., through system-functional linguistics) and generative mechanisms (through critical realism for example; Danermark, 2002). The understanding of intent is not the uncritical association to an efficient cause, but instead, a rigorous argument about the relation between particular forms of expression and their cognitive precursors (using whatever evidence), as is common in cognitive-linguistics discourse.[58]

5.3.6 What Is a System? System as Material Cause

The discussion of the effective and formal causes in previous sections is from the perspective of a researcher. While users may think of their own effective and formal causes, they cannot be said to be seeking systematic conceptualizations. If they do, they can be thought of as taking on the role of a researcher investigating phenomena pertaining to their own particular

---

represent relevant ranges of body-part movements as meaningful—not unlike discourses pertaining to the study of sign language. This is in addition, of course, to the existent work on the linguistics of gestures in general.

58. This is further supported by the ideas in Anton (2012) and McLuhan (1994), which argue that the formal cause must be present to some extent before the act actually takes place. When a formal cause is given, it should relate to the efficient cause as well as giving the forms of actions.

experience. There is indeed a case to be made for studying the relationship between these two modes of analysis: The user or observer-as-researcher examining the contents of their own experience versus researchers observing a user. A study such as this would pertain to the methodology of observation and would be a topic central to foundations research (see section 5.4.2). With respect to the material cause discussed in this section, which is tied to the system, the differentiation and interplay of different observational contexts of user, researcher, and system become explicit in a natural way. Moreover, in moving from system to material cause, the focus expands from technical designs (of applications), to including parts of the world that a user can live in and affect.

The system can be understood from two points of view: that of the user and that of the researcher. The former objectifies the system through their interactions with it, whereas the latter objectifies it through direct knowledge of its technical design. While the search-box and ranked-list combination is a popular system interface, it is nevertheless something that is increasingly superseded by pervasive application contexts. The purpose of systems is moving away from exclusively being to provide ranked lists (Bailey et al., 2010). Furthermore, there is an increasing variety of objects with which to interact, from artificial devices, the built environment, and natural entities, that can be given additional meaning through being augmented visually or as a part of an Internet of Things. The interface therein—the aspect of the system that exposes its functionality and possible modes of change—is thereby becoming fluid and increasingly invisible, and hence is a central aspect of this problematization. While the system takes the place of the material cause, it need not only correspond to those aspects that can be actually touched or felt, but also to virtual aspects that are symbolically touched. From the researcher's perspective, the material cause here is denoted by that part of the world that they seek to study as being responsible for responding to interaction, or that part they want to manipulate to determine an adequate response. Thus the purpose of systems with respect to what it is supposed to present the user—and how—becomes problematized. In general, the traditional notions of what a system is and what it ought to do can no longer be assumed to hold, and hence they require investigation. For Fuhr, IR tools have a specific function: they (on behalf of humans) deal with the ambiguous and provide mechanisms for clarifying ambiguities (Fuhr, 2012). Fuhr's idea can be understood as conceptualizing IR systems as meaning-sharpening entities, which are a qualified form of meaning-suggesting entities, since "clarifying ambiguities" corresponds to preferring a suggested system of relations between ideas/concepts/entities, or a meaning, over another meaning that is less clear (in at least a subjective sense, if not an inter-subjective sense as well).

A more general way to think about a system is in terms of what they are meant to enable. Other than finding relevant documents, they could enable higher levels of retrievability, "findability," and discoverability (Azzopardi and Vinay, 2008). These are general system aspects beyond its behavior upon particular queries (which instead is what the traditional concept of relevance pertains to); they have to do with asking about what kinds of relation a human being (or process) can have with an object, and all the things that may condition this relationship (not just that of being relevant to one of their inquiries). This enabling characteristic of systems can be more generally problematized by asking what the social, political, institutional, economic, and technical conditions are, for the possibility of access, where access is one type of informational experience. This generalization is needed since the embeddedness of a system in a social context makes the technical aspect of the problem of retrievability/findability/discoverability depend strongly on the nontechnical aspect of that problem pertaining public/private data (security, politics, etc.) and the problem of data rights.

In addition to clarifying purposes (as meaning-sharpening or enabling entities), or defining interfaces and new modes of interaction, problematizing the system means to differentiate it sufficiently from other entities. Identifying that part of a socio-technical configuration that is "a system" and that which is "a user" may not always be obvious (Leonardi et al., 2012). This is equally a problem for the physical sciences, in which the object of interest must be differentiated from its environment (see Arafat, 2011b). The significant aspects of a socio-technical configuration that responds to users and therefore constitutes "a system" in the user's and researcher's perspectives, need to be differentiated from other effects.

Construing the system then involves the identification of such significant material aspects in terms of its physical dimensions, interface, and responses, which all serve to identify it in a perceptual and haptic sense. However, particularly from the user's perspective—which is not only important to the user but also to the researcher studying the user—the system is not construed or objectified by ascertaining these fixed material aspects. Instead, its construal happens through its use. The material aspects only become understood as system—that is, the "system" only shows up as a relevant phenomenon—at some point of the user's life and not before. Before this it is simply invisible or without any particular identity or agency.[59] It is only when this entity becomes signified in this way that the human being becomes, technically speaking (from the researcher's perspective), a user.

Construing a system means then to construe an experiential zone of significance, where experience is embodied and embedded in an environment.[60] This construal problem is similar to the problem of understanding the separation versus the togetherness of the observer and the observed in QT. In Bitbol's (2002) analysis, quantum theory is a prototype of participatory science, wherein what is observed is in some strong way brought-out by the observer's way of looking. The observer thus participates in the emergence of the observed: the observer and observed are "entangled" or have become a whole in some sense, and they continue to evolve as one. Following quantum theory, Heelan takes this notion of entanglement seriously, developing a hermeneutical understanding of entanglement that makes the system a mediational instrument that is bound to the user, an instrument allowing one to look at the world in a particular way. Similarly, it can be said that in general, what constitutes a system depends on its use.[61] That is, the user distinguishes the system from a background world by signifying it materially, conceptually, and pragmatically, through their use of it.

From the perspective of IR&S and higher levels of phenomena, beyond understanding the system as device, software, and as a pattern of interaction, the system can be understood as the resultant whole of how the user deals with the world upon learning to use something new; such as a device, a technique, or a system of rules of behavior or a system of thought. Given that a user objectifies a system by their use of it, the definition of the system should be intimately tied to forms of interaction. The user's notion of system is delimited by the degrees of freedom afforded to them by the technical system (i.e., by the system understood from the researcher's technical perspective). These degrees of freedom present to the user a system

59. See Hookway (2014) for a further, extensive discussion on the construal of user versus system, focusing in particular on the 'interface' as the fluid boundary relating humans to technology.

60. The user may not intentionally conceive system use; the use could be nonreflective; see section 5.3.3.2.

61. In some sense, the system consists of those aspects that respond to the user, visually, haptically or otherwise. Just as the meaning of a word corresponds (at least partially) to its use (Wittgenstein, 2010), so the meaning of an interactive system is dependent on the interactions it allows and responds to.

of affordances and enablements, or potentialities, that decide the form that user activities will take. Therefore, in addition to being a material cause for interaction, aspects of what the user takes to be the system relate to what the researcher takes to be the formal cause of interaction.

Any progressive foundations discourse must then understand the material cause for technological activity as something that not only refers to a physical device with respect to its technical specification (e.g., physical characteristics) but also refers to its interactive possibilities, which are actualized by the formal cause. However, in the pervasive technological context where things in the environment constitute a system—the "technology" in a technology-mediated experience—the material cause is constituted by the entire world of a user to the extent that it can be affected by a formal cause. Thus while the formal cause has a public component that goes beyond the individual user, the material cause focuses again on the individual, on the specific loci of activity: the material cause individuates. This has implications for what theories of material causes (of "systems" in the context of IR&S) need to consider. In a pervasive context where a user is walking through a suburb in an augmented-reality space, interacting with several real and virtual entities, which all constitute a user's zone of significance (and hence a material cause or system), mere technical designs of the software elements therein will not do. Instead, the material cause must somehow refer to the spaces and places, which are different aspects of the locus of human experiences.[62]

5.3.7 What Is a Document? Document as Experienced

This section argues for documents having the function of what is brought forth by means of the four causes. As the result of a technology-mediated activity is an experience—along with whatever changes are incurred in the world as a result of this activity (e.g., changes to a software program)—the document must be construed as having a subjective or intersubjective experiential component as well as an objective component referring to an artifact or to physical nature. The different existing notions are first considered before this notion is argued as being more appropriate for the modern context than current notions of document.

Buckland (1997) explores the myriad of understandings of a document. Such a wide range of understandings (as chapter 3 mentioned) is not new

---

62. "Spaces" denote the physical quantifiable locations of a happening, whereas "places" denote the complementary qualitative aspects (Tuan, 1979; Casey, 2013).

(Briet et al., 2006); any object can be a document (Lund, 2009). A document can be a material object existing in the physical world, a digital/virtual object on the computer screen, or a perceived object in the mind of the user. The physical entity can be understood to have multiple representations, from its digital representation, to different views (or perceptible forms; see Levy, 2012). Both the digital representation of a document (e.g., an array of words corresponding to a mathematical set), any forms generated from it (e.g., a small snippet on a screen), and any other nondigital representations all capture something about the meaning of the document. Meaning is additionally conferred to the document by both the social world at large and by the user upon their using/interacting with it. Hence, as a meaningful object admitting multiple coincidental representations of technical and other natures, the document needs to be understood from the perspective of both the mathematical-scientific and humanistic traditions.

Lund (2009) and Olsen et al. (2012) can be interpreted as considering the document from both these perspectives when they conceive of it as an abstract structure that not only depicts the literal contents of an individual logical document but also its life cycle: the process, involving the numerous interactions of multiple factors, that created it or brought it to its current state. Therefore, the signifier of meaning in documents may not just be in the body of the logical document but also in "the structure of an information store, qualifiers of elements of an information store, [and] relationships among information stores,"(Lund, 2009, pp. 9–27) all of which partake in the document's social life. This structure, which is not only a mathematical one, allows one to determine what a particular document is in terms of its concrete content, as well as to say how and why it came to be the way it is. This latter information is not just a statement of document metadata—as stored inside a data store along with the logical document—but also a conceptual cue that would allow one to explain how the document came to be, to create rigorous narratives about the social life of the document. This social-life narrative and the final form of the document's content would then form the document object and constitute the meaning of the document.

The works of Buckland (1991); Briet et al. (2006); Lund (2009); Olsen et al. (2012) raise a general question about documents that is critical to understanding how the notion of "document" should be understood in the context of the four causes. The study of the way documents come to mean what they do is a study of meaning signification. The study of "aboutness" in IR is a study of this type,[63] although in that context, it usually only pertains to the automatic/computational approaches to signification for the sake of computational matching. And it was to this end that chapter 1, stated that the IR system is a meaning-suggesting system. The meaning signifiers of the document of course go beyond the logical document and into a complex structure of things in the world. In the case of the pervasive retrieval systems that are increasingly integrated into human culture, the meaning signification of documents becomes problematized by the document question. Thus the technical/mathematical discourse on aboutness, which works on top of this problematization, would itself have to be reproblematized. Some characteristics of this signification are elucidated next.

What aspect of the document signifies meaning depends on the observer; the overall problematization of the document stems from three views or objectifications of the document, corresponding to the different observers. First, the document from the system's point of view is a technical object for system processing. The second view of the document is from the researcher's perspective, as a theoretical object for research. Finally, from the user's view, the document is a response to interaction, an object with meaningful content that is to undergo interpretation about what it means and how it comes to mean it. The researcher interested in user experience is of course also interested in this third perspective, in what a document means to different users. The first two perspectives pertain mainly to objective construals of document, while the third mainly to subjective and intersubjective construals. Each of these construals specifies both the form or representation of the document and something about its content or meaning. For the system, a quantitative representation of the actual terms/features and the meta-data aspect of this, is all that the document means—the form or stored information in digital format. For the researcher, the document object is a theoretical object for study, whose construal depends on the nature of this study. If the researcher only seeks to build efficient systems, the content or meaning of the document beyond the needs for algorithmic manipulation is of less concern. In this case, the document question is mainly addressed at the level of mathematical foundations and technical

63. Bruza et al. (1999) say that IR "is a reasoning process which is assumed to be driven by determining aboutness" between document and query, and that therefore, investigating aboutness is key to the theoretical setup of IR, which they develop through axiomatizing this notion.

design. Although this view will not be considered here, it closely influences and is influenced by the other two views. For example, if a technical design allows for novel types of document presentations (beyond a ranked list, say), then the researcher would be interested in modeling this and figuring out its ultimate effect on user experience. For the user-centric researcher, it is important to know how the content of a document beyond its form comes to mean something to the user and how that happens through user experience. For the user, each view of the document—whether partial, or full, shown to precede or follow another document, or shown in a particular format—affects what is meant by it. In this case, the context—in particular, the medium through which the document is shown or expressed—is central to the (qualitative) meaning of the document; it confers meaning to the technical/logical document. The document question is thereby important with respect to all three views, especially given the changing, and increasingly pervasive nature of technology.

To understand the place of a document in the Heideggerean picture of technology, consider first that the document is that which is experienced in response to interaction—at least with respect to the user's view of it. Second, from both the user and researcher points of view, documents are human products (artifacts) or objects in nature. These two perspectives of documents are related, as their objective aspects are partially responsible for how they are subjectively or intersubjectively experienced. Finally, as a result, the document is not merely "anything out there," but instead is anything out there that can be experienced as a result of a technologically-mediated activity. Taking these three considerations together, the conception of the four causes suggests that the document is "in the place" of the overall experience itself: the document is therefore that which is brought forth. Hence, a thing out there, if not attachable to an activity explained by the four causes, can only partially be a document. It would fully become a document when in addition to this objective aspect it has an intersubjective/subjective aspect that places it at the end of an activity as something experienced. Without this latter aspect, it is not a document with respect to a technology-mediated activity, but only a document in an objective sense. This is not to suggest that documents, as a coupled subjective-objective entity, can only be subjective—an ultimately private object. Instead, if there is a commonality between two or more such experiences, the document is said to have an intersubjective and not only a subjective component. The meanings suggested in those experiences, would then be shared in some sense. As a practical example, two users following a technology-mediated experience of searching and reading papers could be said to have discovered in them the solution to a longstanding scientific problem. To the extent that both users concur on this, they share some meanings, and their activity has resulted in a meaning being suggested or generated/discovered, a meaning denoting a novel or enlightening proposition, for example (Swanson, 1986).

A document is then the totality of the result or response as experienced, corresponding to that which has been brought forth by the agency of the four causes of a technology-mediated activity (or interaction). This experience is not only something mental—it is also embodied. What has been brought forth are particular meanings (in the language of level three), which can be understood as systems of relationships between meaning signifiers from among virtual, natural, and built objects and processes. Unlike the example of the sculpture (see section 5.3.2) as that which is brought forth by the work of the efficient cause that is the stonemason, in our case there need not be a physical entity. This is instead replaced by meanings that have been brought out or "brought near" (i.e., experienced) by the occasion of all four causes being present. This notion of a document as that which is brought forth is a theoretical conception of document for use in discourse by researchers. To fully specify what a document is, researchers would additionally have to refer to a user type and a technology-mediated activity to capture its concrete subjective aspect.

The next section further discusses this idea of a document object from a researcher's point of view as denoting the totality of the user experience of a response. This is a particularly relevant construal for the modern context. Moreover, it discusses the implications of such a concept of document with respect to where the signifiers of meaning, in the process of meaning-suggestion, are to be located.

5.3.7.1 Implications of understanding document as "experience(d)"   In the pervasive modern context, portions of multiple logical documents could be presented to the user as a response, which may be presented in various visual modes and frames. For example, consider the following use case: the user seeks to know the latest news on reaching their smart home. Suppose their home is equipped with multiple display areas and zones where information can be communicated to them. The same logical document, about the "latest news," can then be split accordingly and displayed in different areas as opposed to on one large screen for scrolled viewing. One snippet of that document, perhaps one with an associated image, can be displayed on their large TV screen, a text-only snippet can be displayed on a smaller device screen that they pass as they move around the house, and that part of the news that elicits interaction can be displayed on their fridge screen, so that they are more likely to interact with it as they seek to consume a beverage. Once they enter an area where visual attention is

unlikely or cognitively burdensome, a part of this news may instead be spoken by playing the associated audio report. And once they are physically settled (e.g., they decide to lounge in bed), the video aspect of the report could also be played on a nearby screen along with the audio. All of this is the response to the implicit query to see latest news that was triggered on entering the user's home. The response here corresponds to portions of information, that can together be understood as one document. Therefore, in addition to the document's objective aspect being an object (that is for IR&S an answer/reply/response to a query), it can also be an event or process. And instead of its objective aspect corresponding to one thing, it can be multiple interrelated objects, or the totality of the flow/process of response and the interactions that follow an interaction. The fluidity of technology-mediated living means that it is more a dynamic sort of experience than static perceptions. Similarly, instead of the subjective side of a document being constituted by a single cognitive correlate, to the extent that an experience persists over time, the subjective side can denote the experience as a whole, over time.

The document in this example—the system's response—from the system's perspective, is a set of representations of one logical document paired with viewing/listening rules. From the user's perspective, it is not so much the different parts but an experienced whole, to be repeated every day on their return home from work. By not being a single object to be viewed at once, but something experienced over time, this type of document breaks away from the classical document paradigm. The way this document comes to mean something—the way its content is interpreted—is quite different from the classical case. The signifiers of meaning are not only the collection of signifiers corresponding to the individual snippets of text, video, and audio, they also correspond to perceptual groupings thereof. For example, that a particular snippet was shown as the user was walking toward the kitchen, and not in audio form as they were standing in the hallway, could significantly affect how the content was interpreted. In general, if the document is the entirety of the experience of a system response, then the signifier of meaning therein is the particular structure of the experience. This structure does not only refer to a mental aspect. As experience is experience of something, all the visual/sense-based aspects of the document are also included, as is the medium and context, along with the relevant cognitive correlates that condition interpretation. It is the user-centric researcher who conceives the document in this way for the sake of studying it as a theoretical object, in order to better understand user experience.

There are other notions of document that appear to support taking meaning-signification as experience structure and are compatible with the document as being an experience (and not only as that which is experienced). A objective part of a document may actually be a search strategy in the form of an application (Gabrilovich, 2012),[64] which then corresponds to an actual usage journey (i.e., usage experience) or a potential (or hypothetical) such journey. The objective part of a document, perhaps controversially, can correspond to a work of (nondigital) art, and not a reproduced/digital version thereof. This is a subtle addition to Briet's list (Briet et al., 2006), as the purpose of such a document is perhaps different from scientific objects (e.g., fossils). But if IR&S is to study technology-mediated user experience, then a study of actual artistic pieces as objective parts of documents would be as a comparative to the study of looking at or experiencing such objects through technology. Whether the mediated experience of a work of art is different from the human experience of it remains unclear, and as the classic work of Benjamin (2008) argues, the general case is that it is not. Even if much is lost in digital or reproduced forms, rich layers of significance (beyond full significance) may still result, and these layers may be evoked as corollaries of modes of access/experience enabled by technology, as opposed to being inherent only in the static reproduced document/object. What is evoked may be an idea; an emotion; or for example, a numinous experience (Latham, 2012), inclining toward Benjamin's notion of the aura of the original pieces (Osborne and Charles, 2015). The document defined as experience works to capture the dynamic structure of the experience of an external/objective entity.

Furthermore, the way a document is used or is to be used should be understood as part of its definition; and how it is infact used depends on our beliefs about it. As Buckland (2012, p. 5) clarifies: "What we believe about a document influences our use of it, and more importantly, our use of documents influences what we believe." The general phenomenon of reading an object or the experience of an object, over and above the object itself, is an important phenomena for study (cf. Dillon, 1992), since as Iser (1979, 1993) holds, the meaning of a document is constructed through the reading experience itself. Latham's (2014)[65] reader-response theory appears to follow from the work of Iser, which is based on a phenomenological account of experience (Iser, 1972).

---

64. This could be seen to go back to the notion of an active document, see Chalmers et al. (1998).

65. See also her more recent works in Lund (2016) and which Gorichanaz and Latham (2016).

What is clear is that although the document may have a material component, or a specific electronic component, this is increasingly insufficient in the modern context to consider only this as its constitutent. The nonmaterial aspect then is of immediate importance to study, meaning those aspects that are other than the list of words or objects in a physical or digital unit of text or other media known as a document. These other nonmaterial aspects then define the document through the reading, use, and general experience of the document. This includes its social context (including information about how it came to be), the way it depicts something in the real world (and what it misses)—and hence how it stands in for the real-world object—and the usage journey it holds. These aspects can be understood, in a semiotic sense, to be represented by a theoretical structure that is an abstract, meaning-signifying structure, which is indicative of what it could mean to experience the document.

Our suggestion that a document should correspond to (a resulting) experience also has some support from one of the original notions of document. While "document" is from the Latin root "docere" ("to teach"), this comes from the Greek deikunai: "to show." As can be interpreted from McNeill (1999, p. 153), the document shows the way (it is a means) to arrive at particular meanings. However, this "showing" is only after a "struggle to know" the document (McNeill, 1999, p. 153). The document as something experienced that imparts meanings (i.e., is meaning suggesting/generating), with subjective (and/or intersubjective) and objective aspects, or as a persisting experience (persisting in the sense it remains over time), constituting and possibly conditioning one's overall lived-experience, is that which is brought forth by virtue of the four causes. As meanings are imparted in this experience, the signifiers of the meanings must be in that experience; they must correspond to the subjective and objective aspects. These signifiers are then responsible, through coming together, for the "showing" to which deikunai corresponds. What then of this struggle to know? The showing, the document, is only as a result of a technology-mediated activity, which can be interpreted as the struggle to know. Thus, the document, the showing, is only such after the effort made by a user to use, to read, or to act in a particular way—as delineated by the four causes; the document is not passively received. The user works to bring-forth or show/unconceal the document.

There are of course many further implications to discourse (to methodology in particular), if "document" is taken as conceptualized here. If a retrieval system is supposed to provide access to documents as things, or to documents as experiences, then IR&S has to first develop a way of talking about (not just representing) the relevant objects or "basic forms" of that thing or experience, respectively. This is basically an investigation of objectification: the study of how things in the world become particularized as things in human experience. This investigation depends on the nature of the observer. What is of concern here is not only the initial objectification of the system on first look, but also its evolution through consequent stages of system use, and any regularities therein pertaining to a particular user or user group. While some users might mainly focus on changed aspects of the interface as the system response—those aspects being their objectification and construal of "response"—others might focus on alternative aspects. For example, in the case of a system offering a simple ranked list as a response: the top few results may be construed by the user as the main response. But, with sponsored results creating a more complex response space, the nonsponsored results below the top results (or indeed the sponsored results outside the ranked list) could instead be construed as the main response; the actual response object could, for example, be formed from information about eye-tracking investigations. However, with more complex interfaces, such as the augmented-reality applications through Google glasses or their equivalent, objectification becomes a much more complex process. The response object may not only be aspects of world-as-augmented, they may also involve the dimension of time by including changes in the augmentation. For example, instead of pages of ranked results, a response could present a set of visible objects and other hidden objects (that would be on other pages in the prior case) that are visible upon head movement. The response is then the immediately visible objects in addition to the objects presented through 'subresponses' upon head movement. It is this ease and fluidity of interaction that makes these subresponses rather than full responses at a perceptual level. Moreover, as capturing the document here is to further consider the subjective component in each of these cases, there has to be fuller understanding of glances than afforded by the physical positions of user eyes captured in eye-tracking research. The works of McNeill (1999) and Casey (2003) provide a rich exploration of glance, on which a methodology for discussing glances and further development of the above concept of document can be based. However, developing such a concept of document requires recourse to discourses whose subject is human experience itself; to particular matters, such as the subjective experience of time within a document (as experience); to the roles of imagination, perception, intuition and other modes of experience in the constitution of a particular experience. This corresponds to discourses characterized as phenomenology.

5.3.8   What Is Relevance?

There are numerous understandings of relevance in IR&S discourse (Huang and Soergel, 2013). They differ according to which aspects they consider to be linked by the relation of relevance and on the nature of that relationship. Relevance is of course beyond being only about topicality; the particular modes of relevance are numerous, for example, relevance as "fresh" or "authoritative" (Inagaki et al., 2010). As the use of IR systems became more pervasive and ubiquitous, there was a need to think of not only the relevance of documents given requests, but also relevance given the further context of user information needs.

The first "relevance revolution," as Borlund (2003) describes it was premised on the idea that relevance should be judged on the information need behind a request rather than on the request itself. This leads to a change in research focus: the user now has to be understood with respect to the "further context" that is their need. Any discussion of relevance ignoring need (given the diversity in the usage of systems) became increasingly perceived as being lacking. Relating queries/requests to documents thereby came to be understood as sufficient only in restricted situations and as not being representative of the diverse ways in which most IR systems were being used. With respect to the four causes, this first revolution can be interpreted as suggesting the need for a richer account of the efficient cause; a minimal formal cause that only considers the forms of queries is not sufficient for the kinds of explanations and discourse sought by an ideal IR&S.

Given the proliferation of social networking, one could infer another such "revolution," pertaining to the "sociological turn" (Cronin, 2008), where the relevance construct expands to give focus not only to the needs of the immediate user (i.e., the personal information need), but also to the social factors influencing the forming of these needs. This second revolution could then be interpreted as calling for a richer formal cause, for a richer description of the public/social/cultural account of queries beyond individual information needs as captured by efficient causes.[66] This is important because the types of phenomena that IR&S addresses, due to their relation to classical search phenomena, are increasing in variety. This increase corresponds to the increase in the portion of lived experience that is technology-mediated, which results in an increase in the number and

---

66. The increasing consideration of the sociological dimension as a second revolution is discussed in section 5.2.4 and also in chapter 2, which relate the trend in IR&S discourse of focus moving (or an understanding therein that it is needing to move) from query-document relations to context-context relations.

complexity of relations that are important for the notion of relevance: relations between information need, request, and system response. This means an expansion of both the field of objects that relevance relates to and the types of relevance considered therein. The question of relevance thus remains significant. As a result, relevance should be understood not as a specific relationship, but instead, as a stand-in concept for any relationship that appears to be of significance in experience.[67]

As a consequence, as the pervasiveness of contexts increases, relevance stands in for increasing types of relations. It becomes increasingly general as a concept by itself, and so it begins to lose its usefulness on its own and requires support from discriminating concepts that would serve to specify it. Thus, to say "x is relevant to y" without specifying the sense of it would just mean that x is related to y, and further specifications would be required. However, the concept of relevance can be improved, especially in light of the above reconceptualizations of basic concepts.

Let "x is relevant to y" denote "x means y," or "x signifies y," or "x and y mean or signify one another." Therefore, the relation between the request, user need, social context, and documents is not just relevance as "relation" with a sense to be further specified. Instead it is relevance as "signification," with the sense of signification to be further specified. In the latter case, all such specification can then be understood as specifications of the senses of significations, of the sense in which something means something else.

Why is this modification an improvement? It better fits with the reconceptualization suggested for the notion of document and also of search as meaning-suggestion. Furthermore, it brings the notion of relevance closer to that in the seminal work by Schutz (Schutz, 1970; Cox, 2012), which influenced relevance theories in IR&S through Saracevic (2007). Schutz was a phenomenologist interested in the intersubjective character of everyday experiences, who concluded that these experiences organize the world in some standard ways, and these ways, or typifications, are a result of habitual modes of experiencing the world. For example, that of taking a thing in the world as some thing, such as the taking of a physical structure as a "toy" or "fun plaything" in one context and as a dangerous object in another (e.g., in the context of such a thing being on a flight of stairs). In these habitual experiences, parts of the world are selected as something: there is a "dynamics of selectivity" (Straßheim, 2010, p. 1412) at play in

---

67. This perhaps fits with the original meanings of the root word of "relevare," which is "to raise up" i.e., signification as raising up or being noticed.

the formation of an experience, which is said to make "certain selections 'relevant' to an individual." Being relevant here is akin to "being signified in a context." As argued in Straßheim (2010), Schutz theory can be seen to complement the seminal theory of Sperber and Wilson (Sperber and Wilson, 1995; Wilson and Sperber, 2002), which instead originates from the area of study bridging linguistics, cognitive science, and anthropology.

In addition to enabling a rigorous characterization of the many senses of relevance corresponding to the various possible technology-mediated experiences, a Schutzian theory of relevance could play a central role in characterizing documents as experiences. For example, if the document is taken to be that which is brought forth to user experience, then as section 5.3.7 argued, the signifier for the meaning of the document no longer pertains to something in the logical document but now corresponds to the structure of that experience. This structure can possibly be characterized according to the habitual typifications it resembles.

The concept of relevance then changes as a consequence of the adoption of Heidegger's conception of technological activity, given the pervasive nature of modern technology. It changes from denoting an arbitrary relation between traditional queries and documents to meaning-signification between formal causes and that which is brought forth (i.e., document as experience).

5.3.9   What Is Context?

At least two senses of "context" apply in IR&S discourse. In the first sense, "context" is used to refer arbitrarily to background factors that are not yet the focus of investigation or are not yet understood as to how they affect an interaction or technology-mediated activity. This is the entirety of the narrative (and factors) explaining system/user action or cognition. These undifferentiated background factors constitute the context from the researcher's observational perspective.

With respect to the user's observational perspective (i.e., their perceiving and interacting with that part of the world that a researcher defines as a system), there is a system context. This term refers to whatever is beyond the person of the user that they observe to be the background world context, from whence interactive possibilities emerge. This system context does not including the interactive or visual components with which the user is already familiar. System context can thus be understood as mainly referring to the background scene of the material cause. While the formal cause is the public/social constituting factors of the form of user expression, the context is the corresponding social constituting factors of the material cause. Similarly, from the system's ("observational") perspective, wherein the system can be understood to be interpreting the world (e.g., through classifying input signals), there is a user context. This context corresponds to the entire set of undifferentiated input signals that are yet to be given meaning as corresponding to the meaningful user interactions of some user. This user context is then the pattern of data representing the world, which could have some relation to meaningful user interaction. But the system does not hold a pattern that can depict a relationship of this type.

In the second sense, context is used to denote the zone of applicability of a proposition; it depicts the possible world (Menzel, 2016) where something is the case. It can denote an arbitrary scope and can either be used explicitly or inferred implicitly. An example of a direct explicit use is "this document is relevant in the context of (i.e., with respect to) the following queries," and an example of an indirect/implicit use with a larger scope is "this system is effective," where the latter statement is true with respect to the immediate context (i.e., the search scenario just observed; see chapter 1). With respect to the first sense of context, the researcher is of course interested in both the user's perspective of the system and the system's perspective of the user. The second sense of context is of use in IR&S discourse, as it employs many types of possible-worlds thinking, such as counter factual arguments about the contexts (or cases/scenarios) in which a system could be more efficient than in others.

There are thus some changes to these notions of context, given the suggestions for expanding the notions of document, query, and so forth, in prior sections. What may have previously been considered to be part of the context (e.g., from the researcher's perspective) would now be conceptualized/objectified specifically as being part of these notions. This can be seen to be a trend in dealing with pervasive applications: more and more aspects of the background world are considered as proper objects for study or automated analyses (for system building). If the context of a document (or of the objective aspect of a document) is sought, then its social role can be mentioned. If the context of the document's social role is sought, then we need to find out how this role compares to the role of other documents or other cultures (i.e., how it is given further meaning). Hence, the richer the concept of document becomes, the more of what was previously considered as context becomes part of the document itself, and the less remains as being beyond this immediate context. The traditional notion of "document collection" has also been part of this context, albeit on the document (system) side as opposed to the user side. As discussed below, this notion also needs to be reconceived.

5.3.10 What Is a Collection?

As with the other aspects discussed above, what a collection is depends on whether the perspective is that of the user, researcher, or system. However, in addition to these actors, the document creator and the collection curator/designer also come into play, as do the cultural processes that make the collection possible. Furthermore, with respect to the perception and conceptualization of a collection, there can be subjective, intersubjective, and objective accounts as in the case of a document. When problematizing the collection, all these viewpoints need to be considered. In general, to the extent that it is accessible through system interactions preceding interaction with a sought-after item or document, the collection partially constitutes the material cause. However, to the extent that the collection is a part of the world made available to a user by means of a system, it is what is brought forth. This interpretation is what IR&S takes a collection to be—the source of the document.

From the perspective of the collection designer/curator and the researcher, the collection is a set of items with a shared meaning, and as with documents, the items correspond to natural, virtual, or produced/designed artifacts, from museum objects to text snippets to videos. Lee (2000, p. 1106) finds that problematizing the collection from this perspective means questioning four key factors that condition the collection: "tangibility, ownership, a user community, and an integrated retrieval mechanism"; he further questions the finitude and boundaries of collections. In addition to these factors, it is important to understand whether the collection refers to a static or changing thing. Most real-life collections are continuously changing; they constitute an open world as opposed to a closed one from the perspective of the content designer and that of the researcher adopting the open-world perspective.

From the user's perspective, the collection is possibly more fluid. Given increasingly pervasive interactive environments, the collection for them—if they have such a concept—is the background from whence documents emerge. It is akin to and undifferentiated from their understanding of system context (part of the overall context of activity; see section 5.3.9). This is the background that offers a set of possibilities for interaction or engagement. It is only through multiple interactive experiences that users may instead differentiate a set of actual or possible entities that can be categorized into semantically related groups, or collections. Simple examples of this are a ranked list (i.e., the collection is what the links point to or represent) and a selection of items on screen that can be clicked. However, these possibilities change through the process of interaction (interaction journeys), and so the user's idea of "collection" or any particular example of it (e.g., the collection responsible for the document they are currently interacting with) is constantly transforming. The user may instead take a collection to be not a multiplicity of logically or semantically linked data items, but simply the collection of all interactive possibilities (i.e., things they interacted with or used, as opposed to facts).

These collections are of course different from what a system would considers to be a collection: the set of definite entities that it can respond to and interact with. Which also differs from the researcher's concept of collection, wherein the collection is not only a set of objects but also includes references to the practices that brought them about. These practices all serve to partially constitute what is traditionally known as the domain (see chapter 2) of a collection. The idea of a domain, not just the understanding of particular domains (Hjørland and Albrechtsen, 1995; Lupu et al., 2014) needs to be problematized, as it is the source of collections. Domains have to do with particular understandings of the cultural processes or activities that result in document creation and collection. As Furner (2015) emphasizes and is further discussed in chapter 6, the study of the act of collecting as a phenomenon identifies what IR&S is about. This act is therefore something that needs to be problematized, along with the acts and cultures of collecting. Moreover, the social mechanisms generative of the formal cause might also be generative of this culture of collecting or indeed that responsible for creating the collection. That is, at the level of IR&S, the communities creating documents have something in common with the communities reading/using them; at the least they have a shared language.[68]

Key constituents of a domain and of the acts/cultures of collecting, are the collection designer/curator or generator, and the processes involved in their creation. These constituents are also important aspects of the collection question and can also be proper aspects of the theoretical object

---

68. To share a social mechanism or formal cause for one's activities means to share a domain, in part at least, and hence possibly to participate in similar or the same discourse, organization, or institution. The significance of institutions is further discussed in chapter 6. To the extent a collection is generated by a discourse, the discipline of discourse analysis is relevant to framing the specific generative mechanisms. These mechanisms would depend on an ontology of conversational and linguistic structures (from an analytical as well as computational perspective; Grosz et al., 1989; Moore and Wiemer-Hastings, 2003), power structures (Foucault and Lewis, 1991; Angermuller et al., 2014), and other aspects (van Dijk, 1997; Wetherell et al., 2001; Angermuller et al., 2014).

of collection that the researcher studies (especially for IS researchers). The collection then has to be understood in terms of its role and function in a context or domain, from the perspective of content creators and users as content consumers. As with documents, the actual collection can be viewed as a set of logically or physically differentiable items; as a set of perceptual or interactive possibilities and concepts; or as the end of a search process.

If the document is interpreted in the way suggested in prior sections (as denoting an experience) then from the researcher's perspective of this user experience, the collection would refer to possible technology-mediated experiences. They are partial constituents (the objective aspects in particular) of potential experiences, and hence indicate potential documents. Ultimately, given the pervasiveness of technology, the collection denotes the world in its totality, i.e. the real-world (built, natural, etc.) "out there," combined with the myriad ways it can appear to a cognitive agent.

Therefore the collection is the many possible ways the world can be revealed, or brought forth: the world in potentia. For example, in early IR research (as discussed in earlier sections of this chapter), the purpose of search technology was to reveal truths, and find connections in a semi-fortuitous way (Swanson, 1986). Meaning that the connections would appear through the system juxtaposing a particular set of information items that had common features—implicitly suggesting the possibility of there being something more than the common features—as opposed to randomly selecting such items. This idea of IR's purpose continues to this day. Doctoral theses on retrieval commonly start out with an articulation of the motivation for IR systems by stating that there is much information in the world, and that this is useless or wasted if it cannot be accessed or made sense of through retrieval technology. What is being suggested is that the information is just sitting there without any use or "life," unless it is given additional meaning as a resource to be retrieved/processed. With the wider notion of collection, this suggestion can be interpreted as the in-potentia state of the larger collection of (all possible) information, including that in books, or natural/built environment objects (i.e., all possible external meaning-signifiers along with all their possible couplings with internal meaning signifiers, denoting all possible documents as experiences).

The collection understood in this way, according to a traditional (and persistent) sentiment in IR research, is precisely the typical worldview of the technologist as Heidegger sees it, that the world (as collection and resource) exists in the mode of *standing reserve*, as a resource to be exploited as means to ends (Heidegger, 1977, 17). That the world is "forced" to be other than it actually is, for the sake of a technical analysis and control. Thus the collection as world is not quite the world, but instead is the world as indexed or captured by our particular devices and algorithms. It is reduced and represented in a way that is not for the purpose of showing it as it is but for another purpose: that of controlling it in some way. Thus, the world is only shown with the function of being a subject of control. That the collection as world referred to these biased depictions, standing there, reserved for us, to be brought forth. Heidegger uses the notion challenged forth, as if they are done violence to: since they are not presented in a natural way and only presented with respect to their being a "resource" to be used. This is as opposed to saying that the world is brought forth corresponding to the world being as it is. This elicits a fundamental question: How are we to know whether that which is called a document, has been brought forth (as has been taken to be the default case) or is instead a result of being challenged forth? This is a question about the authenticity of the technology-mediated experience, relating back to the ethical part of the comportment questions discussed earlier (see section 5.1.1 and section 5.2.4).

The question is indeed relevant. A practical example of its significance is the issue of overdependence on search engines whose results are conditioned by the legal and business policies (such as sponsored results) of the search company, who acts as the curator of results. As a result, a particular image of the world is presented and not another. Consider the effect of this not just on an individual but, as in Heidegger's analysis, on the relation between humans and technology in a particular period of time. Problematizing the question of collection therefore involves asking about how the constant experience of a collection, as that which is brought or challenged forth, informs our worldview, our understanding of ourselves and others (our sociological imagination), and about how authentic or true it is especially with respect to how this affects human living.

5.4 General Issues Pertaining to Comportment

Recall the idea that basic concepts employed in a scientific discourse constitute the center or hard core of the corresponding a research program or tradition, which supports an outer layer of theories (or generative constructs). As already discussed, this outer layer is the main positive aspect of discourse, the part that "grows" the most through employing theories to make new claims and generate new understandings (see chapters 3 and 4). The previous sections considered specific foundational questions. This section instead addresses some implications of their recharacterization on the outer layer, which contains the bulk of what is known as research methodology and constitutes (nonfoundational) research practice. This methodology delineates how the developed foundational concepts would be used to generate these new understandings and findings. However, these implications are still at the foundational level. They are about what is required of outer-layer theoretical frameworks[69] founded on these basic concepts for them to be effective in fulfilling the goals of IR&S, such as those pertaining to the explanation of phenomena and the development of practical solutions.

This section discusses some of the main such implications, with respect to the particulars of scientific observation, research style, and the development of theories or theoretical constructs. First, section 5.4.1 summarizes how the characterization of foundational issues in the preceding section relates to research comportment. Additionally it explains how the structure of the inner layer of discourse might influence that of the outer layer. Second, section 5.4.2 further discusses the methodological implications of the finding above that the foundations researcher needs to consider each relevant research/theoretical object as it would be conceived by different observers: user, system and researcher. Third, given the above discussions suggesting that the place of explanatory research in IR&S is central, section 5.4.3 argues for the important place of a contrastive type of explanatory research (i.e., the strategy of exploring why something happened instead of something else, rather than exploring the why of it in a direct manner) and the implications thereof. It supposes that the contrastive is important due to prior discussions suggesting the need for phenomenological methods combined with simulations. Finally, section 5.4.4 further elaborates the notion of complementary or (actively) coordinated theory growth that chapter 4 suggested was needed for progressive outer-layer growth. This is with respect to

- the wide range of phenomena particular to the modern context,
- the wide range of theory types that have to be employed and actively coordinated or integrated (see chapter 4 and chapter 2, respectively), and
- the discussion in section 5.3 on construing basic concepts.

This section can be interpreted as suggesting what Lakatos calls "positive heuristics" (see chapter 3), that is, suggestions for developing, modifying, and growing the outer layer of discourse, given the characterization of basic

---

69. That is, they are not about specific such theories or theoretical frameworks but instead comment about them as a whole.

questions earlier in this chapter. This is done partly in a direct way by suggesting what kinds of new theories are required and what questions they could answer, and partly indirectly, by indicating what the theory space could look like as a whole relative to the inner-layer discourse.

5.4.1 From Foundations to Nonfoundations

Section 5.1.1 discussed the different types of comportment questions pertaining to the different aspects that constitute the way a typical researcher approaches their phenomena of interest. The typical researcher is of course not the only relevant type of actor or observer. There is the user, whose phenomena of interest is the world and the technology that mediates that world. The typical researcher's phenomena of interest include that of the user's, but in addition they include the cognitive and physical aspects of users to the extent that those aspects are involved in engaging with technology or affecting their technology-mediated experience. The user thereby is part of the researcher's world. Finally, the researcher's perspective also includes the technology being used and the search scenario or usage context. There is also the foundations researcher, whose phenomena of interest in turn include those of the typical researcher's (thereby including that of users). In addition, the foundations researcher's interests includes all those cognitive and physical aspects of the typical researcher that determine their understanding of their phenomena of interest, and all their "outputs" (e.g., phenomena construals, hypotheses and propositions, research discourse as a whole).

The whole of this book is of course from the perspective of foundations research, and as foundations researchers, we also have a comportment, which has an epistemological and ontological aspect, just as does that of the typical researcher, who for us is a phenomenon of interest. The recharacterization of basic concepts of IR&S in the prior sections constitute the ontology of our foundations perspective (i.e., what the phenomena of interest are and how they are construed). In this respect, the characterization of discussions of user cognition (which could be of interest as a phenomenon for typical researchers) as having to do with formal or efficient cause is our characterization of the ontological aspect of a typical researcher's comportment. This book also has much to do with the decision processes of typical researchers, especially the place and use of basic concepts (i.e., in investigating the nature of what is known and discussed by IR&S researchers, and how that happens by means of basic concepts). Thus this book ultimately investigates the epistemological and logical aspects of the typical researcher's scientific-theoretical mode of comportment. The preceding sections grouped basic questions—and the comportment questions they may relate to—by means of a theory of technology, a theory that is at the foundations or inner level. We grouped most of the basic notions into four causes that serve to explain the phenomenon of interest to typical researchers: technology-mediated experience or activity pertaining to user engagement with technology. This is a phenomenon that is higher than the search phenomena particular to traditional IR&S; we argued that moving to this higher level was necessary for progress, given that technology is increasingly pervasive in the modern context.

Yet all of this is still the inner network. If we were to further discuss the mode of comportment pertaining to "making" through the craft that went beyond values into design principles (from interface designs to search-scenario and system design) and the mathematical foundations for technical designs, then we would be a step closer to the outer network (see chapter 3) of discourse. The outer network is instead constituted by specific designs and mathematical models based on these principles and foundations respectively, which can be understood as being akin to the positive theories (or hypotheses) that constituted the outer network of a scientific discourse in chapter 3. In some sense all foundational theories, discussions, and propositions (such as those above), posit something and are amenable to debate and testing. The main difference between them and outer network theories and models are that the latter have more dependencies than the former and are usually of a more restricted scope. For example, consider a cognitive model explaining the behavior of a particular type of user. This model would function as a theory of the efficient cause for those technology-mediated activities in which such users are involved. A foundational or inner-network theory of efficient causes could instead propose the conditions for any successful cognitive theory (e.g., that of considering the embodied nature of cognition, the user's intentionality, or their experience of time). Or, for example, such a theory could argue for the appropriateness of a cognitive-linguistic theory for relating formal and efficient causes, as opposed to some other existing theory. Both such inner and outer theories posit propositions testable by argumentation or empirical tests.

Moreover, the outer network can thereby be structured according to the inner. First, there could be four types of outer-layer theories corresponding to the four causal categories that were used to characterize the objects in the researcher's world. This causal theory stems from an inner/foundational theory of technology. Beyond this, as the foundations layer divided phenomena into four levels, working mainly at the level of technologically-mediated activity/experience, the outer layer theories can additionally be divided according to which level of phenomena they address, and related according to theories that deal with the corresponding phenomena at higher or lower levels. Hence, having outer-level theories that deal with interaction (the interaction level), search and meaning-suggestion (the semantic level), and technology-mediated experience (the mediation level) would obligate IR&S researchers to explore how these theories could inform each other so they would not be mutually incoherent and impede progress.

5.4.2 Observational Contexts
The increasing variation of the relevant phenomena has lead to a reformulation of several classical notions, from search to interaction, to cope with the context of technology-mediated experience. Each such notion admits several objectifications, and there are several observer perspectives to consider. This collectively brings into question the idea and event of scientific observation that enables the researcher to construe, observe, and discuss phenomena in these expanded ways. The scientific observation event is also the means by which the user's and system's observational particulars are determined. Hence, to problematize the event of scientific observation (i.e., the researchers observation context to which they are comported) also means problematizing the other observational contexts. All three observational contexts have to be considered with respect to the nature of objectification therein.

With respect to the researcher's observational context, IR&S scholars are not only interested in users as nominal objects but also as beings who experience the world through technology. What is of interest then is the content of user experience. Hence the researcher is interested in the user's observational context. The researcher is similarly interested in the system's observational context to the extent that the "interpretive process" of the system (e.g., the way the system progressively understands the user's information need through analyzing requests) is of interest. Therefore, given the need for user-centricity in the modern context, the researcher needs to be concerned with issues pertaining to how the user and system get to know and experience the world, and how they come to construe aspects in the world as objects (i.e., their processes of objectification). The researcher also needs to know this from a second-order perspective, from what the user conceives about what the system knows—usually pertaining to what systems know about them (e.g., about their needs)—and what the system "conceives" about what the user knows about, usually pertaining to what the user knows about it (e.g., that the user understands what the interface means and how to use it).

The foundations researcher thereby needs to be concerned with the researcher's objectification process, in both first and second orders, which means being concerned about user and system experience. These various epistemological concerns (about what users, systems, and foundations and other researchers are concerned to know about) are depicted in Figure 5.1. By being concerned with the user's observational context, the foundational researcher is concerned not only with the user's experience of particular scenarios but also with the way people are understood to be users, with what user experience means in the first place, and how IR&S researchers come to construe experience.[70]

Each of these observational contexts affords several ways of knowing for each actor. The researchers know about users from their behavior, but since the user and researcher are the same kind of entity (albeit in different modes; one is using and the other is studying use), the researcher can empathize with the user. Thus the researcher has some understanding of the meaning of and intent behind user behavior due to this similarity, something that is not available in the system's observational context. Hence, the processes of objectification that pertain to a person-as-user would be related, but not equivalent, to the processes of objectification of a person as-researcher or as-scientific-observer. These may be understood as the user and scientific perspectives, or in phenomenological terminology, as constituting different attitudes (Sokolowski, 2000).

In particular, the researcher can put themselves "in the shoes of" the user; they can imagine using a system in the ways a user does, develop insights and explanations through this, and apply them to explain a current user behaviour.[71] This type of analysis involving imaginative variation of (user) experiential scenarios—a kind of "thought experiment"—is something native to the field of phenomenology, where it has been developed as a rigorous technique of analysis (Mohanty, 1991; Sokolowski, 2000). Rich narratives and explanations of hypothetical user experience can be generated from this, as objects for analysis and critique—as hypotheses—to be

---

70. Therefore, not only is the researcher's comportment to the world of interest to the foundations researcher (and thus something to be problematized) but also the user's and system's comportments.

71. Therefore there are methods of studying the user that are available to researchers that would not be available to them if their phenomena of interest pertained, for example, to the natural world.

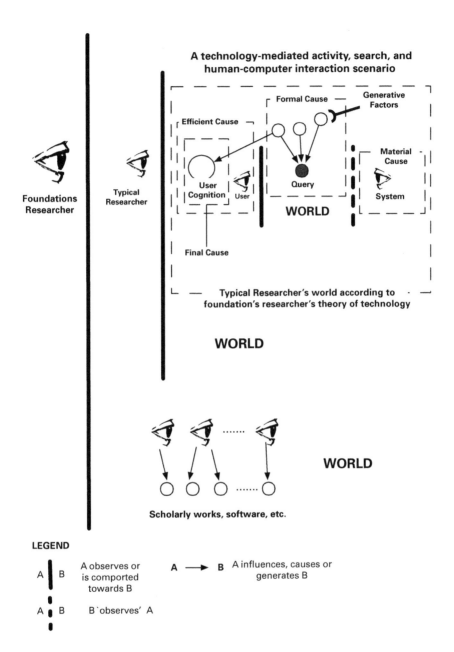

Figure 5.1
A depiction of the main observers and their observation contexts

compared against and to complement actual accounts from user studies or objective statistical accounts of user behavior. While several IR&S works directly employ this method to analyze user experience (Suorsa and Huotari, 2014), there is not yet a standard methodology (as there are for other types of analysis) adapted for the IR&S context.

The phenomenological method of imaginative variations can be used to characterize the user's observational context. Furthermore, the researcher as observer has a special relation to the system because they created it, so knowledge of why it behaves in a particular way and what it is going to do in a given scenario are also known prior to experiment. This is unlike, for example, the observational scenario of the natural scientist, who can neither empathize with a phenomenon nor (generally speaking) have advanced full knowledge of what it would do in different physical contexts. Thus, the IR&S researcher has the ability to investigate scenarios by "mental simulation" of the user entity and by extensively informed computational simulations of the system component.

Thus it would be beneficial to investigate how the phenomenological method could be coordinated with a simulation framework, not so much for the creation of efficient systems, but as a means for generating investigative leads and suggesting different possibilities pertaining to phenomenal variations. The more of this picture one can understand and represent, the more combinations of situations one can simulate or employ in counterfactual argumentation.[72] Knowing the possible variations are useful for the contrastive investigations discussed next, and also for understanding the context of empirical findings.

5.4.3 Explanatory Strategies

As previously discussed (see chapter 2 and prior sections in this chapter), the idea of evaluation in IR&S, with respect to pervasive technology, means looking at final results (such as ranked lists), processes, and events in the context of increasingly larger slices of the technology-mediated life that surrounds it and with respect to an increasingly rich structure of values (Belkin, 2016). The evaluation is not only of individual processes/ systems but also of higher-level activities; it is the evaluation of overall technology-mediated experiences or activities and not only the interactions

---

72. For example, the more possibilities that are known, the more questions of the form "Can this possibility be true and what is its relation to this other possibility?" can be posed and addressed, and as a result, a discourse grown. This type of research strategy is characteristic of the natural sciences, which admit of regular-patterned phenomena.

and systems they refer to. Furthermore, evaluation here does not mean to reduce such complex phenomena and usage contexts to simple quantities, but to elicit comparative critical characterizations that may nevertheless employ quantitative measures.

Given the many variables constituting, for example, efficient and formal causes—beyond information needs and basic queries—and the highly contextual nature of user behavior, the evaluation of a corresponding usage scenario (or the effectiveness of the technological solution employed therein) must first be limited to that scenario. Therefore, instead of broad claims of form "x is the case," the claims ought to be of the form, "x is the case given conditions/variables, a, b, c, ... " Here the variables are not system parameters but mainly socio-cognitive characterizations of the scenario. Thus evaluations have to determine whether a system is "good" with respect to a particular context, and they are required to specify what (for which human activity or mediation context, etc.) the system is actually good for. The respective variables/characteristics would then be of use for explaining why x is the case.

Consider again the case of failure analysis, which seeks to explain failure by asking, for example, why x failed. The salient idea in the explanation of failure is that by chasing the "why question" of failure, the researcher may be lead well beyond the immediate system. As section 2.5.2 discussed, addressing this question means understanding the place of the system in the human context that gives its successes and failures meaning, which presupposes an understanding of the basic concepts used to define these contexts. While there are studies encouraging such deep understandings of system behavior (Harman and Buckley, 2009) and socio-technical processes that failure analysis leads to, such investigations are generally rare because they are difficult. In general, the complex nature of pervasive contexts, which is attributed by many such variables, means that it is clearly not feasible to consider anything but a small selection of factors for everyday explanatory research.

Given this restriction, there are several complementary initial strategies for explanatory research. One strategy is to consider a limited number of variables and then relate the different explanatory theories (or other constructs) to create a larger patchwork; this would be an example of coordinated theory development that chapter 4 suggested as being crucial to progress. The second strategy is to instead work with a limited and more focused form of explanation, the contrastive explanation, which asks a different question: why x instead of y, as if the occurrence of x were unexpected or anomalous. To juxtapose such contrasting situations, there must be an understanding of the different possible situations, different system configurations, interactive pathways, and possible types of user experience. That is, there must be some idea of the contents of each of the causes as well as that which is brought forth (the documents as experience).

There are several related forms, such as the modal or contrastive version: "why still x and not (some) y?" For example, one could ask: "Why does the user keep looking at a particular set of documents and not another?" (e.g., perhaps it was made clear in some other way that the user's need had changed, yet their particular browsing behavior persists). Similarly, "Why did system x fail than not?" is generalizable to "Why did event x occur as opposed to some y?"[73] Moreover, this type of question is particularly suitable for difference analysis as discussed in section 2.5 (i.e., why this particular variation as opposed to that particular variation).[74]

Contrastive investigation/explanation (Lipton, 1990) is particularly useful for social phenomena that do not admit to law-like explanations. It constitutes a fruitful mode of investigation and discovery in the methodology of explanatory economics discourses (Lawson, 1997, p. 26), where finding noncontrastive explanations is more difficult than finding contrastive explanations.[75] Economics and IR&S are related as they deal with socially and culturally conditioned human behavior that is a means to achieving a particular end (Lawson, 1997, 2003; Lehtinen et al., 2012, p. 260).[76]

---

73. According to some, a "why" question is always a contrastive question, where the contrast is implicit if not made explicit (for example, according "to van Fraassen, a why-question is always contrastive" (Weber et al., 2013, p. 41).

74. Recall from the discussion in chapter 2 that statistical hypothesis testing, where the hypothesis is about whether a result differs from another result (e.g., a sample mean from a population mean) is a way to determine that there is a significant variation; it is another matter to ask why this variation occurred.

75. For example, answering why a social process lead to a particular type of consumer behavior or other economic pattern is harder than answering why it leads to that pattern as opposed to some other pattern.

76. Wilson's (2002) anthropologically motivated definition of IR&S certainly allows some overlap between the objects relevant to economics and those relevant to IR&S. Whereas IR&S studies the relations and information flows between material objects, economics studies a particular subset of objects and a particular subset of these flow—those pertaining, for example, to exchange of goods and services. There are indeed applications of models from econometrics and decision theory (Kahneman and Tversky, 1979; Kahneman et al., 1982, 2000; Gilovich et al., 2002) to IR&S, but they are used for ranking improvement as opposed to explanation. In this respect, the methodology for an economic science

Moreover, this form of explanation seems pertinent for IR&S due to the varied nature of search phenomena and the pervasiveness of search-phenomena enabling devices. In particular, it complements the phenomenological method of imaginative variations and the method of computational simulations that are also required to characterize the user- and system-side aspects of technologically mediated activities, especially given the rapidly developing variations of such phenomena in the modern context. These variations refer to the degrees of freedom of the technical design, that is, the ad hoc aspects (q–d relations), and also to the non–ad hoc aspects, such as user-context relationships. This moreover requires understanding the space of possible alternative states: the map of meaningful phenomenological variations or differences (i.e., those pertaining to the researcher's comportment, which includes that of the user).

While each of the four causes in the preceding section come together to explain a technology-mediated activity and experience, they can also serve individually as explanations for each such cause. The seeking out of contrastive explanations for each of these causes, for each level of phenomenon, and for a restricted set or domain of causes can thereby be a method for growing the outer network of discourse. The next section further illustrates the structure of theories on this outer network, where explanatory theories are central but are not the only ones.

5.4.4 Coordinated Theory Growth

This section discusses what theory growth characterizing the outer layer of discourse could mean for IR&S, given the preceding characterizations of the foundations or inner-layer discourse. As chapter 4 argued, the relatively loose notion of theory as generative construct was appropriate—in general—for IR&S. And the coordinated growth of such theories is required for progress, given the modern context of pervasive technology-use. Here coordinated growth means the relating of complementary types of theories, where the relation is with respect to the shared solution of a problem. As the preceding chapters and sections have proposed, the focus of these theories, again for the sake of progressive growth in the modern context, should primarily be technology-mediated activity, a phenomenon at a higher level than users' search and interactive behaviors. Moreover, as prior discourses

---

suggested by Lawson (2003), influenced by the critical-realist perspective in the social sciences, is of significant relevance for IR&S as a whole—especially for the sake of developing explanatory theories.

and sections have argued, progress requires that these theories function to explain the relevant phenomenon, whether user behavior or technology-mediated activity. Explanations of this higher-level phenomenon may of course involve references to the lower-level phenomena constituting it, just as explanations of user behavior within a (pervasive) technology-mediated context would be closely coupled with the interaction possibilities that the system offers, and hence would link to system design. This amounts to the linked or coordinated growth of theories that vary in terms of their subject matter (user, system, behavior, interface) and function (explanation, prediction, interpretation, system building).

The following further elaborates on the notion of complementary or coordinated theories required for progress. It does this by suggesting what it could mean for theories to complement each other, given the preceding discussion of the inner layer, with respect to four of their attributes: their subject matter, function, scope, and style. Theories can of course have other attributes, but these four are sufficient for the purposes of this section.

First, theories can be characterized by their subject matter, or what phenomenon they are about. For example, at the level of search phenomena, theories can be about user (or user groups), documents, collections, systems, or relations therein (e.g., theories of relevance that relate users/judges, queries, documents, and/or collections).[77] However, at the level of technology-mediated activity or experience, these same theories inherit an additional structure that relates/coordinates them with respect to how they together serve to explain that activity or experience. Thus, while an existent theory of information behavior may serve to explain the formal cause for a technology-mediated activity, to the extent that this level of discourse is about explaining such activity, it would not be sufficient except in relation to theories for the corresponding efficient, final, and material causes. This requirement, due to the theory of technology at the foundations level,

---

77. At the level of search phenomena, theories are about what systems or users do, or about how users will experience something (e.g., the satisfaction of or change in information need). Theories of information behavior and information seeking (Fisher et al., 2005) are a common such type of theory. Theories at this level can refer to lower-level phenomena such that the concept of information behavior used could refer to its constituting "information events" (or information related events), which are the loci of manifestation of such behaviors. Information events of course do not only refer to user interactions; user behavior only partially constitutes information behavior. Other constituents could include the behavior of systems, (user/system) communities in general, and the behavior of other agents (Case, 2006).

works to coordinate outer-level theories. It serves as an intellectual demand on IR&S discourse for the sake of progress, as discussed in prior chapters.

Second, theories can be characterized by function, as to what they do or help to do or facilitate. For example, theories can explain, interpret, and predict information events, phenomenal changes, relationships and so forth, or they can facilitate the development of efficient systems and value-oriented policies (e.g., fair policies).[78] The theory of technology that was employed at the foundational level in section 5.3.2 functioned to explain a type of activity. That the modern context seems to particularly call for explanatory theories—at the outer layer, that is—is repeated in several works (Fuhr, 2012; Kelly, 2009) and in prior chapters. At the level of technology-mediated experience/activity, outer-level theories can explain, predict, and interpret such activities/experiences or their causal constituents (e.g., their formal or material causes). For example, a theory that predicts technology-mediated activity can reference a theory about documents (at the level of search phenomena) that instead serves to interpret the document. Thus, theories of one subject matter or function can refer to theories of other subject matters (even if on a different phenomena level) and functions.

Third, theories can be characterized by scope, as to whether a theory is about (or functions to explain or predict) a narrow or wide range of phenomena, and whether it employs a few or many factors to do so.[79] Thus an explanatory theory may explain a subjective, intersubjective, or objective aspect (i.e., one that applies to an individual, to several users, or to a shared attribute of all users, respectively). They may explain something with respect to all three scopes. For instance the theory could be a larger theory linking smaller-scoped theories to form a strong account of the efficient cause for particular types of interactive or technologically mediated scenarios. In this way such theories can account for individual, domain-specific, and typical user experiences.

Finally, theories can be characterized by a style, (or form) with respect to how the theory is expressed, whether as several mathematical propositions, nonmathematical axioms, a rigorous specification of relations, or ambiguous descriptions. Coordinated growth means different styles of

78. That is, theories can function to tell us that something will happen, explain why it happened, what it means, or express how something can happen, e.g., a social change or the building of a system.

79. For example, it can explain the behavior of a group of users or of all users and can do so using one or many types of information need.

theory need to be related for progress, such as mathematical models of efficient or formal causes with first-person phenomenological or interpretive accounts of cognition or language-use/interaction, respectively. The interpretive account here serves to add sufficient meaning to the mathematical model, while the model in turn serves to, for example, show the way for creating technical designs for crafting systems and/or technology-mediated activity (or search) scenarios.

What kinds of theories could be expected to form a progressive outer layer of discourse? Theories pertaining to efficient causes would typically be cognitive theories that are third-person accounts of a neuro-scientific nature (Varela et al., 2017). But they could also be the large-scoped explanatory theories common to the method of thick description (Geertz, 1994), as well as first-person phenomenological accounts (i.e., small-scoped; Varela and Shear, 1999), as are already common in socio-cognitive discourses. However, of particular value are different-scoped theories that complement one another, such that the first- and third-person-accounts of experience cohere (Bitbol, 2002). To seek such complementing theories for the efficient cause is to seek the coordinated theory growth required for a progressive discourse. Consider instead the material cause. Theories capturing material causes correspond to system design, but where the system may include real-world (i.e., built-environment and natural) factors, the theory could correspond to design (as is common in human-computer interaction design) or even architectural theory. For example, in the example in section 5.3.6, an architectural theory of the home could construe the home environment in terms a "center" spot (Norberg-Schulz, 1968; Alexander, 1977, 1979),[80] which may not be the physical center of the home but an experienced or perceived center. It may correspond to what the home users find to be a symbolic congregational spot, such as the living room, that is a nexus between other key areas of the home. And if this center were the first room near the entrance of the house, then the system response would be such that it would be quite different than if this center were farther away from the house entrance. Hence, the user perception of the system would be quite different. The architectural theories relevant here are not those restricted to the physical aspect of the building; but those that focus on the salient aspects of the experience corresponding to

---

80. The work of Norberg-Schulz (1968) in particular considers the intentionality of architectural designs. If such theories were adopted to describe smart-home environments or other built environments that allowed interaction, then the material cause they would depict could also link to efficient causes through formal causes.

living or dwelling (Norberg-Schulz, 1968, p. 5; Heidegger, 1971; Bachelard, 1994) in built environments. In this sense, "dwelling" pertains to the existential result of being in a space/place (i.e., as to what is brought forth to experience, such as is maintained or sustained by the technology-mediated activities or experiences in the modern context). The material cause must therefore partially explain this existential result, and this cannot be merely through reference to physical aspects. Theories of material cause here thus open unto a more variegated space of theories than is characteristic of the existent theory space for classical retrieval systems.

In conclusion, the modern context requires research practice that corresponds to the coordinated growth of a diverse typology of explanatory theories. Each theory would (generally) explain only a limited number of things and use only a limited number of factors, and it would approach its investigation in a contrastive manner.[81] Furthermore, as prior chapters also argued, to the extent the inner network of discourse corresponding to foundations needs to be developed for progress, the corresponding (foundational) generative constructs (and derived foundational propositions) must be constructed in a coordinated manner. Likewise, this book can be understood in terms of theories as generative constructs. Many such theories are of a metatheoretical type (as first discussed chapter 2), meaning that their subject matter pertains to theories and generative constructs.

5.5 Conclusion

This chapter developed a network of foundations questions that correspond to the inner network of a scientific tradition, as a response to the basic question of what a foundation for IR&S should consist of, given the modern context. It differentiated the research culture from the network, suggesting what attributes the culture and network should have to fulfill its function of addressing modern problems. It presented a particular structure to this network, differentiating the disciplinary questions from those pertaining to the researcher's characterization of particular entities, processes, and relationships, which constitute their comportment toward the world. It showed how the purposes and identity of the field, which pertain to disciplinary questions, lay at the root, and how they influence the perusal of other questions. It showed how these questions should be reformulated to reflect

---

81. The middle-range theory (Hedström and Bearman, 2009; Case, 2016) best depicts the scope being referred to here, although these would not be the only type of theories of relevance here.

the modern context, and what is entailed by the modern context with respect to any answers to these questions.

In particular, it reformulated the comportment questions to reflect the need to focus not on classical search or seeking as the key phenomenon, but instead on the encapsulating phenomenon of technology mediation. Thus instead of seeing these questions as corresponding separately either to the instrumental or anthropological aspects of mediation, they were organized according to the part they play in the function of technology as revealing or bringing forth meaning. This is Heidegger's idea of what technology does (beyond being a human activity or a means to an end).

Furthermore, the chapter argued that effectively answering these questions means considering the different but related observational contexts pertaining to how the user, system, and researcher objectify phenomena they observe and/or interact with in technology-mediated scenarios. What a document, query, or other component is depends on which such perspective is taken. The methodological implications of this were discussed, including that of the particular importance of the phenomenological method for rigorously characterizing user experience. To the suggestion of the chapter 4 that progress corresponds to the development of varied types of theories (e.g., in terms of subject matter or function), the present chapter responds with the notion that this amounts to the development of a mixed-method, modular, explanatory scheme.

The foundations network detailed in this chapter is organized according to the overall effect of technology as bringing forth as opposed to its other functions, as the instrumental and anthropological perspectives specify. This serves to identify IR&S discourse in a way that differs from its other, received identities. Chapter 6 explicitly addresses the issue of identity, for both IR&S as a science that studies phenomena and as an art or technological discourse for creating pragmatic solutions to problems pertaining to technology mediation.

6   The Enduring Nature of Foundations

6.1   Introduction

The previous chapter discussed the need for a research culture in addition to a network of foundations questions. It argued that the critical discourse map that such a network provides, while necessary, is not sufficient for a culture (see section 5.1.2). A culture requires scholarly engagement with and the critique and development of such a map. It also requires resolutions to the questions the map depicts and the corresponding enablement of coordinated growth on the outer network. And it is a foundations research culture, more than a static discourse map, that is concomitant with progress, where progress means to effectively solve problems pertinent to the modern context. Such a culture would supposedly work to keep the underlying foundations questions present in discourse and lead them to be asked over and over as their context of application changes. It would do this since the continuous perusal of such questions are necessary for understanding and effecting richer types of technology-mediated experience. A research culture with an intellectual basis in problems and questions that are continuously relevant points to an underlying research tradition with staying power that is worth investing in.

As this chapter will argue, it would be difficult to address newer types technology-mediated experience without reimagining the relationship between IR and IS, by understanding them as integrated, but more significantly (and controversially) by recognizing them as aspects of a hitherto undeveloped science of technology-mediated experience (STME). That is, for there to be progress in foundations discourse, the identity of the discipline needs to be reconstructed. IR&S must be understood as a STME, and this identity—as identity is among the most foundational of issues—needs to be the basis for how other foundational questions are tackled and foundations discourse developed.

It is important to note here at the outset, that a STME should not be thought of as dealing only with experience as mental events. As chapter 5 discussed, employing an embedded and embodied conception of human cognition—whereby experience and act are co-constituted—means that the notion of experience in STME also includes activity. The notion of technology-mediated action (TMA) is used in this chapter to specifically refer to that aspect of the experience which refers to a physical act. Where technology mediated act and technology mediated experience (TME) are referred to separately, this is to focus the reader's attention to the act and cognitive aspects respectively, and denotes an analytic separation. The TMAs and their corresponding TMEs, as mediation-level phenomena, are in turn aspects of technology-mediated living, which partially constitutes the set of human-living phenomena (cf. section 5.3.1). However, a STME in the sense meant here will nevertheless focus on mediation-level phenomena associated with mediation events. That is, it will focus on the mediation aspect—from the perspective of experience or act—of technology-mediated living, and not on technology-mediated living (as a way of human living) as a phenomenon, which would instead be the focus pertaining to a different level of phenomenon (cf. section 5.3.1). Finally, while prior chapters argued that foundations research is crucial for addressing the modern technology-mediation problem, here we will additionally argue for its corresponding culture as necessary in order to prevent IR&S from being isolated.

As Pettigrew and McKechnie (2001) explain, IR&S theory is not well cited outside its field; its problems are not known by others and the commonalities between its problems and those of others are not known. The field is in some way isolated, yet its subject matter of technology-mediated experience is central to modern life. As the main pragmatic purpose of IR is to link contexts and fields—by suggesting relations between otherwise disparate concepts and specialities—one would think that perhaps this purpose would also be reflected in discursive practices in IR&S as an objective to be achieved in its own discourse. Moreover, linking to these other fields is important for progress in IR&S due to external coherence—which mainly refers to sound processes of intellectual borrowing—being an indicator of progress (see chapter 2). External coherence is lacking not only when the borrowed ideas are inadequately structured (relative to their source or with respect to existing IR&S discourse). It is also lacking when irrespective of borrowing, existing ideas internal to IR&S are not adequately related to ideas beyond IR&S.

If IR&S were sufficiently linked to related problems in other disciplines, then its theories at the inner or outer layers (see chapter 4) as constituents of its discourse, would provide an interface to these problems. It would allow others to tackle IR&S problems without excessive specialized training. This interface exists to some extent at the technical level (e.g., machine-learning researchers not working in retrieval can nevertheless grasp retrieval theory and develop retrieval algorithms that use learning techniques). This interface, however, does not extend to all of IR&S with respect to its significant overall problems, which are well beyond the technical. A foundations network and research culture could be understood as instead providing this overall interface, as at the level of foundations, the questions and investigations become somewhat generalized and thereby transcend concerns exclusive to IR&S. For example, consider the question: What is a query? The investigation pertaining to this question would be of use to anyone working in human-computer interaction, technology mediation, and in various other problem contexts concerned with the formal cause of interaction (see section 5.3.5). The prior chapters (chapter 5 in particular) worked to develop an initial such interface. The salient advantage of a foundations research discourse and culture in this sense is this: It has both a generic and specific nature, its generic nature makes it open to discourses external to IR&S, while it specificity keeps it concretely relevant for facilitating progress in IR&S.

An effective foundations research culture is one that is rigorous, authoritative, and adequately expressed; one that uses existing conceptual vocabulary where possible instead of inventing discipline-specific words or being mired in buzzwords. Hence, simply addressing foundations questions in different and unrelated ways (e.g., according to some preferred metatheoretical approach) is not enough for progress, because the inner network would then be incoherent or disconnected. Instead, what is needed is a continuous effort to link up between different uses of a concept, across metatheories and across disciplinary boundaries. Such a culture could then address external coherence, and in doing so allow IR&S to address the issue of isolation and enable it to affect outside discourses—to "trade in the open market of ideas." Without such a culture there is diminished external coherence, insulation, and isolation from other disciplines, and hence stunted progress (Carlin, 2014). In addition to facilitating external coherence across disciplines, a foundations research culture would engender the linking of works across time. That is, the discourse map maps ideas in a timeless way: It links present to past and suggests a future. As Kantor (2015) points out, given the myriad new applications for fundamental IR concepts and technologies, without a proper connection to prior works, researchers are in danger of "reinventing ideas and relationships." This illustrates the importance of a continuing tradition or culture of foundations over and above fragmented works on foundations topics. Without such a culture, the received ideas and wisdoms "may be nothing more than the fossilized residue of lively debates" (Kantor, 2015, p. 1125). What is important in addition to a question being settled or a consensus created is the intellectual journey that lead to it. This journey can be repeated in a continuous way for every period of new applications to refresh the understanding of the underlying basic concepts. A foundations research culture would preserve these journeys, not as residues of prior conversations, but as waypoints of a living dialectic.

Section 6.2 discusses foundations research in the past and how it can be engaged with through an existing research culture, while section 6.3 explores present foundations works, explaining the relative places of different kinds of foundations works and the place of the current work therein. Section 6.4 argues for an integrated IR&S as a precondition for progress. Section 6.5 argues that integration is necessary but not sufficient, that instead the future of foundations lies in seeing it as the foundations of a science of technology-mediated experience. In its function as a craft (what it makes) this science works to enable the creation of meaning-suggestion systems, a purpose through which it becomes a type of *memory craft*. And in its scientific-explanatory function, a STME is argued to be a new kind of science due to both the phenomena it addresses and the methodology required to fulfill this function. Section 6.5 also offers an initial exposition of what this STME could be like in both its functions, and how it could be related to other disciplines. The section thus partially addresses the foundational question of identity, suggesting that, just as notions pertaining to the components of a search need to be rehoused (as elaborated on in chapter 5), the identity and purposes of IR&S ought to rethought. Finally, section 6.6 concludes this chapter.

6.2   Prior Foundations Research

Foundations research has always existed but in different guises. There is a foundations of the past to the extent a conception of foundations research can be read into prior discourse. Through reading some prior works according to modern concerns, this section briefly explores senses in which prior works can be understood to still be of relevance, and what this means vis-à-vis their relation to a contemporary foundations research culture.

That a discourse is foundational could simply mean that it raises a foundational question or discusses the corresponding concept beyond its use in a pragmatic context. To this end, foundations discourse can be understood to be a relatively old discourse. The existence of foundations research however, does not automatically imply the existence of a corresponding culture. Sometimes known by different names, such as "conceptual research" or "theoretical research," foundations research is what the early pioneers of IR&S (e.g., Fairthorne, Farradane, and Brookes) engaged in, and it continues into the present. However, foundations discourse is only taken as foundational for a larger discourse when the latter builds on it. And for that to happen, it has to be more central than peripheral within that discourse— and thus not as diffuse as it is at the present in IR&S. This is not helped of course by research subcultures within IR&S where excessive focus on technology creation diminished concern for basic concepts (as discussed in prior chapters and documented by several authors, e.g., Swanson, 1988).

As to what foundations research looked like in the past, it is the type of discourse already exhibited in the previous chapters or basic questions with respect to questions raised and the discussion that ensued. What then of the foundations research culture? One would suppose that it would be an authoritative discourse culture that continually discusses these questions, their answers, and other related questions. The situation however is more complex.

While what we call "foundations discourse" may have previously found voice under theoretical studies, there is indeed a distinction between the theoretical and the foundational. First, theoretical studies are not only concerned with predicting future trends of IR technology-use, as is sometimes held. They are also for explaining or interpreting current results (i.e., by means of theories). While foundational studies may include theoretical studies, it does not only pertain to theories of limited scope focused on capturing commonalities between a few contexts. It is additionally interested in the overall logical coherence among concepts, praxis, and the different aspects of IR&S research (the subdisciplines, external disciplines, and how they link together) as a whole. As the prior sections argue, given the trend of questions that IR researchers have been asking, it appears that what we need is foundational study and not merely theoretical study. The relation between the foundational and what has previously been taken as theoretical studies is additionally, as follows. While theoretical studies work to capture, study, and create relevant possible phenomena, foundational studies elucidate the conditions that make theoretical study possible.

Numerous prior works can be understood as referring to foundations, several of which have been cited in prior chapters. Apart from works dealing exclusively with one or two foundational questions, there are works with foundational components, such those on mathematical foundations that significantly explore the interpretation of representations (Weissmann, 1986). Some works collect foundational papers about varying topics into one volume (corresponding to a conference proceedings or edited book) such as Debons and Cameron (1975).

Furthermore, some works focus less on understanding individual concepts (e.g., queries, domains, users) and more on fieldwide questions. Fairthorne understood IR&S as a science and not a subdiscipline of mathematics, and suggested that it would be appropriate to characterize it by nonmathematical principles, so that it could be understood without difficulty by non-IR&S researchers (Swanson, 1988). As Swanson (1988) indicates, this was influenced by the work of Whittaker, representative of mid-century foundational discussions on physics (McConnell, 1958). Whittaker sought to capture a discipline in terms of postulates of impotence, that is, the impossibilities or limits in a domain of study with respect to achievements, observations, relationships, properties of objects, and such.[1] The fieldwide foundations-research scope of these works of Fairthorne and Swanson—who further develops postulates of impotence for the IR&S context—can be understood to follow the respective foundations culture in the domain of physics.

As with Debons and Cameron (1975), the problem in such prior works— shared by most prior foundations works—is that there is little interaction between ideas. Instead, each represents an individual foray into important issues according to trending methodologies. As a result, there does not appear to be a critical mass of interacting works constituting a sustained culture of discourse that can be passed on to subsequent researchers. What then is the status of such works? Are they still relevant? Or are they only part of the historical record? And here lies the peculiar nature of the foundational: most questions—adjusted for the modern context—can still be seen as relevant, especially when they have fieldwide concern such as those

---

1. The fundamental laws of physics can be understood as denoting such a limit. Swanson (1988, p. 94) comments about Whittaker's work that he

> noted that any well-developed branch of physics can be exhibited as a set of logical deductions from PI [postulates of impotence]. Numerous examples can be cited, including the impossibility of "perpetual motion." Some progress has been made in other fields as well; the theory of economics follows from the nonexistence of a free lunch, and political theory from the impossibility of fooling all of the people all of the time.

The postulates of impotence can be understood in Lakatosian terminology as negative heuristics.

found in Swanson (1988). They can be seen to be inherited by and hence encapsulated by, their modern expressions. Prior positions regarding them can be seen to create insight for a modern foundation and hence for the modern context. However, it all depends on how the previous works are read. If they are read from the perspective of an effective modern discourse map, then that map can be applied or projected back onto these prior works. This has the effect of picking out and organizing the arguments, so as to give them a proper place in a modern discourse.

Take, for example, the work by Swanson (1988, p. 95) discussing the ultimate limitations of retrieval systems. He notes that there is a limit to the address of the problem of "meeting information needs with items the exact nature and even existence of which are unknown to the requester." This problem is that of the limits of automatic understanding of meaning by systems, and it pertains more generally to the limits of the human-machine relationship. Consider further the problem Swanson raises about how relevance is understood, that documents that may be considered irrelevant independently and may instead be understood to be relevant when considered together. That as a result, research should proceed to develop mechanisms that thereby effectively juxtapose information items, so that creative human thinking can be supported. Then presumably the main goal of the retrieval tool—enabling the making of unexpected connections between disciplines—is fulfilled. This is a problem pertaining to the system question (to the interface aspect, specifically), which is construed in terms of the material and formal causes in chapter 5. Swanson talks about this issue as pertaining to the complexity of human judgments. But it also pertains to efficient causes, the nature of cognition and experience overall (beyond judgments), and especially to the particulars of observation and perception. In a more abstract mathematical sense, this issue relates to whether the rules of combination of observation operators (used to represent the presentation of search results) are commutative or not, as discussed in van Rijsbergen (2004). That is, whether first observing d_1 then d_2 is the same as d_2 then followed by observing d_1. More than merely representing classical presentations of documents, these operators refer to different user experiences, and ask about the difference between one particular experience journey versus another. Note the change in argument, from being about the relevance of documents to being about the relative value and substantial difference in usage experience. And by being about the latter, the argument problematizes in particular the formal and efficient causes—interfaces and cognition—as being of central concern. It also problematizes the documents as presented (i.e., the particulars of technology's role as bringing-forth). Hence it addresses the comparative merits of meaning-suggestion through bringing out several documents at once or in some order rather than presenting one document or documents in some other order.

The other limits and problems of Swanson (1988) equally pertain to the modern context and need to be addressed by a foundations discourse. They also need to be maintained or "kept afresh" by a corresponding research culture, lest they be ignored by modern research trends. If they were to be ignored, the result would be multiple problems and incoherencies in IR&S discourse over time, such as the reinvention of ideas. Section 6.3 discusses similar works of a foundational nature in the modern time, showing how they relate to one another and to the foundations network of the present text.

6.3   Foundations and the Present

Some books address what can be considered to be foundational questions, either in IS or IR. In the IS tradition the closest linked books

- structure a diverse field according to concepts, subfields, theories/paradigms, contexts of application, and research results, trying to grasp why and how the field is the way it is and where it is going;
- address one or two basic questions in depth (e.g., what is information?);
- reconceptualize the field as a whole through one encompassing (meta-)theoretical perspective to create a coherent picture;
- reconceptualize aspects of the field by developing (usually practical) solutions to modern challenges; and finally
- offer indirect appraisal of the field as a whole by historical narratives.

In the IR tradition, even though most works focus on detailing techniques for retrieval processes, other works pertain to foundations research. However, foundations is usually taken to mean mathematical foundations, that is, techniques for representing retrieval objects and processes. The present work takes the scope of foundations research to be both deeper and broader. It is deeper, since it moves beyond mathematical representations to understanding the phenomena being represented. This does not refer to the basic assumptions behind a representation, nor is it primarily concerned with the general discourse about suitable ways to mathematically represent empirical phenomena (see Krantz et al., 2006; Luce et al., 2006; Suppes et al., 2006). Instead, it is concerned with rigorously understanding the objects and processes themselves. Such an approach is more foundational than the discourse about the details of ready-made representations. It is broader in that it considers questions of how the field should be appraised as a whole and not just with respect to particular objects or processes therein.

Sections 6.3.1 and 6.3.2 briefly compare related texts in IS and IR, while section 6.3.3 explains the role of this book and the foundations research culture we are suggesting, with respect to modern works and trends.

6.3.1 Modern Foundational Works in IS

There are several texts, which, by being structured implicitly around basic Foundational questions are consistent with our contention that such an arrangement is important for understanding the overall coherence of the discourse. Bawden and Robinson (2012) offer such a survey of contemporary understandings of basic concepts, theories, and paradigms, subfields of IS, and important conclusions therein. Their work attempts an overall narrative, mainly designed to support a first course in IS. Case (2016) is more extensive in this regard, since he historically contextualizes IR&S concepts and practices by showing their origin and development. Fisher et al.'s (2005) popular survey of theories of information behavior differs by being structured, in encyclopedic style, by methods and approaches. It offers a substantial catalogue of metatheoretical approaches to information behavior, briefly alluding to how basic questions are conceptualized within a particular approach, according to its specific terminology. Although these texts present brief overall critiques of the literature with respect to these questions and provide some suggestions for future research, they remain surveys that focus on breadth of coverage. Our aim in this book has instead been to critically analyze aspects of IR&S in depth, for the purpose of understanding what progress could mean. That is, we have sought to understand the state of the discipline as a whole, and to do this through directly and explicitly addressing the unexamined in existing texts.

At the other end of the spectrum are works offering deep and insightful analysis of several basic questions. Boyce et al.'s (1994) work focuses on basic notions and practices related to measurement and evaluation. It explicates the notion of measurement, extensively detailing its aspects and critically expositing its techniques in the context of IR&S and in general. Day (2008) instead addresses the origin and use of the notion of information. Ibekwe-SanJuan and Dousa (2014) explore approaches to answering basic questions (e.g., about information, knowledge, and communication) from discourses related but external to library and information science. A chapter therein by Hjørland (Ibekwe-SanJuan and Dousa, 2014, chapter 9), like our work, attempts to understand the present state of the discipline. Our work differs from Ibekwe-SanJuan and Dousa (2014) by focusing on developing an explicit framework for understanding this overall state. We do so in a direct analytical style and not indirectly through a historical survey of disciplines related to IS. In its questioning of the overall trajectory of IR&S, Day's (2008) text inspired our explicit exploration of progress in chapters 2–4, but from the "ground-up" perspective of practice that complements and strengthens the "top-down" analyses in Day's book. Finally, while Boyce et al. (1994) does offer some critique of suppositions in existing measures and evaluation paradigms, some of our chapters (chapters 2 and 5, specifically) focused on connecting these suppositions to an overall discourse on foundations.

In addition to these works focused on a few foundational questions, some texts in the IS tradition employ a singular metatheoretical perspective, through which they interpret significant aspects of IR&S over and above addressing some basic questions. Budd's (2001) work offers a historical and conceptual survey of phenomenology, suggesting that a framework based on phenomenology would be particularly suited for understanding epistemological and ontological presumptions in IR&S. We also argue for this premise in section 6.5.4 with respect to the findings in prior chapters. Budd's (2001) work is therefore of critical relevance to the future prospect of developing foundational positions with phenomenological roots. Cornelius's *Meaning and Method in Information Studies* (Cornelius, 1996) seeks to understand IR&S activities as meaning-making activities, and to reconstruct IR&S and LIS by employing philosophical hermeneutics. Cornelius's overall understanding closely matches our idea of search as meaning-suggestion. The next section further discusses this hermeneutical/interpretive aspect of meaning-suggestion.

In general, an overall reconceptualization according to a metatheoretical approach would create a coherent IR&S discourse, which of course would be a sign of progress. However, the above mentioned works focus on providing an initial picture—a picture of IR&S in terms of the concepts of a metatheory. The focus in this text, and with respect to the foundations research culture envisaged, is to enable the development of foundations that does not unduly bias the field toward a specific metatheory, but instead provides a basis from whence metatheories can develop. As then, the corresponding pictures could be compared on the basis of how they conceptually re-present the foundations discourse map. Clearly, no foundations research culture or discourse map is completely unbiased and free of a metatheoretical picture. For example, chapter 4 depended on a metatheory of science taken from Lakatos, and chapter 5 depended on Heidegger's teleological understanding of technology. Yet the goal has not been to adopt any one metatheory wholesale. Instead, as previously discussed, foundations discourse needs to be linked for the sake of progress, and if the foundations were based only on one metatheory, it would then be an isolated, and possibly an increasingly sterile discourse. Therefore, unlike the above texts, our goal in this book has been to provide (by means of the metatheories we employed) a preliminary restructuring of the discipline through a foundations discourse centered on understanding the notion of progress in IR&S. The goal has furthermore been to suggest the rudiments of a foundations research culture for supporting the future development of effective, overall paradigms or conceptualizations of IR&S.

In addition to metatheory-specific texts, there are texts that function to historically contextualize IS discourse through foundational ideas. The historical context and later development of a discipline is crucial for understanding both its present state and potential trajectories for future growth and in general, for deducing ways of appraising new developments in the field. Gilchrist (2009) offers an extensive historical narrative of IS and its subfields. Gilchrist does offer some judgment on the progress of the discipline as a whole or with respect to addressing particular problems. But that text differs from our work: We explicitly explore what progress could mean for IR&S and whether there has been progress in the discipline. Foster and Rafferty's (2011) *Innovations in Information Retrieval* similarly focuses on historical contextualization but bases its analyses on the challenge of modern applications to the received understanding of concepts (e.g., classification, information presentation, information discovery). Finally, Ruthven and Kelly (2011) elaborates on the concepts and approaches constituting interactive information retrieval, a fusion of IR and IS. Like Foster and Rafferty (2011), it is concerned with the implications of modern challenges to received ideas, but it focuses on issues pertaining to users, implying that progress is to be made by a closer link between IR and IS in general. Ruthven and Kelly suggest that the increase in cognizance in IR researchers of user research in interactive information retrieval (and IS) and the subsequent engagement with that research is an important sign that this goal is on its way to being attained. In seeking to understand how well concepts from the IR discourse capture the interactive phenomena observed in modern applications, both Foster and Rafferty (2011) and Ruthven and Kelly (2011) raise the question of phenomena construal. However, the focus of the present book has not been on choosing suitable practical techniques for solving modern problems, but to understand the disciplinary implications that the existence and address of such problems have. The other texts discussed here only consider such implications in a passive manner.

6.3.2   Foundations Texts in IR as Mathematical Foundations

Typical IR texts, such as *Information Retrieval* (Buettcher et al., 2010), discuss techniques for retrieval and evaluation, assuming positions on basic questions (e.g., as to what a document or user is, or what counts as progress). In so doing, they omit foundations studies, which addresses the particulars of those assumptions. As chapter 5 discussed, works such as Huibers (1996); Fang (2007) can be read as addressing a foundations questions, albeit in an implicit sense and mainly as a problem pertaining to representation or technical design. The works of Dominich (2000) are further examples of mathematical foundations. C. J. van Rijsbergen's (2004) *Geometry of Information Retrieval* perhaps comes closest among modern IR works to being a foundations study. Although it primarily aspires to a framework for formal comparison of existing retrieval models, that book also exposes several issues that go beyond mathematical foundations into general foundations research when making its argument. These include the issue of differentiating the cognitive operations of observation and judgment, and that of order effects in interaction (see preceeding discussion about the significance in the order of observing documents in section 6.2).

The validity and coherence of such representational works, and any analysis of the relative merits of representations, especially at a theoretical level, is hinged on a clear understanding of the nature of the phenomena being represented. Furthermore, the fundamental nature and meaning of the relevant phenomena are presupposed in such mathematical-foundations works. This is problematic, since their meanings change readily with the varying contexts of modern applications. A foundations discourse that aims to develop such understandings is then a prerequisite for a progressive mathematical foundation. In addition, a foundations research culture that keeps such a discourse updated amid changing contexts is a prerequisite for keeping representation-focused mathematical-foundations discourse coherent and relevant.

6.3.3   The Place of This Work among Present Works

The type of foundations research the present work suggests, expressed through its initial discourse map (primarily in chapter 5) and through the particular attributes that the corresponding discourse culture should have, can be understood to open up a space for a specific type of research. The above comparison of this work with other contemporary works, can also be understood as a comparison of the respective discourse spaces and cultures (e.g., as to whether it is an in-depth study of one question or a historical narrative for understanding the origin of present concerns). In this respect, the space this book suggests, relative to the others, is as a bridging-space. It anticipates connection not only between foundational concerns in both the present and past, but also among different theories and metatheories, and between foundational and nonfoundational (the inner and outer) aspects of discourse. This is reflected in our arguments for the development of an authoritative foundations discourse—which would require such bridging—as crucial for progress in the field overall, implying in turn that foundations is central for this progress.

6.4   Future of Foundations I: The Requirement of Integrating IR and IS

Thus far, "IR&S" has meant the combination (as a simple juxtaposition) of all that counts as IR with that which counts as IS. Hence "IR&S" does not indicate an integration of IR and IS. There are indeed serious factors in the discourses that stand in the way of an integrated perspective. This section explores some of these factors and discusses what their resolution, enabling an integrated IR&S, could mean. Three major factors separate IR and IS. The first is the historical-pragmatic factor. Growth of the applications of technology (search technology in particular) paved the way for purely pragmatic projects and increasingly lead to a separation with researchers whose focus instead inclined toward the user and issues not pertaining exclusively to the pragmatic context.

The second is the external-schism factor. IR discourse adopted methodologies from computational and natural-scientific discourses. It was influenced directly or indirectly by the mainly positivist philosophical trends. Owing to its focus on the humanistic, IS became associated instead with the humanities and social-scientific discourses. It was influenced by many different schools (and not as much by the positivistic). However, since the scientific and humanistic trends generally do not mix, this external disconnect was inherited by IR&S discourse.

The third is the derived internal schism factor. As a result of the first two factors, a critical-mass of disdain developed for the methodologies, assumptions, and practice of one group by a critical mass in the other group.[2]

---

2. Saracevic (1999, p. 1057) summarizes this poignantly:

On the one hand, the human- (user-) centered side was often highly critical of the systems side for ignoring users and use, and tried valiantly to establish humans as

This was enough to set up, a rarely openly discussed socio-intellectual precedent—a *received attitude*—which resulted in each group perceiving the other group's work as being irrelevant to its own. This precedent is not baseless. It is neither easy nor common for researchers with a natural-science background to appreciate or digest social scientific and humanistic explanations and discourse, which often seem "woolly" and inconcrete to them. And for researchers without mathematical or technical training, detailed experimental works or highly formal works appear to lack sufficient meaning. That this separation needs to be resolved and an integrated IR&S developed is acknowledged by some researchers.

IR and IS largely share the same problem context but approach it from different (and as prior chapters have argued) complementary perspectives. The latter studies the socio-technical context, while the former intervenes in that context by making technology. Yet as some observers argue, there is a sufficiently problematic disconnection, as Saracevic (1999, p. 1055) attests, "these two main clusters are largely unconnected ... there are very few integrating works." Furthermore, Saracevic claims that real progress would be made if this integration were to happen. Saracevic further clarifies the value of research that aims to develop such an integrated picture: "a bestseller is awaiting an author [who] produces an integrative text in information science. Information science will become a full-fledged discipline when the two ends are connected successfully"(Saracevic, 1999, p. 1055).[3]

---

the proper center of IR work (e.g., Dervin & Nilan, 1986; Harter, 1992). The mantra of human-centered research is that the results have implications for systems design and practice. Unfortunately, in most human-centered research, beyond suggestions, concrete design solutions were not delivered. On the other hand, the systems side, by and large, ignores the human side and user studies, and is even often completely ignorant of them. As to design, the stance is "tell us what to do and we will do it." But nobody is really telling, or if telling, nobody is listening.

3. Similarly, Meadows (1990, p. 59) clarifies that the key goal (of theoretical, i.e., foundational in our sense) research is not so much which theories can be applied to aspects of IR&S, but whether various existing theories can be configured to develop an "integrated theoretical picture of the whole subject." Furthermore, Webber (2003) suggests looking at different parts of IR&S as an interconnected whole that share a vision, as without this perspective, there cannot be a unified research community following similar goals. In other words, a discipline (i.e., IR&S) would be lost to myriad subspecialities and submerged in other concerns. Webber suggests reinvigorating collaborative research by bringing different parts of a research community together, so that researchers can work together and identify themselves in such a shared vision.

Is there still a lack of integration (twenty years on)? The growing discourse on interactive information retrieval; (Ruthven and Kelly, 2011), which aims to engage the human and technical aspects more intimately (as this is at the least of pragmatic benefit, given the increasingly pervasive nature of modern technology), seems to suggest otherwise. But, what does it mean to be integrated? What could integration mean?

One meaning of integration could be what chapter 4 argued to be necessary for progress: the coordinated growth of various types of discourses (i.e., coordinated to collectively solve a problem), specifically, between user- and system-oriented discourses. A significant way in which this relation can happen, as chapter 5 alluded to, is when interactions can be explained rigorously in terms of user factors. Explaining interactions rigorously means to consider explanatory theories about the formal cause of technology mediated acts (and hence of interactions that constitute such acts) which relates the interface exposed by the system and user intents (where user intents are additionally exposed by the efficient cause; see section 5.3). However, as chapter 4 also argued, this coordinated growth requires well-developed understandings of shared basic concepts. It is not possible to have an effective theory of formal cause without first having or choosing a theory of cognition and behavior that adequately considers the interface and other system elements. This in effect is a theory that closely intertwines with what was previously an IS phenomenon with a technical phenomenon pertaining to IR.

With the widening remit of what counts as relevant phenomena for study, it is clear that there has to be a discourse that more readily and naturally combines these aspects. And as prior chapters argued, it appears that this has to happen through the development of a foundations discourse that intimately connects social and technical concepts. This combination is what is required to effect the design of pervasive systems, policies, and the analysis of socio-technical situations. This combination is arguably a more principled, active, and a closer integration, than what occurs when user and system notions are simply juxtaposed without the nature of their relationship being rigorously assessed. Hence, proper integration means discovering common presuppositions behind user/system theories, models, and frameworks, followed by readjustments to ensure coherence between system and user aspects. Theories must be developed that employ these aspects to depict the problem context. An adequate theory here would be more integrated than a sum of user and system aspects; its focus need not be the latter aspects, but something else that is nevertheless constituted by them. For example, prior chapters argued for this focus to be technology-mediated living/experience, a phenomenon that encapsulates search and interaction, and where the user-system dichotomy does not predominate, as it does in the encapsulated phenomena. This dichotomy, central to the phenomenon of classical search, reflects the instrumentalist and anthropological perspectives of technology (see chapter 1). But at the level of the higher phenomenon of technology-mediated experience/activity/living, the focus is on what this brings forth. That is, on what the instrumental and anthropological aspects, constituting classical search, come together to occasion at this higher level. This pertains to the meanings suggested to users. As chapter 5 explained, it does not refer to logical or physical documents but to what is understood about them by the user: this understanding is what is brought forth as per Heidegger's theory of technology (see section 5.3.2).

Integration is by no means a trivial task. However, its difficulty not only has to do with issues in IR and IS, but also with external inherited issues. The external-schism factor corresponds to the inherited schism between the two cultures of scientific and humanistic intellectual thought, a schism whose resolution, as Snow explains (Furedi et al., 2009), is important for human progress. As chapter 1 discussed, if any project could call for the systematic blending of methodologies in these cultures, then it is the study of technology, in particular, the study of technology-mediated experience.[4] Thus, even though the inherited schism is understandable and significant (since it is built into the research cultures of IR and IS), it nevertheless needs to be overcome for the sake of progress in IR&S.

If it is accepted that progress in IR&S requires the linking of these two such cultures, and that this is as a result of IR&S needing to deal with the real-world problems that call for such a linking, then this gives IR&S a significance well beyond its current academic context. This is since IR&S thereby acutely manifests longstanding divisions of the parental intellectual cultures of IR and IS. The modern IR&S scholar, working to solve their everyday problems pertaining to radically pervasive socio-technical contexts, is instead confronted by a problem well beyond the confines of their immediate discourse. Moreover, this problem is not just "academic:" it is a fundamental issue for modern human culture. Thus, in its attempt to resolve this problem, aspects of IR&S such as its resultant (integrated) disciplinary setup—the relations between the inner and outer cores—would be important from a general intellectual standpoint beyond disciplines.

---

4. It is perhaps also peculiar that such integration of cultures is crucial for IR&S as a "metaknowledge discipline"—a discipline deliberating on modern knowledge practices, which can be thought of as providing the metaknowledge foundations of the modern information-based human culture.

6.5 Future of Foundations II: A New Kind of Science?

The nontrivial task of integrating IR and IS, of forming a whole by relating between parts, depends first on understanding what that whole is to be like: the question of integration is closely linked to that of disciplinary identity. What is required is a reenvisioning: an appropriation of existing concepts into the vision of a discipline that may be more than its parts (IR and IS). This section proposes such a vision by exploring the question of identity. In particular, it suggests what this new discipline ought to be like. Section 6.5.1 summarizes prior discussions to explain why it is appropriate to call this a science of technology-mediated experience. Section 6.5.2 argues, contrary to prior works, why this is not a subdiscourse of culture studies and why it is other than a science of the artificial. Finally, Sections 6.5.3 and 6.5.4 work to identify the craft and scientific-explanatory functions of a STME. To the extent a STME is supposed to make/modify/design technology and policy (see chapter 5), it should be seen, according to the notion from (Buckland, 2012; see section 5.2.1), as a form of cultural engagement. However, as proposed in section 6.5.3, the craft aspect of the science ought to be understood as pertaining to what in premodern times was known as the craft of memory (as previously alluded to in section 3.3.4). Moreover, as this new discipline is supposed to observe, explain, and predict phenomena, it is a science. But since the phenomena it addresses are complex and mixed, it is not fitting to see it as being a physical, social, or computer (or abstract) science. Perhaps, then, it is a new *kind* of science.

6.5.1 Why a "Science of Technology-Mediated Experience"?

As previously argued, the modern context requires IR&S to be a discourse integrating the humanistic/anthropological and instrumental aspects pertaining to classical search technology. With respect to the notion of search, the central concept in IR&S, chapter 1 argued for a notion that considered the overall ends of search technology: what it ultimately does. It supposed that the purpose of search is meaning suggestion: by mediating experience, technology determines the ways the world is present to us and ways we are present to the world. In other words, technology increasingly determines what the world—and all that is in it—means to us. Search, as the most typical mediating technology, works to determine how the world is presented to us by suggesting what it could mean. It thereby facilitates this meaning-suggestion. However, this is not a detached activity: by interacting in a particular way with technology, we fully participate in the making of the suggested meaning. Therefore, as chapter 5 argued, since meaning-suggestion is a phenomenon pertaining to a human subject, an IR&S addressing the modern context should have as its primary phenomenon technology-mediated experience or activity. Thus, the focus moves from mere search to search as encapsulated in various modern socio-technical phenomena and conceived as technology-mediated experiences or activities. Moreover, there is an upshot to making TME/TMA as the central focus, especially by adopting Heidegger's theory of technology (for structuring this experience and activity, see chapter 5). And that is a framework for principled integration between the instrumental and anthropological aspects of IR&S corresponding to IR and IS, respectively.

The idea of meaning-suggestion as the purpose of activities at the semantic level (see section 5.3.1), corresponds to the idea of being "brought-forth" (to human experience) at the mediation level, where TME/TMA phenomena reside. Thus, the focus of the purpose of IR&S becomes the experience of meaning (the TME), that is, the having of particular experiences and not the traditional documents and their constituents. So the focus moves to cognition, which does not mean "mental content," but the full embodied experience of an agent embedded in an environment. And it is due to this embodied nature that the activity and experience are not separate but instead constitute two aspects of a mediation event. While the focus ought to move to the higher-level phenomenon of TME/TMA, these phenomena are constituted or specified by the lower-level phenomenon (i.e., the documents, the technological design of systems that facilitate these experiences, etc). Thus all such phenomena not on the mediation level are fully included in this new framework, but they play a different role than they did in traditional IR&S.

Therefore, we propose that the practical role and craft aspect of IR&S then needs to be reconceived from being about the suggestion of logical documents to being about the facilitation of meaning-suggestion (as argued in chapter 1) and then toward pertaining to bringing-forth or facilitating TMEs in general (as argued in chapter 5). IR&S's craft aspect ought thereby to be responsible for creating tools and mechanisms for this particular humanistic end. As such a craft aspect would presuppose, the scientific-explanatory role of IR&S ought to instead focus on explaining, understanding, and predicting TMEs and TMAs. The network of foundations questions and this framework of concepts developed in chapter 5 show how the inner part of IR&S discourse—its foundations—ought to be structured according to this repurposing of its scientific and craft aspects. The resultant structure has implications for disciplinary identity.

We contend that if the scientific-explanatory and craft aspects were changed in this way, then IR&S ought to be reenvisioned as a science of technology mediated experience, where this experience is embodied and embedded in an environment and does not only refer to a subjective mental phenomenon (as per the discussion in chapter 5).[5] Hence, the focus is on TME and the corresponding TMA together, not on purely cognitive acts, where "cognition" is understood in a disembodied and dis-embedded sense. It is also not focused only on individual, subjective experience, but also on the intersubjective commonalities between TMEs and the objective technologies that are involved in facilitating these experiences.

The foundations developed in chapter 5 and throughout this book can be understood as only a beginning of a foundations or inner core for such a science. The outer core—the positive aspect of this science that is to be used for observing, explaining, and predicting TMEs/TMAs—was briefly discussed with respect to its structure and how it would grow in chapter 5. The remainder of this chapter instead focuses on the fieldwide foundational question about the identity of an STME; How should this science be thought about and developed, with respect to first its craft aspect and then its scientific aspect? The next section discusses how our conception of a STME differs from recent reconceptualizations of IR&S.

6.5.2   Neither a Science of the Artificial nor a Subdiscipline of Cultural Studies

Furner (2015) construes IR&S as a branch of culture studies that both examines and engenders the cultural practices of collection, preservation, and access (CP&A) (of/to cultural objects). As previously discussed (see section 5.3.10), how a collection is objectified depends on the observer. With respect to the researcher's point of view, a collection is understood not only

---

5. IR&S being identified and reenvisioned as an STME develops Wilson's (2002, p. 11) construal of IR&S as a "fascinating combination of engineering, an odd kind of materials science and social epistemology." First, the engineering aspect is instead construed with respect to its function as meaning-suggestion. Second, the material-science aspect as instead pertaining not only or primarily to the material world but to the experience of that world through a material cause (and other causes, as specified in chapter 5). Thus, as chapter 5 discussed, the material aspect (or material cause) is not the complete signifier of meaning; instead it is the experience in its totality that signifies and confers meaning. Finally, the social epistemology or social-knowing happens as a result of TMEs; it refers to the collective function of using technology to acquire knowledge and information. The following sections relate this function to that of the idea of collective memory (Carruthers, 2000, pp. 7–60).

as a given, fixed mass of objects, but also as including the cultural processes that generated them. This is one of the senses of Furner's notion of collection: it concerns collection-making or collecting with respect to the agency of cultural practices, curators, and the like. There is also the notion of collecting as the gathering together or organizing of things, people, technologies, or works, where the agency may be quite ambiguous; this is discussed further in Cavell (2013) which Furner cites and is itself influenced by Heidegger's conceptualization of the subject.[6] Preservation, if understood as a mode of collecting (i.e., collecting to archive; Furner, 2011) whose corresponding practices can condition technology-mediated experiences (or produce something relevant to them), is also within the purview of the researcher. Finally, "access" (the cultural processes of finding, knowing, perceiving, or looking for, etc.) consists of those practices that are not only of interest to the researcher as objects of study but also those practices that they want to augment through technology.[7] The study of access must also be concerned with the contexts of access with respect to institutional policies that may restrict access, and with the ethics of access such as to do with "equity, justice and diversity" (Furner, 2015, p. 375).

Furner's conceptualization of IR&S appears to at least be partially coherent with Buckland's (2012) proposition that IR&S ought to be seen as a form of cultural engagement, since the subject matter of IR&S is first and foremost cultural objects and practices. This is as opposed to it being a normative science (Buckland, 2012, p. 6) with its subject matter readily amenable to description by means of a propositional calculus or mathematical logic. For a STME, it is supposed that cultural objects and practices become its subject matter through its need to understand the formal and material causes with which to explain/understand a TMA, such as understanding the cultural processes that conditioned user interactions or determined a collection (see section 5.3.10), respectively. The focus for a STME with respect to its scientific-explanatory aspect is the TME/TMA; culture becomes important only in a secondary sense.

---

6. The third type of collecting with ambiguous agency, which refers to "finding the way things are, as organised," is what Heidegger attributes to the technological nature of the modern world (Verbeek, 2010, p. 47–95).

7. The goal of the CP&A researcher/practitioner is similarly, therefore, also to "enhance people's experiences of resource discovery and access, whether one's goal in participating in such an experience is (e.g.) to enjoy a display of cultural heritage artifacts or to learn from a set of astronomical data" (Furner, 2015, p. 373).

However IR&S should be associated with cultural engagement in an additional sense: it not only studies but creates/partakes in and determines that culture; it creates technologies and policies that shape that culture. This is implicit in Furner's conception: the study of CP&A is presumably to inform those very practices. This sense of engagement is associated to the craft aspect of a STME. Culture is therefore of primary concern for a STME with respect to its craft aspect.

Contrary to Buckland (2012, p. 6) and following from the arguments in section 5.2.2, it is supposed that IR&S can indeed be reenvisioned as a science. Even though it would certainly not be a natural or an abstract science, the notion of it being an artificial science as elaborated in Simon (1996) would not work (see Coulter, 2003). Although to the extent that it is about human beings interacting with human ("artificial") creations, a STME is an artificial science: it is not only about the kinds of things being interacted with but is also about the technology-mediated nature of that interaction. Moreover, as a STME would study, for example, the TME of a natural object and its augmented-reality representations, it could not only be a natural science, nor only an artificial science. Yet, given that a STME is expected to employ a variety of existing sciences and humanistic discourses to explain TMEs/TMAs with respect to both technical designs and cultural practices, it is not supposed to be an unstructured and undisciplined discourse—a non-science (see chapter 3). If (as we suppose) there can be such a science, then its type is not quite obvious; the following sections speculate on what such a science could be.

Similarly, contrary to Furner, the scientific-explanatory aspect of a STME is not limited to being a subdiscipline of culture studies. As even though mathematical models are not expected to be sufficient for representing and discussing TMAs from the perspective of positive science, the close link between a TMA/TME and technological designs amenable to mathematical description means that we cannot rely solely on cultural studies.

While the craft aspect of IR&S is not significantly addressed in Furner (2015) or Buckland (2012), it is this craft aspect of a STME that pertains most to cultural practices and cultural engagement. First, consider that the practices of CP&A are memory practices, that is, practices that pertain to the creation and maintenance of a memory institution (e.g., a library or museum) or to collective understanding/memory that is an important constituent of the identity of society (due to which the practices continue). All three of these practices, collecting, preserving and access, are of course increasingly technology mediated. Thus, CP&A can be understood to constitute those technology-mediated activities (i.e., level-two phenomena in chapter 5) that constitute memory practices, which are a type of cultural practice, or personal and communal human activity (i.e., a level-one phenomenon; see chapter 5).[8] The idea of IR&S as mainly being about memory practices and institutions (as opposed to being about information) also finds support in other IS works; see Hjørland (2000). Second, consider that the craft aspect of a STME is tasked to create technology/technique and policy for facilitating particular experiences. If this facilitation is not specific to an individual but is instead for a group, then it corresponds to a memory practice. STME is then responsible for creating/modifying and maintaining cultural practices and institutions and so is directly involved with cultural engagement. In this respect, the craft aspect of a STME would suggest designs that facilitate cultural practices that regularly lead to understandings being brought forth to the experience of several individuals (i.e., facilitating meaning-suggestion). However, the role of this envisaged craft aspect of STME in cultural engagement can be better understood through a more detailed conception of memory practice.

As the following explains, meaning-suggestion as a cultural practice (enabled by technology) can be seen as a modern incarnation of the ancient "arts of memory" or "memory practices." Accordingly, the craft aspect of any STME can be understood as enabling particular types of memory practices; this thereby works to partially identify a STME.

6.5.3 The Craft of STME as a Memory Craft

This section explores the craft aspect of a STME, arguing that it can be identified as a type of memory art or memory craft. However, as section 6.5.3.1 describes, given that the memory arts influenced the discipline of computer science, this may not be surprising. Section 6.5.3.1 introduces the notion of memory craft and its modern influences in addition to computer science, while sections 6.5.3.2 and 6.5.3.3 focus on two salient aspects of the memory arts that are also supposed to be characteristic of the craft aspect of a STME.

---

8. Because these practices condition TMEs in general, their associated institutions are also of interest to the foundations researcher through the foundational question regarding collection (i.e., with respect to the formal and material causes of TMAs). Additionally, to the extent collection and preservation are cultural practices of organization (Glushko, 2013)—of putting things into places and creating narratives—organizational principles and theory are also of relevance to the foundations researcher.

6.5.3.1　The arts of memory and their modern influences　The CP&A practices by which Furner (2015) reenvisions IR&S correspond to memory practices and relate back to the ancient, medieval, and premodern art or craft of memory (Carruthers, 1990, 2000; Yates, 1992; Rossi, 2000). The memory arts cover a wide range of practices with differing purposes. They are usually taken to denote mnemonic principles and techniques (mnemotechnics; Yates, 1992; Danziger, 2008) for organizing memory impressions in order to improve effectiveness of rote memorization by improving recall, such as by providing a scheme for thematically grouping images around a representative image. However, our interest in the memory arts has to do with the techniques therein for associating and traversing a set of images, symbols, or ideas (whether in the mind, in a physical space, or in a combination thereof). This is done for the sake of discovery and invention: This technique of wandering among a cognitive or physical space along with a cognitive attitude (i.e., a way of remembering or imagining) leads to the discovery or derivation of further ideas.[9] A memory art is then not restricted to a specific cognitive act, such as remembering, but involves all of cognition, including in particular imagining and fantasizing,[10] to the extent these have an end. That is, to the extent that cogitation by means of such acts corresponds to a beneficial experience that leads to the knowing or understanding of something or to a preferred state of being. Nor is it limited to mental acts; it could instead correspond to a rich mix of cognitive acts and physical action, behavior—as would be within the ambit of a embodied and embedded understanding of cognition, see sections 6.5.1 and 5.3.3).

In particular, memory techniques employ associations between physical and mental locations (Carruthers, 2000, pp. 10–16). The image employed here need not be a single picture out there or in mind. It also need not be equivalent to something actually seen. Instead it could simply be the cognitive impression left in mind upon the experience of an act as a marker symbolizing that experience. This can be in the form of a visual image or a marker derived from and associated with a recently experienced visual

---

9. An image (which can include letters as well as figures) represents the thing to be remembered. The image is not randomly allocated in memory but is put in a "place" based on its cultural, rational, and emotional significance (Carruthers, 2000, p. 15). Images thus fill a mental structure, that is, "association-fabricated networks of 'bits' in one's memory that must be 'gathered' into an idea." The application of a memory technique leads to a traversal of this structure with a starting point and an endpoint (Carruthers, 2000, p. 23).

10. These cognitive functions can be precisely discriminated; see Casey (2003).

scene, a complex of sounds, emotions or moods, attitudes, or recently thought-about ideas, and so forth. Similarly, the marker image could refer to the overall context of the act—not just the picture in the frame on the wall that was visually experienced but the entire room or building that sets it up to mean what it does. Furthermore, a memory practice does not only refer to looking at a text, for example, extracting some information, keeping it in mind with respect to a mental picture, and then accessing that picture. There are different ways or modes of memorizing, learning, or absorbing a text or object observed; this is since memory practices have different functions, depending on the tradition or institution they support.

These institutions are memory institutions, such as knowledge repositories available to the public; they can be associated with a building, such as a museum or library. Thus, such an institution is constituted by the collecting and organizing, preservation, and access practices referred to in Furner (2015). This can pertain to material objects (books, textiles, bodies, buildings, ruins, etc.). It can also be conceived of more broadly as practices that may not use material objects or pertain to a physical repository like a building into which one can walk. These include written and orally transmitted knowledge traditions—the passing down of knowledge and ways of knowing—through books and ways of reading them that are unwritten (and hence have to be learned through the company of a teacher; Rowlands, 1993; Misztal, 2003; Goody, 2010, 2011). That which is passed down can be an immaterial thing, knowledge (including tacit knowledge), and facts, shared experience, know-hows (e.g., craft, arts, and skills),[11] and the like. These not-necessarily material practices can also be understood as memory institutions. For some such traditions, the corresponding memory art would require more than mental manipulation of juxtaposed images. They could require the memorizer or preservers to enact subtle changes to how they interpret the physical world (imagining it in a particular way) or behave in it, to the way that they are, in order to preserve or remember.[12]

---

11. As would be transmitted through guilds for example (Kilburn-Toppin, 2013).

12. For some to memorize is to "dwell-in" or "dwell-through" a text (Danziger, 2008, 71):

    the sacred text was not a repository of items of 'information' to be extracted and possessed while the source always remained an object separate from the appropriating reader. What medieval advice on reading and remembering stressed was rather the goal of making the text part of oneself. In the words of Gregory the Great: 'We ought to transform what we read into our very selves, so that when our mind is stirred by what it hears, our life may concur by practicing what has been heard.'

Carruthers (1990, 2000) provides a more extensive account; see specifically Carruthers (2000, p. 31).

A rich trajectory or trend of ideas originate from the memory arts, three of which are of particular importance for identifying the craft aspect of STME:

1. Their position as a thinking tool vis-à-vis scientific thinking,
2. The way both their use for rote memorization and invention has been delegated to physical machines and computers, and
3. Their emphasis on the relation between physical locations and memory images that becomes important in later theories of architecture (and in the development of IS).

Firstly, with respect to (1), a strong relationship exists between the memory arts and (systematic) scientific discovery;[13] the former can be seen as a precursor-to the latter (Rossi, 2000, chapter 5). However, the memory arts are not specific to scientific discovery with respect to how that notion came to be considered in the context of the physical sciences. Instead, they were a general craft of thinking for the sake of discovery; they did not come to rely on logic and propositional thinking. As discussed in Krois (2002), Yates (1992, p. 241) held the art of memory as a method of thinking that used imagination instead of arguments: "This art originated in rhetoric, not in logic" (Krois, 2002, p. 152; cf. Carruthers, 2000, pp. 1–6).[14] Whether the images used by the technique are "true representatives" of their referent is not of importance; instead it is their usefulness in leading to—as cues—beneficial understandings or experiences that is of primary importance (Carruthers, 2000, pp. 120–122).

Second, with respect to (2), the memory arts influenced the discipline of computer science through what can be understood as an externalization of memory techniques. The technique is "performed" by a machine, the mechanical (or electronic) operations being the analogue of mental traversals. The machine here can be seen as employing a memory art but for

13. The memory arts have always been used for what can be called "philosophical thinking." Their use for such thinking persists in later philosophy, particularly in the work of Hegel, whose work in turn ends up influencing modern discourses in the philosophy of culture and culture theory (Krois, 2002, p. 153).

14. Oratory was a key application for the memory arts, thus "in antiquity and the middle ages, invention or 'creative thinking' received the most detailed attention in the domain of rhetoric, rather than psychology or what we would now call the philosophy of mind" (Carruthers, 2000, pp. 10–11). The traversal of images as a result of applying a memory technique corresponds in the rhetorical context to taking a particular path through concepts while reading a text or while delivering a speech, i.e., taking the audience through concepts (Carruthers, 2000, pp. 77–82).

recalling something previously "memorized." However, it can also be seen as inventing, where the discovery/invention process is then at least partially delegated to a machine and eventually becomes understood (abstractly) as the state changes of a Turing machine to be implemented on a physical device, a computer. The import of the memory arts to computer science was limited to this sense of creating devices for automatic discovery or calculation.[15] By focusing on the device, much of computer science can be understood as a specialized branch of the traditional memory sciences, whose scope is thus wider: Its subject matter considers human agents, the built environment, and landscapes, among other things.

Third, with respect to (3), the spatial aspect of the memory arts with respect to remembering and imagining entails strong associations between the mental and the physical. It involves both the static and dynamic dimensions, that is, the relating between physical movement and the observation-of-interaction with physical things on the physical side with the (static) in-mind "locations" and mental traversal on the side of cognition. Several trends of thought in architecture, urban design, and cultural geography (see Cosgrove, 2008) use this association to develop their theories. In particular, they can be understood to follow the precedent in premodern memory arts, where physical architecture and architectural motifs had a central role in the memory technique (Carruthers, 2000, pp. 16–24; cf. the discourse on memory theaters and palaces; Rossi, 2000). Related modern ideas include the city as a field of dreams (Buck-Morss, 1991; Benjamin, 1999) and the city as the collective memory of its people (Lynch, 1960, 1984; Rossi, 1982; cf. Schubert, 2016),[16] and the complementary ideas that influenced Paul Otlet and early IR&S (see section 3.3.4).

As section 6.5.3.2 argues, the first and third trends mentioned above give support to identifying the craft aspect of a STME as a memory craft, while the second trend is used to differentiate STME from computer science.

---

15. Prefiguring modern computation was Leibnitz's combinatorial arts and its corresponding hardware, influenced by a fascinating array of prior traditions, from the I-Ching—a Chinese book of divination (von Franz, 1980; Olshin, 2005)—to the work of important figures in the Western memory arts tradition, such as Llull (Maróstica, 1992; Rossi, 2000; Uckelman, 2010), who in turn was influenced by the Arabic astrological and divination tradition (Rosenthal, 1958, 339-380; Link, 2010).

16. One can say that the city itself is the collective memory of its people, and like memory it is associated with objects and places. In particular, the city is "the *locus* of the collective memory. This relationship between the *locus* and the citizenry then becomes the city's predominant image, both of architecture and of landscape, and as certain artifacts become part of its memory, new ones emerge. In this entirely positive sense great ideas flow through the history of the city and give shape to it." (Rossi, 1982, p. 130)

6.5.3.2 Truth seeking is not the primary focus of STME or memory craft

Consider the practical purpose of the search tool as the product of the craft aspect of a STME. For IR, such a tool was originally to enable the fortuitous juxtaposition of ideas to facilitate new discoveries, relate disparate zones of knowledge for the sake of scientific progress, and generally to enable a type of fertile investigation and enrich human creativity (Swanson, 1988). The mental-traversal characteristic of a memory technique also amounts to juxtapositions of a series of images for the sake of discovery. A search tool is a thus a modern means for memory craft. Moreover, with respect to the first trend, as chapter 5 argued, while early IR researchers built their tools to help the project of science and scientific discovery, modern tools not only serve all knowledge pursuits where there is something specific to be learned, but in general, they enable meaning-suggestion and the facilitation of beneficial TMEs. This also characterizes memory craft in at least two ways.

First, the memory craft that identifies with the practical purpose of IR is not the later craft developed in the context of scientific thinking (see Rossi, 2000, chapter 5), but that general, preceding craft, which was not limited to scientific discovery. Thus, in agreement with Buckland (2012, p. 3), the meaning-suggestion tools engendered are not restricted to true meanings or true knowledge. Truth finding was also not the exclusive aim of traditional memory craft. In fact, as Danziger (2008) explains, the post-enlightenment shift in memory arts scholarship came to hold it as not only dealing with true knowledge but also with its distortion (e.g., as phantasms). Similarly, the aim of the classical IR system was not to deliver true knowledge but simply associations; in general, truth seeking is not one of the purposes of meaning suggestion, but of the seeker that uses the tool. Instead, the general goal for memory craft (as for IR&S and the craft aspect of a STME) is to support cognitive acts (imagining, knowing, fanasizing, etc.) or memory practices that pertain at default to the phantasmal and only in a special sense to finding true knowledge.[17]

Second, if the experience of a searcher can be understood as the experience of applying a memory craft (and hence denoting technology-mediated actions/experiences), then generally speaking, TMAs correspond to a type of memory practice with a complementary experience. A TMA is then the application of a memory technique that employs external machines. Hence, in the hierarchy of chapter 5, as a memory practice is a type of human activity and a TMA, it sits between the level-one phenomena of

---

17. The idea of computational tools and media working to support the phantasmal is explored in detail in the seminal work of Harrell (2013).

human activities and the level-two phenomena of TMAs/TMEs. Note that the relation being made here is between the general memory arts—which even though they may involve tools and such are human-centered—and human-centered TMEs/TMAs; not between machines that preceded the modern computer and modern devices as depicted by the second trend mentioned in section 6.5.3.1. Thus, a STME as a craft of memory must consider technology both from a bottom-up device-focused perspective and a top-down policy-focused perspective (see section 1.1). The former perspective addresses the particulars of a user navigating an information space, while the latter addresses the purposes and ends for their engagement in memory practices.

Recall that a TMA/TME, a level-two phenomenon, involves the level-three phenomenon of meaning-suggestion. As a TMA is the application of a memory technique, is it appropriate to infer that memory craft involves meaning-suggestion? Clearly, the use of memory craft for discovery is to acquire new meanings through generating new meanings or new knowledge, where the memory images and practices act as a cue or heuristic for that discovery. This can be understood more precisely. The meaning of something is its place in a system, for example, a ranked list indicates a system of meaning, as it posits both a relation of the query to the list of documents as well as a relation between documents. The form or medium of the response, including the interface, is also a crucial part of this system of meaning. Each such system of meaning, as presented through technology mediation, is interpreted by a user with respect to their preexisting understandings. The meaning suggested is therefore not only what is shown by the system, such as a set of documents on a screen, but this showing as it is interpreted by the user, because that is what is brought forth from technology-use: an experience. Given that it refers not only to words in a classical document but also to an experience, the meaning suggested is also a meaning generation. As chapter 5 also argued, the signifier of meaning here is in the structure of that experience and not the physical documents.[18] Thus, meaning-suggestion corresponds to generation of a meaning as experienced, or to a type of meaningful experience, and is best signified by the structure of that experience. Meaning-suggestion is thus meaning-generation for the sake of discovery or for acquiring (supposedly)

---

18. As the experience is an experience of something, this signifier must also refer to those outer aspects that work to constitute the experience. Hence, the meaning-suggested refers, in terms of the classical IR components, to the user, document (its form and content), and context, but those are secondary aspects.

beneficial experiences. To this extent, the technologies the craft aspect of a STME is responsible for designing, share their purposes with the techniques associated with the classical memory arts. An alternative way to conceptualize the link between meaning-suggestion and memory craft is through recognizing that since meaning-suggestion is the core of many cognitive acts, tools for enabling or augmenting those acts are therefore also a means for their fulfillment in the sense of meaning fulfillment (Beyer, 2015). They are therefore a means for enabling those very acts and experiences (i.e., the experiences of remembering, knowing, imagining, perceiving, fantasizing, searching, etc.) The traditional act of searching, in addition to being encapsulated in such processes as learning and technology-mediated experience, can also be understood as being subsumed or encapsulated in these basic cognitive acts, as these acts result in the fulfillment of meaning (i.e., computer-assisted searching as a means of perceiving, imagining, etc.).

6.5.3.3 The primacy of space and rhetoric With respect to the third trend described in section 6.5.3.1, for a STME purposed in its craft aspect to facilitate beneficial TMEs through designing technology and policy, where the context of technology-use is increasingly pervasive, space and location become particularly significant. There are at least three senses in which this is so. First, space is not just another contextual factor for understanding TMEs (i.e., with respect to the scientific-explanatory aspect of a STME). Instead, the pervasive nature of such technology requires the spatial aspect to play a central part in its design, and it is the craft aspect of a STME that is responsible for this design and for facilitating TMEs with respect to these spatial aspects. Thus conceptions of space—whether the built environment and its architectural principles, landscapes, and their cultural geography, or cities and urban design principles—must be appropriated when designing the material cause for TMAs (i.e., when creating interfaces). These TMAs work to bring forth TMEs, to effect meaning-suggestion—a level-three phenomenon (see chapter 5). This importance of space and place for a STME, also crucial for memory craft, further identifies the craft of STME as a memory craft.

Second, space is not only important for developing a future STME, for engendering beneficial TMEs through its craft aspect, but also for understanding the overall effects of technology-use beyond individual situations of use. As TMEs increasingly constitute human experience in general, the corresponding technology increasingly mediates our experience of space in general (i.e., of the world). Thus, technologies enabling TMAs through tools that enable meaning-suggestion, by bringing-forth particular meanings, serve an interpretive function; they show up the world in a particular way. Both the memory arts and TMAs (as discussed above and in section 6.5.2) work at the personal level and cultural level to preserve, collect, and access both material and nonmaterial memory. Thus, a meaning-suggestion tool such as a pervasive retrieval system/tool, is a tool for practicing the art of memory. And as such, in addition to such a tool being understood in terms of 'what it does', i.e., its immediate effect, it should be understood in terms of the cultures it facilitates (Rauterberg, 2006). This is meant not only in the sense that the system can aid in recall, in bringing-near to experience—as if part of our embodied, embedded, and extended mind—items of knowledge on the fly, but also that it can record prior experiences and play-them back, so that it performs immediate-new-association based recall as well as direct recall of previously seen things as-is. That pervasive systems and social media systems can so readily remember our (increasingly technology-mediated) activities and can bring forth forgotten experiences are significant properties of modern memory practices.

Third, while the way TMEs work to present the world to us is more directly relevant for study with respect to the scientific-explanatory aspect of a STME—which would study experience, e.g., as to whether that which is brought forth to experience is adequate—they are further associated with craft-based concerns that are shared with memory craft. They are based on the observation that the meaning-suggested (i.e., brought forth to experience) is not the literal content being shown, that it is the result of the experience it engenders. Take the modern case of the augmented-reality Google glasses: The meaning of the subway station facing the user is experienced in the context of train-times augmented on top of the real-life station. The system thus acts as a hermeneutic tool. It is constantly responsible for presenting the world in different ways, the world of human-produced objects, the built environment, and the natural world. In the context of pervasive technology-use, this tool facilitates numerous memory arts (i.e., numerous type of regular experiences), but as a whole it is most generally a hermeneutic tool. In a complementary sense, it is essentially a reading tool (i.e., does not simply transfer the actual object to the user, but instead interprets the object); it provides a way of reading, a particular reading. In this sense, the interface does not only present content, it is itself also admixed with the content. The interface's particular way of presenting content, with its colors and font (as in a pervasive context) or, e.g., the way it augments the observation of a museum object, works to persuade the user to "check in" to a location through an app. It leads the user on a journey in some way, such as in a physical space (e.g., inside a library), or leads them to talk or interact with other people and their avatars. The myriad such embodied-cognitive configurations it elicits through augmenting reality all contribute to constituting the content on top of words/images retrieved from prior data or traditional documents. All such possibilities that an interface actualizes along with the underlying data are interacted with as one, as the material cause of a TMA.

The study of such a material cause, given the myriad behavioral possibilities elicited in the user, can then adequately be understood as a study in rhetoric. The orator here is not the interface alone as a technological object but the coupled or entangled whole (see further, Heelan, 2004a, p. 76; Heelan, 2004b) of this object and the user denoted by the corresponding TMA. The interface as material cause—with all its possibilities of interaction and through which the user engages in a memory practice and 'traversal'—would provide the primary source of elements for study. In particular, the interface provides the visual and physical cues for this TMA. The interface brings forth particular aspects of the (real) world "behind it" (by augmenting them) while hiding others (see chapter 1).[19] The TMA

19. Moreover, while the TMA as the application of a memory technique is leading a user through experiences, these cues presented by the interface (the material cause of the TMA) can be understood together to function as ornament, where ornamentation is about "catching a reader's [or user's] attention and orienting his/her cogitative processes" (Carruthers, 2000, p. 117) and is something important for the study of rhetoric. Ornament is other than mere decoration. Whereas decoration is "anything applied to a structure or object that is not necessary to the stability, use, or understanding of that structure or object," ornament is such a decoration without "referent outside of the object on which it is found, except in technical manuals" (Grabar, 1992, pp. xxiii–xxiv). As Carruthers argues, "the manufacture of mnemonic imagery could be analyzed as a process of mental ornamentation" (Carruthers, 2000, p. 122). In particular (Carruthers, 2000, p. 117):

if a thinking human mind can be said to require "machines" made out of memory by imagination, then the ornament and decoration, the "clothing," of a piece will indicate ways in which these mental instruments are to be played. A stylistic figure, an "image," signals not just a subject-matter (res) but a "mood" (modus, color), an 'attitude' (intention), a reading "tempo." Movement within and through a literary or visual piece is performed as it is in music. Choice is involved for the author in placing ornaments in a work, and choice for an audience in how to "walk" among them. And as in all performances, variation from one occasion to another is a given. An essential first step of invention is thus recollective cogitation. For the process of meaning-making to begin at all, one's memory must be hooked-up and hooked-in to the associational play of the mind at work. That is the essential function of any ornament, and it explains why many of the basic features of the ornaments are also elementary principles of mnemonics: surprise and strangeness (for example metaphora, metonymy, allegoria, oxymoron, and, in art, grotesquery).

then can be analyzed as a performative act according to its rhetoric, and by extension, to the extent that TMEs are not only functional experiences (of getting specific things done) but also open to not being function-specific, TMAs/TMEs can be analyzed according to their aesthetic quality (beyond their functionality) according to theories of art.[20]

6.5.4 The Scientific-Explanatory Aspect of a STME

This section seeks to identify the scientific-explanatory aspect of a STME (i.e., STME as a science) by discussing what it would have to be like, given the findings of prior chapters pertaining to its subject matter and worlds of concern, its overall function as a discipline, and its relation to other fields. Sections 6.5.4.1 and 6.5.4.2 discuss what this identity entails, given its focus on experience and Heidegger's theory of technology.

6.5.4.1 Implications for identity due to the centrality of experience   The central phenomenon of STME studies, as already elaborated on in chapter 5, is the TME and corresponding TMA. But because TMAs/TMEs as level-two phenomena are made up of level-three (search-based) phenomena (which are in turn made up of level-four or interaction phenomena), the STME discourse must also be a discourse of these lower-level phenomena. Thus a STME relates to all other technological fields concerned with technology and its human-centered use, where the phenomena therein can be identified with those from one of these levels—even if they do not explicitly refer to TME/TMA. In this sense, the basic questions of IR&S, and hence of STME, are shared by the disciplines of information systems, web science (Hendler et al., 2008), and other technological disciplines. The discipline of human-computer interaction (HCI) has a special consonance with STME, as not only does it share the same subject matter (as do these other disciplines), but it also appears to share trajectory. In its third wave, HCI has moved focus from usability to interaction (Fallman, 2011), including user engagement (O'Brien and Toms, 2008). Beyond this, it is heading toward a more explicit consideration of "individual experience as it develops over time when people carry out activities and use artifacts" (Bødker, 2015, p. 31),[21] that is,

20. Scientific practice along with its use of technology is understood from the perspective of performance in Crease (1993), while Marks (2010) develops an aesthetic theory of ornamentation to understand the mediating nature of modern technology (cf. Grabar, 1992, pp. 234–237).

21. Bødker also mentions the need to consider experiences—individual and shared—of different types of users with different types of artifacts and technological devices (as to

toward the more complete phenomenon of TME as it comes to progressively be the dominant form of human experience. The proliferation of pervasive information seeking/searching contexts that require specific deliberation on interaction and user experience seem to warrant an increasingly intimate convergence between these disciplines. In particular, as the recent fusion conference such as the Conference in Human Information Interaction & Retrieval (CHIIR) and previously the Symposium on Human-Computer Interaction and Information Retrieval (HCIR) and Information Interaction in Context (IIiX) indicate, IR&S research is converging with that of HCI. However, current discourses in HCI suffer (as does current IR&S) from mainly being concerned only with design (of interfaces) and other practical aspects. Several works such as Fallman (2011), Sengers (2005), and Bødker (2006, 2015) argue for the focus of the field to move on to studying the relevant phenomena beyond their immediate use in design. This we contend is ultimately a move toward a STME in both its craft function due to need to produce designs (of tools, interfaces, user experiences, etc.) as well as the need to understand the concomitant user experiences or TMEs.

Moreover, a STME is envisaged as not only being concerned with particular TMAs/TMEs constituting one context of technology-use but also with groups of such phenomena across different contexts or levels. In terms of a causal structure derived from Heidegger's theory of technology (see section 5.3.1), a STME would first inform a discourse of level-one phenomena (human activities/culture and experience). But it would also be informed by cultural discourse for the sake of understanding technology-mediated human living in general. Technology-mediated activities/experiences constituting such human activity or human living span level two, and are themselves constituted by phenomena at lower levels. The four-level breakdown of phenomena and the arrangement of phenomena within levels according to the causal theory in section 5.3.2, together suggest an ontology of phenomena for foundations research, and this works to partially delineate the comportment of the foundations researcher. As to what the epistemology and hence methodology of research is to be, while chapter 5 suggests directions to be followed in this regard, it is not yet clear what it should be without better identifying what STME is supposed to be a

---

how this experience "unfolds over time"), and in particular, that analyses should focus on how "meaning and meaning-making" with respect to these TMAs (Bødker, 2015).

science of: To which region of reality does this TMA/TME belong? This section offers only a preliminary discussion of this question for the sake of relating and differentiating an envisaged STME (its scientific-explanatory part) from IR&S and from other disciplines. As previously discussed, the TME is

- not primarily about mental events, as per traditional cognitive models, since experience is embodied and embedded. The particular nature of the embedded/embodiedness reflects the mediating aspect of the corresponding technology;
- not solely about the subjective experience of individuals (but also "typical experiences," i.e., intersubjective experiential regularities); and
- not solely about momentary aspects of experiences felt emotionally or pertaining mainly to the psychological, or reacted to through simple behaviors.

A STME studies these different aspects of TMEs only with respect to their role in technology-mediated experience. Furthermore, as experience is always the experience of something, STME studies those things that can be experienced and seeks to relate between those things and between experiences of them. Thus, STME is about relating between phenomena in different worlds with respect to their constituting a TMA/TME.

What are these different worlds? They are the (1) mental/cognitive world (2) the world of human activity, (3) the natural world (to the extent it means something due to being something one can interact with, e.g., through an Internet of Things, (4) the world of technological objects, and (5) the world of other human-created objects (including the built world). STME is interested in the latter two worlds both in themselves (e.g., in systems and physical documents) and as interpreted or as observed, by users (e.g., with respect to both researcher views of documents as logical data objects and as the object of user perception). These relate to STME as a study of the four causes of TMA. In particular, world 1 comes into focus when discussing the efficient and the formal cause, world 2 is used to specify the formal cause (but worlds 4 and 3–5 in general are also needed for this). However, world 3–5 mainly relate to the material cause. With respect to the final cause, this can relate back to personal goals (world 1), social goals (world 2), or goals pertaining to world (worlds 3–5). The effect of an interaction is a meaning-suggestion or the bringing-forth (disclosure) of something to appearance (to experience); what is brought forth could belong to any of these worlds. TMEs could bring forth to human experience an understanding by conferring meaning about something, about the world of nature or human activity, or something pertaining to the content of a document, or an understanding of self. Similarly, repeated TMEs work to reveal the world as a whole, that is, they reveal worlds (worlds 1–5) in a particular way, as something. Thus, the study of them as a whole serves to comment on level-one phenomena (human activity/experience). With respect to memory craft, memory techniques and institutions also serve to reveal the world in particular ways. In addition to TMEs, STME would then study TMAs as memory craft enabled by technology, such as that generated through its craft aspect. In coherence with Furner (2015) and Buckland (2012), since memory practices are cultural practices (which inform and are informed by other cultural phenomena), a STME discourse would have to feature cultural analysis without the discipline overall being a subdiscipline of culture studies (as argued in section 6.5.2).

As chapter 5 mentioned, the focus on experience makes the discipline of phenomenology particularly significant for developing a STME. This significance is in fact something that distinguishes a STME from traditional IR&S, especially with respect to Brookes's Popperian conception (see chapter 3) of what matters for IR&S.

Brookes situates IR&S as being concerned with the mental world (world 1) and the world of documents (world 5) (and of course with technology, i.e. world 4). However, although STME pertains to additional worlds, there is a more salient difference. Brookes takes the world of documents to only mean the world of objective documents (i.e., documents as objectively given). However, this would only be a partial account of the document; a STME would additionally consider documents as subjectively given. The view about documents and in general, the world, as objectively given, is a dualist position that must be superseded: The world of artifacts is not objectively given, it is entangled with the mental world. Artifacts such as documents have an objective (e.g., a material) aspect; they are out there. Yet technology mediation is particularly concerned with user experience, which corresponds to the subjective interpretations of documents (and intersubjective regularities of such interpretations), not only their objective aspect. These interpretations result in the artifact being interpreted *as* something (i.e., the artifacts become objectified). Froehlich (1993, p. 228) clarifies the problem by adopting a perspective from phenomenology: *"While it is true that artifacts such as books do have a sort of independent and autonomous life, Popper does not properly address the requirement of interpretation, the social process of understanding and constructing the meaning of an artifact or text."* The ability of phenomenology to accommodate both the subjective (and intersubjective) and objective parts of reality is of particular importance because IR&S deals precisely with such a reality. As Froehlich (1993) explains, phenomenology tends not to overemphasize the subjective, nor does it simplistically define the objective. However, the place of phenomenology for STME is even more crucial. If it is held that the scope of phenomenology as a foundational science or first philosophy "aimed at the careful description of all forms of making meaning and registering meaningfulness" (Husserl, 2002, p. xxxi), then the scientific-explanatory aspect of STME must be founded on and derived from it, or perhaps even be a type of phenomenology. It is not at all clear how this is to proceed, however. Chapter 5 discussed the structure and function of theories that would constitute the outer core of a STME and suggested how the space of these theories could grow. But there is a foreseeable problem—a hard problem. Even though theories can be developed for the four causes determining a TMA, the problem is that linking among these theories means also linking between technical specifications (which include mathematical models) and phenomenological descriptions (or humanistic arguments). Adequate linking would be concomitant with an overarching discourse that functions to couple, combine, or merge quite different types of theories and subdiscourses. This is a hard problem at the heart of the dilemma of Snow's two cultures (see section 6.4). There exist phenomenological analyses of TMAs/TMEs (Selinger, 2012) for specific technological contexts that juxtapose technical design with such analysis, and prior attempts have been made to combine such analyses with mathematical modeling (Petitot, 1999; see Zahavi, 2004, for a critique), but these attempts are still preliminary. With respect to the foundations or inner core of a STME, the current discourse—this book—does work to relate these aspects. Perhaps as such a discourse grows, it can become an overarching discourse informing the growth of outer-core theories, but this would depend on effectively solving the hard problem. Thus, to the extent progress in IR&S depends on reorienting it through developing a STME, it also depends on solving this problem.

That STME requires a methodology that intimately integrates humanistic and technical discourse is partly what makes it a new kind of science. However, an additional reason not only distinguishes it from other disciplines but also support it being a novel kind of science. While the subject matter of a STME concerns several worlds, each already possessing corresponding disciplines and discourses, it is only concerned with these worlds to the extent that they are associated with TMEs/TMAs. And with respect to such phenomena, the scientific-explanatory aspect of a STME is envisaged to be about discovering, characterizing, explaining, understanding, predicting, and in general discussing the nature, relative benefits, and categorizations of TMEs/TMAs, and furthermore, discussing their interrelationships, and the relations between them and other types of experiences.

A STME is moreover going to be involved in evaluating or judging TMEs/TMAs according to values. This is with respect to values pertaining to the fulfillment of the final causes of TMAs (i.e., as to how well such a cause was fulfilled). The scope of this evaluation would not be limited to a system or material cause, but would include the whole TMA and TME. Thus, evaluation as it pertains to TMA/TME, as chapter 5 discussed, involves a complex set of phenomena grouped under the four causes. Although efficiency and effectiveness (in the classical IR case) could still be used as values for evaluation, they will have a different sense for a STME. However, an added aspect is open to evaluation beyond the fulfillment of final causes of TMAs—the experiential component: the meanings brought forth through the corresponding TME. This is also the case for classical IR&S; user interviews and other evidence are used to understand and judge the benefit of usage experiences. The task of a STME yet differs in several ways from that of classical IR&S and traditional user studies. First, it would additionally systematically explain these experiences as subjective experiences along with their intersubjective regularities (see section 5.4). This entails a far more systematic and technical type of interview and first-person account of TMEs, coupled with analyses employing methodology from phenomenology (which entails addressing the hard problem discussed above). Moreover, as the meanings brought forth here are not only the contents or presentation of classical documents as level-three phenomena but the overall TME corresponding to the TMA, the analyses of evidences would be analyses of different phenomena. Second, as discussed next, the judgment about the benefit of what is brought forth takes on a wholly different dimension, particularly when the scope is not one TME but a series of them. This is where the subject of study is that which is brought forth not through one TMA as an application of memory craft, but through many such TMAs that would perhaps constitute a memory culture or memory institution. At this nonindividualized scale, a STME depending on Heidegger's theory of technology needs to relate to his fundamental ontology and a particular notion of truth—as to the 'truth' of what is unconcealed/revealed/brought forth by living through technology with respect to the human-self understanding of their own being and that of the world.[22] That such a STME needs to address these issues is a further reason that it is a different kind of science.

---

22. Thus, unconcealment can be of particular beings or things, and of the world or of beings as a whole (Inwood, 1999, pp. 13–14).

6.5.4.2 Implications for identity due to adopting Heidegger's theory of technology If Heidegger's theory of technology is accepted as a basis for a STME, as a science of TMEs (and corresponding TMAs) with respect to what is brought forth therein, then we contend that a STME is a science that pertains to what Heidegger called the essence of technology. This essence pertains to what technology, through TMEs, reveals to us of the world and ourselves. However, this is not only a static revealing/unconcealing. Heidegger's notion of essence is not a noun but a verb (Verbeek, 2009): It refers to the representative living or dynamic element of something. The essence of technology refers to how technology *holds sway* (how it maintains things, not whether it statically *is* something; Verbeek, 2009, p. 53; cf. Inwood, 1999, pp. 13–15, 209–212). Thus, a culture constituted by TMEs works to reveal the world to us constantly and continually in a particular way, not just in a single experience of technology-use. This notion is increasingly pertinent as technology becomes increasingly pervasive. In the case of a smart-home, the physical and symbolic positioning of the technological devices (pertaining to the interaction design and architectural design of the home and the technologies)—the way of using technology as a whole—conditions our mode of being at home. However, it also works to reveal the home in a particular way. It is not that the house is one thing and the technology in it something else, but that house is experienced (and therefore is) the way it is due to the revealing/hiding pattern engendered by the technology. It furthermore works to reveal us, the observer, in a particular way, as a home dweller.

To this notion of revealing or bringing-forth corresponds a notion of truth that is neither truth as correspondence nor as coherence (as discussed in section 2.2), but a more fundamental notion of truth presupposed by these concepts: truth as unconcealment or uncovery. This is a notion that is not only important to Heidegger's theory of technology but is also crucial to his overall philosophical project of understanding what it means to be. And through this notion, his theory of technology takes a central role for what it means to be in our current historical epoch. For a STME to adopt Heidegger's theory of technology means for it to inherit this concept of truth; a notion that comes into play when explaining TMEs or expressing what TMAs do. And while a foundations discourse on the way to developing a STME would require closely engaging with this notion, this section only seeks to briefly introduce the concept to discuss the disciplinary implications of employing it. Thus the properties of this notion of truth will be discussed in a way that leaves the concept only moderately less tacit than the treatment given to notions of unconcealment, revealing, hiding, concealing, and uncovering in chapters 1 and 5 while explicating aspects of Heidegger's theory of technology.

First, Heidegger's notion of truth does not primarily refer to propositional truth (Dahlstrom, 2001). What is brought forth is not primarily a proposition whose truth can be judged on its way of evaluating the benefits of the associated TME. Propositional truth similarly is not particularly central for IR&S, nor would it be for a STME. As while particular TMEs could be characterized in terms of the raising of propositions and a judgment of their correctness, this is by no means a general feature of such experiences, which instead are of a pre-propositional or pre-predicative nature (Koskela, 2012). This is further supported by section 6.5.3.3, which suggests the importance of such things as the rhetoric of presentation of content in addition to the raw content of physical documents, the experience of which is further removed from being associated to a propositional form.[23] The meanings brought forth that correspond to the combination of this rhetoric (i.e., the particular visual cues in the interface and what they mean in the way they mediate content), raw content, and (as chapter 5 contended) the user's particular way of experiencing (or engaging in the experience of) the TMA are instead best understood as the actualization of a background matrix of relations (Kockelmans, 1984, pp. 7–8) pertaining to a pre-propositional or pre-predicative mode of comportment toward the world (Koskela, 2012, p. 124; Kockelmans, 1984, pp. 1–11).

Second, Heidegger's notion of truth as unconcealment is not a property of objects. Thus for the STME context, it is neither the documents nor their contents that can be said to be "true" in this sense. Instead, it is a property of the human subject, who through their worldly activities (TMAs in our case) disclose themselves (or something about themselves). To ask whether a series of TMEs is beneficial or not means to ask whether they sufficiently disclose (to the user) particular important properties of the user, which are crucial to their humanness, that differentiates them from other beings. Unconcealment has to do with what can be understood as sufficient

---

23. As section 6.5.3.2 discussed, truth seeking is neither a general feature for memory craft nor a purpose for the craft of STME. Thus the corresponding tools are not primarily designed with this goal in mind, but for the more general goal of aiding discovery by providing fortuitous juxtapositions or cues. However, there is no contradiction between this and the suggestion in this section that the scientific-explanatory aspect of a STME has to contend with truth as unconcealment, because this is a more fundamental sense of truth that is always at play in the way a human is living in the world (their being-in-the-world, as Heidegger terms it), whether they are engaged in memory practices or not.

versus insufficient construal; as to whether meanings conferred/suggested together work to construe the world and human beings in an insufficient and reduced way. That is, whether the corresponding set of regular TMEs, through which people live, work to hold a particular construal in sway. Section 5.3.10 showed that a raison d'être of IR&S depends on such an insufficient construal, where the world is information, and this information (hence the world) has little value except once it is organized and made ready for searching and interaction. But the implications are much wider. If the result of a culture of social-media use leads people to relate to one another as merely avatars (i.e., to disclose others and self as such rather than as human beings), or if a technology-infused society that ordered that society on efficiency leads people to construe others as mere resources (for processes), then this is an insufficient construal of human beings: It reduces and disfigures; it could also be judged as dangerous. As while it reveals that aspect of human beings that shows their role in a social-media culture and in social processes, it works to conceal other, more important aspects. In this case, the meaning-suggested through the devices and TMEs they engender is insufficiently complete. It conceals too much of the important meanings. The most important of such meanings pertain not to a person's social standing, psychological state, or such, but to their understanding of their own being.

In particular, Heidegger uses this idea of concealing to differentiate between modern and premodern technology in reference to what they respectively reveal. For him, the essence of modern technology is less a bringing-forth and more a *challenging-forth*, by which is meant that what is revealed with respect to individual things/beings (or the world overall and us) is revealed in a rather peculiar sense. It is presented to us *as* something to be controlled and used, or in its capacity as an object of control and use as a resource for some process.[24] However, this is not the main problem.

---

24. This is not to say that premodern technology had always revealed something as it really is or in an unconditioned way, but that modern technology has a distinctive and peculiar capacity to hide and it does so habitually (it holds sway). What is important to note here is that "technology" here does not only correspond to devices (as if it were only referring to level three-phenomena), but to the effect of technology-use (i.e., more as level-one and -two phenomena). It corresponds to the resultant effect on a society. The effect is that society is ordered in a particular way (top-down; see chapter 1) due to the effect of technological/calculative thinking and is characterized by the systematic use of devices in different arenas of life. This "hiding" serves to reveal the world (as a whole and something particular in it) and the user or the human being (i.e., the meaning of such) in a way that systematically misconstrues them; see (Heidegger, 1977).

Instead the main problem is that for those living in societies where such technology pervades, what is also hidden is the possibility of another way of revealing, let alone that there is an alternative system of meaning pertaining to the world and the human. That is, the fact that these other ways are hidden to them is itself hidden.

But the situation is not dire. Heidegger's critique of modern technology is not a critique of devices or technology-mediation in any absolute sense, but of excessive and misplaced technological/calculative thinking (Dreyfus, 2002). The antidote to such is to become aware that what is revealed is conditioned, that the essence of modern technology is challenging forth. It is to understand how technology challenges forth, so that it can be appropriately situated. This means to understand the place of what is challenged forth and of calculative thinking, vis-à-vis other types of thinking, through focal practices.[25] These practices can be done by means of technology; that is, they can consist of (a culture of) memory practices (TMAs) that work to disclose that which had become concealed. In some sense, one of the purposes of IR&S as a means of making fortuitous connections (see section 5.2.1) can be understood in this way—as a means for revealing hidden relationships and meanings. If this interpretation is accepted, it would perhaps not be a stretch to suggest that this same purpose of classical IR&S is also coherent with the purpose of the aforementioned focal practices and with the purpose of any intellectual discourse that works against concealment and furthermore, against the concealment of concealment.

In the context of a STME, while the result of a single TME is unclear with respect to what it brings forth, the effect of the pervasive use of the

---

25. As Dreyfus (2002, pp. 168–169) argues:

Once we see that technology is our latest understanding of being, we will be grateful for it. We did not make this clearing nor do we control it, but if it were not given to us to encounter things and ourselves as resources, nothing would show up as anything at all and no possibilities for action would make sense. And once we realize—in our practices, of course, not just in our heads—that we receive our technological understanding of being, we have stepped out of the technological understanding of being, for we then see that what is most important in our lives is not subject to efficient enhancement. This transformation in our sense of reality—this overcoming of calculative thinking— is precisely what Heideggerian thinking seeks to bring about. Heidegger seeks to show how we can recognize and thereby overcome our restricted, willful modern clearing precisely by recognizing our essential receptivity to it ... The danger, when grasped as the danger, becomes that which saves us. "The selfsame danger is, when it is as the danger, the saving power." (Heidegger, 1977, p. 39) corresponding technology could be more apparent. The series of TMEs they engender could expose the corresponding technology as suffering from that default character of modern technology (i.e., a means of concealing what is important). The misconstrual here, for our context, should not be understood as a willful one by particular technology designers. Consider the example of Google search results that have been conditioned according to Google's political and economic policies, where the highest-ranked results are ones that are paid for, and furthermore, where many results have been censored. The overall meaning of the search experience is thereby conditioned by Google with respect to economic and political goals. Over time, due to the dependency of society on Google for discovering associations, the assigned associations will become all that the query words mean; the possibility of their meaning otherwise becomes slim. But this misconstrual is willful. It is politically influenced censorship mandated through applications of internal company policy which changes over time. This is not the misconstrual of challenging forth. Instead, consider the pervasive use of augmented-reality devices such that users progressively only experience the world through such augmentation. For example, let the object that is perceived/experienced be a house plant as a game object, such that its growth is the subject of a social game, a competition. Over the course of game play by a sufficient number of players, the meaning of the plant beyond its dimensions and role in a such a game will become distant to the set of observers. The possibility of a nongame meaning will also gradually become distant.[26] This is not due to the policy of the game makers or application makers, but a side effect of it. That modern technology misconstrues is a problem. In a technology-pervasive world, human beings are lead to understand the world and themselves through TMEs, and if such experiences were to misconstrue, then this would call into question all that is understood through these experiences.

There are several upshots of a STME adopting such a theory of technology. First, the analysis of TMEs in a STME adopting Heidegger's theory of technology is not only phenomenological but also has an existential aspect.

---

26. Similarly, relations between the subject and the plant, beyond their game roles—game participant and game object—would also become distant. The distancing of the corresponding meanings would also affect the subject's understanding of their own being, since the world they experience has changed.

That is, the pertinent question for a STME in its scientific-explanatory function is not only what explains a TME but also what does it mean to be a subject who lives in the world through TMEs: What does it mean to exist in that way that is determined through TMEs (Gelven, 1989, pp. 14–20)?[27] Moreover, in this second sense, the study of TMEs is not primarily an ontic study (about entities) but an ontological one, that is, the study of the being (of human beings) by means of TMEs/TMAs. Thus, the practice of STME involves the study of four levels of phenomena (now including level-one phenomena of understanding the human being or living in the age of TMEs/TMAs) and the different methods for analyses typical to each level. This range of phenomena and analyses, which are required to fulfill the overall function of explaining/engendering beneficial experiences, serve to distinguish a STME as a new kind of science.

Heidegger's theory of technology and his overall project has the ethical function of being an antidote to the doubly concealing nature of modern technology through the corresponding philosophical discourse and through being a means for developing other antidotal focal practices. A second upshot of adopting Heidegger's theory is that a STME can be understood to also inherit this function. This suggests that a STME in its scientific-explanatory function ought consider not only individual but also multiple TMEs. In its evaluation of them (as to whether they are beneficial) it should also consider in some capacity whether what is brought forth through technology-use is sufficiently unconcealing (and hence offers sufficient construals); too concealing; or at worst, concealing that it is concealing and thereby hiding other ways of revealing/construing. Moreover, such a STME discourse would be of use for supplanting a discourse that seeks to understand modern human life in general. Thus, as TME is an increasingly large part of human experience (and where the human subject is increasingly a user), the findings of STME about typical user experiences increasingly would be necessary for employment in most of the human sciences, since they now have to be concerned with technology. It would be

---

27. With respect to the trajectory of modern IR&S, which has come from understanding query-document relations and is heading toward understanding context-context relations (see section 5.2.1), the most fundamental such relations are between existential contexts. These contexts are presupposed by relations between, for example, contexts expressed in terms of their socio-historical dimension. That a STME would need to study TMEs with respect to their existential aspects in its scientific-explanatory function thus coheres with this trajectory.

particularly relevant for writing history to document the present by characterizing the modern human living experience, perhaps through being incorporated into a historical method.

As Ortega y Gasset (1958) explains, history is understood through regularities in human living that people in any time or place can relate to.[28] It is the particular similarity and difference between an old regularity and a modern one that allows us to empathize with and understand past lives. Regularities can be understood as archetypes or typicalities,[29] which can be constructed at many levels (e.g., at the social or psychological levels), creating histories that for Ortega y Gasset correspond to forming typical narratives that collect and organize human phenomena. A STME, to the extent it can be used to understand typical human experiences, and hence to create narratives thereof, would then be of importance for making possible Ortega y Gasset's Galilean project of history for the modern time; see (Ortega y Gasset, 1958, pp. 9–29). If a STME is conceived in this way, then it appears to be a human science and is something that is not just for the use of technologists. However, owing to the importance it must give to both measure and technical design, it would be a peculiar human science, and perhaps a new kind of human science.

---

28. These regularities are the common responses to the shared dramas of life that pertain to any period of time (Ortega y Gasset, 1958, p. 28):

> History busies itself with finding out what human lives were like; but the expression is usually misunderstood, as though this were a matter of inquiring into the character of human subjects. Life is not solely man, that is to say, the subject which lives. It is also the drama which arises when that subject finds himself obliged to fling his arms about, to swim shipwrecked in that sea which is the world. History, then, is not primarily the psychology of man, but the refashioning of the structure of that drama which flares between man and the world. In a specific world, confronted by it, men of the most diverse psychologies find themselves possessed of a common and inevitable repertory of problems which gives to their existences an identical basic structure. The psychological differences, subjective in nature, are subordinate, and do no more than bring minor deviations to the plot of their common drama.

For the current period, technology has a significant role to play in the drama of human life.

29. This typicality (i.e., shared structure) is a condition of possibility for history: *"The investigation of human lives is not possible if the wide variety in these animals does not hide an identical basic structure; in short, if human life is not, at bottom, the same in the tenth century before Christ as in the tenth century after Christ, among the Chaldeans of Ur as in the Versailles of Louis XV"* (Ortega y Gasset, 1958, p. 18). A detailed study of the structures that make historical explanation possible can be found in White (1975).

6.6 Conclusion

A foundations discourse map is a necessary but insufficient factor for a foundations research culture. The initial treatment of foundational questions and the corresponding discourse map; the detailing of overall research focus at (from queries and documents to causes); the considering of the subjective, objective, and the intersubjective; and the examining of the phenomenological, existential, and technical can be collectively understood to constitute an *aspirational paradigm* for a foundations research culture. It suggests a foundation for what appears to be a new kind of science pertaining to technology-mediated experience and activity. This chapter discussed the importance of such a culture for facilitating a critical engagement between IR&S and outside fields that give intellectual credence to IR&S as a serious discipline. While foundations research has always existed, and while its questions are continually relevant, such a culture is still forthcoming. As we have argued in this chapter, for there to be a future for a foundations culture, it has to be understood as a foundations not of IR&S as classically understood, but for an integrated IR&S, reimagined as a science of technology-mediated experience (STME). Furthermore, the practical purpose of such a science has to be understood as enabling/facilitating and constructing memory cultures that are cultures of meaning-suggestion. The practical or craft aspect of a STME is such that it can be called a memory craft in the premodern sense. This corresponds to the facilitation of types of technology-mediated experiences (as opposed to the classical purpose of displaying relevant documents).

A STME would be a new kind of science for several reasons: it requires to combine methodologies across the humanities and the technical/mathematical sciences; its being about embedded, embodied experience and activity (thereby at once being about technical and humanistic matters), and its having an ethical function that goes beyond understanding TMEs. It can be understood to pertain to the essence of technology (and modern human living as mediated by technology), whereas IR and IS pertain to instrumental and anthropological aspects. A STME does not refer to the instrumental and anthropological aspects of technology-use but to a phenomenon that is their synthetic-whole: the technology-mediated experience. Thus it presents one way to conceive "the whole" that an integrated IR&S could pertain to, beyond being a sum of the instrumental and anthropological. Not only can a STME be understood to absorb several technical disciplines into one (e.g., HCI, information systems, and web science), its disciplinary space also demands rigorous integration of Snow's two cultures.

This is neither an artificial nor an academic demand. It is a direct result of the practical problems, given the pervasive nature of technology and the resulting human-machine relationship that characterize the modern context. Progress in IR&S depends on developing a strong foundations culture, which is concomitant on a reenvisioning of the identity of IR&S and developing a STME. Yet the development of such a STME is concomitant on solving hard problems pertaining to a rigorous merging between discourses that are divided according to Snow's two cultures.

Finally, by being a root science for studying TME, a STME would serve the humanities because discourses therein seek to understand the modern human condition as it is conditioned by technology. The discussion in this chapter merely forms an initial proposal as to what an STME could be like or has to be identified with. The goal of a foundations research culture is to elaborate on its specifics.

7 Foundations as the Way to the Authoritative against the Authoritarian: A Conclusion

7.1 Introduction

Modern people live through technology. Technology mediates their lives in an increasingly pervasive and comprehensive manner. Technology thus becomes responsible for all matters that pertain to human-living, and particularly responsible for human actions and experience associated with the desire to know. Any discipline poised to develop and critique modern technology would increasingly find itself responsible for creating technology for human living as a whole and not only one aspect of it. It would also find the scope of its critique increasingly extending to address technology-mediated human living as a whole beyond, presumably, a previously narrowly scoped concern. This responsibility is not conferred explicitly by any authority. Instead it is acquired by simply seeking to make more effective or efficient technology, or by seeking to understand and explain how this technology is received by its increasingly ubiquitous and intimate usage contexts. The expansion of responsibility and research interest is a natural effect of discovery and exploration in the technological domain, just as the development of research concerns in physics proceeded from the world of large objects to the microworld, and from phenomena in the visible spectrum to those in other spectra.

Information retrieval and science (IR&S) has been responsible for assisting people to effectively cope with knowledge and knowing, with being informed and being aware. It has done this by developing technology and techniques, knowledge characterizations and collections, institutional and access policies, memory practices, and information cultures, all in the service of this responsibility. It has also evolved from being a profession and craft to being a discourse that comments on, critiques, and contextualizes on its own work—whether that work is on the cultural significances of institutions, knowledge practices, access policies, or the effectiveness of its technology and techniques. Thus IR&S faces a rapidly expanding space of concerns. By simply attempting to design effective search technology for an arbitrary, pervasive context, IR&S increasingly needs to be concerned with the full human context of technology-use. By seeking to comment on the use of its technologies in general, its scope of concern goes beyond that single use-context to understanding the effect of such technology on human living. These concerns are not unique to IR&S, but instead are something IR&S shares with an increasing number of disciplines, discourses, and cultures of technical development in industry. This is to be expected due to the encroaching ubiquity of technology-mediated living. What may have been problems mainly pertaining to IR&S now concern everyone. Studies of society or the human condition, whether through sociology, politics, history, or philosophy, cannot ignore the technological dimension, as it increasingly defines the modern human condition. The conduct of scientific practice, whether natural or otherwise, is intimately entangled with technology-use: Both scientific knowing/discovery and experimentation pertain to technology-mediated experiences.

What then is IR&S to do when its disciplinary space has been encroached on from all sides; its boundaries permanently changed? When its problems concern numerous other players and its different responsibilities are thereby redistributed and scattered? And when as a result, its authority with respect to these problems and concerns (pertaining both to the creation of technologies and the analyses of its use contexts) is ambiguous at best? As many have recognized these problems indicate a crisis (Warner, 2001; Nolin and Åström, 2010). And nothing seems to indicate that the situation is changing except to intensify the problem. Is this however, a problem? If research concerns were scattered, would this matter, as long as the respective problems were being solved?[1] That is, is there any point in intervening in the process? And is there something therein that has become lost and is really worth saving? If there were something lost, then this would correspond to a particular way that IR&S characterizes a research problem and solves it (i.e., problem construal and resolution), that is feared to be lost or inadequately transmitted or translated in the chaotic yet natural process of

1. At the scientific level, it does not matter what the problem solvers are called—information scientists, computer scientists, or technologists—or from where—industry or academia—they hail. What matters is the characterization and solution of the problem. Disciplines are born, they develop, they perish; they have their functions and uses, and intellectual-social or practical-political conditions from which they are born and through which they are "recycled."

intellectual redistribution. This particular perspective, to be saved, would have to be defended by an argument. Yet such a problem and its solution (e.g., a matching algorithm) could become a specific part of a whole in a different discipline; it could simply be adopted as, for example, a statistical learning problem, with the matching problem becoming a learning problem. What would be defended here may not be the particular expression that the general problem finds as a specific one, but the application-specific meaning it has (i.e., that it captures the idea of "matching," a semantic relation between queries and documents) and not just learning.

We contend that what is ultimately worth saving is the way IR&S looks at the world: how it construes the world through its ontology of phenomena, a construal that serves to identify the discipline in a particular way. Thus, what is of general benefit in this regard is to analyze insights generated by looking at a problem as "matching" (such as a learning problem as in the above case), construe technological behavior as information seeking or search behavior, and to analyze the particular interrelationships between phenomena thus construed. In both such cases, the insights would together reflect a IR&S specific world-picture. However, as this book argues—and as summarized below—what is of particular benefit, is a generalized picture that evolves out of addressing IR&S's own foundational questions for the modern context. This picture, the foundations discourse map—which works to identify IR&S and its key phenomena in a different way—imparts a particular organization to its main ideas that reflects a "whole." This whole pertains to understanding IR&S as a science of technology-mediated experience. While aspects of the whole are of concern to various fields, bringing them together under this whole is a beneficial project that keeps relevant the central concerns of IR&S in a way that preserves some salient aspects of the identity of IR&S. Section 7.2 reiterates the overall justifications of this book that lead to the development of a foundations map and the suggestion of reimagining the identity of IR&S. Section 7.3 explains some of the positive implications of developing a foundations research culture that is based on such a map and the implications of not doing so. Section 7.4 concludes this chapter.

7.2 Foundations as Characterizing the World Picture of IR&S

Chapter 1 contextualized the key phenomenon of search, which is the focus of IR&S. It reconstrued search, such that—in addition to it referring to an algorithmic, mathematical, and in general, instrumental phenomenon—it should also be understood as having a semantic function. That it had to do with signifying meanings, that while the user is searching, the event of search is that of meaning-suggestion.[2]

Search functions to relate a user behavior (user interactions) to data in a meaningful way; it is a function that is presupposed in many applications through which devices are used. Search as a phenomenon is then the means through which much of modern technology is used. In particular, it can be understood to be a significant phenomenon of modern technological mediation, and in some sense it is the most typical such phenomenon as it captures a relationship between the key actors of technological mediation: the human user, technological device, and the world. In capturing the evolving set of such applications that condition the use of the devices they inhabit, search captures the changing nature of the human-machine relationship. This relationship, is in particular characterized by mediation. Technology-mediated experience (TME) accounts for an increasingly large portion of human living. This means that the study of technology mediation is important, and hence the study of search and its encapsulating (see chapter 6) phenomena is important. Search is (1) the technical phenomenon that is the means by which devices are able to mediate experience, and (2) the semantic phenomenon of meaning-suggestion, which explains that TME is a meaning expanding (through suggestion) experience. In capturing the relation between user, technology and world central to mediation, and hence depicting mediation, search is a phenomenon that captures both the human and the system or instrumental aspects of technology.

The study of search as represented by IR and IS (as IR&S) can be understood to be important with respect to their studying technological mediation, except that IR&S does not study mediation in any explicit manner. Yet as chapter 1 discussed, IR&S is trending away from ad hoc research with instrumental goals and toward understanding users and contexts, resulting in broader research concerns. This trend is characterized by the increased generality of its representative research questions, which in going toward the foundational problematizes the basic concepts and the construal of basic phenomena. This overall trend thereby can be understood to be moving toward problematizing technology mediation as the central concern for modern IR&S. To understand this trend, it is necessary to problematize foundations: the presupposed concepts in IR&S research. One of the key

---

2. Chapters 5 and 6 refined this notion to indicate that the meaning suggested does not refer to what a system offers in response to a query but to the user experience of a user–system interaction event; or more generally, to a mediation event.

questions characterizing this problematization has to do with the purpose of IR&S—what it is that IR&S scholars seek to do—as a way to disambiguate its goals, differentiate it from other fields, and to ultimately see whether it is important for addressing mediation. However, the question of purpose is not easy to address directly. Instead we asked a related question: What do people find beneficial about IR&S and what it does? This question is related to the issue of purpose, as what is beneficial is only so with respect to a set of purposes. This is the question of progress: What developments in IR&S are beneficial and progressive? The chapters that follow chapter 1 examined how progress can be construed. The premise was that notions of progress would hopefully lead to understanding purpose, and together these two concepts would allow us to understand the overall foundations of modern research trends in IR&S, trends that point to understanding mediation.

Chapter 2 developed notions of progress presupposed in IR&S discourse from several key works in information retrieval. It used what can be understood as visions for IR from the work of Crestani et al. (2003) as indicating ideas of progress: (1) internal (theoretical) coherence; (2) effective objectification or construal of relevant phenomena; and (3) external coherence, which is not only about the appropriate borrowing of approaches from other disciplines but also about the clear understanding of the place of the discipline among other disciplines. Chapter 2 showed that numerous IR&S works can be read as suggesting notions of progress along the lines of these aims. It also captured several other notions of progress presupposed in discourse, such as the notion that progress requires considering additional values and evaluation techniques. This further demonstrated the modern trend away from ad hoc research that focuses on a narrowly scoped pragmatic context and toward the non–ad hoc, which ultimately ends at technology mediation.

Chapters 3 and 4 sought instead to understand what progress could mean from a normative angle, in terms of how HPoS construed progress in a discipline. Chapter 3 suggested how existing methodologies that work with science can be used to develop a normative theory of progress for the mixed scientific–humanistic discipline that is IR&S. An analysis of the works of HPoS scholars lead to the general idea of progress as problem solving, which chapter 4 then refined into a more exact normative account. The refinement was done with respect to notions of progress that were developed in chapter 2, so that the result is a normative yet relevant account. Progressive research in IR&S depends on the stage of the discourse. In the normal stage, it was argued to be research that solves IR&S-specific problems, which are meant to address both humanistic and technical aspects of problems (i.e., not sacrificing one for the other). This focus primarily requires explanatory research to explain why users behave as they do. The result is research that ties together findings in humanistic and technological disciplines; research that clarifies the relation between basic concepts (which form the inner network) and the outer network of discourse. However, if the stage of discourse is other than this, then progress corresponds to actively improving the relation between the outer and inner networks (i.e., working out what is presupposed in research) and then developing the ideas in a rigorous fashion.

Given the modern context as discussed in chapter 1 and the particulars of modern research trends in IR&S as discussed in chapter 2, it could be argued that IR&S is not in the "normal stage" of discourse, that it is in the stage of seeking its foundations. Thus, in addressing the foundational question of progress those chapters serve to indicate that IR&S at this current juncture, is at the stage of finding and address its foundations questions (beyond the foundational question of progress).

Chapter 5 presented an idea of what the foundations for IR&S as a whole (as a discourse map) might look like—how a foundations discourse could be structured. It suggested building on the idea of discourse as network from prior chapters. It suggest that a foundations research discourse would have to be a network of interrelated questions and concerns. The chapter explained that the function of such a discourse map would be to enable a type of discursive engagement that would work to suggest the overall (not only foundations research) research directions given (1) the particular relational structure developed between foundational concepts and (2) the necessary stances suggested for the resolution of each foundational question given the modern context. The foundations network developed in chapter 5 is ordered in such a way as to reorient IR&S. This reorientation takes IR&S further into the current trend of considering TME as its central phenomenon over classical search. Chapter 6 then discussed the implications of reorienting basic concepts in this way; in particular, it suggests that the identity of IR&S has to be reimagined. Not only does IR&S have to be seen as an integrated discourse, but the modern context—making progress therein—and the expected end of current trends in IR&S also suggest that the shift from classical search to mediation means that IR&S will likely become a science of technology-mediated experience (STME). IR&S would then be responsible for creating systems and mechanisms for meaning-suggestion. Chapter 6 shows how these conceptions capture both the received identities (of IR and IS) and the notion of memory arts, where the latter depicts IR&S as supporting memory institutions and practices. Chapter 6 also shows how a STME could relate to the function of technology as a whole as a means for bringing-forth, which is in addition to (and more essential than) its instrumental/anthropological function.

The next section summarizes the book's discussion of the effect of having a strong foundation and the implications of not having one. It argues that, given the modern significance of TME, the discipline that works to solve TME problems through resolving foundational concerns would have an advantage and an authority over other related disciplines that do not.

7.3 Implications for an IR&S Discourse with and without Foundations

A foundations research discourse and culture reveals the nature of the discipline by showing how it deals with its key problems, problems which at the foundational level can be shown to relate more easily to problems outside the field. It thereby allows the field to be more easily differentiated and related to by nonspecialists. A coherent foundation confers an authoritativeness to the overall discourse. It imparts a stable identity to the field and its practitioners, and it gives them a sense of respect and worth. Finally, it confers identity and respect to its institutions, in terms of its standing in academia or industry. Our contention is that if these questions and concerns were made explicit, related to one another, and problematized, then the resulting discursive framework around foundations questions would be beneficial. It would act as a bridging discourse between IR, IS, and other disciplines, and would perhaps serve to create a discourse on STME that goes beyond the mere juxtaposition of IR and IS. In particular, it would

- address problems brought out from the modern context that we contend are foundational in nature;
- work to understand IR and IS in an integrated manner, so that research projects can be mutually beneficial (as the instrumentalist and anthropological aspects are indeed complementary) and to prepare the ground for an extensive discourse on STME; and
- relate IR&S research concerns directly to similar concerns in other fields, allowing IR&S to contribute to the larger discourse on technology.

Without a strong foundation, several risks exist: a lack of authoritative discourse, dissolution, scattering or redistribution of the discipline and its concerns to other fields, and the breakdown of related institutions. The following sections detail the implications associated with these risks.

7.3.1   Lack of Authoritative Discourse

Discussions of foundations are important throughout the life of a discipline; the nature of it is therefore open-ended. This should not be taken to mean that it is an unending discussion for its own sake that never settles. Instead, an authoritative, rigorously argued consensus about certain issues is possible, while always open to reasonable debate.[3]

If concepts are not open to reasonable debate, then there is always the danger of assumptions being made that are no longer acceptable. For example, one may think that a document can no longer be understood in its classical technical sense as a set of words, that they are a different kind of entity: they are cultural objects first and foremost. But the lack of an authoritative discourse on what documents as cultural entities could mean—especially practically speaking—works to maintain the prior classical technical meaning because of a pervasive authoritarian attitude. This attitude refers to the perceived political difficulty of imagining any foundational discussions of the nature of documents as having the power to affect technological research, even though document models are central to this research. This difficulty manifests in several ways: It is indicated by the implicit shunning through labeling as "irrelevant" (or "theoretical," "impractical," "abstract," "difficult," etc.) without sufficient reason, any model that is not strictly within the (often not very well-justified) parameters of the current center of discourse. Because of the lack of an authoritative discourse, preexisting conceptions help support an authoritarian attitude.

For example, consider the contention that there is a tacit expectation, in any discussion of the nature of documents, that it be followed or concluded by a mathematically representable model that reduces this nature to a set of features. And moreover that this is often the purpose and only acceptable resultant "concrete contribution" of any such discussion. This is an expectation that proliferates with an authoritarian attitude (as opposed to an

---

3. In this way we would respond to Nolin and Åström (2010) and Warner (2001) by suggesting that while a strong foundations—that would work to effect Nolin et al.'s "convergent turn" (Nolin and Åström, 2010, pp. 16–17)—might appear to be a move engendering an exclusivity, that it need not be. Any consensus reached about an idea can be quite variegated so as to give a proper place to contrasting ideas, with the place and preference given therein being always up for debate. This we contend is something that would be a hallmark of an authoritative research culture. An authoritarian culture would instead be of an exclusivist type, and is less likely to be the characteristic of a rigorous foundations. It would instead characterize a research discourse that worked with an unquestioned or 'presumed foundations,' an uncritically developed foundations.

authoritative way) the idea that discussions that do not immediately show such models are incomplete, not sufficiently conclusive, and not ultimately useful. This in turn begets an attitude of indifference towards such discussions, and this attitude often reifies into the unjustified belief that this is the only reasonable attitude towards such discussion, and that such discussions must be ambivalent until and unless augmented or completed by a mathematical model. The intuition here is that if researchers are not comfortable (in a foundations research culture) talking about particular issues, then they incline to a dogmatic/authoritarian attitude toward those issues, which contributes to a process of degeneration in research output. In addition to encouraging such unhealthy attitudes, a non authoritative discourse does not have the same rhetorical force as an authoritative one. As a result, it is liable to be taken apart and redistributed into more authoritative discourses.

7.3.2 Dissolution of the Discipline

A lack of foundation means that the field may become submerged or absorbed into other fields (Vickery, 2009), which usually means that its particular solutions and findings may become lost in some sense. Competition from other fields and other factors may mean the disappearance of IR&S (Nolin and Åström, 2010),[4] or what we think is more problematic, the loss of IR&S-specific insights into solving problems that IR&S shares with other fields. Disciplines have shifting boundaries, especially technology-related disciplines. It could be argued that the endeavor of actively seeking foundations, or understanding progress, is an exercise that will rapidly become irrelevant. But in spite of shifting boundaries, the foundations discourse largely survives; and to be of continual relevance it needs constant reexpression in a way that accounts for changing contexts.

7.3.3 Breakdown of Institutions

What is the unique contribution from academia vis-à-vis industry in IR&S? If the main technical contribution to IR&S comes from industry, what would be the unique selling point of IR or IS research groups, or of information schools (iSchools), that may contain them? Foundations research would clearly be the defining concern in academia, as it is concerned with lasting intellectual issues regardless of whether they have monetary value. However, the academia–industry dichotomy, may not mean what it used to, because the functions of these institutions are radically shifting.

---

4. In particular, that "a less developed research field takes on the role of the underdog" (Nolin and Åström, 2010, p. 16).

Nevertheless, without a foundation to support a continually relevant discourse on basic ideas, there would be no intellectual resistance to the myriad social, political, and economic factors that work to restructure and/or dissolve institutions. There would be no way to preserve IR&S as a perspective defining a research institution, a profession, or a type of scholarship.

7.4 Conclusion

At this juncture, progress in IR&S requires developing a rigorous foundations research culture that generalizes the identity of IR&S to make it a science of technology-mediated experience that works to enable the cultural practice of meaning-suggestion, and generalizes its focus to then be technology-mediation over and above the encapsulated phenomenon of search. It is not sufficient to develop isolated solutions to foundational questions but to actively relate between solutions—whether within IR&S or beyond it—to create an authoritative foundations representing a particular world-picture that differentiates it from other disciplines. This means enlarging the scope of research, and in some sense, opening a "Pandora's box of problems" (Järvelin, 2011, p. 18). But in response to the fear that science is thereby at risk (Järvelin, 2011, p. 29), we say—given our findings in this book about what progress entails—that it is science that is at risk from not opening that box. Instead, progress is concomitant with boldly opening the box and dealing with the challenges therein, through a research culture that is not only intellectually stimulating but also radically relevant to any effective engagement with the modern context.

References

Adams, Fred, and João Antonio de Moraes. 2016. Is there a philosophy of information? *Topoi* 35 (1): 161–171.

Adriaans, Pieter. 2013. Information, Fall 2013 edn. In *The Stanford Encyclopedia of Philosophy*, ed. Edward N. Zalta.

Agamben, Giorgio. 2012. What is a Paradigm? *Lecture at European Graduate School*. A transcribed text of the Agamben lecture that can be seen on [Youtube]: http://www.youtube.com/watch?v=G9Wxn1L9Er0

Albertson, Dan. 2015. Visual information seeking. *Journal of the Association for Information Science and Technology* 66 (6): 1091–1105.

Alexander, Christopher. 1977. *A pattern language: Towns, buildings, construction*. Oxford: Oxford University Press.

Alexander, Christopher. 1979. *The timeless way of building*. New York: Oxford University Press.

Allan, James, Bruce Croft, Alistair Moffat, and Mark Sanderson, eds. 2012. Frontiers, challenges, and opportunities for information retrieval: Report from SWIRL 2012 the second strategic workshop on information retrieval in LORNE. *SIGIR Forum* 46 (1): 2–32.

Andersen, Olivia C., and Hendrik C. Andersen. 1918. *Creation of a world center of communication*. Rome, Italy: Private Printing. Original published in Paris in 1913.

Angermuller, Johannes, Dominique Maingueneau, and Ruth Wodak. 2014. *The discourse studies reader: Main currents in theory and analysis*. John Benjamins Publishing.

Anton, Corey. 2012. Mcluhan, formal cause, and the future of technological mediation. *Review of Communication* 12 (4): 276–289.

Antonacopoulou, E. 2008. Actionable knowledge. In *International encyclopedia of organization studies*, eds. S. Clegg and J. Bailey, 15–18. Thousand Oaks, CA: SAGE Publications.

Apel, Karl-Otto. 1984. *Understanding and explanation: A transcendental-pragmatic perspective*. Cambridge, MA: MIT Press.

Arafat, Sachi. 2008. Foundations of information retrieval inspired by quantum theory. PhD diss, University of Glasgow, Glasgow, UK.

Arafat, Sachi. 2011a. Fundamental research questions in information science. In *Proceedings of the 74th meeting of the American Society for Information Science and Technology*, Vol. 48, 1–3. Wiley Online Library.

Arafat, Sachi. 2011b. Senses in which quantum theory is an analogy for information retrieval and science. In *Quantum Interaction—5th International Symposium, QI 2011, Aberdeen, UK, June 26-29, 2011*, eds. Dawei Song, Massimo Melucci, Ingo Frommholz, Peng Zhang, Lei Wang, and Sachi Arafat. Vol. 7052 of *Lecture Notes in Computer Science*, 161–171. New York: Springer.

Arafat, Sachi, Michael Buckland, Melanie Feinberg, Fidelia Ibekwe-SanJuan, Ryan Shaw, and Julian Warner. 2014. Pluri, multi-, trans-meta and interdisciplinary nature of LIS. Does it really matter? In *Proceedings of the 77th meeting of the American Society for Information Science and Technology* 51 (1): 1–5.

Arguello, Jaime, Matt Crane, Fernando Diaz, Jimmy Lin, and Andrew Trotman. 2016. Report on the SIGIR 2015 Workshop on Reproducibility, Inexplicability, and Generalizability of Results (RIGOR). *SIGIR Forum* 49 (2): 107–116.

Armstrong, Timothy G., Alistair Moffat, William Webber, and Justin Zobel. 2009. Improvements that don't add up: Ad-hoc retrieval results since 1998. In *Proceedings of the 18th ACM conference on information and knowledge management*, 601–610. New York: ACM Press.

Aronowitz, Stanley. 2003. A Mills revival. *Logos* 2 (3): 67–93.

Ashoori, Elham. 2009. Using topic shifts in content-oriented XML retrieval. Ph.D. diss, Queen Mary, University of London, London.

Ashoori, Elham, and Terry Rudolph. Commentary on Quantum-Inspired Information Retrieval. arXiv:1809.05685 [cs.IR]. Sep. 2018.

Atreya, Avinash, and Charles Elkan. 2011. Latent semantic indexing (LSI) fails for TREC collections. *ACM SIGKDD Explorations Newsletter* 12 (2): 5–10.

Attfield, Simon, Gabriella Kazai, Mounia Lalmas, and Benjamin Piwowarski. 2011. Towards a science of user engagement (Position paper). In *Proceedings of the Workshop on User Modelling for Web Applications at the 4th ACM International Conference on Web Search and Data Mining*, 8. New York: ACM.

Azzopardi, Leif, and Vishwa Vinay. 2008. Retrievability: An evaluation measure for higher order information access tasks. In *Proceedings of the 17th ACM conference on information and knowledge management. CIKM '08*, 561–570. New York: ACM Press.

Bachelard, Gaston. 1994. *The poetics of space* (Maria Jolas, Trans.). Boston, MA: Beacon Press.

Baeza-Yates, Ricardo A., and Berthier Ribeiro-Neto. 1999. *Modern information retrieval*. Boston: Addison-Wesley Longman Publishing Limited.

Bailey, Lee W. 1989. Skull's darkroom: The camera obscura and subjectivity. In *Philosophy of technology*, ed. P. T. Durbin, 63–79. New York: Springer.

Bailey, Peter, Nick Craswell, Ryen W. White, Liwei Chen, Ashwin Satyanarayana, and S. M. M. Tahaghoghi. 2010. Evaluating search systems using result page context. In *Proceedings of the third symposium on information interaction in context. IIIX '10*, 105–114. New York: ACM.

Bains, Paul. 2014. *The primacy of semiosis: An ontology of relations*. Toronto: University of Toronto Press.

Bar-Hillel, Y. 1962. Theoretical aspects of the mechanization of literature searching. In Hoffmann W. (eds), *Digital Information Converters / Digital Information Processors / Dispositifs traitant des informations numériques. Vieweg + Teubner Verlag, Wiesbaden*.

Barwise, Jon, and John Perry. 1983. *Situations and attitudes*. Cambridge, MA: MIT Press.

Bates, M. J. 2005. An introduction to metatheories, theories, and models. In *Theories of information behavior*, eds. Karen E. Fisher and Lynne McKechnie, 1–24. Medford, NJ: Information Today.

Bawden, D., and L. Robinson. 2012. *Introduction to information science*. London: Facet Publishing.

Bawden, D., and L. Robinson. 2013. 'Deep down things': In what ways is information physical, and why does it matter for information science? *Information*, 18 (3) paper CO3.

Belkin, N. J. 2008. Some (what) grand challenges for information retrieval. *SIGIR Forum* 42 (1): 47–54.

Belkin, N. J. 2010. Challenges for information retrieval research in the 21st century. Keynote presentation. *11th annual meeting of Brazilian graduate programs in information science*. Rio de Janiero, Brazil.

Belkin, N. J. 2016. People, interacting with information. *SIGIR Forum* 49 (2): 13–27.

Bellogín, Alejandro, Pablo Castells, Alan Said, and Domonkos Tikk. 2014. Report on the workshop on reproducibility and replication in recommender systems evaluation (REPSYS). *SIGIR Forum* 48 (1): 29–35.

Benjamin, Walter. 1999. *The arcades project*. Cambridge, MA: Harvard University Press.

Benjamin, Walter. 2008. *The work of art in the age of mechanical reproduction.* London: Penguin UK.

Beuchot, Mauricio, and John Deely. 1995. Common sources for the semiotic of Charles Peirce and John Poinsot. *The Review of Metaphysics* 48 (3): 539–566.

Beyer, Christian. 2015. Edmund Husserl, Summer 2015 edn. In *The Stanford encyclopedia of philosophy*, ed. Edward N. Zalta.

Bhaskar, Roy. 2010. *Reclaiming reality: A critical introduction to contemporary philosophy.* New York: Taylor & Francis.

Bird, Alexander. 2013. Thomas Kuhn, Fall 2013 edn. In *The Stanford encyclopedia of philosophy*, ed. Edward N. Zalta.

Bitbol, Michel. 2002. Science as if situation mattered. *Phenomenology and the Cognitive Sciences* 1 (2): 181–224.

Blair, David C. 2006. *Wittgenstein, language, and information: "Back to the rough ground!"* New York: Springer.

Blom, Björn, and Stefan Morén. 2011. Analysis of generative mechanisms. *Journal of Critical Realism* 10 (1): 60–79.

Bødker, Susanne. 2006. When second wave HCI meets third wave challenges. In *Proceedings of the 4th Nordic conference on human-computer interaction*, 1–8. New York: ACM.

Bødker, Susanne. 2015. Third-wave HCI, 10 years later—participation and sharing. *Interactions* 22 (5): 24–31.

Bodoff, David. 2012. Fuhr's challenge: Conceptual research, or bust. *SIGIR Forum* 47 (1): 3–16.

Boellstorff, Tom. 2008. *Coming of age in second life: An anthropologist explores the virtually human.* Princeton, NJ: Princeton University Press.

Borgmann, Albert. 2009. *Technology and the character of contemporary life: A philosophical inquiry.* Chicago: University of Chicago Press.

Borlund, Pia. 2003. The concept of relevance in IR. *Journal of the American Society for information Science and Technology* 54 (10): 913–925.

Boyce, B. R., C. T. Meadow, D. H. Kraft, and R. M. Hayes. 1994. *Measurement in information science.* San Diego, CA: Academic Press.

Brabazon, Tara. 2006. The google effect: Googling, blogging, wikis and the flattening of expertise. *LIBRI* 56 (3): 157–167.

Braman, Sandra. 2006. The micro- and macroeconomics of information. *ARIST* 40 (1): 3–52.

Brier, Søren. 2008. *Cybersemiotics: Why information is not enough!* Toronto: University of Toronto Press.

Briet, Suzanne, Ronald E. Day, Laurent Martinet, and Hermina G. B. Anghelescu. 2006. *What is documentation? english translation of the classic french text.* Metuchen, New Jersey: Scarecrow Press.

Brogan, Walter. 2005. *Heidegger and Aristotle: the twofoldness of being.* Albany, New York: State University of New York Press.

Brookes, Bertram C. 1980a. The foundations of Information Science part I. philosophical aspects. *Journal of Information Science* 2 (3-4): 125–133.

Brookes, Bertram C. 1980b. The foundations of information science part II. Quantitative aspects: Classes of things and the challenge of human individuality. *Journal of Information Science* 2 (5): 209–221.

Brookes, Bertram C. 1980c. The foundations of information science part III. Quantitative aspects: Objective maps and subjective landscapes. *Journal of Information Science* 2 (6): 269–275.

Brookes, Bertram C. 1981. The foundations of information science part IV. Information science: The changing paradigm. *Journal of Information Science* 3 (1): 3–12.

Bruza, Peter, Dawei Song, and Kam-Fai Wong. 1999. Fundamental properties of aboutness (poster abstract). In *Proceedings of the 22nd annual international ACM SIGIR conference on research and development in information retrieval*, 277–278. New York: ACM.

Buck-Morss, Susan. 1991. *The dialectics of seeing: Walter benjamin and the arcades project.* Cambridge, MA: MIT Press.

Buckland, Michael. 2012. What kind of science can information science be? *Journal of the American Society for Information Science and Technology* 63 (1): 1–7.

Buckland, Michael K. 1991. Information as thing. *Journal of the American Society for Information Science* 42 (5): 351–360.

Buckland, Michael K. 1997. What is a 'document'? *Journal of the American Society for Information Science* 48 (9): 809.

Buckland, Michael K. 2012. Interrogating spatial analogies relating to knowledge organization: Paul Otlet and others. *Library Trends* 61 (2): 271–285.

Buckland, Michael K., and Z. Liu. 1998. History of information science. In *Historical studies in information science*, eds. Trudi Bellardo Hahn and Michael Buckland, 272–295. Medford, NJ: Information Today, Inc. Published for the American Society for Information Science.

Buckley, Chris. 2009. Why current IR engines fail. *Information Retrieval* 12 (6): 652.

Budd, John M. 2001. *Knowledge and knowing in library and information science: A philosophical framework*. Lanham, MD: Scarecrow Press.

Buettcher, S., C. L. A. Clarke, and G. Cormack. 2010. *Information retrieval: Implementing and evaluating search engines*. Cambridge, MA: MIT Press.

Butts, Robert E., and William Whewell. 1968. *William Whewell's theory of scientific method*. Pittsburgh: University of Pittsburgh Press.

Bynum, Terrell. 2015. Computer and information ethics, Winter 2015 edn. In *The Stanford encyclopedia of philosophy*, ed. Edward N. Zalta.

Caldwell, Bruce. 1991. The methodology of scientific research programmes in economics: criticisms and conjectures. In *Economics, culture and education: Essays in honour of Mark Blaug*, ed. G. K. Shaw, 95–107. Hants, UK: Edward Elgar.

Callan, J., J. Allan, C. L. A. Clarke, S. Dumais, D. A. Evans, M. Sanderson, and C. Zhai. 2007. Meeting of the minds: an information retrieval research agenda. *ACM SIGIR Forum* 41 (2): 25–34.

Campbell, I., and C. J. van Rijsbergen. 1996. The ostensive model of developing information needs. In *Proceedings of the 2nd Conference on the Conceptions of Library and Information Science*, 251–268.

Capurro, Rafael, and Birger Hjørland. 2003. The concept of information. *Annual Review of Information Science and Technology* 37 (1): 343–411.

Carlin, Andrew P. 2014. Theories of information, communication and knowledge: A multidisciplinary approach, eds. Fidelia Ibekwe-SanJuan and Thomas M. Dousa. London, UK: Springer, 2014. *JASIST* 65 (6): 1299–1302.

Carruthers, Mary. 1990. *The book of memory: A study of memory in medieval culture*. Cambridge: Cambridge University Press.

Carruthers, Mary. 2000. *The craft of thought: Meditation, rhetoric, and the making of images, 400–1200*. Cambridge: Cambridge University Press.

Cartwright, Nancy. 1983. *How the laws of physics lie*. Cambridge: Cambridge University Press.

Case, Donald O. 2006. Information behavior. *Annual Review of Information Science and Technology* 40 (1): 293–327.

Case, Donald O. 2016. *Looking for information: A survey of research on information seeking, needs and behavior*, 4th ed. Bingley, UK: Emerald Group Publishing.

Casey, Edward. 2013. *The fate of place: A philosophical history*. Berkeley: University of California Press.

Casey, Edward. 2003. Imagination, fantasy, hallucination, and memory. *Imagination and its pathologies*. Cambridge, MA: MIT Press.

Castells, Manuel. 2000. *The rise of the network society: The information age: Economy, society, and culture*, Vol. 1. Oxford: Blackwell.

Cavell, Stanley. 2013. The world as things: Collecting thoughts on collecting. In *Contemporary collecting: Objects, practices, and the fate of things*, ed. Kevin M. Moist and David Banash, 99–130. Lanham, MD: Scarecrow Press.

Chakravartty, Anjan. 2001. The semantic or model-theoretic view of theories and scientific realism. *Synthese* 127 (3): 325–345.

Chalmers, David J. 2002. The first person and third person views (part I). http://consc.net/notes/first-third.html.

Chalmers, M., K. Rodden, and D. Brodbeck. 1998. The order of things: Activity-centred information access. *Computer Networks and ISDN Systems* 30 (1–7): 359–367.

Chang, Yu-Wei. 2013. The influence of taylor's paper, question-negotiation and information-seeking in libraries. *Information Processing Management* 49 (5): 983–994.

Clark, Andy, and David Chalmers. 1998. The extended mind. *Analysis* 58 (1): 7–19.

Clarke, Charles L. A., Maheedhar Kolla, Gordon V. Cormack, Olga Vechtomova, Azin Ashkan, Stefan Büttcher, and Ian MacKinnon. 2008. Novelty and diversity in information retrieval evaluation. In *Proceedings of the 31st annual international ACM SIGIR conference on research and development in information retrieval*, 659–666. New York: ACM.

Cleverdon, Cyril W. 1970. The effect of variations in relevance assessments in comparative experimental tests of index languages. *Cranfield Library Report 3*. Cranfield Institute of Technology, UK.

Cohen, Robert S., Paul K. Feyerabend, and Marx W. Wartofsky. 1976. *Essays in memory of Imre Lakatos*. New York: Springer.

Cole, Charles. 2012. *Information need: A theory connecting information search to knowledge formation*. Medford, New Jersey: Information Today, Incorporated.

Collins, Harry. 1992. *Changing order: Replication and induction in scientific practice*. Chicago: University of Press.

Coltman, Rodney R. 1998. *The language of hermeneutics: Gadamer and Heidegger in dialogue*. New York: State University of New York Press.

Cornelius, Ian. 2002. Theorizing information for information science. *Annual review of information science and technology* 36 (1): 392–425.

Cornelius, Ian V. 1996. *Meaning and method in information studies*. Norwood, NJ: Ablex Publishing.

Corradetti, Claudio. 2012. The Frankfurt school and critical theory. *The Internet Encyclopedia of Philosophy*. Retrieved from https://www.iep.utm.edu/.

Cosgrove, Denis. 2008. *Geography and vision: Seeing, imagining and representing the world*. New York: IB Tauris.

Coulter, Jeff. 2003. Projection errors and cognitive models. *The Journal of the Learning Sciences* 12 (3): 437–443.

Cox, Ronald R. 2012. *Schutz's theory of relevance: A phenomenological critique*. New York: Springer.

Crease, Robert P. 1993. *The play of nature: Experimentation as performance*. Bloomington: Indiana University Press.

Crease, Robert P. 1997. Hermeneutics and the natural sciences: Introduction. *Man and World* 30 (3): 259–270.

Crestani, F., S. Dominich, M. Lalmas, and C. J. van Rijsbergen. 2003. Mathematical, logical, and formal methods in information retrieval: An introduction to the special issue. *Journal of the American Society for Information Science and Technology* 54 (4): 281–284.

Croft, W. Bruce, Donald Metzler, and Trevor Strohman. 2010. *Search engines: Information retrieval in practice*. New York: Pearson.

Cronbach, Lee J., and Paul E. Meehl. 1955. Construct validity in psychological tests. *Psychological bulletin* 52 (4): 281–302.

Cronin, Blaise. 2008. The sociological turn in information science. *Journal of Information Science* 34 (4): 465–475.

Cuadra, C. A., and R. V. Katter. 1967. Opening the black box of 'relevance'. *Journal of Documentation* 23 (4): 291–303.

Currás, Emilia. 1993. The need for theoretical studies in information science. *Journal of the American Society for Information Science* 44 (7): 430–430.

Dahlstrom, Daniel O. 2001. *Heidegger's concept of truth*. Cambridge: Cambridge University Press.

Danermark, Berth. 2002. *Explaining society: Critical realism in the social sciences*. London: Routledge.

Danermark, Berth, Mats Ekstrom, Liselotte Jakobsen, and Jan ch. Karlsson. 2001. *Explaining society: An introduction to critical realism in the social sciences*. New York: Routledge.

Danziger, Kurt. 2008. *Marking the mind: A history of memory*. Cambridge: Cambridge University Press.

Dar, Reuven. 1987. Another look at Meehl, Lakatos, and the scientific practices of psychologists. *American Psychologist* 42: 145–151.

David, Marian. 2015. The correspondence theory of truth, Fall 2015 edn. In *The Stanford encyclopedia of philosophy*, ed. Edward N. Zalta.

Dawson, Neal V., and Fredrick Gregory. 2009. Correspondence and coherence in science: A brief historical perspective. *Judgment and Decision Making* 4 (2): 126–133.

Day, Ronald E. 2008. *The modern invention of information: Discourse, history, and power*. Carbondale and Edwardsville, Illinois: Southern Illinois University Press.

Day, Ronald E. 2011. Death of the user: Reconceptualizing subjects, objects, and their relations. *Journal of the American Society for Information Science and Technology* 62 (1): 78–88.

Day, Ronald E. 2014. *Indexing it all : The subject in the age of documentation, information, and data*. Cambridge, MA: MIT Press.

De Mey, Marc. 2012. *The cognitive paradigm: Cognitive science, a newly explored approach to the study of cognition applied in an analysis of science and scientific knowledge*. New York: Springer.

Debons, Anthony, and William J. Cameron, eds. 1975. *Perspectives in information science, NATO advanced study institute series E: Applied science*, Vol. 10. New York: Springer.

Deely, John N. 2005. *Basics of semiotics*. Tartu, Estonia: University of Tartu Press.

Dervin, Brenda. 1999. On studying information seeking methodologically: The implications of connecting metatheory to method. *Information Processing & Management* 35 (6): 727–750.

Di Buccio, Emanuele, Giorgio Maria Di Nunzio, Nicola Ferro, Donna Harman, Maria Maistro, and Gianmaria Silvello. 2015. Unfolding off-the-shelf IR systems for reproducibility. In *Proceedings of the SIGIR workshop on reproducibility, inexplicability, and generalizability of results (RIGOR)*, 107–116. New York: ACM.

Dillon, Andrew. 1992. Reading from paper versus screens: A critical review of the empirical literature. *Ergonomics* 35 (10): 1297–1326.

Dominich, Sandor. 2000. Foundation of information retrieval. *Mathematica Pannonica* 11 (1): 137–153.

Dong, Hai, Farookh Khadeer Hussain, and Elizabeth Chang. 2008. A survey in semantic search technologies. In *2008 2nd IEEE international conference on digital ecosystems and technologies*, 403–408. Phitsanuloke, Thailand: IEEE.

Dourish, Paul. 2004. *Where the action is: The foundations of embodied interaction*. Cambridge, MA: MIT Press.

Dourish, Paul, and Genevieve Bell. 2011. *Divining a digital future: Mess and mythology in ubiquitous computing*. Cambridge, MA: MIT Press.

Dow, John T. 1977. A metatheory for the development of a science of information. *Journal of the American Society for Information Science* 28 (6): 323–332.

Dowden, B., and N. Schwartz. 2016. The philosophy of social science. In *The internet encyclopedia of philosophy*, eds. James Fieser and Bradley Dowden. Retrieved from https://www.iep.utm.edu/.

Dretske, Fred. 1981. Knowledge and the flow of information. Cambridge, MA: MIT Press.

Dreyfus, Hubert L. 2002. Heidegger on gaining a free relation to technology. In *Heidegger reexamined*, Vol. 3. *art, poetry, and technology*, eds. Hubert L. Dreyfus and Mark A. Wrathall, 163–173. London: Routledge.

Dreyfus, Hubert L. 2007. Why Heideggerian AI failed and how fixing it would require making it more Heideggerian. *Artificial Intelligence* 171 (18): 1137–1160.

Dreyfus, Hubert L. 2014. *Skillful coping: Essays on the phenomenology of everyday perception and action*. Oxford: Oxford University Press.

Drotner, Kirsten, Hans Siggaard Jensen, and Kim Schrøder. 2008. *Informal learning and digital media*. Newcastle, UK: Cambridge Scholars.

Dumais, Susan T. 2009. An interdisciplinary perspective on information retrieval. In *Proceedings of the 32nd international ACM SIGIR conference on research and development in information retrieval*, 1–2. New York: ACM.

Eggins, Suzanne. 2004. *Introduction to systemic functional linguistics*. New York: Continuum.

Ellis, D. 1984. Theory and explanation in information retrieval research. *Journal of Information Science* 8 (1): 25–38.

Ellis, D. 1996. The dilemma of measurement in information retrieval research. *Journal of the American Society for Information Science* 47 (1): 23–36.

Ellis, Paul D. 2010. *The essential guide to effect sizes: Statistical power, meta-analysis, and the interpretation of research results*. Cambridge: Cambridge University Press.

Elman, Colin, and Miriam Fendius Elman, eds. 2003. *Progress in international relations theory: Appraising the field*. Cambridge, MA: MIT Press.

Evans, Vyvyan, and Melanie Green. 2006. *Cognitive linguistics: An introduction*. Edinburgh: Edinburgh University Press.

Falcon, Andrea. 2015. Aristotle on causality, Spring 2015 edn. In *The Stanford encyclopedia of philosophy*, ed. Edward N. Zalta.

Fallman, Daniel. 2011. The new good: Exploring the potential of philosophy of technology to contribute to human-computer interaction. In *Proceedings of the SIGCHI conference on human factors in computing systems*, 1051–1060. New York: ACM.

Falzon, Christopher, Timothy O'Leary, and Jana Sawicki. 2013. *A companion to Foucault*. Oxford: Wiley-Blackwell.

Fang, H., T. Tao, and C. Zhai. 2011. Diagnostic evaluation of information retrieval models. *ACM Transactions on Information Systems (TOIS)* 29 (2): 7.

Fang, Hui. 2007. An axiomatic approach to information retrieval. Ph.D. diss. University of Illinois at Urbana-Champaign.

Farradane, J. 1961. The challenge of information retrieval. *Journal of Documentation* 17 (4): 233–244.

Faye, Jan. 2014. *The nature of scientific thinking: On interpretation, explanation and understanding*. London: Palgrave Macmillan.

Feenberg, Andrew. 2002. *Transforming technology: A critical theory revisited*. New York: Oxford University Press.

Feenberg, Andrew. 2009. Critical theory of technology: An overview. In *Information technology in librarianship: New critical approaches*, eds. Gloria J. Leckie and John Buschman, 31–46. Westport, CT: Libraries Unlimited.

Feenberg, Andrew. 2010. *Between reason and experience: Essays in technology and modernity*. Cambridge, MA: MIT Press.

Ffytche, Matt. 2011. *The foundation of the unconscious: Schelling, freud and the birth of the modern psyche*. Cambridge: Cambridge University Press.

Fisher, Karen E., Sanda Erdelez, and Lynne McKechnie, eds. 2005. *Theories of information behavior*. Medford, NJ: Information Today.

Flanagan, Mary, Daniel Howe, and Helen Nissenbaum. 2008. Embodying values in technology: Theory and practice, eds. Jeroen van den Hoven and John Weckert, 322–353. Cambridge: Cambridge University Press.

Floridi, Luciano. 2008a. Information ethics: Its nature and scope. In *Information technology and moral philosophy*, eds. Jeroen Van den Hoven and John Weckert, 40–65. Cambridge: Cambridge University Press.

Floridi, Luciano. 2008b. The method of levels of abstraction. *Minds and Machines* 18 (3): 303–329.

Floridi, Luciano. 2011. *The philosophy of information*. Oxford: Oxford University Press.

Floridi, Luciano. 2017. Semantic conceptions of information, Spring 2017 edn. In *The Stanford encyclopedia of philosophy*, ed. Edward N. Zalta.

Flynn, Bernard. 2011. Maurice Merleau-Ponty, Fall 2011 edn. In *The Stanford encyclopedia of philosophy*, ed. Edward N. Zalta.

Foster, Allen, and Pauline Rafferty. 2011. *Innovations in information retrieval*. London: Facet Publishing.

Foucault, Michel, and A. Lewis. 1991. *Politics and the study of discourse*. Chicago: The University of Chicago Press.

Freeman, Walter J. 1999. *How brains make up their minds*. London: Weidenfeld & Nicolson.

Freeman, Walter J. 2012. *Neurodynamics: An exploration in mesoscopic brain dynamics*. New York: Springer.

Frické, Martin. 2015. Big data and its epistemology. *Journal of the Association for Information Science and Technology* 66 (4): 651–661.

Friedman, Michael. 1974. Explanation and scientific understanding. *The Journal of Philosophy* 71 (1): 5–19.

Frigg, Roman, and Stephan Hartmann. 2012. Models in science, Fall 2012 edn. In *The Stanford encyclopedia of philosophy*, ed. Edward N. Zalta.

Froehlich, Thomas J. 2004. A brief history of information ethics. *BiD: Textos universitaris de biblioteconomia i documentació* 13.

Froehlich, Thomas J. 1993. Review of 'dilemmas in the study of information: Exploring the boundaries of information science-Samuel D. Neill'. *The Library Quarterly: Information, Community, Policy* 63 (2): 228–230.

Fuhr, Norbert. 2012. Salton award lecture: Information retrieval as engineering science. *SIGIR Forum* 46 (2): 19–28.

Fuller, Steve. 2006. *The new sociological imagination*. London: SAGE.

Furedi, Frank, Roger Kimball, and Raymond Tallis. 2009. *From two cultures to no culture: C. P. Snow's "two cultures" lecture fifty years on*. London: Civitas: Institute for the Study of Civil Society.

Furner, Jonathan. October 10, 2011. *Fundamental research questions in information science*. Talk given as part of the panel session at 74th Annual Meeting of the American Society for Information Science and Technology, New Orleans.

Furner, Jonathan. 2014. The ethics of evaluative bibliometrics. In *Beyond bibliometrics: harnessing multidimensional indicators of scholarly impact*, eds. Blaise Cronin and Cassidy R. Sugimoto. Cambridge, MA: MIT Press.

Furner, Jonathan. 2015. Information science is neither. *Library Trends* 63 (3): 362–377.

Gabrilovich, Evgeniy. 2012. From information needs to action needs: Towards contextual app search and recommendation. In *Workshop on the appification of the web at the 21st World Wide Web Conference*.

Garfinkel, Harold, and Anne Rawls. 2015. *Toward a sociological theory of information*. London: Routledge.

Garland, David. 2014. What is a history of the present? on Foucault's genealogies and their critical preconditions. *Punishment & Society* 16 (4): 365–384.

Gavroglu, Kostas, Pantelis Nicolacopoulos, and Yorgos Goudaroulis. 1989. *Imre Lakatos and theories of scientific change*. New York: Springer.

Geertz, Clifford. 1994. Thick description: Toward an interpretive theory of culture. In *Readings in the philosophy of social science*, 213–231. Boston: MIT Press.

Gelven, Michael. 1989. *A commentary on Heidegger's being and time (rev. ed.)*. DeKalb, Illinois: Northern Illinois University Press.

Gilchrist, Alan, ed. 2009. *Information science in transition*. London: Facet Publishing.

Gilovich, Thomas, Dale Griffin, and Daniel Kahneman. 2002. *Heuristics and biases: The psychology of intuitive judgment*. Cambridge: Cambridge university press.

Glanzberg, Michael. 2014. Truth, Fall 2014 edn. In *The Stanford encyclopedia of philosophy*, ed. Edward N. Zalta.

Glazebrook, Trish. 2000. *Heidegger's philosophy of science*. New York: Fordham University Press.

Glushko, R. J. 2013. *The discipline of organizing*. Cambridge, MA: MIT Press.

Goguen, Joseph. 1997. Towards a social, ethical theory of information. In *Social science, technical systems and cooperative work: Beyond the great divide*, eds. Susan Leigh Star Les Gasser Geoffrey Bowker Geoffrey Bowker and William Turner, 27–56. New York: Psychology Press.

Goguen, Joseph. 1999. Tossing algebraic flowers down the great divide. In *People and ideas in theoretical computer science*, 93–129. New York: Springer.

Goldman, Alvin, and Thomas Blanchard. 2016. Social epistemology, Winter 2016 edn. In *The Stanford encyclopedia of philosophy*, ed. Edward N. Zalta.

Gonzalez, Wenceslao J. 2014. The evolution of Lakatos's repercussion on the methodology of economics. *HOPOS: The Journal of the International Society for the History of Philosophy of Science* 4 (1): 1–25.

Gonzalez, Wenceslao J. 2015. Prediction and novel facts in the methodology of scientific research programs. In *Philosophico-methodological analysis of prediction and its role in economics*. Theory and Decision Library A: (Rational Choice in Practical Philosophy and Philosophy of Science), 103–124. New York: Springer.

Goody, Jack. 2010. *Myth, ritual and the oral*. Cambridge: Cambridge University Press.

Goody, Jack. 2011. Memory in oral and literate traditions. In *The collective memory reader*, eds. Jeffrey K. Olick, Vered Vinitzky-Seroussi, and Daniel Levy, 321–324. Oxford: Oxford University Press.

Gordon, Michael, and Praveen Pathak. 1999. Finding information on the world wide web: the retrieval effectiveness of search engines. *Information processing & management* 35 (2): 141–180.

Gorichanaz, Tim, and Kiersten F. Latham. 2016. Document phenomenology: A framework for holistic analysis. *Journal of Documentation* 72 (6): 1114–1133.

Gorton, William A. 2015. The philosophy of social science. In *The internet encyclopedia of philosophy*, eds. James Fieser and Bradley Dowden. Retrieved from https://www.iep .utm.edu/.

Grabar, Oleg. 1992. *The mediation of ornament*, Vol. 35. Princeton, NJ: Princeton University Press.

Grosz, Barbara J., Martha E. Pollack, and Candace L. Sidner. 1989. Discourse. In *Foundations of cognitive science*, ed. M. L. Posner. Cambridge, MA: MIT Press.

Guha, Ramanathan, Rob McCool, and Eric Miller. 2003. Semantic search. In *Proceedings of the 12th international conference on world wide web*, 700–709. New York: ACM.

Gupta, Bina. 2000. *The empirical and the transcendental: A fusion of horizons*. New York: Rowman & Littlefield.

Gutting, Gary. 1989. *Michel Foucault's archaeology of scientific reason: Science and the history of reason*. Cambridge: Cambridge University Press.

Haack, Susan. 1978. *Philosophy of logics*. Cambridge: Cambridge University Press.

Hansen, Preben, and Soo-Young Rieh. 2016. Recent advances on searching as learning: An introduction to the special issue. *Journal of Information Science* 42 (1): 3–6.

Hansson, Sven Ove. 2015. Science and pseudo-science, Spring 2015 edn. In *The Stanford encyclopedia of philosophy*, ed. Edward N. Zalta.

Harman, Donna, and Chris Buckley. 2009. Overview of the reliable information access workshop. *Information Retrieval* 12 (6): 615–641.

Harmon, Glynn. 1971. On the evolution of information science. *Journal of the American Society for Information Science* 22 (4): 235–241.

Harrell, D. Fox. 2013. *Phantasmal media: an approach to imagination, computation, and expression*. Cambridge, MA: MIT Press.

Harter, S. P. 1992. Psychological relevance and information science. *Journal of the American Society for information Science* 43 (9): 602–615.

Harter, S. P. 1996. Variations in relevance assessments and the measurement of retrieval effectiveness. *Journal of the American Society for Information Science* 47 (1): 37–49.

Hedström, Peter, and Peter Bearman. 2009. *The Oxford handbook of analytical sociology.* Oxford: Oxford University Press.

Hedström, Peter, and Richard Swedberg. 1998. *Social mechanisms: An analytical approach to social theory.* Cambridge: Cambridge University Press.

Heelan, Patrick A. 1965. *Quantum mechanics and objectivity.* Dordrecht, The Netherlands: Springer.

Heelan, Patrick A. 1970. Complementarity, context dependence, and quantum logic. *Foundations of Physics* 1 (2): 95–110.

Heelan, Patrick A. 1987. The primacy of perception and the cognitive paradigm: Reply to De Mey. *Social Epistemology* 1 (4): 321-326.

Heelan, Patrick A. 1989. *Space-perception and the philosophy of science.* Berkeley: University of California Press.

Heelan, Patrick A. 1991. Hermeneutical phenomenology and the philosophy of science: Science, Culture, Literature, ed. Hugh J. Silverman, 213–228. New York: Routledge.

Heelan, Patrick A. 1997. Why a hermeneutical philosophy of the natural sciences? *Man and World* 30 (3): 271–298.

Heelan, Patrick A. 2003. Husserl, lonergan, and paradoxes of measurement. *Journal of Macrodynamic Analysis* 3: 76–96.

Heelan, Patrick A. 2004a. Hermeneutical phenomenology and the natural sciences. *Journal of the Interdisciplinary Crossroad* 1 (1): 71–88.

Heelan, Patrick A. 2004b. The phenomenological role of consciousness in measurement. *Mind and Matter* 2 (1): 61–84.

Heelan, Patrick A. 2015. *The observable: Heisenberg's philosophy of quantum mechanics.* New York: Peter Lang.

Heelan, Patrick A., and B. E. Babich. 2002. *Hermeneutic philosophy of science, Van Gogh's eyes, and God: Essays in honor of Patrick A. Heelan.* New York: Springer.

Heidegger, Martin. 1977. *The question concerning technology and other essays*, William Lovett, trans. New York: Harper & Row Publishers.

Heidegger, Martin. 1962. *Being and time.* New York: Harper & Row.

Heidegger, Martin. 1971. Building dwelling thinking. In *Poetry, language, thought*, 143–159. New York: Harper and Row.

Hendler, James, Nigel Shadbolt, Wendy Hall, Tim Berners-Lee, and Daniel Weitzner. 2008. Web science: an interdisciplinary approach to understanding the web. *Communications of the ACM* 51 (7): 60–69.

Hjørland, Birger. 1996. Rejoinder: A new horizon for information science. *Journal of the American Society for Information science* 47 (4): 334–335.

Hjørland, Birger. 2000. Documents, memory institutions and information science. *Journal of Documentation* 56 (1): 27–41.

Hjørland, Birger. 2004. Domain analysis: A socio-cognitive orientation for information science research. *Bulletin of the American Society for Information Science and Technology* 30 (3): 17–21.

Hjørland, Birger. 2008. What is knowledge organization (KO)? *Knowledge organization. International journal devoted to concept theory, classification, indexing and knowledge representation* 35 (2/3): 86–101.

Hjørland, Birger. 2010. Domain analysis in information science. In *Encyclopedia of library and information sciences*, 1648–1654.

Hjørland, Birger. 2011a. The importance of theories of knowledge: Browsing as an example. *Journal of the American Society for Information Science and Technology* 62 (3): 594–603.

Hjørland, Birger. 2011b. The importance of theories of knowledge: Indexing and information retrieval as an example. *Journal of the American Society for Information Science and Technology* 62 (1): 72–77.

Hjørland, Birger. 2014. Information science and its core concepts: Levels of disagreement. In *Theories of Information, Communication and Knowledge*, eds. Fidelia Ibekwe-SanJuan and Thomas M Dousa, 205–235. Dordrecht: Springer.

Hjørland, Birger. 2016. Informetrics needs a foundation in the theory of science. In *Theories of informetrics and scholarly communication*, 20–46. Berlin: Walter de Gruyter.

Hjørland, Birger, and Hanne Albrechtsen. 1995. Toward a new horizon in information science: Domain-analysis. *Journal of the American Society for Information Science and Technology* 46 (6): 400–425.

Hodges, Wilfrid. 2013. Model theory, Fall 2013 edn. In *The Stanford encyclopedia of philosophy*, ed. Edward N. Zalta.

Holler, Jan, Vlasios Tsiatsis, Catherine Mulligan, Stefan Avesand, Stamatis Karnouskos, and David Boyle. 2014. *From machine-to-machine to the internet of things: Introduction to a new age of intelligence*. San Diego, CA: Academic Press.

Hookway, Branden. 2014. *Interface*. Boston, MA: MIT Press.

Hookway, Christopher. 2015. Pragmatism, Spring 2015 edn. In *The Stanford encyclopedia of philosophy*, ed. Edward N. Zalta.

Hopkins, Burt. 2015. *The philosophy of Husserl*. London: Routledge.

Huang, Xiaoli, and Dagobert Soergel. 2013. Relevance: An improved framework for explicating the notion. *Journal of the American Society for Information Science and Technology* 64 (1): 18–35.

Huibers, Theodorus Wilhelmuskn Charles. 1996. An axiomatic theory for information retrieval. Ph.D. diss, University of Utrecht, University of Utrecht.

Huizinga, Johan. 1949. *Homo ludens: A study of the play-element in our culture*. London: Routledge & Kegan Paul.

Husserl, Edmund. 1969. Philosophy as rigorous science. In *Perception: selected readings in science and phenomenology*, Paul Tibbetts, ed., 209–233. Chicago: Quadrangle Books.

Husserl, Edmund. 2002. *The shorter logical investigations*. London: Routledge.

Ibekwe-SanJuan, Fidelia. 2012. The french conception of information science: "une exception française"? *Journal of the American Society for Information Science and Technology* 63 (9): 1693–1709.

Ibekwe-SanJuan, Fidelia, and Thomas M. Dousa. 2014. *Theories of information, communication and knowledge: A multidisciplinary approach*. New York: Springer.

Ihde, Don. 1979. *Technics and praxis: A philosophy of technology. Boston studies in the philosophy of science*, Vol. 24. New York: Springer.

Inagaki, Yoshiyuki, Narayanan Sadagopan, Georges Dupret, Anlei Dong, Ciya Liao, Yi Chang, and Zhaohui Zheng. 2010. Session based click features for recency ranking. In *Proceedings of the 24th AAAI Conference on Artificial Intelligence*, 1334–1339. Menlo Park, CA: AAAI Press.

Ingwersen, P., and K. Järvelin. 2005. *The turn: Integration of information seeking and retrieval in context*. New York: Springer.

Introna, Lucas. 2011. Phenomenological approaches to ethics and information technology, Summer 2011 edn. In *The Stanford encyclopedia of philosophy*, ed. Edward N. Zalta.

Inwood, Michael J. 1999. *A Heidegger dictionary*. Oxford: Wiley-Blackwell.

Iser, Wolfgang. 1972. The reading process: A phenomenological approach. *New Literary History* 3 (2): 279–299.

Iser, Wolfgang. 1979. *The act of reading*. London: Routledge and Kegan Paul.

Iser, Wolfgang. 1993. *Prospecting: From reader response to literary anthropology.* Baltimore, MD: Johns Hopkins Uinversity Press.

Ishii, Hiroshi, and Brygg Ullmer. 1997. Tangible bits: Towards seamless interfaces between people, bits and atoms. In *Proceedings of the ACM SIGCHI conference on human factors in computing systems,* 234–241. New York: ACM.

Jameson, Fredric. 2005. *Archaeologies of the future: The desire called utopia and other science fictions.* New York: Verso.

Janoff-Bulman, Ronnie, ed. 1990. *Psychological inquiry: An international journal for the advancement of psychological theory,* 1 (2). New York: Taylor & Francis.

Jansen, Bernard J., and Soo Young Rieh. 2010. The seventeen theoretical constructs of information searching and information retrieval. *Journal of the American Society for Information Science and Technology* 61 (8): 1517–1534.

Järvelin, Kalervo. 2011. IR research: systems, interaction, evaluation and theories. *SIGIR Forum* 45 (2): 17–31.

Johnson, Christopher D. 2012. *Memory, metaphor, and aby warburg's atlas of images.* Ithaca, NY: Cornell University Press.

Jonze, Spike. 2014. *Her* [Motion picture]. United States: Annapurna Pictures.

Jung, Carl Gustav. 2014. *The archetypes and the collective unconscious.* London: Routledge.

Kahneman, D., and A. Tversky. 1979. Prospect theory: An analysis of decision under risk. *Econometrica* 47 (2): 263–291.

Kahneman, Daniel, and Amos Tversky, eds. and R. S. Foundation. 2000. *Choices, values, and frames.* Cambridge: Cambridge University Press.

Kahneman, Daniel, Paul Slovic, and Amos Tversky, eds. 1982. *Judgment under uncertainty: Heuristics and biases.* Cambridge: Cambridge University Press.

Kantor, Paul B. 2015. Revisiting the foundations of IR: Timeless, yet timely. In *Proceedings of the 38th international ACM SIGIR conference on research and development in information retrieval,* 1125–1127. New York: ACM.

Kelly, Diane. 2009. Methods for evaluating interactive information retrieval systems with users. *Foundations and Trends in Information Retrieval* 3 (1–2): 1–224.

Kelly, Diane, Jaime Arguello, and Robert Capra. 2013. NSF workshop on task-based information search systems. *SIGIR Forum* 47 (2): 116–127.

Kelly, Diane, Filip Radlinski, and Jaime Teevan. 2014a. Choices and constraints: Research goals and approaches in information retrieval (Part II). In *Proceedings of the 37th international ACM SIGIR conference on research and development in information retrieval,* 1284–1284. New York: ACM.

Kelly, Diane, Filip Radlinski, and Jaime Teevan. 2014b. Observational approaches to information retrieval. Slides to their SIGIR 2014 Tutorial on Choices and Constraints: Research Goals and Approaches in Information Retrieval (Part II).

Kelly, Sean Dorrance. 2002. Merleau–Ponty on the body. *Ratio* 15 (4): 376–391.

Kember, Sarah, and Joanna Zylinska. 2012. *Life after new media: Mediation as a vital process*. Boston: MIT Press.

Khalil, Elias. 1987. Kuhn, Lakatos, and the history of economic thought. *International Journal of Social Economics* 14 (3/4/5): 118–131.

Kilburn-Toppin, Jasmine. 2013. Material memories of the guildsmen: Crafting identities in early modern london. In *Memory before modernity: Practices of memory in early modern Europe*, 165–181. Leiden: Brill.

Kindi, Vasso P. 1995. Kuhn's "the structure of scientific revolutions" revisited. *Journal for General Philosophy of Science* 26 (1): 75–92.

Kitcher, Philip. 1993. *The advancement of science–science without legend, objectivity without illusions*. New York: Oxford University Press.

Knox, Jean. 2003. *Archetype, attachment, analysis: Jungian psychology and the emergent mind*. New York: Routledge.

Kochen, M. 1967. *The growth of knowledge: Readings on organization and retrieval of information*. New York: John Wiley & Sons.

Kockelmans, Joseph J. 1984. *On the truth of being. Studies in phenomenology and existential philosophy*. Bloomington: Indiana University Press.

Kolodny, Niko, and John Brunero. 2013. Instrumental rationality, Fall 2013 edn. In *The Stanford encyclopedia of philosophy*, ed. Edward N. Zalta.

Korfhage, Robert R. 1991. To see, or not to see—is that the query? In *Proceedings of the 14th annual international ACM SIGIR conference on research and development in information retrieval*, 134–141. New York: ACM.

Koskela, Jani. 2012. Truth as unconcealment in Heidegger's being and time. *Minerva—An Internet Journal of Philosophy* 16: 116–128.

Krantz, David, Duncan Luce, Patrick Suppes, and Amos Tversky. 2006. *Foundations of measurement, Vol. I: Additive and polynomial representations*. New York: Dover.

Krois, M. J. 2002. Ars memoriae, philosophy and culture: Frances yates and after. *Philosophy and Culture: essays in honor of Donald Phillip Verese*. Charlottesville: Philosophy Documentation Center.

Kuhn, Thomas S. 2012. *The structure of scientific revolutions*. Chicago: University of Chicago Press.

Kulka, Tomas. 1977. Some problems concerning rational reconstruction: comments on Elkana and Lakatos. *British Journal for the Philosophy of Science* 28 (4): 325–344.

Lakatos, Imre, and Alan Musgrave. 1970. *Criticism and the growth of knowledge.* Cambridge: Cambridge University Press.

Lakatos, Imre, John Worrall, and Gregory Currie. 1980. *The methodology of scientific research programmes.* Cambridge: Cambridge University Press.

Lakatos, Imre. 1971. History of science and its rational reconstructions, In *PSA: Proceedings of the Biennial Meeting of the Philosophy of Science Association* Vol. 1970: 91–136. eds. Roger C. Buck and Robert S. Cohen, 91–136. Dordrecht: Springer.

Lalmas, Mounia, Heather O'Brien, and Elad Yom-Tov. 2014. *Measuring user engagement. Synthesis lectures on information concepts, retrieval, and services.* San Rafael, CA: Morgan & Claypool Publishers.

Larvor, Brendan. 1998. *Lakatos: An introduction.* London: Routledge.

Latham, Kiersten F. 2012. Museum object as document: Using buckland's information concepts to understand museum experiences. *Journal of Documentation* 68 (1): 45–71.

Latham, Kiersten F. 2014. Experiencing documents. *Journal of Documentation* 70 (4): 544–561.

Laudan, Larry. 1981. A problem solving approach to scientific progress. In *Scientific revolutions*, ed. Ian Hacking. Oxford: Oxford University Press.

Laudan, Larry. 1986. *Science and values: The aims of science and their role in scientific debate.* Berkeley: University of California Press.

Laudan, Larry. 1989. From theories to research traditions, 2nd ed. In *Readings in The Philosophy of Science*, Baruch A. Brody and Richard E. Grandy, eds., 368–79.

Lauden, Larry. 1977. *Progress and its problems: Towards a theory of scientific growth.* Berkeley: University of California Press.

Law, Effie Lai-Chong, Virpi Roto, Marc Hassenzahl, Arnold P. O. S. Vermeeren, and Joke Kort. 2009. Understanding, scoping and defining user experience: A survey approach. In *Proceedings of the SIGCHI conference on human factors in computing systems*, 719–728. New York: ACM.

Lawson, T. 1997. *Economics and reality.* London: Routledge.

Lawson, T. 2003. *Reorienting economics.* London: Routledge.

Lee, Hur-Li. 2000. What is a collection? *Journal of the American Society for Information Science* 51 (12): 1106–1113.

Lehtinen, Aki, Jaakko Kuorikoski, and Petri Ylikoski, eds. 2012. *Economics for real: Uskali Mäki and the place of truth in economics.* London: Routledge.

Leonardi, P. M., B. A. Nardi, and J. Kallinikos. 2012. *Materiality and organizing: Social interaction in a technological world*. Oxford: Oxford University Press.

Levy, David M. 2012. *Scrolling forward: Making sense of documents in the digital age*, 1st edn. New York: Arcade Publishing.

Lin, Jimmy, Matt Crane, Andrew Trotman, Jamie Callan, Ishan Chattopadhyaya, John Foley, Grant Ingersoll, Craig Macdonald, and Sebastiano Vigna. 2016. Toward reproducible baselines: The open-source IR reproducibility challenge. In *Advances in information retrieval: 38th european conference on IR research, ECIR 2016, Padua, Italy, March 20–23, 2016. proceedings*, eds. Nicola Ferro, Fabio Crestani, Marie-Francine Moens, Josiane Mothe, Fabrizio Silvestri, Maria Giorgio Di Nunzio, Claudia Hauff, and Gianmaria Silvello, 408–420. Springer.

Link, David. 2010. Scrambling truth: Rotating letters as a material form of thought. *Variantology* 4: 215–266.

Lipton, Peter. 1990. Contrastive explanation. *Royal Institute of Philosophy Supplement* 27: 247–266.

Little, Daniel. 1993. On the scope and limits of generalizations in the social sciences. *Synthese* 97 (2): 183–207.

Losee, John. 2004. *Theories of scientific progress: An introduction*. New York: Routledge.

Luce, R. Duncan, David H. Krantz, Patrick Suppes, and Amos Tversky. 2006. *Foundations of measurement, Vol. III: Representation, axiomatization, and invariance*. New York: Dover.

Lund Niels W., Tim Gorichanaz, and Kiersten F. Latham. 2016. A discussion on document conceptualization. In *Proceedings from the document academy* 3 (2): 544–561.

Lund, Niels Windfeld. 2009. Document theory. *Annual Review of Information Science and Technology* 43 (1): 1–55.

Lupton, Deborah. 2013. Understanding the human machine [commentary]. *Technology and Society Magazine, IEEE* 32 (4): 25–30.

Lupu, Mihai, Michail Salampasis, and Allan Hanbury. 2014. Domain specific search. In *Professional search in the modern world: Cost action IC1002 on multilingual and multifaceted interactive information access*, eds. Georgios Paltoglou, Fernando Loizides, and Preben Hansen, 96–117. New York: Springer.

Lykke, Marianne, and Anna G Eslau. 2010. Using thesauri in enterprise settings: Indexing or query expansion? In *The Janus faced scholar: A Festschrift in honour of Peter Ingwersen*, Birger Larsen, Jesper Wiborg Schneider, and Fredrik Åström, eds., 87–97. Copenhagen: Det Informationsvidenskabelige Akademi (Royal School of Library and Information Science).

Lynch, Kevin. 1960. *The image of the city*. Cambridge, MA: MIT press.

Lynch, Kevin. 1984. Reconsidering the image of the city. In *Cities of the mind*, 151–161. New York: Springer.

Ma, Lai. 2012. Meanings of information: The assumptions and research consequences of three foundational lis theories. *Journal of the American Society for Information Science and Technology* 63 (4): 716–723.

Ma, Lai. 2013. Is information still relevant? *Information Research* 18 (3) paper C33.

Mahon, Michael. 1992. *Foucault's Nietzschean genealogy: Truth, power, and the subject*. Albany, NY: SUNY Press.

Manning, Christopher D., Prabhakar Raghavan, and Hinrich Schütze. 2008. *Introduction to information retrieval*. Cambridge: Cambridge University Press.

Marchionini, Gary. 2010. *Information concepts: From books to cyberspace identities. Synthesis lectures on information concepts, retrieval, and services*. San Rafael, CA: Morgan & Claypool Publishers.

Marks, Laura U. 2010. *Enfoldment and infinity: An Islamic genealogy of new media art*. Cambridge, MA: MIT Press.

Maron, M. E., and J. L. Kuhns. 1960. On relevance, probabilistic indexing and information retrieval. *Journal of the ACM (JACM)* 7 (3): 216–244.

Maróstica, A. 1992. Ars combinatoria and time: Llull, leibniz and peirce. *Studia Llulliana* 32 (2): 105–134.

Marturano, Antonio. 2002. The role of metaethics and the future of computer ethics. *Ethics and Information Technology* 4 (1): 71–78.

Marx, Karl. 1971. *A contribution to the critique of political economy*. London: Lawrence and Wishart.

Matheson, Carl, and Justin Dallmann. 2015. Historicist theories of scientific rationality, Summer 2015 edn. In *The Stanford encyclopedia of philosophy*, ed. Edward N. Zalta.

McCarthy, John, and Peter Wright. 2007. *Technology as experience*. Boston: The MIT Press.

McConnell, J. 1958. Whittaker's correlation of physics and philosophy. In *Proceedings of the Edinburgh mathematical society*, Vol. 2, 57–68. Edinburgh: Oliver and Boyd, and Edinburgh Mathematical Society.

McLuhan, Marshall. 1994. *Understanding media: The extensions of man*. Cambridge, MA: MIT press.

McNeill, William. 1999. *The glance of the eye: Heidegger, Aristotle, and the ends of theory*. Albany, NY: Suny Press.

Meadow, Charles T. 2006. *Messages, meanings and symbols: The communication of information*. Oxford: Scarecrow Press.

Meadows, A. J. 1990. Theory in information science. *Journal of Information Science* 16 (1): 59–63.

Meadows, A. J. 2016. Apologia pro theoria sua. In *Theory development: In the information sciences*, ed. Diane H. Sonnenwald, 300–318. Austin: University of Texas Press.

Meehl, Paul E. 1967. Theory-testing in psychology and physics: A methodological paradox. *Philosophy of science* 34 (2): 103–115.

Meehl, Paul E. 1978. Theoretical risks and tabular asterisks: Sir Karl, Sir Ronald, and the slow progress of soft psychology. *Journal of Consulting and Clinical Psychology* 46 (4): 806–834.

Meehl, Paul E. 1990. Appraising and amending theories: The strategy of Lakatosian defense and two principles that warrant it. *Psychological Inquiry* 1 (2): 108–141.

Menzel, Christopher. 2016. Possible worlds, Spring 2016 edn. In *The Stanford encyclopedia of philosophy*, ed. Edward N. Zalta.

MezeI, Balázs M. 1986. Yves simon's understanding of Aristotle: Some comments. *Hungarian Philosophical Review* 57 (4): 86–94.

Miller, J. Mitchell. 2008. Otherness. In *The sage encyclopedia of qualitative research methods*, ed. Lisa M Given. Los Angeles: Sage Publications.

Mills, C Wright. 2000. *The sociological imagination*. Oxford: Oxford University Press.

Mills, Jon. 2014. *Underworlds: Philosophies of the unconscious from psychoanalysis to metaphysics*. London: Routledge.

Misztal, Barbara. 2003. *Theories of social remembering*. Maidenhead, U.K.: Open University Press.

Mitcham, Carl, and Alois Huning, eds. 1986. *Philosophy and technology II: Information technology and computers in theory and practice*. New York: Springer.

Mizzaro, Stefano. 1996. On the foundations of information retrieval. In *Proceedings of aica'96*, 363–386. Roma, Italy.

Mohanty, Jitendra Nath. 1991. Method of imaginative variation in phenomenology. In *Thought experiments in science and philosophy*, ed. Gerald J. Massey Tamara Horowitz, 261–272. Savage, MD: Rowman & Littlefield Publishers.

Mohanty, Jitendra Nath. 2012. *Edmund Husserl's theory of meaning*, Vol. 14. New York: Springer.

Monton, Bradley, and Chad Mohler. 2014. Constructive empiricism, Spring 2014 edn. In *The Stanford encyclopedia of philosophy*, ed. Edward N. Zalta.

Moore, Johanna D., and Peter Wiemer-Hastings. 2003. Discourse in computational linguistics and artificial intelligence. In *Handbook of discourse processes*, eds. Arthur C. Graesser, Morton Ann Gernsbacher, and Susan R. Goldman, 439–486. Lawrence Erlbaum Associates.

Moylan, Tom. 2000. *Scraps of the untainted sky: Science fiction, utopia, dystopia*. Boulder, Colorado: Westview Press.

Mulligan, Kevin, and Fabrice Correia. 2013. Facts, Spring 2013 edn. In *The Stanford encyclopedia of philosophy*, ed. Edward N. Zalta.

Nigel, Ford. 2013. Information need: A theory connecting information search to knowledge formation by Charles Cole. Medford, NJ: Information today, 2012. 224 pp. $59.50 (ISBN 978-1-57387-429-8). *Journal of the American Society for Information Science and Technology* 64 (12): 2595–2596.

Niiniluoto, Ilkka. 2011. Scientific progress, Summer 2011 edn. In *The Stanford encyclopedia of philosophy*, ed. Edward N. Zalta.

Nolin, Jan, and Fredrik Åström. 2010. Turning weakness into strength: Strategies for future lis. *Journal of Documentation* 66 (1): 7–27.

Norberg-Schulz, Christian. 1968. *Intentions in architecture*. Cambridge, MA: MIT press.

O'Brien, Heather L., and Elaine G. Toms. 2008. What is user engagement? A conceptual framework for defining user engagement with technology. *Journal of the American Society for Information Science and Technology* 59 (6): 938–955.

O'Brien, Heather L., and Elaine G. Toms. 2010. The development and evaluation of a survey to measure user engagement. *Journal of the American Society for Information Science and Technology* 61 (1): 50–69.

Oddie, Graham. 2014. Truthlikeness, Summer 2014 edn. In *The Stanford encyclopedia of philosophy*, ed. Edward N. Zalta.

Oddy, R. N., N. J. Belkin, and H. M. Brooks. 1982. Ask for information retrieval: Part 2 results of a design study. *Journal of Documentation* 38 (3): 145–164.

Oksala, Johanna. 2003. The birth of man. In *Metaphysics, facticity, interpretation*, 139–163. New York: Springer.

Olsen, Bernt Ivar, Niels Windfeld Lund, Gunnar Ellingsen, and Gunnar Hartvigsen. 2012. Document theory for the design of socio-technical systems: A document model as ontology of human expression. *Journal of Documentation* 68 (1): 100–126.

Olshin, Benjamin B. 2005. The I Ching or 'Book of Changes': Chinese space-time model and a philosophy of divination. *Journal of Philosophy and Culture* 2 (2): 17–39.

Ong, Walter J. 1971. *Rhetoric, romance, and technology*. Ithaca, NY: Cornell University Press.

Ortega y Gasset, José. 1958. *Man and crisis*. New York: W. W. Norton & Company.

Osborne, Peter, and Matthew Charles. 2015. Walter Benjamin, Fall 2015 edn. In *The Stanford encyclopedia of philosophy*, ed. Edward N. Zalta.

Otlet, Paul. 1990. *International organisation and dissemination of knowledge: Selected essays of Paul Otlet*. Amsterdam: Elsevier for the International Federation of Documentation.

Owens, Joseph. 1978. *The doctrine of being in the Aristotelian metaphysics: A study in the greek background of mediaeval thought*. Toronto: PIMS.

Parrinder, Patrick. 2000. *Learning from other worlds: Estrangement, cognition, and the politics of science fiction and utopia*. Liverpool: Liverpool University Press.

Pauen, Michael. 2012. The second-person perspective. *Inquiry* 55 (1): 33–49.

Petitot, Jean. 1999. *Naturalizing phenomenology: Issues in contemporary phenomenology and cognitive science*. Stanford, CA: Stanford University Press.

Pettigrew, David, and François Raffoul, eds. 2012. *Heidegger and practical philosophy*. Albany, NY: SUNY Press.

Pettigrew, Karen E., and Lynne E. F. McKechnie. 2001. The use of theory in information science research. *Journal of the American Society for Information Science and Technology* 52 (1): 62–73.

Pickering, W. Roy. 1996. Principia informatica: Conversations with R.T. Bottle. *Journal of Information Science* 22 (6): 447–456.

Pietarinen, Ahti-Veikko. 2006. Interdisciplinarity and Peirce's classification of the sciences: A centennial reassessment. *Perspectives on Science* 14 (2): 127–152.

Pirolli, Peter, and Stuart Card. 1999. Information foraging. *Psychological review* 106 (4): 643–675.

Polanyi, Michael. 1964. *Personal knowledge*. New York: Harper & Row.

Polanyi, Michael. 1967. *The tacit dimension*. New York: Doubleday.

Porpora, Douglas V. 1998. Four concepts of social structure. In *Critical realism: Essential readings*, eds. Margaret Archer, Roy Bhaskar, Andrew Collier, Tony Lawson, and Alan Norrie, 339–355. London: Routledge.

Randolph Mayes, G. 2015. Theories of explanation. In *The internet encyclopedia of philosophy*, eds. James Fieser and Bradley Dowden. https://www.iep.utm.edu/, July 14, 2016.

Rauterberg, Matthias. 2006. From personal to cultural computing: How to assess a cultural experience. In UDayIV : Information nutzbar machen : Information der Beitrage zum Usability Day IV 09. Juni 2006 (pp. 13–21), eds. G. Kempter, P. von Hellberg. Lengerich: Pabst Science Publisher.

Rayward, W. Boyd. 2008. *European modernism and the information society: Informing the present, understanding the past*. Aldershot, UK: Ashgate Publishing.

Salmon, M. H., ed. 1979. *Hans Reichenbach: logical empiricist*. New York: Springer.

Rescher, Nicholas. 2000. *Kant and the reach of reason: Studies in Kant's theory of rational systematization*. Cambridge: Cambridge University Press.

Robertson, S. E. 1979. Between aboutness and meaning. In *Proceedings of The Analysis of Meaning: Informatics 5*, eds. M. MacCafferty and K. Gray, 202–205. Aslib.

Robertson, S. E. 2008. On the history of evaluation in IR. *Journal of Information Science* 34 (4): 439–456.

Robertson, S. E., M. E. Maron, and W. S. Cooper. 1982. Probability of relevance: A unification of two competing models for information retrieval. *Information Technology—Research and Development* 1: 1–21.

Robertson, S. E., and H. Zaragoza. 2009. The probabilistic relevance framework: BM25 and beyond. *Foundations and Trends in Information Retrieval* 3 (4): 333–389.

Rosenthal, Franz. 1958. *Ibn khaldun: The muqaddimah, an introduction to history*. New York: Pantheon.

Rossi, Aldo. 1982. *The architecture of the city*. Cambridge, MA: MIT press.

Rossi, Paolo. 2000. *Logic and the art of memory: The quest for a universal language*. London: Continuum International. Trans. Stephen Clucas.

Roth, Michael S. 1994. Foucault's 'history of the present.' *Michel Foucault Critical Assessments* 1: 97–110.

Rowlands, Michael. 1993. The role of memory in the transmission of culture. *World archaeology* 25 (2): 141–151.

Ruthven, I., and D. Kelly. 2011. *Interactive information seeking, behaviour and retrieval*. London: Facet Publishing.

Sakai, Tetsuya. 2016. Statistical significance, power, and sample sizes: A systematic review of SIGIR and TOIS, 2006–2015. In *Proceedings of the 39th international ACM SIGIR conference on research and development in information retrieval*, 5–14. New York: ACM.

Salice, Alessandro. 2016. The phenomenology of the Munich and Göttingen circles, Winter 2016 edn. In *The Stanford encyclopedia of philosophy*, ed. Edward N. Zalta.

Salton, Gerard. 1996. A new horizon for information science. *Journal of the American Society for Information science* 47 (4): 333–333.

Saracevic, Tefko. 1992. Information science: Origin, evolution and relations. In *Conceptions of library and information science I*, eds. P. Vakkari and D. Cronin, 5–27.

Saracevic, Tefko. 1999. Information science. *Journal of the American Society for Information Science and Technology* 50 (12): 1051–1063.

Saracevic, Tefko. 2007. Relevance: A review of the literature and a framework for thinking on the notion in information science. part III: Behavior and effects of relevance. *Journal of the American Society for Information Science and Technology* 58 (13): 1915–1933.

Savolainen, Reijo. 2016. Contributions to conceptual growth: The elaboration of Ellis's model for information-seeking behavior. *Journal of the Association for Information Science and Technology* 68 (3): 594–608.

Sayre-McCord, Geoff. 2014. Metaethics, Summer 2014 edn. In *The Stanford encyclopedia of philosophy*, ed. Edward N. Zalta.

Scharff, Robert C., and Val Dusek. 2014. *Philosophy of technology: The technological condition: An anthology*, 2nd edn. Oxford: John Wiley & Sons.

Schoefegger, Karin, Tanel Tammet, and Michael Granitzer. 2013. A survey on socio-semantic information retrieval. *Computer Science Review* 8: 25–46.

Schubert, Dirk. 2016. *Contemporary perspectives on Jane Jacobs: reassessing the impacts of an urban visionary*. London: Routledge.

Schutz, Alfred. 1970. Reflections on the problem of relevance, ed. Richard M. Zaner. New Haven: Yale University Press.

Selinger, Evan. 2012. *Postphenomenology: A critical companion to Ihde*. Albany, NY: SUNY Press.

Sengers, Phoebe. 2005. The engineering of experience. In *Funology: From Usability to Enjoyment*, eds. Mark A. Blythe, Kees Overbeeke, Andrew F. Monk, and Peter C. Wright, 19–29. Dordrecht: Springer.

Serlin, Ronald C., and Daniel K. Lapsley. 1985. Rationality in psychological research: The good-enough principle. 40 (1): 73–8.

Simon, Herbert A. 1996. *The sciences of the artificial*. Cambridge, MA: MIT Press.

Simon, Yves René Marie. 1986. *The definition of moral virtue*. New York: Fordham University Press.

Simon, Yves René Marie. 1996. *Foresight and knowledge*. New York: Fordham University Press.

Simon, Yves René Marie. 1999. *Practical knowledge*. New York: Fordham University Press.

Simon, Yves René Marie. 2001. *The great dialogue of nature and space*. Southbend, IN: St. Augustine Press. Reprint. Translated by Paule Simon, Originally published 1970 by Magi Books, New York.

Singhal, Amit, and Marcin Kaszkiel. 2001. A case study in web search using trec algorithms. In *Proceedings of the 10th international conference on world wide web*, 708–716. New York: ACM.

Smeaton, Alan. 1993. Report on TREC-2 conference. *IR Digest* 10 (42).

Smith, B. C. 1996. *On the origin of objects*. Cambridge, MA: MIT Press.

Smith, David Woodruff. 2013. Phenomenology, Winter 2013 edn. In *The Stanford encyclopedia of philosophy*, ed. Edward N. Zalta.

Snyder, Laura J. 2012. William whewell, Winter 2012 edn. In *The Stanford encyclopedia of philosophy*, ed. Edward N. Zalta.

Sokolowski, R. 2000. *Introduction to phenomenology*. Cambridge: Cambridge University Press.

Song, D., M. Lalmas, C. J. van Rijsbergen, I. Frommholz, B. Piwowarski, J. Wang, P. Zhang, G. Zuccon, P. D. Bruza, S. Arafat, and L. Azzopardi, E. Di Buccio, A. Huertas-rosero, Y. Hou, M. Melucci, and S. Rüger. 2010. How quantum theory is developing the field of information retrieval. In *Proceedings of AAAI-Fall 2010 Symposium on Quantum Informatics for Cognitive, Social, and Semantic Processes (QI)*, 105–108.

Sonnenwald, Diane H. 2016. *Theory development in the information sciences*. Austin: University of Texas Press.

Spärck-Jones, Karen. 1988. A look back and a look forward. In *Proceedings of the 11th annual international ACM SIGIR conference on research and development in information retrieval*, 13–29. New York: ACM.

Spärck-Jones, Karen. 2001. Automatic language and information processing: Rethinking evaluation. *Natural Language Engineering* 7 (1): 1–18.

Spärck-Jones, Karen. 2007. Statistics and retrieval: Past and future. In *Computing: Theory and applications, 2007. ICCTA '07. international conference on*, 396–405.

Spärck-Jones, Karen, Steve Walker, and Stephen E. Robertson. 2000. A probabilistic model of information retrieval: development and comparative experiments: Part 1. *Information Processing & Management* 36 (6): 779–808.

Sperber, Dan, and Deirdre Wilson. 1995. *Relevance: Communication and cognition*, 2nd edn. Oxford: Blackwell.

Spielberg, Steven (Director). 2002. *Minority Report* [Motion Picture]. United States: 20th Century Fox.

Stapp, H. P. 2007a. *Mindful universe: Quantum mechanics and the participating observer*. In The Blackwell Companion to Consciousness, eds. Max Velmans and Susan Schneider, 300–312. New York: Springer.

Stapp, Henry. 2007b. Quantum mechanical theories of consciousness, eds. Max Velmans and Susan Schneider, 300–312. Malden, MA: Blackwell.

Straßheim, Jan. 2010. Relevance theories of communication: Alfred Schutz in dialogue with Sperber and Wilson. *Journal of Pragmatics* 42 (5): 1412–1441.

Stroud, Barry. 1996. Mind, meaning and practice. In *The Cambridge companion to Wittgenstein*, eds. H. D. Sluga and D. G. Stern. Cambridge: Cambridge University Press.

Suorsa, Anna, and Maija-Leena Huotari. 2014. Knowledge creation and the concept of a human being: A phenomenological approach. *Journal of the Association for Information Science and Technology* 65 (5): 1042–1057.

Suppe, Frederick. 1989. *The semantic conception of theories and scientific realism.* Bloomington: University of Illinois Press.

Suppes, Patrick, David H. Krantz, R. Duncan Luce, and Amos Tversky. 2006. *Foundations of measurement, vol. II: Geometrical, threshold, and probabilistic representations.* New York: Dover.

Swanson, D. R. 1986. Undiscovered public knowledge. *The Library Quarterly* 56 (2): 103–118.

Swanson, D. R. 1988. Historical note: Information retrieval and the future of an illusion. *Journal of the American Society for Information Science* 39 (2): 92–98.

Tague-Sutcliffe, Jean. 1992. Measuring the informativeness of a retrieval process. In *Proceedings of the 15th annual international ACM SIGIR conference on research and development in information retrieval*, 23–36. New York: ACM.

Taube, Mortimer. 1965. A note on the pseudo-mathematics of relevance. *American Documentation* 16 (2): 69–72.

Thagard, Paul. 2007. Coherence, truth, and the development of scientific knowledge. *Philosophy of science* 74 (1): 28–47.

Toulmin, Stephen. 1982. The construal of reality: Criticism in modern and postmodern science. *Critical Inquiry* 9 (1): 93–111.

Trotman, Andrew, and David Keeler. 2011. Ad hoc IR: Not much room for improvement. In *Proceedings of the 34th international ACM SIGIR conference on research and development in information retrieval*, 1095–1096. New York: ACM.

Tsou, Jonathan Y. 2015. Reconsidering the Carnap-Kuhn connection. In *Kuhn's structure of scientific revolutions—50 years on*, eds. William J. Devlin and Alisa Bokulich, 51–69. New York: Springer.

Tuan, Yi-Fu. 1979. Space and place: Humanistic perspective. In *Philosophy in geography*, 387–427. New York: Springer.

Turkle, Sherry. 2005. *The second self: Computers and the human spirit*. Cambridge, MA: MIT Press.

Turkle, Sherry. 2011. *Life on the screen*. New York: Simon & Schuster.

Turpin, Andrew H., and William Hersh. 2001. Why batch and user evaluations do not give the same results. In *Proceedings of the 24th annual international ACM SIGIR conference on research and development in information retrieval*, 225–231. New York: ACM.

Turpin, Andrew H., and Falk Scholer. 2006. User performance versus precision measures for simple search tasks. In *Proceedings of the 29th annual international ACM SIGIR conference on research and development in information retrieval*, 11–18. New York: ACM.

Uckelman, Sara L. 2010. Computing with concepts, computing with numbers: Llull, Leibniz, and Boole. In *Programs, proofs, processes*, eds. Fernando Ferreira, Benedikt Löwe, Elvira Mayordomo, and Luís Mendes Gomes, 427–437. Berlin: Springer.

Vakkari, Pertti. 1998. Growth of theories on information seeking: An analysis of growth of a theoretical research program on the relation between task complexity and information seeking. *Information Processing & Management* 34 (2): 361–382.

Vakkari, Pertti, and Kalervo Järvelin. 2005. Explanation in information seeking and retrieval. In *New directions in cognitive information retrieval*, 113–138. New York: Springer.

Vakkari, Pertti, and Martti Kuokkanen. 1997. Theory growth in information science: applications of the theory of science to a theory of information seeking. *Journal of Documentation* 53 (5): 497–519.

Van Acker, Wouter. 2012. Architectural metaphors of knowledge: The mundaneum designs of Maurice Heymans, Paul Otlet, and Le Corbusier. *Library trends* 61 (2): 371–396.

Van Dijck, José. 2013. *The culture of connectivity: A critical history of social media*. Oxford: Oxford University Press.

van Dijk, Teun A. 1997. *Discourse as structure and process*. London: Sage.

van Fraassen, B. C. 1980. *The scientific image*. New York: Oxford University Press.

van Rijsbergen, C. J. 2004. *The geometry of information retrieval*. Cambridge: Cambridge University Press.

van Rijsbergen, C. J. 2006. Quantum haystacks. In *Proceedings of the 29th annual international ACM SIGIR conference on research and development in information retrieval*, 1–2. New York: ACM.

van Rijsbergen, C. J., and M. Lalmas. 1996. Information calculus for information retrieval. *Journal of the American Society for Information Science* 47 (5): 385–398.

Varela, Francisco, Evan Thompson, and Eleanor Rosch. 2017. *The embodied mind: cognitive science and human experience*, Revised edn. Cambridge, MA: MIT Press.

Varela, Francisco, and Jonathan Shear. 1999. First-person methodologies: What, why, how. *Journal of Consciousness studies* 6 (2–3): 1–14.

Varzi, Achille. 2016. Mereology, Winter 2016 edn. In *The Stanford encyclopedia of philosophy*, ed. Edward N. Zalta.

Verbeek, Peter-Paul. 2009. Moralizing technology: On the morality of technological artifacts and their design. In *Readings in the philosophy of technology*, ed. David M Kaplan, 226–243. New York: Rowman and Littlefield.

Verbeek, Peter-Paul. 2010. *What things do: Philosophical reflections on technology, agency, and design*. College Station, PA: Penn State University Press.

Verbeek, Peter-Paul. 2016. Toward a theory of technological mediation: A program for postphenomenological research. In *Technoscience and postphenomenology: The manhattan papers*, eds. J. K. Berg, O. Friis, and R. P. Crease, 189–204. London: Lexington Books.

Vickery, B. C. 2009. Meeting the challenge. In *Information science in transition*, ed. Alan Gilchrist. London: Facet Publishing.

Visker, Rudi. 1995. *Michel Foucault: genealogy as critique*. New York: Verso.

Volpi, Franco. 2007. In whose name? Heidegger and 'practical philosophy.' *European Journal of Political Theory* 6 (1): 31–51.

von Franz, Marie Louise. 1980. *On divination and synchronicity: The psychology of meaningful chance*. Toronto, Canada: Inner City Books.

Voorhees, Ellen M. 2000. Variations in relevance judgments and the measurement of retrieval effectiveness. *Information Processing & Management* 36 (5): 697–716.

Voorhees, E. M., D. K. Harman, and National Institute of Standards and Technology. 2005. *TREC: Experiment and evaluation in information retrieval*. Cambridge, MA: MIT Press.

Wagner, David G., and Joseph Berger. 1985. Do sociological theories grow? *American Journal of Sociology* 90 (4): 697–728.

Walker, Percy B. 1974. Robert Arthur Fairthorne: An appreciation. *Journal of Documentation* 30 (2): 127–138.

Warner, Julian. 2001. W (h) ither information science?/! *The Library Quarterly* 71 (2): 243–255.

Warner, Julian. 2010. *Human information retrieval*. Cambridge, MA: MIT Press.

Watkins, John. 1989. The methodology of scientific research programmes: A retrospect. In *Imre Lakatos and theories of scientific change*, ed. Goudaroulis-Yorgos Nicolacopoulos P. Gavroglu Kostas, 3–13. New York: Springer.

Webber, Sheila. 2003. Information science in 2003: A critique. *Journal of Information Science* 29 (4): 311–330.

Weber, Erik, Jeroen Van Bouwel, and Leen De Vreese. 2013. *Scientific explanation*. New York: Springer.

Weidenfeld, Matthew C. 2011. Heidegger's appropriation of Aristotle: Phronesis, conscience, and seeing through the one. *European Journal of Political Theory* 10 (2): 254–276.

Weissmann, V. E. 1986. Statistics in information retrieval experiments. *Information processing & management* 22 (1): 29–37.

Wells, Herbert George, and Alan James Mayne. 1938. *World brain*. London: Methuen & Company.

Wetherell, Margaret, Stephanie Taylor, and Simeon J. Yates. 2001. *Discourse theory and practice: A reader*. London: Sage.

Wheeler, Michael. 2014. Martin Heidegger, Fall 2014 edn. In *The Stanford encyclopedia of philosophy*, ed. Edward N. Zalta.

Whewell, William. 1847. *The philosophy of the inductive sciences: Founded upon their history*, 2nd edn. London: John W. Parker.

White, Hayden. 1975. *Metahistory: The historical imagination in nineteenth-century Europe*. Baltimore, MD: Johns Hopkins University Press.

Wiener, Norbert. 1954. *The human use of human beings*. Boston: Houghton Mifflin.

Wilson, Deirdre, and Dan Sperber. 2002. Relevance theory. In *Handbook of pragmatics*, 606–632. Oxford: Blackwell.

Wilson, Patrick. 2002. On accepting the asist award of merit. *Bulletin of the American Society for Information Science and Technology* 28 (2): 10–11.

Wilson, Tom D. 1994. Information needs and uses: fifty years of progress. In *Fifty years of information progress: a journal of documentation review*, ed. Brian C. Vickery, 15–51. London: Aslib.

Wilson, Tom D. 1999. Models in information behaviour research. *Journal of Documentation* 55 (3): 249–270.

Winograd, Terry, and Fernando Flores. 1986. *Understanding computers and cognition: A new foundation for design*. Norwood, NJ: Ablex Publishing.

Winther, Rasmus Grønfeldt. 2015. The structure of scientific theories, Spring 2015 edn. In *The Stanford encyclopedia of philosophy*, ed. Edward N. Zalta.

Wise, John A., and Anthony Debons, eds. 1987. *Information systems: Failure analysis. NATO Advanced Study Institute series F: Computer and systems sciences*, Vol. 32. New York: Springer.

Wittgenstein, Ludwig. 2010. *Philosophical investigations*. John Wiley & Sons.

Wolfram|Alpha. Wolfram Alpha LLC.

Yates, Frances Amelia. 1992. *The art of memory*. New York: Random House.

Young, James O. 2013. The coherence theory of truth, Summer 2013 edn. In *The Stanford encyclopedia of philosophy*, ed. Edward N. Zalta.

Zahavi, Dan. 2004. Phenomenology and the project of naturalization. *Phenomenology and the cognitive sciences* 3 (4): 331–347.

Zhai, C., and J. Lafferty. 2004. A study of smoothing methods for language models applied to information retrieval. *ACM Transactions on Information Systems* 22 (2): 179–214.

Zhai, ChengXiang. 2011. Beyond search: Statistical topic models for text analysis. In *Proceedings of the 34th international ACM SIGIR conference on research and development in information retrieval*, eds. Wei-Ying Ma, Jian-Yun Nie, Ricardo Baeza-Yates, Tat-Seng Chua, and W. Bruce Croft, 3–4. ACM Press.

Zhai, ChengXiang. 2015. Towards a game-theoretic framework for information retrieval. In *Proceedings of the 38th international ACM SIGIR conference*, 543–544. Bejing, China: SIGIR.

Index